The Many Cinemas of Michael Curtiz

The Many Cinemas
of Michael Curtiz

EDITED BY R. BARTON PALMER
AND MURRAY POMERANCE

University of Texas Press ᗊᗎ *Austin*

Requests for permission to reproduce material from this work should be sent to:
Permissions
University of Texas Press
P.O. Box 7819
Austin, TX 78713-7819
utpress.utexas.edu/rp-form

⊗ The paper used in this book meets the minimum requirements of
ANSI/NISO Z39.48-1992 (R1997) (Permanence of Paper).

Library of Congress Cataloging-in-Publication Data

Names: Palmer, R. Barton, 1946–, editor. | Pomerance, Murray, 1946–, editor.
Title: The many cinemas of Michael Curtiz / edited by R. Barton Palmer and
Murray Pomerance.
Description: First edition. | Austin : University of Texas Press, 2018. |
Includes bibliographical references and index. | Filmography.
Identifiers: LCCN 2017046035
    ISBN 978-1-4773-1554-5 (cloth : alk. paper)
    ISBN 978-1-4773-1555-2 (pbk. : alk. paper)
    ISBN 978-1-4773-1556-9 (lib e-book)
    ISBN 978-1-4773-1557-6 (non-lib e-book)
Subjects: LCSH: Curtiz, Michael, 1888–1962—Criticism and interpretation. |
Motion picture producers and directors—United States.
Classification: LCC PN1998.3.C87 M36 2018 | DDC 791.4302/32092—dc23
LC record available at https://lccn.loc.gov/2017046035

doi:10.7560/315545

To Hollywood's unsung metteurs en scène,
and those who cherish them

If you want something done, give it to a busy person.
—*Attributed to Benjamin Franklin and Lucille Ball*

Contents

Acknowledgments

We wish to express sincere gratitude to our colleagues and friends at University of Texas Press, including Nancy Bryan, Jim Burr, Lynne Chapman, Derek George, Cameron Ludwick, Sarah McGavick, and Sarah Mueller, as well as to Dan Sacco (Toronto), without whose energies and generosity this work could not have been completed. We thank, as well, the staff of the Margaret Herrick Library, Academy of Motion Picture Arts and Sciences, Beverly Hills, including Jenny Romero and Louise Hilton; the staff of the Warner Bros. Archives at the University of Southern California, especially Brett Service; and the staff of Photofest New York, especially Derek Davidson and Todd Ifft.

Our families have given us support in this work, as well as great joy — that fuel nonpareil for powering an appreciation of Michael Curtiz.

R. Barton Palmer, Atlanta
Murray Pomerance, Toronto

The Many Cinemas of Michael Curtiz

INTRODUCTION

The Many Cinemas of Michael Curtiz

R. BARTON PALMER AND MURRAY POMERANCE

With the British, French, and German economies severely strained, even wrecked, in victory, the Great War settled—permanently, as it transpired—the question of which national film industry would assume a leading position in the world market. Hollywood attained a dominance that would never be surrendered. By the early 1920s, film distribution had become intensely international, offering the prospect of immense profits to those producers who, through industry, talent, and guile, were able to develop and carry out strategies of filmmaking and distribution that garnered screen time and a disproportionate share of ever-increasing box-office receipts. American troops had been decisive in the defeat of Germany on the western front, but the accidental spoils of war were economic, not territorial. In the course of the 1920s, the United States found itself enjoying an economic boom that, fueled in part by the misfortune of recent allies, brought the country to global dominance. Britain and France owed Wall Street huge sums to cover the purchase of war materiel, and Germany, their principal enemy, was required by the Treaty of Versailles to make substantial reparation payments. The network of international finance in the West found itself badly strained and eventually in need of steadying by the strangest of solutions.

Designed by an international committee headed by soon-to-be-president Herbert Hoover, the Dawes Plan (the Dawes Committee was chaired by the banker Charles Gates Dawes [1865–1951]) stipulated that the United States lend money to the vanquished Germans, who then used the funds to make reparation payments, which would enable Britain and France to repay Wall Street bankers. (Wall Street was in effect moving money toward itself.) One of the effects of this arrangement (which helped end a Continental hyperinflation crisis) was to financially subordinate European

Michael Curtiz on set. Courtesy PhotoFest New York.

economies to that of the United States. This development was mirrored in the film industry. Hollywood in the 1920s was becoming the cinema that in one way or another absorbed the many cinemas of Europe. Political developments on the Continent during the 1930s increased the speed with which US filmmaking, more and more the desired professional destination of many, perhaps most, who were working in European national traditions, became interestingly syncretic. A thoroughly internationalized community making films for both the home and overseas markets quickly emerged from what had only a decade earlier been an industry much more narrowly American in its national identity.

Filmmakers recently installed in California soon found themselves in an unexpectedly advantageous position. The industry followed a business model that aimed at making back the production costs of individual films in domestic distribution, whose design, built around an elaborate scheme of time-valued releases (the run-zone-clearance system), meant that almost all films could be marketed to their full earning-value potential. Profits would come from distribution overseas (yet another "zone"), where the expensively produced Hollywood product, its costs already covered, could be leased at bargain rates that local producers or distributors could hardly match, since their releases started out in the red in the home market, not in the black, and in any case they could not put as much money on the screen as did Hollywood.

To make movies for the world, the American industry recognized the advantage of enlisting the world (which in effect meant Europe) in their making, adopting and adapting important styles and trends that had proved their worth abroad. From other industries, the studios signed up talented, proven filmmakers who could extend the range and depth of the national talent pool, in the process denying their services to would-be competitors. Alfred Hitchcock making films for David O. Selznick was ipso facto not making them for Gaumont-British or British International Pictures. By the time hostilities were renewed in 1939, sending the Continent into a near-suicidal spiral whose finale would again advantage US filmmakers, Hollywood had become the site of a complexly internationalized industrial-artistic practice, reflecting, among other cultural influences, Continental tastes, styles, and thematic obsessions that were brought to North America by an émigré community of considerable size and ever-growing importance. In a strange synergy that would further serve Hollywood's interests in cornering talent from erstwhile competitors, the worldwide depression ruined the Weimar film industry, and the advent of National Socialism in 1933, for obvious reasons, provided many of German cinema's most renowned figures with further encouragement to emigrate to the United States, where they could continue their careers with the best resources then available anywhere in the world. Fritz Lang, Ernst Lubitsch, Billy Wilder, Douglas Sirk, and myriad more filmmaking talents were reborn in America (Portuges 2013).

A Generalist of Note

Among the most talented of European cineastes who made their way in California after the end of the Great War was a Hungarian named Mihaly Kerteszh, or Michael Curtiz, as, once ensconced in Hollywood, he wanted to be known. An interesting odyssey through several national film industries ended with Curtiz being headhunted by, and then accepting employment as a contract director at, Warner Bros. Producing for an increasingly sophisticated domestic audience, and eager as well to release films that would do well in lucrative foreign markets (it was at the time not uncommon for scenes to be retaken several times in different languages), production heads at the emerging studios welcomed experienced and talented refugees from European cinemas that were seemingly in a constant state of crisis. This trend accelerated after filmmaking required more complex forms of drama with the conversion to sound (pioneered by Warner Bros., eager to more firmly establish its niche in a highly competitive business). At the Warners studio—originally on Santa Monica Boulevard in Hollywood—Curtiz quickly made his mark as the most competent and consistently successful of Hollywood generalists. His remarkable work ethic—focus one's attention intensively; keep things moving at a fast clip; economize, economize, economize—perfectly suited the fast-paced system of production, and he had an enviable talent for quickly and effectively resolving the innumerable granular problems that arose in the course of shooting. With a truly catholic breadth of interest in different forms of narrative and spectacle, this sophisticated and well-educated central European specialized in not specializing; this increased his value to the studio and enabled him to deploy his considerable artistic talents in turning out some of the classic studio era's finest examples across an impressive variety of genres.

In fact, it would hardly be an exaggeration to say that Curtiz, more than any of his foreign-born colleagues, exemplified Hollywood's internationalism during the classic studio period (1920–1965). Born in 1886, Curtiz had (remarkably) already made about seventy films for the nascent Hungarian and Austrian industries before arriving in America in 1926; an important part of his résumé was that, as filmmaking in the early teens was turning to feature-length production, Curtiz had spent some time in Denmark working with August Blom, one of the pioneers of this emerging form of cinematic narrative. Already with more experience than most— perhaps all—of his new colleagues in Hollywood, he went on to make more features (about one hundred, including projects with more than one directorial credit) than any other American director. These include a number of the most enduringly popular films of the studio era in all the industry's principal genres: spectacular actioners (*Captain Blood*, 1935; *The Charge of the Light Brigade*, 1936; *The Adventures of Robin Hood*, 1938; *Santa Fe Trail* and *The Sea Hawk*, both 1940); biopics (*The Private Lives of Elizabeth and Essex*, 1939; *Yankee Doodle Dandy*, 1942; *Young Man with a Horn*, 1950; *Jim Thorpe: All-American*, 1951; *The Story of Will Rogers*, 1952); melodramas and film noir (*Four Daughters*, 1938; *Daughters Courageous*, 1939; and *Mildred Pierce*, 1945); musicals (*Night and Day*, 1946; *White Christmas*, 1954; *King Creole*, 1958); and westerns (*Dodge City*, 1939; *Virginia City*, 1940; *The Proud Rebel*, 1958). It is also significant that *Casablanca* (1942), likely the classic industry's most beloved dramatic film, and certainly—with Humphrey Bogart, Ingrid Bergman, Paul Henreid, Claude Rains, Conrad Veidt, Sydney Greenstreet, and Peter Lorre—one of the great paradigms of ensemble performance, was directed by Curtiz. Simply put, the history of US studio filmmaking is unimaginable without him.

Curtiz was born Kaminer Manó Kertész to a middle-class Jewish family in Budapest, then the second capital city of the Austro-Hungarian Empire and a cosmopolitan center where the cinema, though slow to start, quickly gained a substantial hold in the immediate prewar period. A university graduate who trained also in the National Theater, Kertész (now styling himself "Mihály," perhaps to seem less Jewish: although Jews were prominent in the Hungarian arts community, the larger culture suffered from anti-Semitism) began an acting and directing career in the nascent industry in 1912. His speedy management of staging, on scales both large and small, as well as the rapport he established with actors, made him an immediate and continuing success; escaping from military service after a brief stint in the imperial army, he managed to turn out more than fifty films before the advent of the Béla Kun communist regime in 1919 meant the nationalization of the industry, to which he was opposed. Hardly missing a beat, Kertész made his way west, where he quickly established himself in the Austrian industry. Despite his limited ability to speak German, he directed more than fifteen additional projects for Sascha-Film. Deteriorating economic conditions, and the prospect of better working conditions, likely made him decide in 1926 to relocate from Vienna to the United States.

His name now anglicized, Curtiz was hired by Jack Warner on the basis of his biblical epic *The Moon of Israel* (1924; released in the United States in 1927). This story of Moses and the Exodus featured ingenious art design and set construction, as well as a compelling story effectively communicated by the director's spare style. It was a prestige package assembled on time and under budget by the always well-organized director, who tolerated no slackness in himself or others. In effect, *Moon of Israel* rivaled the much more expensive version of this material released several years earlier by Paramount: Cecil B. DeMille's *The Ten Commandments* (1923). Nothing could have been more appealing to the budget-minded Jack Warner than the film's deceptively inexpensive epic grandeur. Because of chronically limited resources and the legendary parsimony of the Warners, the studio's films needed to be made less expensively than competitors' releases featuring more generous production values. One of Curtiz's first projects for Warner Bros. was a film similarly based on Old Testament material, *Noah's Ark* (1928), a "part-talking" film with some sequences shot silent and others furnished with a soundtrack. A reserve-seat engagement was followed by a more conventional release, and the very expensive production (over $1 million, a huge budget for Warners) made back twice its costs in box-office receipts. Jack Warner's investment in Curtiz paid dividends from the beginning.

Technically proficient and with a flair for effective dramatizing, the hard-driving Curtiz perfectly suited the studio's not easily reconciled needs for efficient, rapid production and palpable aesthetic value. Curtiz had learned how to quickly make films that were both inexpensive and good. In the course of the 1930s, he turned out forty-five features for the studio in an impressive demonstration of energy and competence that was not matched by any of his contemporaries. Curtiz's virtues were the virtues of the system. As was the case for the other majors, twice-weekly program changes at theaters owned and operated by Warner Bros. (the Warner Bros.–First National chain) meant that production required volume and speed, and there was little time or money to explore stylistic alternatives or rectify all the problems with scripts, art design, casting, and so forth that inevitably emerged once shooting started. Not every production was destined or indeed needed to be a masterpiece that bore the personal imprint of an auteur imagined as (at least artistically) resisting a system designed to Taylorize his desire for originality. Almost all of Curtiz's films, especially those made while he was under Warner Bros. contract, are good enough, and because he made so many, a considerable number are among the best turned out by Hollywood during the period. It is a testimony to Curtiz's craftsmanship that the films themselves rather than his direction of them are what have always been most memorable. The *Cahiers du cinéma* auteurists contended that a true film author kept making the same film over and over again. Curtiz's talent was quite different, one they (and film criticism in general) found it difficult to appreciate. He was a man of many cinemas, not just of one, and his achievements were marked by substantial differences rather than recognizable similarities or signatures. He was the very best of the flexible, multitalented *metteurs en scène* upon whom the industry depended for its continuing success.

The *metteurs* were jacks-of-most-trades, and perhaps masters of one or two. In Hollywood of the golden age, the identifiability of films as belonging clearly and sharply to genre categories was no small element in studios' carefully conceived arrangements for production and marketing geared toward profit. By shaping films to genre patterns—adventure pictures, swashbucklers, romances, melodramas, westerns, and so on—producers could opt for well-known formulae that would, on one side, make casting, rehearsing, shooting, and editing conventional and straightforward; and on the other, make the look of films recognizable for audiences who wanted to repeat pleasurable experiences with variation. Any filmmaker who could demonstrate remarkable skill in directing successful films in a number of genres (by watching the budget and the narrative structure simultaneously) could be a real boon in an industry where constant demand existed for production in many genres at once. In the big studios, directors learned to move swiftly from picture to picture, regardless of the script, but to do this with facility in a wide range of genres and with a sharp eye to the speed of production was not everyone's forte.

Equally comfortable with indoor and outdoor genres, Curtiz demonstrated a special talent for large-scale costume dramas, especially those that required mounted figures en masse. Steady, reliable, fast-moving competence was the order of the day. The ablest of such studio men could make occasional silk purses from sow's ears; more importantly, however, they were able to turn not-so-wonderful projects into acceptable, profitable releases, taking full advantage of all the resources that the studio provided. At least, for the most part: no studio-era filmmaker avoided failures. Arguably, no one was better than Curtiz in maximizing the potential of each of the very different projects he was assigned; the productions he oversaw were characteristically untroubled, not requiring his dismissal and replacement. And he was sometimes called on to work uncredited with his studio colleagues, as, for example, on Mervyn LeRoy's splashy costume drama *Anthony Adverse* (1936).

His unstrained fluency in managing all the resources of cinematic narrative can be glimpsed most readily in "ordinary" releases like *The Kennel Murder Case* (1934), a detective programmer starring a pre-*Thin Man* William Powell and based on one of S. S. Van Dine's Philo Vance mysteries. In only seventy-three minutes of running time, Curtiz manages to condense an extraordinarily complex plot (seven suspects emerge in connection with a double murder) that required numerous, very different setups. Some scenes required framings with up to five interlocutors. For the film to make any sense, a huge number of plot points had to be clearly communicated, which Curtiz manages with ease (a stunning feat, given that his English was at best fractured), using blocking and mise-en-scène to full advantage. *Man in the Net* (1959) is a routine thriller starring an Alan Ladd in obvious decline. The narrative is almost devoid of interest-sustaining twists and turns, but Curtiz prevents the film from being unbearably dull by emphasizing how Ladd, falsely accused of murdering his wife, is hidden from police in a nearby cave by a gang of local children he has befriended. Once again, his ease in communicating narrative information in ways other than through dialogue comes to the fore; if the project in the end must be counted a failure, Curtiz, who made the best of a bad deal, can hardly be blamed, and the talent on evident display in *Man in the Net* merits recognition.

Despite his importance to Hollywood history, Curtiz has not been well served by critical protocols underwritten by the neoromantic view of artistic single-mindedness. The French never liked him because he exemplified the system they were determined (wrongly, to a great degree) to see as a barrier to true artistic expression. The one comprehensive monograph devoted to Curtiz, James C. Robertson's *The Casablanca Man: The Cinema of Michael Curtiz* (Routledge, 1993), provides a useful overview of his long career, but concentrates on his several notable productions rather than considering the range of value to be found in his extensive oeuvre. R. J. Kinnard and R. Vitone's *The American Films of Michael Curtiz* (Scarecrow, 1986) offers accounts, sometimes very brief, of all the director's Hollywood productions. It thus shows Curtiz off as the mastermind behind such films as *Casablanca*, *Yankee Doodle Dandy*, *The Sea Hawk*, and *Mildred Pierce* but neglects the full, rather astonishing range of his accomplishments. By emphasizing multiplicity rather than singularity, and by offering discussions of his films and artistic practice from a variety of angles (including politics, gender, and genre) that add up to a collective portrait of considerable subtlety and complexity, *The Many Cinemas of Michael Curtiz* aims to shed new light on an all-but-unknown cinematic genius. Key popular films are examined with fresh eyes, and hitherto neglected releases of substantial historical interest such as *Noah's Ark*, *Night and Day*, *Virginia City*, *Black Fury*, *Female*, and numerous other films are given their proper due. Curtiz, the editors and contributors agree, simply cannot be properly understood, or his achievements properly valued, from the conventional "The Cinema of _____" approach. Offering a thorough and provocative reassessment of one of classic Hollywood's most important figures, this volume offers more than yet another author study of a notable director. *The Many Cinemas of Michael Curtiz* is more properly understood as a contribution to the writing of studio-era history than as a narrow tribute to one of its principal personalities. The editors and contributors are all major figures in contemporary film studies, and the interest in this project of those who are thoroughly versed in the history of Hollywood's classical era must be counted as further evidence of the value to be found in Curtiz's films.

It is time, we all agree, that he receives his proper critical due, and one of the features of this volume is that with Bill Krohn's chapter on *Casablanca* and Bob Miklitsch's on *Young Man with a Horn*, it provides updated and detailed readings, based on production histories, of notable Curtiz productions. For Krohn, *Casablanca* is a film without a "directional auteur" in the classic sense, and Curtiz worked closely with the producer, Hal Wallis, and others involved to make it a studio classic. *Young Man*, as Miklitsch recounts, plays interestingly and creatively with its literary source as much as with its much-praised engagement with the early history of jazz. Katharina Loew's assessment of *Noah's Ark* reveals, as reviewers at the time noted, that it is "an uneven film," but one filled with "impressive individual episodes like the flood sequence, the train wreckage, or God's instructions to Noah." These sequences, Loew concludes, "testify to Curtiz's visual mastery and remain noteworthy today." Kristen Hatch's detailed examination of the production files for *Mildred Pierce* confirm the view that, as he proclaimed himself, the producer, Jerry Wald, was largely responsible for the project's most notable feature: the substantial transformation of the James M. Cain source novel. But Wald made clear that the changes were done "not by suppressing the director's vision but by synthesizing it with his own and adapting it to the limitations of the Production Code and the imperatives of the star system." *Yankee Doodle Dandy* is an iconic film for the industry and for its director, as well as a showcase for the many talents of its star, James Cagney. Yet as Julie Grossman argues, the film's "fascination with alternating figures of sameness and difference points not only to melting-pot universality and can-do Yankee individualism but also to collaborative artistic creativity, eclecticism, and flexibility—all values at least partially in tension with an easy patriotism." And so, she continues, "Cagney's body art, if we could call it that, is complemented by Curtiz's emphasis on performance and nimbleness in the film's style."

Auteurism, we are reminded, depends on a problematic literary metaphor—"writing" in both its material and compositional senses—that is in large measure peculiarly unsuited to describe the varied creative acts required of filmmakers like Curtiz in the classic era. The point made in one way or another by the contributors to this volume is that to conceive of directors as authors is to obscure the many senses in which the work they do is representational. Directorial work largely consists of assisting in the bringing of multifarious materials to the screen—making cinema from dialogue, images, music, performance—while helping the system showcase the attractions on which its continuing popularity depended. Because neoromantic notions of individual genius are imported from literary studies, they simply do not speak fairly to forms of visual artistry, of which, during the classic studio era, Curtiz was arguably one of the most talented and flexible practitioners.

An assessment of the contributions of Michael Curtiz to European and Hollywood cinemas must engage with this question, and a number of the essays in this volume take up that challenge. Murray Pomerance, evaluating Curtiz's contribution to the success of *White Christmas*, refuses to "put forward the argument that in helming *White Christmas* Michael Curtiz contributed signally to the mythic structure of our culture or played in fascinating new ways with important sociological or psychological themes." Instead, what Curtiz accomplished was to make the film "in every sense a matter-of-fact, businesslike, and clean-cut illustration of its story"; moreover, "its deeper purpose was to show off VistaVision, creating for other filmmakers dreams of what they might do and for audiences charge up anticipation of VistaVision pleasures to come."[1] Similarly, as Homer Pettey argues, Curtiz's assays of the western genre, especially in the 1930s, "represent profound cinematic experiments with color and sound, all indicative of Curtiz's willingness to exploit the latest technologies available for filmmaking." John Ford is usually given full credit for this development, but there is also a case to be made that "Curtiz ushered in the great age of the feature-length western." Nathan Holmes demonstrates that with *Captain Blood* and a handful of other swashbucklers, Curtiz contributed substantially to Hollywood's exploration of "the 'edge zones,' of modernity." Thus, "Curtiz's small corpus of maritime cinema takes us to sea to put us out of touch with the world, if only to see it anew." For Colin Williamson, *Mystery of the Wax Museum* figures as more than a late entry in the horror film cycle that was prominent in the 1930s. It was not coincidental, he suggests, that "*Mystery* was released at the end of Hollywood's transition to synchronized sound." With "its illusion of life," the wax museum "provided a natural space for investigating . . . the mysteries of the cinema during a major transitional period in film history."

David Desser's chapter on *Life with Father* offers a detailed production history of one of Curtiz's most enduringly popular films, focusing on his effective coaching and management of the actors involved. In addition, Desser emphasizes how this film belongs to a production trend, of which it was one of the most significant entrants: "The film version of *Life with Father* was part of a cycle of nostalgic films intended not only to offer up visions of a kind of prelapsarian America, but also to reintegrate men into the feminine sphere." In the 1930s, and later during the war, Curtiz directed a number of releases that prominently featured political themes, both domestic and international. Barton Palmer argues that the problem they posed for him, and that he successfully resolved, was presentational rather than intellectual. It was to manage an effective balance between the politically charged backgrounds that, with their action scenes, were meant to provide viewers with topical interest and visual pleasure, and the love relationship between the male and female leads in the foreground, where star power and the erotic were meant to offer irresistible hooks.

For Landon Palmer, Curtiz's late-career work with Elvis Presley reveals how the director "played an instrumental role in developing the screen persona of a star who portended a new industrial design of Hollywood performance, an 'electronic age' star whose screen image united media commodities and cultural industries." *King Creole*, as he shows, "speaks profoundly to the ways in which the gatekeepers of a former studio system transitioned to a Hollywood characterized by wider screens and growing competition from other forms of media leisure." Steve Rybin finds that two of the films Curtiz made with the star Kay Francis, *Mandalay* and *Stolen Holiday*, offer "notable case studies for exploring how a director and a performer work together to creatively negotiate the strictures of studio censorship and repression," marking the films with a "contrapuntal style." Also exploring Curtiz's work with the principal players at Warners, Constantine Verevis explores the director's contributions to the studio's "Merrie England" cycle, in which Errol Flynn persistently played "a man for whom moral and political decisions are unambiguous, and who is provided with the chance to put these decisions into practice through direct physical action." Accordingly, Flynn becomes the "embodiment of Warners' philosophy of individual morality . . . [whereby] the heroic acts of an individual [are at] both the core of the narrative and the bearer of the film's ideology." Verevis's essay considers how two of these pictures—*The Charge of the Light Brigade* and *The Adventures of*

Robin Hood — "harnessed Flynn's flawless physiognomy and Curtiz's energetic visual style to (respectively) consolidate and mark out the pinnacle of the cycle." Since Curtiz can be justly credited with making substantial contributions to the production trends of the era, it is perhaps inevitable that his projects sometimes reflected something of Hollywood history as well. Deron Overpeck sees Curtiz's late-career project *The Egyptian* as informed by the postwar demise of the studio system. Here is a film, Overpeck argues, that "contains Curtiz's traditional thematic concerns about the abuses of power," but "it is also marked by a sense of decline that is uncommon in the director's works," even if it is entirely appropriate to the story he was assigned to tell. As his career wound down in a period of institutional change, Curtiz might be forgiven for this personal, perhaps unconscious signing onto a project whose theme was the ultimate pointlessness of an artistry deployed in the service of others.

Lamenting that the remake is "perhaps the most critically debased form for creative ingenuity," Seth Friedman carefully analyzes how in Curtiz's 1950s revision of the famous Warners early sound release *The Jazz Singer*, key elements of the original "are shifted in order to nuance the film's presentation of a postwar American Judaism far from irrelevant to Curtiz's experience in his adopted country." The film, Friedman argues, thus "exemplifies a form of authorship crucial to the continuing function of a filmmaking sector in which re-use and extension of various kinds play vital roles." Rebecca Bell-Metereau argues that two of the projects from the last stages of Curtiz's Hollywood career, *The Helen Morgan Story* (a musical biopic) and *The Scarlet Hour* (a noirish melodrama), "stretched and bent both gender and genre boundaries in complex and potentially progressive ways," disappointing filmgoers eager for the more conventional pleasures of genre filmmaking. Her close readings of the films, informed by a detailed recovery of production history, point to a conclusion about Curtiz's peculiar artistry that is supported by other chapters in this book, namely, that in many of his superficially ordinary films, he nonetheless "shaped his material—particularly off-beat depictions of gender and suggestive, ambiguous narrative conclusions for characters—in a way that challenged conventions, leaving viewers in the same liminal space Curtiz occupies as auteur—or not—with details unsettled and subject to interpretation."

Curtiz was successful in working within the system because he made the most of the sometimes rather limited possibilities that a project presented. Mark Glancy's archive-based account of the making of *Night and Day*, the Cole Porter biopic in which Cary Grant played the lead, reveals that "what is remarkable about this film is the extent of the star's control and also, in keeping with the idea that the auteur expresses his own personality, the extent to which the rewritten film represents Grant's own life." Yet as Glancy demonstrates through a reading of key scenes, the film belongs "firmly within" the director's oeuvre, manifesting "his eye for detail and his scrupulous attention to dialogue and performance." Similarly, critics have customarily understood *Elizabeth and Essex* as a deglamorized and, hence, somewhat problematic showcasing of Warners leading lady, Bette Davis. David Greven's analysis of the production emphasizes how "at every turn Curtiz facilitates her effort to inhabit and realize Elizabeth's advanced age and strange, at times fright-making appearance." He concludes that the film depends on a complex partnership between star and director, who "worked together to create a cinematic effect, one with both feminist and misogynistic implications." Approaching the film in this way leads Greven to identify its thematic connections with two later Curtiz projects (*Flamingo Road* and *Mildred Pierce*), which can be seen as constituting a triptych focusing on "the body as the site of struggle, conflict, possibility, and change." Focusing on the representation of women in the director's oeuvre, Michele Schreiber finds that his two *Daughters* films "depict a Curtiz woman whose decisions are guided by a strong moral compass and whose sexuality goes unspoken," in the manner of family melodrama. These female portraits contrast strongly with the "autonomous, bold, libidinous Curtiz woman to be seen in *Female* and *Flamingo Road*."

The impressive diversity of approaches to Curtiz's huge oeuvre in this volume suggests two important, related practical truths about the Hollywood studio era of the talented *metteur en scène*. First, that an indispensable employee can be resolutely "above the line," that is, no simple craftsman. At the same time, however, the *metteur* is not "authorial" in the senses promoted by auteurism, following the aesthetic protocols promoted by neoromanticism, especially its antiestablishmentarian ethos, which demanded the promotion of self over system. To be sure, in the literary metaphor invented by Alexandre Astruc, Curtiz disposed of a "caméra-stylo," but his multifaceted creativity cannot be fairly described by this narrow notion of style. In fact, his framing and photographic strategies in general do not add up to some substantial claim on uniqueness. He did not "sign" his projects. Second, and more importantly, as an exceptional *metteur*, whose profession involves, as the word's etymology suggests, "placing" or "putting," Curtiz implicitly valued diversity and multiplicity—his career might be seen as what happened when a talented director proved inimical to either aesthetic immutability or thematic monologism, in the spirit of the institution that lent him many voices to speak. If Curtiz spoke eloquently, it was because he was energized by the worldliness of an industry that was opposed to self-restricting commitments. He was most fortunate to have belonged for most of his professional life to a thoroughly internationalized community of "makers" committed, like him, to ever-evolving forms of cinematic eloquence.

Note

1. Note *Variety*'s prediction of August 27, 1954: "VV's impact, while giving a full-stage effect to this musical, should be even greater when applied to outdoor and action-drama stories."

Work Cited

Portuges, Catherine. 2013. "Jewish Immigrant Directors and Their Impact on Hollywood." In *Hollywood's Chosen People: The Jewish Experience in American Cinema*, ed. Daniel Bernardi, Murray Pomerance, and Hava Tirosh-Samuelson, 35–51. Detroit: Wayne State University Press.

CHAPTER 1

Bending It Like Curtiz: Gender and Genre in *The Scarlet Hour* and *The Helen Morgan Story*

REBECCA BELL-METEREAU

Michael Curtiz once bitterly claimed, "You are only appreciated so far as you carry the dough into the box office. They throw you into gutter next day" (Harmetz 1992, 76). Famously and repeatedly acknowledged for his ability to work within the restrictive studio system in a variety of genres, Curtiz always tried to entertain people enough to make a profit, which was key to survival at Warner Bros. The counterbalancing motivation Curtiz confessed—to "put all the art into my pictures I think the audience can stand" (Kinnard and Vitone 1986, 2)—merits attention as well, particularly in regard to genre and gender. Although his skill at discovering and working with actors in minor roles was legendary, Curtiz was never viewed as a "woman's director," along the lines of George Cukor. Some writers note accusations of sexual harassment during his long career, and he purportedly lost a lawsuit for failure to provide child support (Robertson 1993, 116). Nevertheless, a number of his films exhibit a pattern of sympathetically exploring female points of view. Some of the most interesting films directed by Curtiz are neither well known, nor were they lucrative, but they defy conventions in groundbreaking ways. It might seem odd to pick female protagonists from two relatively obscure Curtiz films with shocking scenes of men hitting women as artistically innovative exemplars of transgressive gender roles, but close analysis of *The Helen Morgan Story* (1957) and *The Scarlet Hour* (1956) reveals how Curtiz stretched and bent both gender and genre boundaries in complex and potentially progressive ways.

It may be argued that many of the financial disappointments among Curtiz's films resulted from a failure to fulfill a genre formula demanded by studios and fans. Judith Hess accounts for the tension between genre films' reactionary messages and simplistic conclusions, often wedded to their financial success, and their avoidance of artistic complexity: "Genre films . . . serve the interests of the ruling class by assisting in the maintenance of the status quo and they throw a sop to oppressed groups who, because they are unorganized and therefore afraid to act, eagerly accept the genre film's absurd solutions to economic and social conflicts. . . . Genre films address themselves to these conflicts and resolve them in a simplistic and reactionary way" (1974, 1). Although film noir is not a precise genre, some of Curtiz's most intriguing films, marked by noir styles and conventions, frustrate audiences' expectations for ordinary crime dramas.

The Scarlet Hour

During the making of one such film, *The Scarlet Hour*, the filmmaker's life was marred by a series of threatened legal actions. He had left Warner Bros., gaining more freedom in his subsequent contract with Paramount. Hal Erickson (n.d.) describes the film as a "bold experiment" for Paramount pictures in the midfifties, noting how the new Fujinon lenses, with their larger apertures, provided superior images in low-light conditions. This technical advance is noticeable in the unusual opening of the film, set in medias res on a hilltop lovers' lane, beginning with a long shot of city lights below and cutting to a medium shot of Tom Tryon as the darkly handsome bachelor Marsh, standing by the car door, smoking what seems like a postcoital cigarette. His manner reveals how hopelessly he loves the vampy blonde married woman Paulie Nevins (Carol Ohmart), who is in the driver's seat. Her masculine-sounding name fits her offhandedly commanding tone and her position at the wheel of a snazzy Plymouth convertible. It is obvious that she is in the metaphorical driver's seat in their relationship, since she tells Marsh what to do (and not do) and complains about her loveless marriage to wealthy Ralph Nevins (James Gregory), the owner of a real estate development business and Marsh's boss. The immediate appearance of two other cars compels the lovers to hide in the bushes, where they overhear a plot to rob a nearby house, a chance event that sets the stage for their adulterous romance to turn into larceny. As the couple hunkers down, barely out of sight, to eavesdrop on the planning, the lighting is just a shade brighter than that of an ordinary film noir, making the scene at once suspenseful yet almost darkly comical. When they retire to a local bar to contemplate their future, Leith Stevens's orchestral scoring of "Never Let Me Go" begins as a nondiegetic soundtrack, switches to diegetic accompaniment as Marsh chooses the tune on the jukebox, and then provides the nondiegetic background to their passionate parting embrace, subtly foreshadowing the theme of obsessive love for listeners who recognize the song.

This opening resembles a typical film noir setup, but several elements make *The Scarlet Hour* more nuanced than the standard noir narrative and also render Paulie's character more complex than an archetypal femme fatale. Because circumstances lure her into crime as the plot unfolds, she doesn't come across as a heartless temptress devoid of romantic feeling. Moreover, after the introduction of the lovers' plight, Curtiz provides a shocking view of Paulie's life with Ralph that engenders sympathy for her situation. She returns home, where we see an enormous shadow of her suspicious husband lurking behind her. He grills her about where she has been until two in the morning, and she offers the lame alibi of having gone to a movie. The conversation becomes heated, and when she asks him why he won't give her a divorce, he slaps her face, not once but twice. In a minor key, the musical motif from the bar scene crescendos in the soundtrack as Ralph pushes Paulie to the garage floor and proceeds to beat her up. We watch this in another shot of his menacing silhouette against the wall. This kind of violence against women is not unusual in 1950s films, but Curtiz's rendition stands out as brutal and disturbing in a way that creates potential sympathy for Paulie as a battered woman, rather than disapproval of her as an adulterous wife. The scene foreshadows the film's climax, when Ralph hits her and tries to kill her during a jewel heist. These two scenes echo near the conclusion, when Paulie finds herself humiliated, rejected by Marsh, and emotionally cornered. In a gender reversal, mirroring her husband's actions, she slaps Marsh for saying he no longer loves her.

The path to this conclusion follows Curtiz's typically breakneck pattern of punchy action interspersed with slower interludes of character exposition. As Paulie tries to cajole Marsh into stealing the money from the robbers and running away with her, another layer of complexity in her backstory emerges. She takes him to a seedy part of town to show why she feels she must have money before leaving her husband. Standing beside him and pointing to a slum apartment complex, she says, "That's where I come from," declaring, like a modern Scarlett O'Hara, that she refuses to be poor ever again. This pause for character exposition explains Paulie's desperation, and her later displays of obsessive jealousy suggest that she is not merely using Marsh to get money or as a means of escape. Soon she begins to imitate her husband's pitifully possessive behavior, a response suggesting that she loves Marsh, in her own pathological way.

As is characteristic of Curtiz films, *The Scarlet Hour*'s integration of music, significant lyrics, and nightclub entertainment scenes into narrative themes and plot is subtle and economical. On the evening of the heist, Paulie arranges a double date at a swank nightclub as her alibi. To leave Ralph without a car, she disconnects an essential part of the engine—displaying yet another stereotypically masculine skill—and then sends him to his office to untangle a work crisis that she and Marsh concocted. She then joins her longtime pal Phyllis (Elaine Stritch), a wisecracking, good-hearted gold digger, and Phyllis's chubby sugar-daddy husband, Tom (played with charming befuddlement by Billy Gray), at the club. In their jovial camaraderie, Phyllis and Tom serve as perfect foils to the calculating Paulie and her viciously possessive spouse. When Phyllis—"Phyl," as Paulie calls her—sends Tom to fetch drinks, Paulie says she needs to slip out to say good-bye to "someone" before her husband takes her on a long vacation. Phyl expresses reservations, but then accepts her role and wonders at how attached Paulie is to this apparent lover. The comfortable intimacy of their conversation demonstrates their longtime friendship, another unusual asset for a femme fatale.

Throughout this development phase, Curtiz uses music to underscore shifting emotional registers. The bouncy Latin music that Phyl and Tom dance to contrasts with the motif of entrapment expressed in the lyrics to "Never Let Me Go" (sung by the popular Nat King Cole), which was played without lyrics in the opening bar scene. As Cole croons about desperate love, the words are laden with irony, in light of Paulie's plot to abandon her husband, even as she grasps for complete possession of her new lover, Marsh. *The Scarlet Hour* contains a series of plot twists, some of which are predictable, but Curtiz keeps the action flowing so rapidly and seamlessly that the picture maintains suspense through the constantly shifting nature of relationships and characters. When Ralph discovers Paulie and Marsh's love affair, he follows Paulie to the heist, taking along his gun. He drags her into his car. They struggle, the gun goes off, and he is accidentally killed. Marsh assumes the robbers have shot Ralph, and when he finds Paulie genuinely shaken he becomes assertive and tells her they must leave the scene. By the time she returns to the nightclub and finds Phyl and Tom dancing the rumba, she recovers her poise enough to go back home and provide a convincing alibi to a detective (played with dogged determination by the well-cast E. G. Marshall).

Marsh loses his veneer of certainty when he returns to the office the next day and the secretary, Kathy (Jody Lawrance), moves into position as an alternative love interest for him. Curtiz complicates Kathy, unveiling how she has secretly loved Marsh and divined most of his secrets all along, hidden evidence from the police, and lied to provide him with an alibi as her overnight companion, even at the cost of her reputation. Although she is depicted as relatively innocent, she acts as the sexual initiator with Marsh—just as Paulie did—even if her aggression takes milder forms of tenderly straightening his collar and inviting him to dinner at her apartment.

In contrast to these bold women, Marsh becomes increasingly passive and resistant, refusing to further involve Kathy in his sordid life and rejecting her attentions. The ambiguous nature of their relationship is revealed early on when he stays at her apartment until two in the morning (an echo of Paulie's tardy arrival home in the opening scene). After spying on them, Paulie bribes her way into Marsh's apartment and gets drunk while he is out. When he finally returns from Kathy's, she flies into a jealous rage, becomes vicious, and hits him, eventually going along with police suggestions that he and Kathy were having an affair. As the final plot pieces fall together, revealing that the robbery was self-staged to conceal the fact of the wife's jewels having been secretly sold, everyone appears to be trapped in the perfect noir ending. But a few unresolved plot details and distorted visual elements in the closing shots cause the depiction of Paulie to veer away from the stereotypical femme fatale persona.

Sidney Rosenzweig notes the expressionist style of Curtiz, which features windows "that stand between the camera and the human characters and seem to surround and entrap them" (1982, 157). Not every window in a Curtiz film is a trap, though. For example, when Ilsa visits Rick's room in *Casablanca*, the shot out the window hints at escape to a nostalgic past and an imminent sexual liaison. *The Scarlet Hour* offers one of the director's most artful uses of a window as entrapment in the film's closing shot. Once the convoluted events unfold and all the guilty parties receive their just deserts, Paulie asks the police for a moment to put on "something decent" before they take her to jail. She enters her elegant bedroom and gazes through an upstairs window at the scene below. The man she loves is about to enter a police car just as his devoted new girlfriend drives up, runs to him, and tries to hug him. He stands stoically, refusing to return her embrace. The camera cuts to a close-up of Ohmart's face through the window as tears course down her cheeks. About to exchange her gilded cage for prison bars, she bends her forehead to the windowpane and smashes the bangs of her perfect coif against the glass, making it look as if her head is melting into the window itself. In a surreal vision of agony the shot fades to black.

Staring out through a signature Curtiz window, Paulie looks down at her lover, her face contorted in a grimace of regret that melts the hard-boiled shell of the femme fatale, in *The Scarlet Hour* (Paramount, 1956). Digital frame enlargement.

The ending of *The Scarlet Hour* was in part dictated by Production Code requirements, under which a fallen woman should be punished, preferably by death or at least prison. Despite these conventional demands, Curtiz makes the eventual outcome for all characters involved uncertain, with enough ambiguity to trigger concerns from censors. Ambiguity because, after all, the couple stole worthless fake jewels, Paulie claimed the shooting was accidental, and, as was obvious, she would make a comely and sympathetic defendant. She could explain how her husband was physically abusive and refused to grant her a divorce, how she was driven by fear and a desire to escape his threats. If Marsh overcame his self-loathing guilt, he could make a case for a short prison sentence for theft of fake jewels, especially in light of his confession and obvious remorse. The open-ended quality of this modulated conclusion caused disappointment on both ends of the viewing spectrum, from censors eager to enforce a strict "crime doesn't pay" resolution and from cynical noir fans expecting the unrepentant stance of morally bankrupt characters. On close examination, somehow the noir conclusion melts before our eyes into an almost corn-fed version of the genre.

Such loose ends were not the whole story behind the film's drab box-office reception. The industry and studio system as a whole were under continued pressure from censors and growing competition from television fare, and *The Scarlet Hour* may have seemed out of date to audiences, in spite of the film's creative take on the classic genre. It featured relatively inexperienced actors and thus received sparse critical attention, in spite of a number of strong performances. It has remained so little known that one volume on Curtiz describes it as "a minor western" (Kinnard and Vitone 1986, 99), perhaps confusing it with *The Proud Rebel* (1958). This meager description contrasts with John Baxter's view that Curtiz was "inescapably one of the best directors ever to emerge in the cinema" (quoted in Kinnard and Vitone 1986, 99). Despite citing Paul Henreid's claim that Curtiz was "among the top seven, or so, directors of all time," Kinnard and Vitone conclude that Curtiz met his own modest goal of making "the best pictures I can that will give audiences their money's worth: to please myself as much as I can without forgetting that the pleasure of my audiences comes first" (7). *The Scarlet Hour*'s clever take on the genre may have pleased Curtiz and his screenwriters, the highly ironic and self-reflexive Frank Tashlin, John Meredyth Lucas, and Rip Van Ronkel, but it didn't make money.

The Helen Morgan Story

After leaving Warner Bros. and directing *White Christmas* (1954), *We're No Angels* (1955), and *The Vagabond King* (1955), Curtiz returned to the studio for *The Helen Morgan Story*, an apparent labor of love that intrigued Jack Warner and perhaps Curtiz. *The Helen Morgan Story* contains multiple homages to the life, career, and films of the actor and torch singer Helen Morgan (1900–1941), particularly in the biographical connections apparent in Morgan's depiction of an alcoholic singer in Rouben Mamoulian's *Applause* (1929), a film that Jean-Marie Lecomte describes as creating "a sense of dysphoria and, above all, of musical disenchantment" (2008, 159). Curtiz's film stands as a convoluted and self-reflexive background metanarrative that echoes elements of the filmmaker's own troubled relationship with Warner Bros. The film lost $500,000, a financial disaster that James Robertson describes as "a sad and unjust way for Curtiz finally to leave the studio he had served so well" (1993, 122).

As in *The Scarlet Hour*, the narrative focuses on a character obsessed with an amoral narcissist, but instead of a man falling for a femme fatale, the female protagonist, Helen Morgan (Ann Blyth), falls for bad boy Larry Maddux (played with a convincing combination of huckster charm and sadistic sexual magnetism by Paul Newman). Like Carol Ohmart's femme fatale, Newman's con man is more complex than the stereotype, and he does seem to be "stuck" on Helen. He returns repeatedly with money-making schemes that prompt bad decisions and engineer devastating emotional disappointments for her, yet his one-dimensional image grows more nuanced through the course of the narrative, as does Helen's.

The Helen Morgan Story had a substantial enough cast to capture attention, but it flopped at the box office, largely because it failed to meet audiences' expectations for the genre. With too much melodrama for a musical and too much music for a melodrama, the film's strong points—such as the seamless wedding of characters, themes, and music—went generally unnoticed or at least unappreciated. Yet the music in this film is so thoroughly integrated into the narrative that it broadens the social context and at times subtly undermines or complicates the simplicity of stock types and gender role portrayals. A varied visual style moves from realist segments in the opening carnival scenes to a sudden downpour that recalls Tod Browning's ominous revenge scene in *Freaks* (1932) to hyperbolic cringe-making genre conventions in the musical numbers, as Helen sobs her way through the torch songs she made famous, and finally to canted frames in the penultimate, expressionist scenes that show her hitting rock bottom.

Like the secondary characters of *The Scarlet Hour*, minor figures in *The Helen Morgan Story* come to life through an extraordinarily strong group of actors. Powerful scenes and small gestures reveal not only their relationship to Helen but also their standing in a larger social context. Curtiz films often convey the suggestion that so-called little people are important, even if he was reputed to be ruthless in his treatment of extras and actors who did not seem to him like true stars or consummate professionals. Sometimes he concocted set designs and stunts that, in the heat of shooting, endangered and injured actors and animals, especially in early films such as *Noah's Ark* or *The Charge of the Light Brigade*.

Playing Helen, Ann Blyth didn't face physical danger but she did have to fall physically and emotionally, cast as a codependent figure in a film that undermined her emotional and professional confidence. As in *The Scarlet Hour*, the female lead has a longtime female friend, this time Dolly (Cara Williams), with whom she used to work in show business. Once again, the two women have an intimate and revelatory relationship. The secondary romantic couple serves as a model for how the main duo ought to mature and grow. In Dolly, Williams plays a type very similar to the role played by Stritch in *The Scarlet Hour*: a big-boned blonde with a brusque, fun-loving manner and utter loyalty to her volatile friend. Dolly is paired with a regular guy, an apprentice con man named Benny Weaver (played with bluff good spirits by Alan King), who is neither handsome nor ambitious but is willing to play the sidekick and no-questions-asked husband, happy to be told what to do by the woman he loves. While this kind of relationship is unusual in film noir, it occurs with regularity in the musical genre, and Curtiz adds greater depth to these minor characters than is customary.

In a spirit of egalitarian populism and with a nod toward realism, Curtiz gives other minor characters a role in depicting the seamier realities of show business (one scene includes a girl's silhouetted suicide by hanging). Unlike the typical glitz of many musical settings, depictions of Morgan's life in early scenes emphasize the speakeasy environment of the Prohibition era. The introduction of Larry in the opening scene sets the stage for their future relationship. After a downpour, Helen enters his trailer and changes clothes behind a transparent screen. Soon, Larry turns out the lights and grabs her, in a tussle that turns from resistance to a helplessly passionate embrace. She wakes the next morning to find a curt note, beginning what is for her a recurring pattern of disappointment.

At every turning point, Larry reappears to inveigle Helen into another moneymaking scheme that relies on her talent and someone else's money. He convinces her to enter a fixed beauty contest for Miss Canada as a front for his bootlegging operation. Judges discover she is not Canadian, so Russell Wade (Richard Carlson), the contest's outside American legal counsel, strips her of the title. Later on, Wade falls for her, in spite of his amicable marriage of convenience. In typical musical montages, upbeat songs such as "On the Sunny Side of the Street" signal her rise, but soon enough we find the police smashing cases of liquor, in extravagant physical displays connecting Helen's addiction and her performance environment.

In the midst of Helen's success, Larry shows up with another woman at an upscale nightclub where Helen is asked to perform, and the musical turns into expressionist melodrama. Staring at the couple, Helen slugs back a couple of extra drinks and wobbles up to the stage, where she sings George Gershwin's "The Man I Love." Grabbing a table to keep from falling down, she croons with a sob in her voice, her eyes glistening as she gazes the whole time at Larry. He stares back, riveted, in spite of his date's attempt to block his view of Helen's dramatic final notes. An abrupt

Helen and Larry face off, trapped emotionally and visually in expressionist pools of light and shadow that look like bars, as they stand in front of a window that offers no hope of escape, in *The Helen Morgan Story* (Warner Bros., 1957). Digital frame enlargement.

fade-out and cut shows Helen staggering into her darkened apartment, the profile of an unidentified man (who turns out to be Larry) shrouded in shadows dominating the right side of the frame, watching her undress. In contrast to these rather sinister visuals, nondiegetic music in the background is oddly upbeat, like a whimsical score from a Doris Day comedy. When Helen hears a noise—the clink of Larry's drink falling over—the soundtrack turns menacing as he approaches, grabs her, and insists that she wants him.

Throughout the scene, Curtiz uses expressionist pools of light in the midst of darkness, the shadow of Helen's venetian blinds like bars against the wall. The actors take turns in the light, with the other as a black silhouette, mesmerized in a dance of love and hate. Trapping Helen against the blinds, Larry grabs her, and what looks like a potential rape soon turns to mutual desire, in a reprise of the film's opening. As Helen tries to escape, Larry knocks over a lamp, and the scene closes with him crouched over her small body as she eagerly returns his passionate embrace. Following a fade-out, the next scene finds Larry at Wade's law office, offering to front a nightclub for Helen, with Wade as secret investor and silent partner. Thus the Helen Morgan Club is born, and her star begins to rise while she and Larry seem to be lovers again. Revolted when she finally discovers this scheme, Helen tells Larry she loves Wade. Like the scorned Ralph or Paulie in *The Scarlet Hour*, Larry jealously strikes out, slapping Helen twice before storming out.

A number of writers have criticized Curtiz for manufacturing events that deviated from the facts of the real Helen Morgan's story. Paul Newman's Larry condenses several shady lovers and two husbands, and the narrative focuses on a single obsessive love and hate as characters career in and out of one another's lives. Curtiz justified his choice to have Gogi Grant—famous for her 1956 hit "The Wayward Wind"—dub Blyth's voice, because "the kind of high-pitched, low-voiced torch singing" that the original singer used to perform "wouldn't go over today, it's outmoded" (Landazuri, n.d.). Blyth declared publicly that she "wasn't hurt by the decision," describing herself as "disappointed but not heartbroken" (ibid.). This was to be Blyth's last film, and she may well have been humiliated by Curtiz's refusal to use her own voice. She received generally negative reviews for her acting, and Curtiz was faulted for taking Hedda Hopper's suggestion to cast Blyth in the role. More significantly, Blyth's process of embedding herself in the role of a self-denigrating character convinced that her life was doomed may have taken its toll. The timing of the popular television premiere of Polly Bergen in a live performance of the role of Helen Morgan on *Playhouse 90* (for which she won an Emmy) did not help the film's chances for success, coming on May 16, 1957, around four months before the movie's theatrical release on October 5.

The film diminishes Morgan's career by overlooking her film performances. Amy Lawrence observes that at least one writer's analysis of Helen Morgan's film performance "seems to address Morgan's speaking and singing," whereas "most contemporary critics focused exclusively on her musical abilities, often in ways that linked femininity with victimization" (2013, 5). Life imitated art when directors forced Morgan into roles as helpless women, and Curtiz's version of her life repeats this pattern, perhaps dooming the film to failure. Viewers wanted a happy musical, not a chronicle of the singer's decline, topped by an unconvincingly arbitrary redemptive ending. The comments about Morgan's voice reveal many critics' lack of musical sophistication, with some describing it as "thin." But in *Applause*, the real Morgan's performance is close to the delicate power of coloratura operatic style, not surprising since the director, Rouben Mamoulian, previously directed operas. In *The Helen Morgan Story*, Gogi Grant heightens the melodrama by ranging from pleading anguish to silky purr or full-throated belting wail, all styles that are a far cry from the real voice of Morgan as we hear it in *Applause*.

As Curtiz's Helen hits bottom, her diminished voice takes center stage in a cascade of scenes that feature a degree of expressionist surrealism unparalleled in musicals until Bob Fosse's *All That Jazz* (1979). Canted frames reveal Helen's abject disorientation as an orchestral version of "The Man I Love" plays and a passing car drenches her with water. In a bar, with the camera tilting back and forth, Helen hears a radio playing Jerome Kern's

"Why Was I Born?" Turning to other drunken patrons, she insists, "I made that song famous. I'm Helen Morgan, the star." As she starts to warble the final high notes and emits a hoarse off-key screech, they tell her to shut up. Leaving the bar, she staggers through an alley, canted frames tilting at greater extremes as she faints, harp strings jangling in the background, a policeman blowing his whistle when he finds her among the trashcans. An abrupt cut shows a close-up of her strapped down, racked with delirium tremens, sweating, shivering, hallucinating, and screaming, "Let me have a drink! Please."

With the magic of montage, Helen's suffering ends in a cut to a snow-covered window, a shot of her quiet and calm in bed. She receives a visit from Larry, who has sent flowers, pretending they are from famous people who still remember her. After his stint in jail, he can finally tell her, "You come first. We'll dig up a justice of the peace," but she replies, "It's too late now." Ignoring her rejection and whisking her off for one last look at her club, Larry leads her inside, where applause suddenly explodes from the darkened show floor and lights go up. This maudlin triumphant closing of *The Helen Morgan Story* is unable to override the relentless sadness and seemingly inevitable path of deterioration in the central character's life. Nevertheless, the popularity of public acclamation scenes reflects the timeless emotional appeal of such acknowledgment. Imitating his own glory when he won an Oscar for *Casablanca*, Curtiz presents a roomful of celebrities applauding Helen's professional life. So far removed from the scenes of her previous struggle with rehab and shivering hallucinations that it has an almost surreal quality, this conclusion reifies the oneiric fantasy of public acceptance and adoration. With dreamlike ease, as she takes the stage, she sings as she did before her descent into alcoholism, effortlessly and smoothly, the pianist magically sensing the song she wants, Kern and Hammerstein's "Can't Help Lovin' Dat Man," the masochistic emotional core of her story.

In *The Helen Morgan Story* and *The Scarlet Hour*, Curtiz paints vivid portraits of male and female characters whose self-destructive attachments doom themselves and others in scenes that violate gender roles and confound the genre expectations of audiences. Rather than attempting to settle the debate whether Curtiz is an undervalued auteur or simply a skilled technician, the analysis of these two films has explored a different argument, focusing on how he shaped his material—particularly offbeat depictions of gender and suggestive, ambiguous narrative conclusions for characters—in a way that challenged conventions, leaving viewers in the same liminal space that Curtiz occupies as auteur, or not, with details un-settled and subject to interpretation. Some scholars claim there are no references to Curtiz's own life in his films, whereas others, such as Catherine Portuges, see in his depictions a deep identification with the outsider, an artifact of his position as a Jewish exile (2011, 168). Even if a reading of transgressive gender portrayals is speculative, it may enrich and deepen our perception of these films to hear echoes of the young Hungarian immigrant director in Paulie's vow never to be poor again, or to see traces of Curtiz's own wish fulfillment in his fantasy ending for Helen Morgan, at long last receiving the love and public recognition of talent, both longed for and deserved.

Archive

Warner Bros. Archives, University of Southern California, Los Angeles (WB). Files consulted included the Michael Curtiz Legal File 2875.

Works Cited

Erikson, Hal. n.d. Synopsis of *The Scarlet Hour*. AllMovie.com, www.allmovie .com/movie/the-scarlet-hour-v109031.

Harmetz, Aljean. 1992. *Round Up the Usual Suspects: The Making of "Casablanca"; Bogart, Bergman, and World War II*. New York: Hyperion.

Hess, Judith. 1974. "Genre Films and the Status Quo." *Jump Cut: A Review of Contemporary Media* 1:1–18. www.ejumpcut.org/archive/onlinessays/JC01folder /GenreFilms.html.

Kinnard, Roy, and R. J. Vitone. 1986. *The American Films of Michael Curtiz*. Metuchen, NJ: Scarecrow.

Landazuri, Margarita. n.d. "*The Helen Morgan Story*." Turner Classic Movies website, www.tcm.com/this-month/article.html?id=628634|636890.

Lawrence, Amy. 2013. "Bruised and Confused: Helen Morgan and the Limits of Pathos." *Film History* 25, no. 3: 1–31.

Lecomte, Jean-Marie. 2008. "Rouben Mamoulian's *Applause* and the Birth of the Disenchanted Musical." *Studies in Musical Theatre* 2, no. 2: 147–161. Clipping in Michael Curtiz Legal File 2875, WB.

Portuges, Catherine. 2011. "Curtiz, Hungarian Cinema, and Hollywood." In *Comparative Hungarian Cultural Studies*, edited by Steven Tötösy de Zepetnek and Louise Olga Vasvári, 161–170. West Lafayette, IN: Purdue University Press.

Robertson, James C. 1993. *The Casablanca Man: The Cinema of Michael Curtiz*. London: Routledge.

Rosenzweig, Sidney. 1982. *"Casablanca" and Other Major Films of Michael Curtiz*. Ann Arbor, MI: UMI Research Press.

CHAPTER 2

Making a *Life with Father*

DAVID DESSER

When Warner Bros. bought the screen rights to *Life with Father*, a 1939 Broadway show running at the Empire Theatre that went on to become Broadway's longest running nonmusical play (3,224 performances), the studio intended to release the film version in 1941. The studio records do not indicate exactly why it was delayed until August 1947.[1] It is possible that, upon further thought, Warners delayed the release until the Broadway show closed, on July 12, 1947, although studio records do not reflect this, and production heads could not have predicted its unprecedented success on the Great White Way. The film was certainly not shot for a 1941 release. Indeed, production did not begin until 1946. Perhaps the studio's all-out support for the war effort put this relatively modest story of late nineteenth-century New York on the back burner: Warner Bros. was unquestionably the most gung ho of the majors in its prowar offerings. It gave the country *Confessions of a Nazi Spy* (Anatole Litvak) as early as 1939; John Huston's noir-tinged *Across the Pacific* (1942); Howard Hawks's paradigmatic *Air Force* (1943) and *To Have and Have Not* (1944), the filmmaker's first foray into both noir and Ernest Hemingway's masculine world; and from Raoul Walsh, *Objective, Burma!* (1945), surely the grimmest war film made until Sam Fuller returned from the European front.

The studio head, Jack Warner, was involved with the project from the start. So much did he want the rights that he gave up not only a lot of money but also, and more unusually, a great deal of creative control to the property owners, Mrs. Clarence Day and the theatrical authors, Howard Lindsay and Russel Crouse. Mrs. Day (as she insisted on being called) held the rights to the literary properties upon which the Broadway show was based (their author, Clarence Day Jr., having died in 1935), a hugely successful series of short stories that had appeared in many of the most prominent literary magazines of the day, including, most particularly, the

New Yorker, but also *Harper's Magazine* and the *New Republic.* Many of these sketches were compiled into a collection in 1935, similarly to huge success, and these became the basis of the loosely connected vignettes in the play and subsequent film.

Casting discussions went on early in the preproduction process. The original idea was to have the Broadway leads, co-author Howard Lindsay and his wife, Dorothy Stickney, as the principals in the film. Even after Stickney dropped out of consideration, Lindsay remained in the running. Following a screen test, however, he determined that his voice was unsuitable for film. Bette Davis was Warners' top female star, and she wanted the role of Vinnie: "She worked hard on her makeup, hair, and characterization, but simply could not convey the daintiness and innocence that conceal Lavinia's will of iron" (*Magill's Survey of Cinema* 1995). Mary Pickford was also tested.

Michael Curtiz was long attached to the project. But his production of patriotic and war films seems to have left *Life with Father* somewhat in the lurch. From 1941 through 1944, Curtiz directed eight war-themed films, including, of course, *Casablanca,* and also the Americana-tinged patriotic biopic *Yankee Doodle Dandy.* Given the studio's substantial investment in the project, however, it was no surprise that they put it on the front burner right after the war.

Although Irene Dunne was early on signed for the role of Mother, Vinnie Day, she apparently did not like the part.[2] Asked by James McCourt, "Which directors discussed motivation with you a lot?" she replied, "Michael Curtiz, for instance, in *Life with Father,* because I didn't like the role very much, and he had to placate me and make it more palatable" (McCourt 1980). Indeed, as Richard Schickel concurs, "She particularly, and correctly, despised the ditsiness of Vinnie Day" (1981, 50). Yet as Maria DiBattista perceptively notes, "Dunne was always, morally and temperamentally, a wife" (2003, 203). Of course, a wife did not have to be scatterbrained and ignorant, even in the early 1880s, but Dunne had the ability to make Vinnie both ditsy and shrewd at the same time. Dunne was still, at the time, one of the top female stars of the era. Although she had never won an Oscar, she had been nominated three times, for *Theodora Goes Wild* (1936), *The Awful Truth* (1937), and *Love Affair* (1939). She was a smart businesswoman, and she and her agent, Charles Feldman, were among the pioneers of freelance work in the studio era, often agreeing to a percentage of the box office in lieu of an upfront salary (see Carman 2012). This she did for *Life with Father,* a successful gambit on her part, since the film went on to great success.

The casting of the role of Father—Clarence Day Sr.—took a bit longer.

According to one source, William Powell wanted the role—apparently, he had wanted it for years—and urged his studio, MGM, to buy it for him. Although, it should be noted, had MGM gotten it, the studio would likely have cast Spencer Tracy (*Magill's Survey of Cinema* 1995). At this point, Warner Bros. asked MGM to lend out Powell, as well as Elizabeth Taylor for a supporting role. As it happened, by the time Powell landed the role he was fifty-four years old; the official playbook describes Clarence Day Sr. as being in his forties. Other roles were cast fairly quickly: the popular Edmund Gwenn in the role of the slightly befuddled Reverend Dr. Lloyd, and silent-film legend Zasu Pitts in the rather underdeveloped role of Cousin Cora.

The veteran screenwriter Donald Ogden Stewart was assigned the perhaps unenviable task of adapting the play—unenviable because he was hamstrung by contractual obligations to leave it as untouched as possible or to have Mrs. Day and Lindsay and Crouse approve any changes. Stewart tried to do what any screenwriter does when adapting a play, which is to open it up, and get away from the limited sets that were typical of a Broadway play at the time. Besides changing locales in the Day's house (the play used only the morning room), Stewart found success by setting scenes in locales that are only alluded to in the play, such as the Reverend Lloyd's church, a department store where Clarence is fitted with a new suit, and a restaurant in which a major plot point is revealed. As studio memos reveal, these scenes were well thought out by the production: to ensure historical accuracy, permission was secured to use the names of Lewis & Conger, a department store still in business in 1947; McCreery's & Co., one of the most upscale stores of its era; and Delmonico's, a restaurant synonymous with fine dining. The scene in Delmonico's emphasizes the plush luxury and glamour of the interior and the solicitude of the waiters. It is also here that we see Father speaking French, a reminder of the kind of education he would have received (no doubt at Yale, which Young Clarence [Jimmy Lydon] is to attend in the upcoming fall). It is also at Delmonico's that we learn Father was never baptized; thus, almost forty-three minutes into the film we get the semblance of the plotline that will form the spine of the narrative as Father's unbaptized status comes to be important. A later scene in McCreery's department store further embeds the feelings of nostalgia the film has all along been careful to create, with the array of hats and suits demonstrating the shifts in fashion, and with the variety of bathing suits and corsets clearly indicating to the contemporary audience the freeing of women's bodies from Victorian strictures. It is worth noting that McCreery's and Delmonico's were almost exclusively the province of the well-to-do in the late nineteenth century. For Cousin Cora and her traveling companion, Mary Skinner, visiting from bucolic, faraway Ohio, it was a virtual dreamworld.[3]

Of course, in Hollywood's Golden Age, screenwriters were also constrained by that most dreaded of institutions: the Production Code Administration. Though the stage play was family friendly in every respect, the PCA had two problems with the film script. The first was the frequent "swearing," with the words "God" and "damn" sounded on occasion (though never as one word) by Father. The Code specifically addressed this: "Resolved, That those things which are included in the following list shall not appear in pictures produced by the members of this Association, irrespective of the manner in which they are treated: Pointed profanity— by either title or lip—this includes the words 'God,' 'Lord,' 'Jesus,' 'Christ' (unless they be used reverently in connection with proper religious ceremonies), 'hell,' 'damn,' 'gawd,' and every other profane and vulgar expression however it may be spelled." This concern was dealt with by eliminating the offending words from the film script and substituting "Oh, Gahd!" Apparently "Gahd" was a spelling the censors could live with. In fact, given Father's clipped, formal speaking voice, the substitution worked better than having him use words that might have sounded both more profane and more modern.

The other issue was trickier. The Code states, "No film or episode may throw ridicule on any religious faith." Here the characterization of the Reverend Doctor Lloyd became the concern. From today's perspective, he is a bit flighty, but harmless and well meaning. As portrayed by Gwenn, Doctor Lloyd is in every respect a kind and decent man who happens not to recall the exact value of the land acquired for the new church uptown. To the PCA censors, his seeming absentmindedness and gentle manner needed careful handling. Interestingly, they were right insofar as at least two letters to the studio after the film's release wondered why the characterization of the minister had to be so negative. (What today seems charming was perhaps a more problematic characterization at the time.)

As is well known, the Production Code couldn't prevent sexual innuendo, and there is much of that in the film. When Father sees his youngest son Harlan's dog, the boy tells him its name is "Princess." Holding him up, Father notes, "He looks more like a Prince to me." More directly, when innocent fourteen-year-old Mary visits with Cousin Cora, she sees naïve, sixteen-year-old Clarence (i.e., Clarence Jr.) holding a violin. After establishing that he plays the violin and that she plays the piano, she asks, "Do you ever play"—breathless pause—"duets?" Clarence replies, "Well,

I haven't up to now." Mary responds, "Neither have I . . . up to now." The use of close-ups on the two juveniles emphasizes the quick development of puppy love. Even in her early teens, Elizabeth Taylor already had the sex appeal—the stunning figure and the dark blue eyes that appeared violet—that would soon make her among the most beautiful women in the world. Her line delivery, with the intake of breath and the meaningful pause, make for humor and an innuendo impossible to overlook. Later, when she sits on Clarence's lap and he cries out, "Get up, get up!" as if scalded by a hot drink, he may attribute it to the fact that she is sitting on Father's old suit, and the suit won't do anything that Father wouldn't do (like kneel in church). But there are clearly other reasons for Clarence's sudden eruption. Finally, we might note Vinnie's horrified realization that if Father has not been baptized, then perhaps she and he are not married. A glance over at her two youngest sons in their cozy bed horrifies her. That scene ends with a fade-out, allowing us to fill in the implications, remembering, too, the Production Code's guideline that "the sanctity of the institution of marriage and the home shall be upheld. Pictures shall not infer [*sic*] that low forms of sex relationship are the accepted or common thing."

Principal photography began under Curtiz's direction in August 1946, with a generous twelve-week shooting schedule. Shooting in Technicolor presented problems in preproduction; many rolls of test footage were shot to get things like the hair color of the family (all different shades of red) correct and to match the production design to hair color and costume. The use of Technicolor indicates the prestige with which the studio endowed the film, the saturated colors adding to the nostalgic appeal and getting away from the rather drab use of black-and-white in the war films and home-front melodramas. With the problems of Technicolor solved, Curtiz worked with his usual intensity, though problems with illnesses (minor for both Dunne and Taylor, but at the cost of shooting delays) and the strange repeated absences of William Powell (who, unbeknownst to the studio and crew, was undergoing treatment for rectal cancer) pushed back the completion of principal photography by four weeks. Given that all the principals were owed money should the film go over its allotted shooting schedule, the studio was concerned, though not panicked, by these delays.

Overall, however, the veteran Curtiz kept things moving and the production flowing. Jimmy Lydon liked to tell the story of his experiences working with Curtiz on the film:

> Mike Curtiz was a wonderful, crazy, marvelous man. He could barely speak English and had a violent temper. If anything went wrong, he

would sometimes stand in the middle of the set and scream at the top of his lungs: "Who gets the big dough, you or me?" And he'd never go to lunch. So when the actors would come back from eating, he'd be mumbling "Damn no good actors, why do you always have to feed your faces?" But when you got used to him, he was wonderful, just the most marvelous director. (Thomas 2016)

At one point, Elizabeth Taylor could not get her blocking right in the scene where she sits on Lydon's lap. As Lydon recalls it:

By the eighth take, the director had had enough and started screaming. Poor Elizabeth began to cry and ran off the set to her dressing room, which was in a trailer outside the sound stage. Curtiz followed the distressed Taylor out and unleashed a mixture of rage and regret. Here's this great, huge man who looked like a wrestler, with not a hair on his head, pacing up and down in front of Elizabeth's dressing room screaming at the top of his lungs and swearing like a marine. "Son-of-a-bitch! Don't cry, damn it! You break my heart—I kill myself—I'm sorry!" Well, that was Mike Curtiz. (Thomas 2016)

The one true problem that arose had to do with Zasu Pitts. Curtiz wanted to replace her after a few days of shooting her scenes. Since virtually all of these were with Elizabeth Taylor, who would be owed extra money if the film went over schedule and who was proving a bit delicate, the studio vetoed this idea. Now most famous for her leading role as Trina in the contested classic *Greed* (1924), Pitts was one of the busiest actresses in Hollywood during the 1920s and 1930s. Most of her films of the early sound era, however, were B features in which she was accustomed to working quickly and with minimal effort—no surprise, since in one three-year stretch (1932–1934), she appeared in about fifty films. By 1946, her career was winding down, and she appeared in no A features before or after *Life with Father.* She went on to become one of the most active former movie stars to work in television in the 1950s. There is nothing at all wrong with her performance in the film, however, that one can see from this juncture.

Curtiz exhibited more meticulousness than perhaps he had previously—owing most likely to the set design and the use of Technicolor—and he and the studio were rewarded with solid, often glowing reviews and a terrific box-office return. Though Warner Bros. had hoped for a bit more recognition from the Academy at Oscar time, William Powell had been right to covet the role of Father, since he received a nomination for

Best Actor (he lost to Ronald Colman and was also competing against Gregory Peck, John Garfield, and Michael Redgrave). Max Steiner was nominated for Best Dramatic or Comedy Score. In addition, the film received nominations for art direction–set decoration (color) and cinematography (color).[4]

Curtiz found a way of opening up the play beyond the use of a variety of sets and locales. To avoid staginess, he frequently employs a moving camera. Thus, instead of cutting, he employs follow shots with a dolly, along with the frequent use of panning. He uses a dolly-in or a dolly-out to reframe characters, rather than cutting. A crane is employed from time to time, as, for instance, when Vinnie accompanies Cora and Mary out of the music room and up the stairs to show them the room in which they will stay. This sequence employs many of the stylistic strategies apparent throughout the film. From a static three-shot, the camera pans with them as they exit the music room, and then dollies forward as they approach the staircase. As Vinnie and Cora move up the stairs, the crane is employed to continue to follow them. The two go up, but since Mary lags behind, the camera movement drops her out of the frame. The whole sequence lasts a mere seventeen seconds, a long take by Hollywood's standards since the 1980s, but hardly Wellesian in its duration. Still, in its relative complexity it indicates Curtiz's break from the stage and his keen sense of the cinema. The comparison to Welles is not unwarranted, since Curtiz employs a technique seen frequently in *The Magnificent Ambersons* (1942), as well as in Vincente Minnelli's *Meet Me in St. Louis* (1944) and Jean Renoir's *La Règle du Jeu* (1939), and that is to make a transition from one character to another by having the new character enter the frame from off-screen while the camera is moving as the other characters exit the frame. In addition, Curtiz uses deep focus on a number of occasions. This has the effect, on the one hand, of reproducing the multilayered focal planes on which a stage play may rely, and yet, on the other, of giving the feeling of opening up the film away from the typical guided views of classical decoupage. Curtiz, then, did everything he could to remove staginess from the material, aided by the few scenes inserted by Donald Ogden Stewart with the blessing of Lindsay, Crouse, and Mrs. Clarence Day.

The question of billing, which arose before production began, was solved in an interesting way, apparent only at the time of release. The discussion about who would be billed first—Irene Dunne or William Powell—had become so well known that it was reported in the trade papers at the time. Although it could be argued that Dunne was the bigger star of the two and that Powell might have been a gentleman about the whole thing,

The use of deep focus works to create a more cinematic effect precisely through theatrical staging while continuing to emphasize the sets, props, and costumes that create a nostalgic patina over the film, in *Life with Father* (Warner Bros., 1947). Digital frame enlargement.

once agents were involved (as they usually were), things became more contentious. The problem was finally solved when the studio agreed that top billing would shift between the two of them. This was not a big problem when it came to newspaper advertising. Dunne would get top billing on the ad copy one day, and Powell on the next. But for release prints of the film, the situation was both trickier and more expensive. Powell would receive top billing on the print shown for the New York premiere, and Dunne would have her name first on the print for the Los Angeles premiere. Otherwise, the studio made prints with one or the other listed first and sent them out around the country. Oddly, the film was never officially copyrighted. Although there is a copyright statement on the film, it is not listed in the US Catalog of Copyright Entries for Motion Pictures (*AFI Catalog of Feature Films*, n.d.). During the videotape years, many inferior copies of the film were available for sale at very low prices. A restoration, with copyright, appeared in 2007, and DVD versions have appeared from a number of companies, but not Warner Bros.[5]

A Little Life Reading

It would be easy to see the huge success of the Broadway play as a response to the looming dark days of World War II. The gradual easing of the Great Depression was due, in large part, to the gearing up of war production, and although many forces in the United States lobbied for continued isolation, events in Europe, especially after September 1, 1939, could not be ignored. The play clearly offered a vision of a simpler time, for both families and the country. There is nothing in the studio records about what Warner Bros. thought of the meaning of the play, no discussion of theme or significance. Yet by the time it was released, we may see it as an important contribution to the culture of the postwar era.

The film version of *Life with Father* was part of a cycle of nostalgic films made at the end of, and just after, the war. Rejecting the cynicism of film noir and the domestic melodramas insisting that a woman's place was in the home, these films intended not only to offer up visions of a kind of prelapsarian (white) America but also to reintegrate men into the feminine sphere. With millions of American men returning from the European and Asian theaters of war, battle-hardened and baptized by fire, the country potentially had a huge social problem on its hands. The GI Bill, which encouraged these men to study a trade or attend college, was one way of meeting the challenge of demobilized vets. Another was an ideology of consumerism and family values. Many women's films preached an ideology of home and family to women who had recently been on factory assembly lines, free from the tyranny of patriarchy for the first time in their lives. They had to be convinced to return to it — although a softening of male attitudes was also apparent in the postwar cultural shift. Films were in the forefront of trying to shape these attitudes about the place of men (and women) in peacetime.

Twentieth Century–Fox, long the master of Americana, entered the cycle at the same time as *Life with Father* with the Betty Grable vehicles *The Shocking Miss Pilgrim* and *Mother Wore Tights* (both 1947). Irene Dunne, star of *Life with Father*, evened up the gender balance with perhaps her most famous role in RKO's *I Remember Mama* (1948). Over at MGM, also in 1947, the reliable Charles Walters directed *Good News*, a Roaring 20s–set musical (which had opened on Broadway in 1927), and in 1948, twenty-eight-year-old Mickey Rooney returned to small-town America, this time at the turn of the century, for Rouben Mamoulian's *Summer Holiday*. Paramount, seeing the end of the war in sight, released the now little-known *Our Hearts Were Young and Gay* (1944), a story of young women sailing to Europe in the peaceful days of 1923. The film was something of a success, since there was a sequel, *Our Hearts Were Growing Up* (1946). Even the cynical Billy Wilder found settings in his native Austria for *The Emperor Waltz* in 1948. The nostalgic value of the turn-of-the-century Austrian Alps setting would be interesting to gauge. I suggest, too, that the musical biopic comes into its own in this period, precisely for its nostalgia value rather than because of any sudden interest in performers or composers. A good example is *Incendiary Blonde* (1945), Paramount's account of the arguably now-forgotten Texas Guinan. Probably long forgotten as well are the Dolly Sisters, twin Hungarian immigrants in New York, whose vaudeville career is recounted in a Betty Grable–June Haver Technicolor spectacular.[6] We learn little about the composer Jerome Kern in *Till the Clouds Roll By* (1946), but are treated to many of his most famous songs of yesteryear. The same is largely true of Irving Rapper's *Rhapsody in Blue*, with Robert Alda in the role of George Gershwin (1945), and of Cary Grant playing Cole Porter in *Night and Day* (1946), directed by Michael Curtiz and released while *Life with Father* was in production.

Yet it is Minnelli's colorful classic *Meet Me in St. Louis* that set the standard not only for small-town nostalgia but also for the hardly noted undercurrent of the reintegration of men into an all-female world. Though *Life with Father* began as short stories of Father's antics in old New York, one can detect the manner in which Father is isolated, even alienated, from his family. The same is no less true for Mr. Smith (Leon Ames) in *Meet Me in St. Louis*. It may be more than trivial or coincidental that Ames went on to appear as Clarence Day Sr. in the television series *Life with Father*, which ran for twenty-eight episodes on CBS in 1953–1955. *Meet Me* demonstrates the manner in which Mr. Smith is an outsider in the almost all-woman world (Alonzo Jr. is a minor character, and Grandpa, although important, is clearly already integrated into the female world, as seen at the start when he continues the song "Meet Me in St. Louis," picking it up from his granddaughter Agnes). Mr. Smith is even willing to move the family to New York before the world's fair takes place in St. Louis—thus robbing the whole family of a thrill they are eager to experience. Of course, he changes his mind when little Tootie (Margaret O'Brien) destroys the snowman family in the famous Christmas scene.

Clarence Day Sr. is no less alienated from his family and the household goings-on. Maids continually leave the family's employ because of his berating them; he does not take kindly to overnight guests in his home; he condemns his wife's purchases (e.g., a rubber plant, a pug dog statue) and the manner in which she keeps the household accounts; he allows his son

Whitney to skip catechism practice to play baseball; and, as noted, he has not been baptized. Vinnie may be horrified at hearing this, but Clarence refuses to give in: "I won't be baptized," he loudly insists. Father's notion that baptism is all right for "savages and children" belies the obvious implication that since the women he knows *are* baptized, they must be one or the other.[7] His refusal, then, continues to set him apart from his wife and sons.

We see that this alienation is only superficial. He loses every argument to his wife. The rubber plant, though it shifts rooms, remains in the house. Cora and Mary stay for an entire week. Vinnie spends more money on the household accounts when she convinces Father to open up charge accounts, especially at McCreery's. She and her son go shopping there and charge a fifteen-dollar pug-dog statue, initiating a kind of "pug-dog economics." Father rejects the statue, so Vinnie has Clarence Jr. return it in exchange for a new fifteen-dollar suit, which Father had previously refused to buy. Father insists he told Vinnie not to buy the suit, and she replies that they didn't buy the suit, they exchanged the statue for it. Father becomes flustered while trying to understand what happened to his fifteen dollars. When Clarence insists that they must pay for the statue, Vinnie rightly points out that they no longer have it. And most importantly, Mother convinces Father that he will be baptized: their trip uptown to the church in a fancy horse-drawn cab closes the film. What does it mean for Father to be baptized into the world of savages, children, and women?

For Minnelli's Mr. Smith and Curtiz's Clarence Day, their return to the family realm, the world of women and domesticity, is a subtle lesson for returning veterans of World War II. They must put aside their adventurous ways, their commanding presence and patriarchal control, in order to achieve an appropriate balance of gender relations.

Of course, there was no need to be subtle about this: plenty of films made in the immediate postwar period dealt with the problem directly. The point about setting this tale in the past, playing around the edges of a nostalgic glow, is to insist that men were always already part of the domestic realm, feminized into the consumer culture dominated by women. The famed historian Ann Douglas influentially wrote about the "feminization of American culture" during the Victorian era, claiming that middle-class women and liberal clergymen exerted a great degree of influence on literature and art while the men took care of business. No surprise then that it is precisely Vinnie Day and the Reverend Lloyd whose taste and values eventually reform and reintegrate the irascible but lovable Father (and indeed it is that most sentimental of values—love—that we feel for and attribute to him). Michael Curtiz, who had done much to rouse America in support of the war, was no less important in helping America win the peace.

Notes

1. Unless otherwise noted, all references to studio records and memoranda derive from the *Life with Father* box, Warner Bros. Archives, USC. The *AFI Catalog of Feature Films* tells a different story: "HR [*Hollywood Reporter*] news items add the following information about the production: In 1940, Samuel Goldwyn offered $200,000 for screen rights to the Oscar Serlin production of the play, but the purchase did not take place because Serlin demanded a three-year clearance clause before the exhibition of the film. In July 1944, Mary Pickford negotiated with Serlin for rights, planning to star in the film with William Powell. Warner Bros. acquired the screen rights to the play in Nov 1944 for a reputed down payment of $500,000 plus a percentage of the net proceeds. As part of the agreement, the film was not to be released before 1947 and the property was to revert back to Oscar Serlin after a period of seven years." But nothing in the files reflects this, and some studio memos indicate Warner Bros.' acquisition and preproduction discussions as I outline them. It is true that the studio paid $500,000 for the rights.

2. The IMDb indicates that Mary Pickford made several screen tests for the role of Vinnie, and all agreed that she would be perfect in the role, since Lavinia was a variant upon many of her silent-screen roles. But the studio felt that her thirteen-year absence from the screen made her box-office appeal problematic (www .imdb.com/title/tt0039566/trivia?ref_=tt_trv_trv). There is nothing in the studio files about screen tests for other actresses, but it is worth noting that Pickford was the same age as William Powell, though at least six years older than Dunne. The IMDb and other sources, noncredited (e.g., www.threemoviebuffs.com/review /life-with-father), claim that Curtiz preferred Dunne over Pickford. Studio files do not indicate that Curtiz was involved in casting at the preproduction stage. Other sources indicate that Curtiz pursued Dunne for the role after the studio wavered over Pickford.

3. The department store would have been especially nostalgic for many in the audience because of the goods (and prices, e.g., a man's suit for $15) on display. By 1900, stores like Sears, Roebuck and many of the famous emporia in America's cities and towns had made the department store a usual haunt for upper- and middle-class Americans, who no longer made their own clothes or built their own furniture. By the 1940s, most audience members would have had the experience of shopping at department stores from the time they were young.

4. Edmund Gwenn was awarded the Best Supporting Actor Oscar for his role as Kris Kringle, a.k.a. Santa Claus, in *Miracle on 34th Street*. It was felt by some that his lightly comic turn in *Life with Father* contributed to his award for the Christmas Day family classic.

5. My copy was issued by Alpha Video, a company that specializes in low-budget, out-of-copyright films and television shows. See its website, www.oldies .com.

6. It must be noted that many of the musical biopics, as well as other nostalgic

musicals, were produced in Technicolor. As mentioned earlier, this was not only a question of prestige but also a way of further embedding nostalgia in the very fabric of the film.

7. Vinnie's insistence at the dinner table at Delmonico's that "everybody's baptized" is, of course, patently untrue—it is notably untrue, for instance, of the film's director and the Warner Bros. studio head.

Works Cited

AFI Catalog of Feature Films. n.d. *Life with Father*. www.afi.com/members/catalog/DetailView.aspx?s=&Movie=25245.

Carman, Emily. 2012. "Women Rule Hollywood: Ageing and Freelance Stardom in the Studio System." *Celebrity Studies* 3, no. 1: 13–24.

DiBattista, Maria. 2003. *Fast-Talking Dames*. New Haven, CT: Yale University Press.

Douglas, Ann. 1977. *The Feminization of American Culture*. New York: Knopf.

Magill's Survey of Cinema. 1995. "*Life with Father*." June 15. curtiz.tripod.com/life.htm.

McCourt, James. 1980. "Irene Dunne: The Awesome Truth." *Film Comment* 16, no. 1: 26–32.

Schickel, Richard. 1981. "We Remember Irene." *Film Comment* 27, no. 2: 48–52.

Thomas, Nick. 2016. "Jimmy Lydon Remembers *Life with Father*." June 16. The Spectrum, www.thespectrum.com/story/entertainment/2016/06/16/jimmy-lydon-remembers-life-father/85830388.

CHAPTER 3

The Jewish Jazz Singer Remakes His Voice: Michael Curtiz's Update of the Warner Bros. Classic

SETH FRIEDMAN

The Jazz Singer (1927) is difficult to remake. As Krin Gabbard explains, this is attributable to historical conditions of production and reception that became unrenewable or unfashionable, including the novelty of synchronized sound, the acceptability of blackface, Jews' struggle to assimilate into whiteness, and Al Jolson's enormous popularity (95). Regardless, *The Jazz Singer* has been remade three times for commercial US film and television. The first remake was a 1952 Michael Curtiz–directed film starring Danny Thomas. This was followed by a version featuring Jerry Lewis, for the second episode of the anthology show *Startime* (1959–1960), in 1959. The final film iteration was a 1980 Neil Diamond vehicle. The significance of these ostensibly misguided remakes has been of interest to scholars such as Gabbard, who highlight their differences. In this essay, I examine how *The Jazz Singer*'s remakes provide provocative case studies for exploring questions of authorship. Of the three remakes, Curtiz's version is the richest for discussions of auteur theory, because he directed films exclusively for Warner Bros. for decades. Through an analysis of how Curtiz's *The Jazz Singer* was constructed in response to changing conceptions of Jewish identity and the crumbling studio system, I argue that it exemplifies how conventional notions of auteurism often fail to account for how artistry can be expressed in a studio remake, perhaps the most critically debased form for creative ingenuity.

A Beautiful Friendship: Warner Bros. and Curtiz's Authorship

Curtiz has figured in debates about authorship primarily because of his remarkable career in the studio system. Before arriving in Hollywood, just before the conversion to sound, he directed a plethora of known silent films in several European film industries (Kinnard and Vitone 1986, 2). Warners prompted his move to Hollywood, since the studio had successfully lured another Jewish émigré in flight, Ernst Lubitsch; however, the studio did not re-sign its then "foremost director" in 1926, the year it hired Curtiz (Robertson 1993, 11). Curtiz's timing was fortuitous: the studio subsequently turned into a major, thanks to its gambles on synchronized sound, which reached an apotheosis with *The Jazz Singer*. Curtiz thus became a contract player at a time in the studio's history that dovetailed with his strengths, of which the most renowned was his productivity. He directed an astonishing 100 films in Hollywood between 1926 and 1961, most of which were made solely for Warner Bros. after it became one of the Big Five (Kinnard and Vitone 1986, 2). In fact, Warners exclusively backed his films from 1926 until his 1947 flirtation with an independent production unit, Michael Curtiz Productions (MCP), in which the studio had minority ownership (Robertson 1993, 95). After shuttering MCP in 1949, the director returned to Warners until 1954, when he broke his streak of eighty-seven consecutive films with no other major in order to helm Fox's *The Egyptian* (Wollen 2003, 67).

Curtiz's *The Jazz Singer* therefore represents a significant moment in both his and the studio's histories. His remake of the film most responsible for turning Warner Bros. into a powerhouse, at practically the culmination of his faithful career with it, signals the end of an era. The studio's decision to back a Curtiz remake to celebrate the twenty-fifth anniversary of *The Jazz Singer* encapsulated both the trajectory of the director's Hollywood career to that point and the changing strategies of a studio system in transition before its collapse. The circumstances that contributed to the fall of the studio system, including the 1948 Paramount decree, suburbanization, and the advent of commercial television, are well documented. These conditions ultimately led to a media consolidation governed by synergy and the package-unit model, in which creative personnel were attached to films on a one-off basis. Consequently, studio-era, long-term contracts evaporated, spurring Curtiz's 1954 split from Warners. As James Robertson chronicles, "His position at Warners gradually became less secure as he grew older and more difficult film-making economics emerged" (1993, 94). Apparently, the separation was mutual. After MCP failed, Robertson reports, "Curtiz was resentful against the studio because he believed he had been sabotaged" (102).

At the time of *The Jazz Singer* remake, then, the halcyon days of Curtiz as a prized studio director were done. He had risen to eminence with

Warners after *Captain Blood* (1935), a lavishly budgeted ($1.2 million) costume drama that performed well at the box office and netted five Oscar nominations, making him, as well as its stars Errol Flynn and Olivia de Havilland, valuable studio properties (Internet Movie Database). Warner Bros. capitalized by reteaming the three in hit films in several genres, such as *The Charge of the Light Brigade* (1936), *The Adventures of Robin Hood* (1938), and *Dodge City* (1939). *The Charge of the Light Brigade*'s $1.5 million box-office haul demonstrated that *Captain Blood* was no fluke, catapulting Curtiz into, in Robertson's words, "the top flight of Hollywood directors," a position he retained until the studio system began to fall apart in the late 1940s (1993, 39). Yet the shrewd remobilization of such elements at the studio's bidding is evidence central to Curtiz's legend as a hired hand who favored the studio's agenda over his own. Peter Wollen summarizes these sentiments by claiming that the "consensus" explanation credits "the studio system, with its discipline, its routine, its standard code of practice, and its teams of professional employees" for the director's success (2003, 62). As Wollen retorts, however, "It is simply mistaken to believe that Curtiz was no more than a studio hack without authority over the films he made" (64).

Curtiz is often still referred to as a gun-for-hire director of the studio era, one who never replicated the brilliance of *Casablanca* (1942), which, although it won him the Best Director Oscar, is typically cited as an anomaly. This conception has been bolstered by scholarship on *Casablanca* that characterizes it as pastiche, epitomized by Umberto Eco's essay on its cult appeal. For Eco, the film's disjointedness renders it cultish because fans easily recognize its assembled fragments, which often pay homage to earlier films. Much of this is attributable, claims Eco, to Curtiz's lack of a coherent artistic vision, since the director was unsure how to conclude it until the ending was actually shot (1985, 6). In addition to its potential to devalue the merits of ad-libbing and pastiche, Eco's assessment that *Casablanca* is irregular disregards how its success resembles that of other highly revered films Curtiz directed for Warner Bros., such as *The Adventures of Robin Hood*, *Angels with Dirty Faces* (1938), *Yankee Doodle Dandy* (1942), and *Mildred Pierce* (1945). *Casablanca* is not atypical of the director's oeuvre, and its recycling and reimagining of aspects of earlier films are key aspects of many of his other works, especially his remakes.

Despite Curtiz's reputation, his output with Warners bears the conventional hallmarks of an auteur's. Such traditional evaluations of authorship derive from post–World War II *Cahiers du cinéma* critics, who self-interestedly wrestled artistic credit from collaborators, primarily screenwriters. *Cahiers* critics argued that auteurs were distinguished by their thematic preoccupations and stylistic tendencies, particularly when constrained by commercial imperatives. Following the logic of the *Cahiers* auteurists, Sidney Rosenzweig contends that Curtiz's films display formal regularities, including "high crane shots to establish a story's environment; unusual camera angles and complex compositions in which characters are often framed by physical objects; much camera movement; subjective shots, in which the camera becomes the character's eye; and high contrast lighting, with pools of shadows" (1982, 6–7). In their thematic preoccupations, Wollen claims that Curtiz's films "favor the underdog and frequently portray resistance against cruel or corrupt authority" (2003, 74). The director's oeuvre thus aligns with the auteurist notion of authorship, irrespective of his proclivities for appropriation and script improvisation, which might be taken to belie coherency of narrative vision.

A major reason why Curtiz is not hailed as an auteur anyway is that his thematic preoccupations mirrored those of the studio. As Robertson notes, "the Warners 1930s style" was characterized by "a concern with contemporary social issues from the viewpoint of the underdog" (1993, 13). This makes it challenging to untangle the studio's agenda from Curtiz's artistic interventions. Robertson posits that "because his individualism was hidden from public view and he could not be associated with any one genre," Warner Bros. gets much of the credit (2). The director similarly suffers in evaluations of his stylistic tendencies. Wollen maintains that his generic range led to formal variation, "as each genre required its very own appropriate style" (2003, 74). He contends, therefore, that it is misguided to dismiss Curtiz's authorial merits because his company-man approach diversified his output. Wollen thus deploys André Bazin's "genius of the system" argument, in which the legendary theorist diverged from Truffaut in postulating that artistry in "classical Hollywood cinema stemmed from its relationship with popular culture rather than the opportunities it gave for self-expression" (65). Instead of valorizing mavericks who defy studio mandates, Wollen leverages Bazin to claim that "the auteur might almost be seen as the quintessential genre artist," since "the skill of the popular artist consists of fulfilling predictable expectations while introducing a renovatory degree of variation" (65). For Wollen, Curtiz's expression of the same thematic preoccupations as the studio's affirms his authorial standing: the congruence enabled the director to innovate within a highly restrictive framework in ways that fused with his directorial talents.

Updating Reputations: Curtiz and the Remake

According to this Bazin-inspired alternative, a director's effectiveness is linked with a tension that underscores genre and elicits its primary pleasure: a blend of sameness and difference. The remake might be the greatest test of this logic, since its restrictive template highly constrains the director's freedom. Interestingly, then, one of the most notable but overlooked aspects of Curtiz's career is the prominence there of remakes. His first outing for Warner Bros., *The Third Degree* (1926), had been made into a film in 1913 and 1919 (Robertson 1993, 13). The choice to have Curtiz helm a remake on his maiden voyage, as it were, was wise because it exploited the director's aptitudes and concealed his weaknesses. Besides aligning with Curtiz's productivity, remakes allowed him to focus on modifying existing content with narrative and formal innovations instead of using new scripts. Curtiz acknowledged his shortcomings as a writer, which mostly derived from his not being a native speaker of English. As Robertson summarizes, the director "apparently possessed only a sketchy command of spoken English"; he had surmounted a similar problem in earlier filmmaking contexts, since "his poor spoken German in 1919 had not prevented his swift success in Vienna" (8–9). While conquering language barriers in European silent film industries was impressive, it was more remarkable that Curtiz thrived prolifically in Hollywood after the conversion to sound, without ever mastering English.

The remake figured conspicuously in the director's career partly because presold narratives inoculated Curtiz from working with unproven commodities. Of his collaborations with Flynn and de Havilland, for example, *The Adventures of Robin Hood*, a remake of *Robin Hood* (1922), was arguably the most successful, garnering $4 million at the box office and three Academy Awards. As Constantine Verevis surmises about that remake, it "is not only a vehicle for co-stars Errol Flynn and Olivia de Havilland, *but also* a sound and Technicolor update of the Douglas Fairbanks silent epic" (2006, 6; emphasis in the original). Robertson likewise stresses the director's knack for updating originals, arguing that Curtiz's *The Breaking Point* (1950), an adaptation of Ernest Hemingway's book *To Have and Have Not* (1937), was consequently a remake of the 1944 Howard Hawks–directed adaptation for Warners, and was, "from a purely artistic standpoint, arguably his best film of all" (1993, 105). The remake as form figured prominently in Curtiz's career from his start with Warners to the height of their mutual success and his subsequent decline with the studio. This helps explain the director's endurance: the remake jelled with the productivity demands of both the studio era and the sub-sequent transitional period, when presold, studio-owned properties miti-gated post-vertical-integration economic risk.

In light of the remake jibing with Curtiz's competencies and figuring extensively in his oeuvre, *The Jazz Singer* is especially germane to examine in relation to authorship. According to Verevis's approach, in which he de-ploys Thomas Leitch's subgeneric categories to differentiate remakes fur-ther, *The Jazz Singer* seems best labeled an "update" (2006, 12). In contrast to the "readaptation," which "seeks to subordinate itself to the 'essence'" of the original, the update, Verevis argues, "'competes directly' with its . . . source by adopting an overly revisionary and transformational attitude toward it" (12). Although critics and fans often decry the update for being unfaithful, its potential to alter the original provides more explicit oppor-tunity for authorial expressivity than do remakes beholden to fidelity. Yet it is not clear-cut that Curtiz's *Jazz Singer* should qualify as an update. In Gabbard's charting of differences between *The Jazz Singer*'s versions, for instance, Curtiz's appears faithful because the only discrepancies Gabbard cites in a table full of similarities are the following: it centers on middle- rather than lower-class Jews; and the protagonist does not sing jazz, wear blackface, or fall for a Gentile (1998, 99). Putting aside the love interest's identity—I subsequently contend that in the Curtiz film, it is intentionally ambiguous—those changes in race and class representation epitomize the film's status as an update. The elimination of blackface and the elevation of the Jewish protagonist's class standing are significant alterations that highlight its broader reimagining of the original.

Of course, the 1927 *Jazz Singer* is itself an adaptation that alters its source material. It is based on Samson Raphaelson's 1925–1926 Broadway play *The Day of Atonement*, which was derived from his short story of the same name (Gabbard 1998, 100). That title reveals how the original film and Curtiz's remake maintained key aspects of their source. It refers to the Yom Kippur climax beginning with Kol Nidre at sundown: this is the holi-est Jewish holiday, in which Jews seek forgiveness for their sins. As Gab-bard observes, the biggest change from the play to the original film was the contrived ending. Raphaelson's story, which was, ironically, inspired by Al Jolson's life, has the protagonist, at the Kol Nidre service, aban-don his entertainment career to honor the family tradition of becoming a cantor; by contrast, the original film's outlandish and Oedipal conclusion enables Jakie to accomplish the seemingly irreconcilable objectives of as-similating into whiteness by becoming a theater star, and of maintaining his Jewish heritage by reuniting with his doting mother after his dogmatic father dies (100). Gabbard declares that the commercially motivated finale "helped cement a tradition that we now call classical Hollywood cinema" (110). This claim is buttressed by *The Jazz Singer*'s canonical place in film history, established by its revolutionary popularization of synchronized sound. Indeed, just as *The Birth of a Nation* (1915) was most responsible for codifying the classical film's narrative and formal elements, *The Jazz Singer* calcified them, since the conversion to sound bolstered Hollywood power by further marginalizing independent competitors.

Michael Rogin memorably made this now-conventional Hollywood history seem culturally salient by theorizing that these seminal moments in the classical film's development were inextricably linked with larger racial discourses. Specifically, both films influentially employing innovations like sound leverage them to depict white supremacy; African Americans are dehumanized or vilified by the films' narrative and associated formal devices. As Rogin documents, *The Jazz Singer*'s featuring of Al Jolson performing in blackface was more prominently advertised than its use of synchronized sound in promotional material (1992, 418). For Rogin, this was not a narratively irrelevant, purely spectacular element that simply mobilized Jolson's popular use of minstrelsy in his music career to augment the film's performance at the box office. Instead, Rogin contends, it was the donning of blackface that enabled the Jewish protagonist to win his Gentile lover, get on the popular stage, and concurrently sustain his Jewish heritage; the consequences of using blackface showed that Jews were more capable of assimilating into hegemonic "white" cultural status than African Americans (441). The elimination of blackface from Curtiz's version is therefore not just a minor discrepancy. Combined with other significant changes, Curtiz's remake dramatically transforms the ideological message contained in the original film while concurrently maintaining much from it.

Rogin correctly maintains that the 1927 version, by making the traditionalist father, not the arch-white girlfriend, the protagonist's primary obstacle, conveniently ignored the anti-Semitic, white-supremacist nativism dominant at the time, when severe quotas limited Jewish immigration and American Jews faced oppression (427). Vincent Brook's analysis of Curtiz's remake in relation to its contexts begins to suggest why it had become prudent to update the original. As Brook notes, although the intergenerational conflict remains the main obstacle impeding the satisfactory resolution of Curtiz's narrative, that struggle had become unrelated—by the early 1950s—to Jews being represented as an inferior ethnicity made up of poor immigrants (2011, 403). Curtiz's film is instead predicated on the notion that Jews are already fully assimilated into middle-class white-ness, by depicting a post–World War II utopia in which they are not forced to abandon tradition to become Americanized. Brook theorizes that such a mediation was situated in postwar conditions that elevated Jews' status, including the 1948 founding of Israel, the revelations of the Holocaust (the ultimate horrors of anti-Semitism), and an economic boom that im-proved many Jews' standing but *elided* discrimination that Jews faced dur-ing the Red Scare, when they were disproportionately conflated with com-munism (as exemplified by the Rosenberg trial) (402). At the same time, as Mary Dudziak charts, the civil rights movement was accelerating, and US officials were concerned that racial inequality positioned the country poorly in relation to communist egalitarianism. This left racist traditions like blackface distinctly less appealing to some (2000, 12). These cultural conditions and the aforementioned industrial shifts that altered Holly-wood demonstrate that the circumstances influencing Curtiz's version of *The Jazz Singer* were distinct from those affecting the original.

You Ain't Seen Nothing Yet:
Curtiz's Innovation and Convention

Despite these shifting contexts, the three screenwriters of the remake—Frank Davis, Leonard Stern, and Lewis Meltzer—largely honored the original script by centering Curtiz's *The Jazz Singer* on the Jewish aspiring entertainer and underdog's struggle to overcome his oppressive father's demand that he respect Jewish tradition. The story still had appeal, as the film grossed a respectable $4 million at the domestic box office. Like the original film and in standard Hollywood fashion, structural problems im-peding Jews as a group are ignored by being displaced onto individuals, to fit the classical, protagonist-driven narrative and to avoid grappling with questions of discrimination. Specifically, David Golding (Eduard Franz), who is on the verge of retirement, plans for his only child, the returning Korean War veteran Jerry (Danny Thomas), to replace him as the synagogue's cantor. Jerry is reluctant to fulfill his patrilineal destiny because he wants to be on Broadway, putting his mother, Ruth (Mildred Dunnock), in the middle of the conflict. Jerry's loyal girlfriend, Judy Lane (Peggy Lee), an already-renowned stage performer and recording artist, amplifies his chances, thanks to her connections. The tension between re-specting his heritage and accomplishing his professional objective propels Jerry's narrative, as it did for the original *Jazz Singer*'s protagonist. Yet there were major formal changes to the production. Chief among these: it was shot in Technicolor and featured more spectacular musical segments than the original, which, despite being the first Hollywood musical, contains only rudimentary song and dance numbers. Both these modifications were mainly driven by industrial objectives, because television's threat prompted both a movement away from black-and-white cinematography and the growth of Technicolor musicals.

Other production decisions affecting Curtiz's version, particularly the casting, were influenced by industrial motives, and consequently had cultural ramifications. Interestingly, Doris Day, the top female box-office draw of the 1950s and a star of four Curtiz films—*Romance on the High Seas* (1948); *My Dream Is Yours* (1949); *Young Man with a Horn* (1950), about an aspiring music performer; and, alongside Thomas, *I'll See You in My Dreams* (1951)—was the first choice for Judy's part (Robertson 1993, 114). Day turned down the role and, in an exhibition of a synergistic logic that was gaining momentum in the industry, it went instead to Lee, a successful recording artist who had never before starred in a Hollywood film. This casting history reveals that producers felt no qualms about hiring an actress who didn't look stereotypically Jewish, because both Day and Lee appeared Gentile. Like the original version's love interest, Mary Doyle (May McAvoy), who, Rogin argues, is depicted, primarily by her costuming, as a paragon of whiteness in relation to the ethnic protagonist, Judy is garbed in decadent white gowns in two of her musical numbers, including her introduction (1992, 442). The growing postwar acceptance of Jews as culturally white makes it difficult to determine whether these costuming decisions were designed to portray her as a Gentile in comparison to Jerry, but she is made to appear whiter than white in those gowns.

Such ambiguity about her identity is not assuaged by the only explicit reference to her potential Jewishness. During her visit to the middle-class Golding house for Passover, Judy casually remarks that she "hasn't been at a Seder since she left home." For Gabbard, this confirms that she is Jewish and works to resolve "the problem of intermarriage" (1998, 104). It is as plausible, however, to surmise that she is referring to another guest visit to a Seder. The vagueness of Judy's background is unsurprising; industrial tactics in response to the studio system being in flux, along with the increasing acceptance of Jews' cultural whiteness, encouraged the avoidance of alienating content such as interethnic romance. The seed is planted that Judy is Jewish, but ambiguously enough that she might also be Gentile.

There is little uncertain about the ethnicity of Jerry or the persistence of his religious faith. When he first confronts his father about abandoning his cantorial lineage, Jerry stresses that he is "not being blasphemous," even though he claims that performing onstage gives him greater satisfaction than leading prayers. This is a key difference from the original's protagonist, who runs away as a child to escape oppressive tradition and then jettisons any semblance of Jewishness or Judaism, even Anglicizing his name (from Rabinowicz to Robin), until he later appeases his dying father by temporarily leaving the theater to perform Kol Nidre. In contrast, Jerry is not banished after departing the first time. He accepts his father's prayer book gift and returns home for Passover. Put simply, he is forced neither to conceal his ethnicity nor to forsake Judaism in order to succeed professionally and be accepted into the dominant culture. Although Jerry is unambiguously Jewish and consistently reveres his heritage, the casting of Thomas is notable for accentuating emerging synergistic strategy: in real life, he was an established comic in radio who subsequently became a television star. The film alludes to this star image by having Jerry dabble in radio and portraying him in two stand-up comedy routines.

The Lebanese Thomas is also, significantly, the only non-Jew cast as the lead in any iteration of the film. As Brook observes, though, Thomas, in relation to other actors, "ironically *looks* the most Jewish of any in the film" (2011, 404). In fact, at one point Thomas removes a prosthetic nose, breaks the fourth wall by staring into the camera, and exclaims, "You know, I didn't even need this. I could've done it on my own hook."[1] These coinciding narrative and formal choices that emphasize a Jewish stereotype are indicative of the film's biggest departure from the original, which reveals Curtiz's authorial hand. Rather than have the protagonist hide his Jewish identity or downplay his Judaism to fit into the dominant culture, the remake abides largely by the original's narrative while depicting Jews, in line with changing ideology, as successfully assimilated, irrespective of ethnic difference.

The Seder scene, which is not in the first film version, is a good example of how even though the remake incorporates much of the original's story, Curtiz uses additions and modifications to transform its meaning. It is critical narratively because it allows Judy to refer to her Seder history and inspires Jerry's existential crisis, which threatens the satisfactory resolution of the classical dual plotlines highlighting a professional quest and heterosexual romance. It also enables Curtiz to feature an explicit discussion of Judaism that would have been comparatively incongruous with the original's narrative of compulsory assimilation. The fact that broader cultural conditions of the time made it plausible—though also somewhat incongruous—to depict Jews as fully incorporated into middle-class white-

Jerry Golding (Danny Thomas) removes his prosthetic nose to reveal his natural hook in *The Jazz Singer* (Warner Bros., 1952). Digital frame enlargement.

ness from the start permitted Curtiz to foreground Judaism as something to be cherished rather than as an archaic religion that had to be phased out for the ethnic group to be accepted into the dominant culture. The scene begins with a shot of David lecturing the bourgeois guests about the meanings and origins of Passover. Then, in a film with few close-ups, Curtiz cuts to one when David informs the attendees about the symbolic significance of matzah (unleavened bread) and other items on the Seder plate. Such a formal choice is noteworthy because it is a clear departure that draws the audience's attention closely to the Jewish cultural content, imparting David's lesson directly to the imagined viewer, who receives the visual information in close-up through the eye of the omnipotent camera in even greater detail than is offered the characters.

This scene is the most blatant example of Curtiz's teachings about Judaism (in the Seder tradition, interestingly). It is not anomalous, though it is more explicit than most other instances. Another moment transpires when Jerry confronts his father for the second time about refusing the cantorial position, prompting David to proclaim his son dead to him. David then hurries to the synagogue to perform the mourner's Kaddish (Prayer for the

Dead), which—the viewer learns through Jerry's shocked dialogue—is a sin to recite for the living. The film's opening scenes depict Rosh Hashanah services, the start of the High Holidays that culminate in Yom Kippur. These moments position the Jews as fully integrated Americans, but at the same time capitalize on the opportunity to educate viewers about Judaism. After the opening credits and establishing shots, which show the synagogue—a site of Golding cantorial presence for several generations—the film cuts to Jerry exiting a taxi. The Irish-accented working-class driver, seemingly less assimilated than the fully integrated Jerry (whose military attire unequivocally confirms his American identity), wishes his passenger happy holiday in Yiddish: "*Gut yontiff*, me lad."[2] The cabbie then exclaims that "it's twice he'll be celebrating" the New Year. Such an unrealistic depiction of widespread acceptance and understanding of Judaism in the opening scene is telling in relation to how the film naïvely disregards persistent ignorance and bigotry. The meanings of almost all Jewish holidays and Yiddish sayings elude most non-Jewish Americans to this day. Few of even the small percentage of contemporary Americans who are aware that Rosh Hashanah marks the start of the Jewish year, adhering to its own calendrical logic, would claim to celebrate that New Year in addition to the standard one. Regardless of the drawbacks of inaccurate minority portrayals, such instances allow Curtiz to teach the primarily Christian audience subtly by not being overly didactic about Judaism's specifics.

The notion that the mass audience would readily accept an idealistic representation of Jews as completely Americanized informs the changes that Curtiz incorporates to modify the original film's significance. If, as Gabbard notes, the Oedipal addendum in the ending of the original film was central to its commercial success and to the reification of the classical style, then it is important to see that it was altered in the remake. As Rogin theorizes, one thing that makes the original culturally significant is that the Jewish patriarch pays with his life for trying both to thwart the protagonist's jazz-singing goals and, by extension, to stop synchronized sound—because the film becomes silent for its duration after he demands that Jakie cease suggestively serenading his wife (with "Blue Skies") (1992, 423). This is what gives the original film its Oedipal dimension; the protagonist is disconcertingly close to his mother and kills his father, with sacrilege, enabling his mother to requite his love. Similar events transpire much differently in the remake. Instead of singing his adoring mother a jazz song, Jerry serenades her with a traditional lullaby, which he later innovatively peps up with Judy for a play, marking his affections as appropriate rather than taboo. Additionally, even though David becomes gravely ill on the eve of Yom Kippur, forcing Jerry to return home just before a new musical's opening, he survives rather than dies after hearing his son perform Kol Nidre in his absence. In contrast to the original protagonist, who risks his career to see his dying father, Jerry's abandonment of the play does not threaten his professional goals. Gabbard speculates that a primary reason Curtiz's version was less memorable than the original was that it did not contain the narrative tension underscoring its predecessor, making David's opposition to Jerry bear "the marks of a neurotic symptom, a familiar convention during Hollywood's romance with psychoanalysis in the 1950s" (1998, 102–103).

Although Freudian psychology undoubtedly had a massive influence on Hollywood at the time of Curtiz's remake, and although David's survival is less dramatic than the cantor's death in the original film, such assessments downplay what drove the update's alterations as well as why those modifications made sense culturally and industrially. Curtiz was a Jewish director who, like the original film's protagonist and many other Jews in Hollywood at the time, had largely concealed his heritage and Anglicized his birth name into a more marketable moniker (Rosenzweig 1982, 5).[3] To that end, he virtually avoided grappling directly with his Jewishness onscreen before being given the opportunity to remake *The Jazz Singer*, at a time when Jews' relationship to the dominant culture was changing drastically in the popular imagination. His remake expresses this experience by depicting a protagonist who is able to succeed in the entertainment industry while maintaining his Jewish identity, albeit by pragmatically rendering it subservient to career needs.

What is even more remarkable, though, is how the film presages the full shift to the package-unit system. Today, as the economic risk of the dominant blockbuster logic precipitates seemingly endless reboots and remakes, Curtiz's acumen with the update could retrospectively reposition him as an artistic vanguard more than a hack. On the heels of directors such as J. J. Abrams and Ryan Coogler garnering box-office success and critical praise in many circles for reimagining, respectively, the *Star Wars* and *Rocky* franchises by simultaneously underlining the originals' traditions and creatively infusing them with novelty in relation to their cultural contexts, it is time to acknowledge Curtiz's similar aptitude for updating films for their times.

Notes

1. Such a joke aligns with Thomas's broader star image at the time; he frequently made self-deprecating jokes about the size of his nose in his comedic performances and appearances.

2. For more Irish Yiddishism onscreen, see James Cagney in Roy Del Ruth's *Taxi* (1932).

3. Non-Jews did the same; Danny Thomas was born Amos Muzyad Yakhoob Kairouz (in Michigan).

Works Cited

Brook, Vincent. 2011. "The Four *Jazz Singers*: Mapping the Jewish Assimilation Narrative." *Journal of Modern Jewish Studies* 10, no. 3 (November): 401–420.

Dudziak, Mary L. 2000. *Cold War Civil Rights: Race and the Image of American Democracy.* Princeton, NJ: Princeton University Press.

Eco, Umberto. 1985. "*Casablanca*: Cult Movies and Intertextual Collage." *SubStance* 14, no. 2: 3–12.

Gabbard, Krin. 1998. "Ethnic Oedipus: *The Jazz Singer* and Its Remakes." In *Play It Again, Sam: Retakes on Remakes*, edited by Andrew Horton and Stuart J. McDougal, 95–114. Berkeley: University of California Press.

Kinnard, Roy, and R. J. Vitone. 1986. *The American Films of Michael Curtiz.* Metuchen, NJ: Scarecrow.

Robertson, James C. 1993. *The Casablanca Man: The Cinema of Michael Curtiz.* London: Routledge.

Rogin, Michael. 1992. "Blackface, White Noise: The Jewish Jazz Singer Finds His Voice." *Critical Inquiry* 18, no. 3 (Spring): 417–453.

Rosenzweig, Sidney. 1982. *"Casablanca" and Other Major Films of Michael Curtiz.* Ann Arbor, MI: UMI Research Press.

Verevis, Constantine. *Film Remakes.* Edinburgh: Edinburgh University Press, 2006.

Wollen, Peter. 2003. "The Auteur Theory: Michael Curtiz and *Casablanca*." In *Authorship and Film*, edited by David Gerstner and Janet Staiger, 61–75. New York: Routledge.

CHAPTER 4

"Don't Fence Me In": The Making of *Night and Day*

MARK GLANCY

On December 11, 1945, the last day of filming for *Night and Day* (1946), the cast and crew broke into spontaneous applause when the final shot was completed. Cary Grant, however, took the opportunity to make a point to Michael Curtiz. Speaking so that everyone on the set could hear him, Grant told the director, "Mike, I want you to know that if I'm chump enough ever to be caught working for you again, you'll know I'm either broke or I've lost my mind" (quoted in Waterbury 1947, 38). He was not joking. Over the course of the previous six months, the production had faced a succession of crises, and these served to exacerbate some basic differences between the director and the star. Curtiz was unquestionably the most highly regarded director at Warner Bros. His films brought critical acclaim and huge returns at the box office, and the studio's executives admired his work ethic on the set. Curtiz never wanted to stop shooting and even resented breaking for lunch. Yet his lack of interest in actors and his impatience with the cast and crew often led to shouting and occasionally to explosions of anger. Cary Grant, meanwhile, was one of the most popular leading men in Hollywood, and Warners had gone to great lengths to secure him as the star of *Night and Day*. He was a freelance rather than a contract star, and this enabled him to insist on an unusual degree of influence over each film that he made. He prided himself on his quiet professionalism, his eye for detail, and his scrupulous attention to dialogue and performance.

The conflict between Curtiz and Grant, and the troubled production of *Night and Day*, is well documented in the Warner Bros. Archives, housed at the University of Southern California. In this chapter, I use these documents to explore the film's production history. My interest is to examine the process of filmmaking within the studio system, and particularly the questions of authorship and agency that arose on this film. Although some of the troubles that plagued *Night and Day* were unusual—or at least unusually severe—some were quite ordinary in 1940s studio filmmaking. At this point in Hollywood history, Cary Grant's interventions can be seen as an unusual factor; very few stars carried such influence. A bitter labor dispute and the illnesses of key members of the cast presented further unusual problems. By contrast, other troubles and complications were commonplace. The script was assigned to several screenwriters, who competed to establish their own visions of the story. The musical numbers were directed by the choreographer, LeRoy Prinz. The Breen Office applied the Production Code with zealous rigor, with the result that the "suggestive" lyrics of songs such as "Love for Sale," "Miss Otis Regrets," "Anything Goes," and "Let's Do It" had to be modified for the film (see, for example, Breen to Warner, January 16, 1945; all cited correspondence is in the Warner Bros. Archives). And of course the studio's executive producer, Jack Warner, made many key decisions and held the ultimate authority over the production. But whether the challenges that the filmmakers faced were unusual or commonplace, they raise the question of the extent to which one of the studio's top directors was able to make a film uniquely and distinctively his own. We must also take into account the nature and range of the evidence found in the archive. Although it is a rich source of information about this and many of the studio's other films, any archival source is inevitably encumbered by bias and limitations, and these must be considered alongside the information that emerges.

The production documents indicate that the original idea for *Night and Day* did not come from Michael Curtiz or Cary Grant. In fact, they joined the production more than a year after Jack Warner and Cole Porter began corresponding about the film in May 1943 (Porter to Warner, May 17, 1943). Jack Warner's proposal for a musical biopic of Porter fit well within the studio's production strategy during World War II. Before the war, Warners was well known for its biopics of great men of letters and science, including *The Story of Louis Pasteur* (1936), *The Life of Emile Zola* (1937), and *Dr. Ehrlich's Magic Bullet* (1940). During the war, it turned to musical biopics, beginning with life stories of the composers George M. Cohan, in *Yankee Doodle Dandy* (1942), and George Gershwin, in *Rhapsody in Blue* (released in 1945 but filmed in 1943). The studio scored its biggest hit of the war years with the musical *This Is the Army* (1943), not a biopic but nevertheless a film closely associated with the popular composer Irving Berlin (Glancy 1995, 64). In contemporary parlance, these films would be termed "jukebox musicals"; that is, backstage musicals centered on a popular performer or composer who used either the life story or the drama of putting on a show as a means of drawing together a succession of popular songs. Cole Porter's music made him an ideal subject for such a film. Beginning with the Broadway musical *Paris* in 1928, he had written a string of hit musicals for Broadway and the West End, and he had contributed many well-known songs to Hollywood films. By the mid-1940s, his back catalogue included some of the best-known songs of the previous fifteen years and certainly more than enough to fill a musical biopic.

From the beginning, Warner Bros.' primary interest in *Night and Day* was to make a film that would capitalize on the popularity of Porter's music. In August 1943, the studio reached an agreement with the composer that allowed any of his songs to be used in the film in return for a flat payment of $300,000. Porter was given script approval, but at this point the story was unwritten; getting the rights to use Porter's music in a film was the primary objective. The screenwriter Jack Moffitt had begun working with the executive producer Hal B. Wallis to develop a treatment, but Moffitt made it clear that Porter's life story posed challenges. It lacked the rags-to-riches struggle that fueled popular biopics such as *Yankee Doodle Dandy*. "Porter is a rich man who inherited a great fortune from his grandfather, married a wealthy woman, and prefers to live a life of luxury," Moffitt observed. He warned that although the public appreciated Porter's "sophisticated" music, they would not like the man if he was characterized as a sophisticate, and they would not like the film if it had an "atmosphere of supercilious luxury" (Moffitt to Wallis, July 6, 1943). What remained unspoken for Moffitt—and in all the production documents and script materials surrounding the film—was that Cole Porter was predominantly, probably entirely, homosexual. Although he was married, his affairs with men were known to his wife and known more generally in show-business circles (McBrien 2000, 102–103). The filmmakers, too, were undoubtedly aware of Porter's sexuality, but knew that the Production Code rendered it completely off-limits as subject matter for the film. His life story would have to be dramatized in other terms.

Moffitt met with Porter and ascertained that the composer "recognizes the plot needs of movie entertainment" and would not object if his life story were told formulaically and not altogether accurately. Hence, Moffitt's fifty-eight-page treatment took a fanciful and contrived approach to Porter's life story. He framed it as "the triumph of the hick"; that is, the story of an ordinary American who "made the grade" on Broadway. Porter's background in rural Indiana was portrayed as central to his character, and while his family's wealth was not denied, it was emphasized that his grandfather was a self-made man. Although Porter and his wife would be seen to travel frequently in Europe, they would be shown to be homesick for the United States ("An American can be happy just so long in Europe," he would say). The inspiration that fueled Porter's songwriting would be his love for his wife. And the story would be given a wartime relevance by dramatizing Porter's struggle to recover from the severe injuries he suffered in 1937 when his legs were crushed beneath a horse in a riding accident. This would be achieved through a flashback structure. In the opening scene, set in World War II, Porter would visit a veterans' hospital, and the injured servicemen would be surprised to learn that he, too, is in a wheelchair. In the closing scene, he would be inspired by war news to get out of his wheelchair and walk with a cane and leg braces.

Wallis disliked the flashback structure and the wartime scenes, and Moffitt was soon taken off the film (Moffitt to Wallis, August 12, 1943). Nevertheless, Moffitt rightfully received a screen credit for "adaptation": many of the story points that he argued for remained in the story. Onscreen, for example, early scenes set in Indiana establish that Porter's formidable grandfather disapproved of show business, but in a later scene, on his deathbed, he commends his grandson for his hard work and success. The film shows Porter meeting his youthful wife, Linda (Alexis Smith), when she visits the Porter family home in Indiana for Christmas, and then meeting again when he is wounded in World War I and she is working as a nurse in a French hospital. Yet Linda was actually eight years older than Porter, and they met at a party at the Paris Ritz after the war. Similarly, the film shows Porter struggling to establish himself as a songwriter, including a scene in which he works as a sheet music demonstrator in a department store, but in fact the couple were very wealthy. Linda had received a large divorce settlement from her first husband, and this allowed the Porters to live a life of luxury in Paris and Venice during the 1920s (McBrien 2000, 65–66).

The film departed from Moffitt's treatment in its celebratory approach to show business. This change of tone came when Wallis left Warners and the film was assigned to Arthur Schwartz in April 1944 (Schwartz to Warner, April 13, 1944). Schwartz was a noted Broadway composer ("By Myself," "Dancing in the Dark," "That's Entertainment," and many other songs), and he was not as wary of New York sophistication as Jack Moffitt had been. He thought that *Night and Day* should be a lighter and brighter film. Moffitt had emphasized Porter's personal creativity through scenes in which he is seen composing his songs and performing them privately for Linda. Schwartz argued to Jack Warner that this would be "monotonous" and that the film should instead have fully staged musical numbers. He also suggested having Monty Woolley play himself in the film. Woolley and Porter had attended Yale University together and had been friends ever since, but more importantly for Schwartz, Woolley had recently become a popular screen personality as a result of prominent roles in *The Man Who Came to Dinner* (1942) and *Since You Went Away* (1944). His dry, sardonic humor—already well known from these earlier films—could figure significantly in *Night and Day*. Schwartz envisaged cameos for other famous personalities who had worked with Porter during his career, including Eve Arden and Mary Martin. They would also appear in the film. Schwartz's more upbeat version of the story was approved by Warner, and two new writers, Charles Hoffman and Leo Townsend, were assigned to write a script based on it (Schwartz to Warner, April 13, 1944).

It was not until August 1944 that Warner assigned Michael Curtiz as the director of *Night and Day*. Having also directed *Yankee Doodle Dandy* and *This Is the Army*, Curtiz was the natural choice for the film, but nevertheless Schwartz and Porter were both "delighted" to hear the news, and they thanked Warner profusely (Schwartz to Warner, August 16, 1944; Porter to Warner, August 29, 1944). Having Curtiz as director was a sure sign of the film's importance to the studio. So, too, was the choice to film in Technicolor, another decision proudly reported to Porter (Warner to Porter, February 16, 1945). Warner took another key decision in the same month: to pursue Cary Grant to play Porter. Casting Grant was partly a matter of box office. His previous films for Warners, *Destination Tokyo* (1943) and *Arsenic and Old Lace* (1944), were among the studio's highest-grossing films and continued his long winning streak at the box office (Glancy 1995, 64). True, he was not a musical star. It was Grant's debonair image and his flair for light, sophisticated comedy that made him ideal for the role of Cole Porter. He fit perfectly with Schwartz's vision of the film. Hence, Warner was willing to agree to Grant's standard contract demands. As well as a $100,000 fee, these included approval of both the script and the director (Warner to Roy Obringer, a principal lawyer at Warner Bros., August 17, 1944). Grant therefore joined the project knowing that Curtiz would direct but also with his own authority clearly set out. Extraordinarily, Warner agreed to a method of freeing Grant from a long-standing obligation to Columbia Pictures. While he was still an up-and-coming star, Grant had signed a multifilm, nonexclusive deal with the no-frills Columbia and its autocratic chief executive, Harry Cohn. Now, as one of Hollywood's most bankable stars, Grant was "very anxious to clear out of the Columbia set-up," but he owed one more film to the studio (Steve Trilling, Jack Warner's lieutenant, to Warner, August 8, 1944). Jack Warner stepped in with a deal. Grant would fulfill his obligation to Columbia by making a film at Warners, and in return Warners would lend its leading male star, Humphrey Bogart, to Columbia for a single film (*Dead Reckoning*, 1947). Bogart had no say in the matter—he was under an exclusive, long-term contract to Warners—but Grant was thrilled to be "taken out of bondage" by this exchange (Trilling to Warner, September 28, 1944).

If the deal between Warners and Columbia did not clearly establish that *Night and Day* had become a Cary Grant film first and foremost, the events that followed certainly did. Warners planned to start filming on November 15, 1944, but late in September, and just before agreeing to the Columbia exchange, Grant's manager informed Warners that the star was taking a six-month hiatus from work (Trilling to Warner, September 28, 1944). This was because Grant's marriage to his second wife, the Woolworth heiress Barbara Hutton, had begun to unravel. Hutton complained that Grant's only interest was in his work and that when he was not at the studio filming he was at home studying scripts (Higham and Moseley 1989, 171; Nelson 2003, 138). Grant was determined to take time off and repair his marriage. He promised Warners only that his first film after this hiatus would be for them (Trilling to Warner, September 26, 1944). The studio countered that it could not put *Night and Day* on hold for so long, and that it could not guarantee Curtiz's availability so far into the future (Trilling to Warner, September 28, 1944). The response from Grant's manager was that if the mid-November starting date was definite, the studio should "make other plans for the casting of Cole Porter" (Trilling to Warner, September 28, 1944). The studio capitulated. It agreed to both the Columbia exchange and Grant's hiatus, and *Night and Day* was delayed for six months. In the meantime, Curtiz directed *Mildred Pierce* (1945). When he returned to *Night and Day*, he found himself encumbered with a star who had both the authority and the inclination to question every aspect of the filmmaking process.

Grant's perfectionism could make him a difficult collaborator at the best of times, but the summer of 1945 was far from the best of times at Warners. In March, the Conference of Studio Unions had initiated one of the bitterest and most prolonged strikes in Hollywood history (Horne 2001, 14–15). It lasted for six months—throughout the filming of *Night and Day*—and severely limited the studio's ability to build new sets. Original estimates called for *Night and Day* to have sixty-two sets, but the number was reduced throughout filming by recycling sets from other films, by shooting on the back lot at Warners and other studios, and by filming on location (Schwartz to Warner, January 29, 1945). Grant found fault with the sets built at Warner Bros. and refused to shoot a scene until the problems were addressed. The daily progress reports written by the production manager, Eric Stacey, are a catalogue of the star's criticisms. In the final month of filming, Stacey remarked, "I don't think there has been a set in this picture that has not been changed by Cary . . . and it has cost this studio a terrific amount of money" (Stacey to T. C. Wright, head of production at Warner Bros., September 5, 1945). The famously well-dressed star kept a keen eye on wardrobe and costuming as well, including the attire of his co-stars, and on two occasions stopped filming while his criticisms were addressed by the wardrobe department (Stacey to Wright, July 21, 1945, and August 18, 1945). Technicolor was another source of contention. This was Grant's first Technicolor film, and despite the makeup and lighting tests done before the start of filming, he was alarmed by his appearance. In the third week of filming, he saw rushes of the scene in which Porter visits his dying grandfather, and complained that he looked more ill than the grandfather. "Something better be done about this!" he said as he left the screening room (Stacey to Wright, July 6, 1945). It was not the first or the last time the filmmakers were faced with his demands.

Many of the problems on set concerned the script, which went through innumerable drafts. Cole Porter was unimpressed with the version he read in September 1944, and Curtiz, Hoffman, Schwartz, and Townsend were dispatched to New York, where they spent a week in conference with him, in his suite at the Waldorf-Astoria, listening to his objections and promising to address them (Schwartz to Warner, September 29, 1944). Cary Grant read a revised script in January 1945 while he was on hiatus, and was concerned enough to invite the same team to his home on a Sunday, where they had a "long session" and departed with another list of objections (Schwartz to Warner, January 29, 1945). In April, weeks before Grant went on the payroll, he began attending story conferences at the studio to voice his concerns (Grant to Warner Bros., May 2, 1945). Nevertheless, problems remained when filming began on June 16, 1945. The first scene to go before the camera, set at the New Haven railway station, involved a long dolly shot of Porter and his girlfriend, Gracie (Jane Wyman), talking as they walk through the station. Curtiz got the shot to his satisfaction on the first day, but Grant protested that the dialogue was weak and the characterization was "lousy." He insisted that the scene be rewritten and filmed again (Stacey to Wright, June 16, 1945).

This proved to be a pattern throughout the filming. Curtiz would set up scenes and rehearse them with stand-ins, but when it was time for Grant to step in, he would find fault. In a scene set during a pep rally at Yale University, for example, Curtiz intended Grant, as an enthusiastic cheerleader, to lead a choir singing "Bulldog, Bulldog." But Grant, perhaps feeling uncomfortable as a forty-one-year-old playing an undergraduate, insisted that instead he should play the scene with his back to the camera in the main shot (Stacey to Wright, July 11, 1945). Changes such as these required new camera and lighting setups, and the production rapidly fell behind schedule as production costs mounted.

In July, a "big meeting" was held to address the faults of the script fully and finally, with the aim of avoiding further delays. Grant, Curtiz, Prinz, and Schwartz conferred well past midnight, outlining extensive revisions of the scenes that remained to be filmed (Stacey to Wright, July 14, 1945). Yet these revisions also proved inadequate. As filming continued in August, Stacey reported that the "script situation" was still "extremely bad," and that even the newly revised scenes were "being rewritten at the suggestion of Cary Grant" (Stacey to Wright, August 9, 1945). Two weeks later, Stacey observed that Curtiz was "just about frantic" because the writers were being called to the set to revise scenes three or four times each day. This was the result of "Cary Grant picking at and criticizing the script" (Stacey to Wright, August 22, 1945). Grant's concerns were not limited to his own scenes. A scene in which Linda watches the premiere of *50 Million Frenchmen* with Porter's cousins (Dorothy Malone and Donald Woods) originally included the cousins' eight-year-old son. Grant read the scene on the morning it was due to be filmed and insisted on cutting the child's part, even though the young actor had been cast and his wardrobe fitted (Stacey to Wright, September 5, 1945). Curtiz was apparently unnerved by the authority the star wielded. Stacey reported friction on the set between Curtiz and the cameramen (Peverell Marley and William V. Skall), the art director (John Hughes), and the musical director (Prinz) (Stacey to Wright, June 27, 1945; July 24, 1945; and August 18, 1945). Curtiz could "get very upset" and "act very silly" when the cast refused to work past six (Stacey to Wright, June 30, 1945).[1] Finally, on the last day of filming, Grant insisted on yet more dialogue changes, and Curtiz lost his temper. Knowing that he could not vent his anger at Cary Grant, he instead "bawled out the crew" in frustration. Curtiz then stormed off the set as he was "booed by the crew," and Stacey had to coax the director back (Stacey to Wright, September 29, 1945).

Thus, despite the fact that Curtiz had won the Academy Award for Best Director just a few months before filming began, and despite his long-term status at Warners, the production documents indicate that Grant assumed control of many key decisions. Does this make Grant an auteur and reduce Curtiz's role to that of a "studio hack"? (see Robertson 1993, 1–4). The film historian Patrick McGilligan has argued that within the Hollywood studio system, some actors could be auteurs. Writing about James Cagney, another Warners star who worked frequently with Curtiz, McGilligan stipulates that an actor can be considered an auteur if he is "so powerful that he changes lines, ad libs, shifts meanings, influences the narrative, and altogether means something definite to the public regardless of the intent of the director" (McGilligan 1972). Cary Grant certainly fit these criteria long before he made *Night and Day*. What is remarkable about this film is the extent of the star's control and also, in keeping with the idea that the auteur expresses his own personality, the extent to which the rewritten film represents Grant's own life. His character became a man who is so single-mindedly preoccupied by his work that he ultimately alienates his neglected wife. This was of course the story of Grant and Barbara Hutton, too, except that Hutton filed for divorce while *Night and Day* was in production, whereas the film ends on a note of bittersweet reconciliation between Cole and Linda Porter.

Revealing as production documents may be, and intriguing as it is to see a filmmaker's personal concerns expressed in his work, these areas of interest often do little to illuminate a film's visual style. The legal files, script files, and progress reports in the Warner Bros. Archives offer little information about the director's work on set. Although the records of the Art Department can offer plans for the visual design of a film, the decisions made about camerawork, lighting, staging, and color are seldom recorded. With *Night and Day*, an exception to this occurred when Selena Royle, playing Porter's mother, suddenly became ill on the sixth day of shooting. She had a kidney infection, and it was unclear how long she would be away from the production. At the time, Curtiz was in the midst of filming a Christmas Day scene at the Porter family's Indiana home, at which the entire family opens presents and then sings the Cole Porter song "Old Fashioned Garden." With Royle suddenly absent, Curtiz had two choices. He could replace the actress and shoot her scenes again, thus losing several days' work, or he could shoot around her. He decided on the latter tactic, and Eric Stacey observed approvingly that the director did "a wonderful job of cheating" by "inventing shots, using a double . . . and being very ingenious" (Stacey to Wright, June 21, 1945). The ingenuity involved intercutting to show the scene from several different characters' points of view. This took the action away from the piano, where the

Throughout *Night and Day* (Warner Bros., 1946), Cole Porter (Cary Grant) shows more interest in his music than he does in his wife Linda (Alexis Smith). Digital frame enlargement.

mother was singing, but also invested the scene with the film's characteristic restless energy. The scene ends not by focusing on the family gathered around the piano, but with a dolly shot that moves across the living room and past the Christmas tree, and ends by looking out the window onto a snowy front yard. This choice of shots not only masked Royle's absence but also suggested Porter's restlessness and his urge to leave home as soon as he could.

The scene was in keeping with the broader visual design of the film. Curtiz was well known for his use of a mobile camera (Rosenzweig 1982, 27, 54), and throughout *Night and Day* crane shots and dollying are employed to ensure that the lengthy film (128 minutes) has a dynamic pace and mood. The director was also well known as a master of crowd scenes (Robertson 1993, 140), and in *Night and Day* a huge number of extras populate the spaces around the main characters. Moreover, these characteristics of style—the mobile camera, the pace, and the crowd scenes—are used more prominently than in Curtiz's other films, and they are used to represent show business as a transient, restless life of continual movement and ever-present crowds. Porter is forever traveling—from Yale to Indiana to New York to France to London and back again—and the camera seems to be as restless as he is. Moreover, Porter is almost always surrounded by people. Whether he is in rehearsals, backstage, in a theater audience, or at a postperformance party, the camera must move through crowds to find him. It dollies through these spaces, passing all varieties of plausible activity, seemingly in search of him. Once he is found within a space, he is often on the move again, and the camera must once again follow him.

Thus, it appears that Curtiz chose one of Porter's most famous songs, "Don't Fence Me In," as a visual metaphor for the composer's refusal to follow conventional career and family expectations. It is notable, for example, that the film comes to a standstill when Porter's grandfather puts pressure on him to give up show business and become a lawyer. This scene is shot in a more staid manner than the rest of the film: the static, shot-reverse-shot sequence is unusual in a film that otherwise maintains fluid movement. Similarly, when Porter is writing the song "Night and Day," Linda joins him at the piano and proposes that they retreat to a quiet life in a secluded villa. Once again, the camerawork becomes more staid. They are shown in a static medium shot as they converse. But then Porter finds the chord progression he has been searching for on the piano, and as he plays the melody of "Night and Day" for the first time, he loses interest in their conversation. He turns subtly away from her, and the camera moves up and back in a smooth crane shot that suggests that his music will always take him away from her.

Scenes of Porter and Linda discussing the future of their relationship are more typical of the film's restless camerawork. In two separate scenes, they walk down the street together after a premiere, and a dolly shot follows them closely, highlighting their movement as well as the public nature of the space. There are other people walking around and past them, observing, and this emphasis on movement and a lack of privacy foreshadows the problems they will face as a couple. They will never settle down, and they will never have the privacy that Linda seeks. This tension culminates in the rehearsal scenes for Porter's most popular musical, *Anything Goes*. He invites the company to rehearse at their Long Island home. In the first shot of the scene, he appears entirely content, sitting at a desk on his wide lawn while some members of the company swim and dive in the pool in the foreground and others practice a dance routine behind them. Next, by contrast, comes a long shot from Linda's point of view, in which the same activity seems more distant, chaotic, and invasive. When she joins him, Cole promises yet again that they will soon spend time alone together, but she is quickly jostled out of the way by the performers that crowd nearly every scene of the film, and frequently come between the couple.

It is intriguing to imagine how difficult filming many of the crowd scenes must have been. Moving the camera through and around these dense crowds, in time with the performers acting on cue, could only have been a labyrinthine process. The daily reports, however, offer no indication that this method of filming caused delays. Rewriting the script, seeking the approval of the Breen Office for every changed scene, and altering the sets and costumes did cause delays, and principal photography was not finished until September 29, 1945. By that time, *Night and Day* was twenty days behind schedule and its costs had ballooned to $4.4 million, the highest budget recorded for Warner Bros. at that time (Glancy 1995, 64). Yet Jack Warner's box-office instincts paid off. When it was released in August 1946, *Night and Day* proved to be an extraordinarily popular film. Worldwide earnings of $7.7 million made it one of the biggest hits of the decade (ibid.).

The production documents in the Warner Bros. Archives reveal a great deal about the making of this very popular film. In addition to documenting many conflicts and delays, they reveal the collaborative nature of studio filmmaking in this era, since key creative decisions were taken by an array of filmmakers. They also foreshadow the beginning of a new era of studio filmmaking. The postwar period saw more stars seeking the power that Cary Grant had achieved. The paper trail of documents, however, reveals more about matters relating to scripting, personnel, costs, and contracts than about matters of visual style. The creative decisions taken by Curtiz are seldom noted, and so the true extent of his influence is submerged beneath the weight of other forms of evidence. Yet this is a film that belongs firmly within Curtiz's oeuvre. Its pace, its ever-moving camerawork, and its crowd scenes are characteristic of the director's best work, and the story would not have been as fully or vividly realized without his distinctive direction. If this fact has been overlooked by Curtiz's admirers, it is perhaps because the bright Technicolor palette of *Night and Day* seems far removed from the *noir*-ish, black-and-white visual design of his more celebrated films, such as *Casablanca* and *Mildred Pierce*. It may also be that interest today is diminished by the film's inability to engage with the realities of Porter's life. Nevertheless, examining the film serves as a reminder of the diversity of Curtiz's talents, and examining the production papers serves as a reminder that they often fall short of documenting the director's role and influence.

Note

1. The working hours may have irritated Curtiz especially in the case of Grant, whose contract always stipulated that he did not work after six (except for night scenes).

Archive

Warner Bros. Archives, University of Southern California, Los Angeles. The specific files consulted include the Cary Grant legal file; *Night and Day* Daily Progress Reports; Story: Memos and Correspondence file, *Night and Day*; and Story Treatment file, *Night and Day*.

Works Cited

Glancy, Mark. 1995. "Warner Bros. Film Grosses, 1921–51: The William Schaefer Ledger." *Historical Journal of Film, Radio and Television* 15, no. 1: 55–73.

Higham, Charles, and Roy Moseley. 1989. *Cary Grant: The Lonely Heart*. New York: Harcourt Brace Jovanovich.

Horne, Gerald. 2001. *Class Struggle in Hollywood, 1930–1950*. Austin: University of Texas Press.

McBrien, William. 2000. *Cole Porter*. New York: Vintage.

McGilligan, Patrick. 1972. "James Cagney: The Actor as Auteur." *Velvet Light Trap* 7 (Winter): 3–15.

Nelson, Nancy. 2003. *Evenings with Cary Grant*. New York: Citadel Press.

Robertson, James C. 1993. *The Casablanca Man: The Cinema of Michael Curtiz*. London: Routledge.

Rosenzweig, Sidney. 1982. *"Casablanca" and Other Major Films of Michael Curtiz*. Ann Arbor: University of Michigan Press.

Waterbury, Ruth. 1947. "Notorious Gentleman." *Photoplay*. January, 38.

CHAPTER 5

Long Love the Queen: Bette Davis, Curtiz, and Female Melodrama

DAVID GREVEN

Bette Davis made several movies with Michael Curtiz in the 1930s: two in 1932: *The Cabin in the Cotton* (notable for its famous Davis line "I'd love to kiss you, but I just washed my hair," delivered in a southern accent) and *20,000 Years in Sing Sing* (starring Spencer Tracy); *Jimmy the Gent* (1934), starring James Cagney; *Front Page Woman* (1935); *Kid Galahad* (1937), in which Davis plays the girlfriend of boxing manager Edward G. Robinson; and *The Private Lives of Elizabeth and Essex* (1939), based on Maxwell Anderson's play and co-starring Errol Flynn, or, as the Hungarian émigré director famous for his malapropisms and heavy accent called him, "Earl Flint." While there is much to be said about all these films and about Curtiz and Davis's relationship, my focus here is on *The Private Lives of Elizabeth and Essex*. In my view, it has not been given its critical due as one of the major women's films, a genre that Curtiz brilliantly shaped, as *Elizabeth*, *Mildred Pierce* (1945), and *Flamingo Road* (1949) evince. *Front Page Woman* anticipates *Elizabeth*'s showcasing of strong female roles as well as gender play, fluidity, and ambiguity, and I discuss it briefly before moving on to the 1939 film.

The Curtiz-Davis Collaboration

Born Kaminer Manó Kertész in 1886 in Hungary to a Jewish family, Curtiz made films such as *The Charlatan* (1917) in his native land before his arrival in Hollywood in 1926, where he thrived and became a prolific studio-system filmmaker until the 1960s. Davis became one of the major stars of classical Hollywood, but she had inauspicious beginnings, as a contract player first at Universal and then at Warner Bros.; she was given lackluster parts before commencing her reign as the studio's box-office queen from the late 1930s to the mid-1940s. Even her breakthrough performance, while on loan to RKO, as the slatternly and manipulative Mildred in John Cromwell's *Of Human Bondage* (1934), did not ensure good roles, though she won a compensatory Oscar the following year for *Dangerous*.[1] It took Davis's 1937 lawsuit against Warners, an attempt to break her contract for being given bad parts, to change the course of her career. Unsuccessful though it was, the suit (which went to trial in England) inspired a shift in the studio's attitudes, and Davis finally began to get the top roles she craved.

Curtiz's initial reaction to Bette Davis, whom he did not want for *Cabin in the Cotton*, emblematized her frustrating early experiences. Rejections for supposedly being unattractive ("a little brown wren") were frequent. Curtiz was "abusive to Bette personally, barking at and needling her in heavily Hungarian-accented tones," writes Ed Sikov, though in *Cabin*, his first film with her, "he lights her with great finesse" (2007, 47). Confronted with the decision to cast Davis as the southern belle Madge in that film, Curtiz exploded: "Goddamned nothing no good sexless son of a bitch!" (47). While Curtiz clearly misjudged both his star's talent and her beauty (the latter always a controversial point), his initial apprehension haunts her performance—or, better put, his treatment of her performance—in *Elizabeth*. Davis stated the matter this way: "Mr. Curtiz, I must say, monster as he was, was a great European moviemaker. He was not a performer's director. I made quite a few pictures with him. You had to be very strong with him. And he wasn't fun. He could humiliate people, but never me. He was a real BASTARD! Cruelest man I have ever known. But he knew how to shoot a film well" (Chandler 2006, 83). Curtiz may not have been a "performer's director" in Davis's eyes, but when he filmed her in *Elizabeth*, he gave free rein to her artistic impulses, and her perhaps sadomasochistic desire to punish her own appearance (and the audience along with it). Curtiz's film is notable for several unflinching close-ups of Davis as the aged queen. Her appearance—white plaster face and shock of red hair—is frequently described as ugly.[2]

As Martin Shingler has argued, Davis's performances offer ironic pleasures. Her role in Vincent Sherman's *Mr. Skeffington* (1944) exemplifies Davis's gender ambiguity and ironic detachment. The unconventionally attractive Davis plays a woman famed for her beauty. This vain and morally vacuous woman becomes not only old but also disfigured by illness. *Elizabeth* anticipates Davis's transformation into physical decrepitude in *Skeffington* and, most famously, in Robert Aldrich's *What Ever Happened to Baby Jane?* (1962). There, the aged Jane Hudson, a former child star ("Baby Jane") and failed movie actress, lives with her wheelchair-bound sister, Blanche (Joan Crawford), whom she terrorizes out of jealousy and despair. Davis's Jane is a theatrical, Kabuki-like creature whose unkempt appearance is offset by an overapplication of white make-up (a self-homage to the performer's own Elizabeth), a delusional older woman's attempt to re-create her child-star looks.

Curtiz allowed for a new realism onscreen in his collaboration with Davis. At every turn he facilitated her effort to inhabit and realize Elizabeth's advanced age and strange, at times fright-making appearance. I emphasize this aspect of the film because, first, it chiefly reflects how the director and the star worked together to create a cinematic effect, one with both feminist and misogynistic implications, and, second, it speaks to Curtiz's work in the woman's film genre generally. *Elizabeth* heralds the director's penchant for exploring the meanings of shifting female appearances, as well as the transformation from dowdiness to glamour found in *Mildred Pierce*.

While Joan Crawford, the star of *Mildred*, could never really look dowdy, her initial scenes, in which Mildred struggles to make enough money to support her family after her divorce, are striking in their verisimilitude, especially the montage of the exhausted heroine trudging from one failed job prospect to another. (Mildred makes her way on a series of pitiless, scorchingly bright urban streets before finally arriving at the restaurant where she will begin to make her fortune.) Curtiz, who balked at Crawford's casting, and forced her, humiliatingly at this point in her career, to take a screen test for *Mildred*, presented the once-glamorous MGM star, attired in everyday clothes before her meteoric rise in the diegesis, in a realistic, humanizing light suitable not only for this role but for Crawford's transition to the hardboiled Warners milieu. Similarly, in *Flamingo Road*, directing Crawford as a heroine who goes from squalor to success (in an echo of her role as Mildred), Curtiz initially presented Crawford's Lane Bellamy, a carnival dancer, in a literally unflattering light as she examines her aging appearance with the help of a hanging lightbulb in a tent. Lane goes on to become a prosperous society wife who lives on the titular road, though perpetually preyed upon by Sydney Greenstreet's malevolent, corrupt sheriff.

Taken as a triptych, *Elizabeth*, *Mildred Pierce*, and *Flamingo Road* are films about women's physical and emotional transformations that place special emphasis on the body as the site of struggle, conflict, possibility, and change.[3] Along the way, a considerable potential for gender ambiguity emerges in these films and continues in other Curtiz works such as *The Proud Rebel*, a 1958 Technicolor western that reunited the director with one of his major female stars of the 1930s, Olivia de Havilland. This beautiful, deeply moving, and quite underrated film concerns the efforts of a former Confederate soldier, John Chandler (Alan Ladd), to get help for his young son, David, who has been mute since witnessing his mother's death in a fire. Chandler ends up working for an embattled, tough, but kindhearted farmwoman, Linnett Moore (de Havilland), who becomes involved with him and acts as a second mother to his son. What is especially notable for our purposes is Curtiz's and de Havilland's willingness to make Linnett nonstereotypically female. De Havilland starred in a number of popular Curtiz-helmed films as Errol Flynn's gorgeous love interest, but she was also willing to be less than femininely glamorous onscreen, as her tough-minded later performances demonstrated. Not presented as anything like an idealized beauty, Linnett is as tough and formidable as her name until she is softened by romantic and maternal love. While this redemptive pattern is a familiar one in Hollywood narrative, it is nevertheless striking that Linnett, a solitary, aging woman, is presented in such a lifelike manner. It is this interest in deglamorizing the female star and offering more realistic portrayals of femininity that links *Elizabeth* and Curtiz's later works.

Front Page Woman

The Curtiz-Davis film that is most thematically linked with *Elizabeth*, however counterintuitively, is *Front Page Woman*. The chief overlap between the films, one a newspaper comedy, the other a female melodrama, is the theme of a solitary, driven woman attempting to make her mark in a male-dominated world and also to negotiate romantic and sexual desire (heterosexual in both works) within this world. Davis and her frequent co-star George Brent (whose acting talents were, regrettably, subpar, though he was blandly handsome and winsome) play rival newspaper reporters, Ellen Garfield and Curt Devlin, who are also in love and engaged to be married. He doesn't believe that women make good reporters, certainly not as good as men. The film, Davis recalled with incredulity years later, was originally called *Women Are Bum Newspapermen* (Chandler 2006, 107). The woman's situation and experiences within a male-homosocial world is a theme that both *Front Page Woman* and *Elizabeth* render visually. In a striking shot early in *Front Page*, Davis's reporter, the lone woman in a sea of male reporters, makes her disoriented way to the symbolic shore of the prison news office after having witnessed a woman's execution in the gas chamber. As Ellen tries to walk and keep her composure, men in hats swim hurriedly and indifferently past her. Once in the newsroom, she tries to phone in the details of the story, only to faint dead away. *Elizabeth* is full of scenes in which the singular, embattled queen must contend with a gathered group of male officials who pay her reverence but are clearly attempting to undermine her.

Front Page Woman shows us female collaboration, albeit strictly for expedient purposes on Ellen's behalf. Devlin tricks her by fudging the jurors' decision in a big murder trial they are both covering, leading Ellen to phone in the wrong results, bring disaster upon her paper, and get fired by her irate boss. This escapade lands Devlin in jail, although he is confident that his editor will soon get him out. Ellen, however, cozies up to Inez Cardoza (Winifred Shaw), whose lover, Maitland Coulter (Gordon Westcott), has been convicted of murder and whom she swears is innocent. Ellen notices Inez in a bar, buys her a drink, and gets her to confess to the murder. The scoop restores Ellen's career. She visits Devlin in jail and breaks the news to him, getting him to admit that, yes, women do make good reporters. A comic-relief friend of Devlin's, the photographer Toots (Roscoe Karns), takes their photo as they kiss with the prison bars between them; they keep kissing even after Toots says he has the shot. Curtiz creates a striking visual allegory of their relationship—they will always have to find ways of overcoming essential barriers to their intimacy and desire, but in the end, however strenuous the effort, they will succeed. (At least, that is my optimistic reading. One could argue that Toots's allegorical shot implies imprisonment of another kind for Ellen once she is married to the sexist Devlin.)[4]

The Heroic Elizabeth

Front Page Woman charts a woman's difficulties in negotiating not only a man's world but also a romantic relationship with a man whose ambition threatened to kill her career. She triumphs in the end. The heroine of *Elizabeth* triumphs as well, but her victory is decidedly Pyrrhic, for in maintaining her rule she loses her love. *Elizabeth* opens with Robert Devereux, the Earl of Essex (Flynn), returning to England after the capture of Cádiz in 1596, a famous event in the Anglo-Spanish War. To prevent the Anglo-Dutch forces from claiming their spoils, the Spanish burned their own fleets, prompting Essex to sack the city of Cádiz. He returns to cheering crowds lined up outside Elizabeth's palace, and beams at them proudly, a pride that will be his undoing. Inside the palace, Elizabeth, who is being dressed for her meeting with him, bristles with rage—although we are left to decide whether she is angry at Essex personally or at the complications of the situation, which force her to rebuke him for actions that have brought fame to him but have left the English population overtaxed and starving so that his army could be funded.

Curtiz introduces us to Davis's Elizabeth in a stylized manner: we see only her silhouette through the screen behind which she is changing her clothes, accompanied by the actress's English-accented though recognizable voice and by her recognizable gestures. (I suspect Davis herself stood behind the screen and gestured, unless someone was found who could precisely imitate the actress; on doubling Bette Davis, see Pomerance 2013, 111–123.) Immediately, we are barred access to Elizabeth's image, though we hear her commanding voice and see her shadow. It is another of Curtiz's effective visual allegories, here of the central problem of *Elizabeth*: the lonely female ruler's conflict between her desire and her obligations to state and throne.

Proceeding with great anticipation across a lengthy space to the enthroned ruler, Essex does not expect the reception that he is about to receive from his queen. Believing that he will be hailed as a hero, he is stunned to hear Elizabeth's accusatory demand, "Where is my Spanish treasure fleet?" She accuses him of having done all he did chiefly for the glory of Essex, not the glory of England. I argue that *Elizabeth* has a richly metatextual quality, being an allegory of Davis's Warner Bros. career as "Queen of the Studio." Elizabeth's criticisms of Essex echo Davis's own regarding Flynn, whose casting she bitterly opposed, since he seemed to her inadequate, unprofessional, and shallow. (Maxwell Anderson's play, on which the screen treatment is based, is written in blank verse, which had to be rewritten in order for Flynn to play the role. He gives a fine performance nonetheless, as I see it; he is utterly convincing as a shallow but alluring figure.) Instead, she wanted Laurence Olivier, whom she had seen in films such as *Fire Over England* (1937), to be her co-star. (In that film, Flora Robson plays the aging Queen Elizabeth, enmeshed in ongoing conflicts with Spain; Olivier plays Michael Ingolby, the spy whom Elizabeth loves; Vivien Leigh, one of the queen's ladies-in-waiting, also loves Ingolby, a scenario quite similar to the queen's.) At the end of their first scene, Elizabeth slaps Essex across the face for his insolence. As Flynn reports in his autobiography, Davis was furious that despite her stature at

A portrait of ardent and impossible desire. Bette Davis as Queen Elizabeth, looking up at Essex (Errol Flynn), in *The Private Lives of Elizabeth and Essex* (Warner Bros., 1939). Digital frame enlargement.

Warner Bros. at the time, Flynn was still being paid more for this picture than she was. As he tells it, Davis retaliated against him—perhaps for this slight, perhaps because he was cast at all—by *actually* hitting him across the face with a bejewelled hand (indeed, the big gaudy rings look like brass knuckles) (Flynn 1979, 224). Later in life, Davis softened her opinion of Flynn's performance, saying he was both well cast and good in the role, but the animosity these actors felt toward each other in life gives their powerful onscreen chemistry its charge, I imagine.[5]

Interestingly, Davis and Flynn had co-starred the previous year in Anatole Litvak's film *The Sisters*, a beautifully made melodrama in which Davis gives a quiet, subtle performance as a woman in love with a charming layabout who abandons her and his own life to drink. The plot of *Elizabeth* corresponds with remarkable poignancy to that of *The Sisters*, as the aging queen, despite her clear, rational view of Essex's limitations and dangerous ambition, pines over and longs for him. *Elizabeth* provides a template for one of the major dynamics of the woman's film, the heroine's longing for a man, sometimes a most unworthy man, whom she cannot possess. Joan Crawford's films such as *Humoresque* (1946), *Possessed* (1947), *Sudden Fear* (1952), and *Autumn Leaves* (1956) are especially redolent of this theme, as, in its own fashion, is *Mildred Pierce*, which is notable for its depiction of its heroine's romantic and sexual ambivalence.

Elizabeth reveals what interested Curtiz and inspired his artistic creativity, and what did not. Surprisingly, given the homosocial, male-adventure quality of most of his best-known films, such as the Robin Hood, western, and pirate movies he made with Flynn in the 1930s, Curtiz demonstrates very little visual interest in the scenes between Essex and his men or in those depicting military battle in Ireland as Essex attempts to crush Tyrone's (Alan Hale) rebellion. These scenes come across as stagy and artificial, the action haphazard.

Curtiz's distinctive visual genius comes through in the scenes depicting Elizabeth's conflicted responses to Essex. In their first scene together, when the queen berates Essex for his seeming victory at Cádiz, Essex is associated with sustained movement as he and his entourage make their way through the palace largely in real time. In contrast, we do not see the queen herself until Essex is before her. We in effect become Essex at that final moment, looking at the queen at last. Curtiz introduces Elizabeth through a shot that begins at a low angle and rises up to take in the full image of the queen, richly and lavishly attired, seated on her throne. Her visual introduction confirms that first, last, and always, this woman is regal. Curtiz renders their first confrontation in a collage of visual styles, shifting from long shots to close-ups and two-shots, giving the scene and its increasing emotional (and political) violence a gathering momentum. As the scene ends, the camera dollies into a close-up of Elizabeth as Essex storms off. Her expression is at once resolute, iconic, infuriated, and suffused with suffering.

Another crucial scene soon follows. In most representations of Elizabeth I, the queen is shown intriguing with her male advisers and courtiers. While she has conferences with a crucial Essex ally, the arch and condescending Francis Bacon (Donald Crisp), and others, Davis's Elizabeth is, importantly, depicted in an extended scene with her ladies-in-waiting, including the treacherous Lady Penelope Grey (Olivia de Havilland), who loves Essex, too. After Elizabeth knocks chess pieces to the floor, angry that Lady Penelope has rendered her "powerless" during the game, the ruler asks her gathered ladies to cheer her up. Penelope suggests that she and Mistress Margaret Radcliffe (Nanette Fabray) sing versions of the English poet Christopher Marlowe's poem "The Passionate Shepherd to His Love," famous for its first line, "Come live with me and be my love," and Sir

Walter Raleigh's parodic "The Nymph's Reply to the Shepherd." Penelope skillfully plots her revenge on the queen this way, singing Raleigh's song so that its verses will wound the aging and insecure monarch:

> If all the world and love were young,
> And truth in every Shepherd's tongue,
> These pretty pleasures might me move,
> To live with thee, and be thy love.

Though the diversion is initially in bawdy good humor, suggesting a "tournament of song," the queen becomes enraged when she perceives that she is being mocked.[6]

Again, Curtiz's visuals are daring. From a shot of Davis fulminating at the singing women and then one of their reaction, he cuts—shifting the position of the actor and the scene's emotional logic—to a shot of Elizabeth staring at her strange, ghost-white pallor and red-hair-wreathed face in a mirror. Her apoplectic reaction as she inspects her image evokes a moment in a fairy tale: "Smash them!" she commands her minions regarding all the mirrors in the palace. What follows, however, is a tender scene between women. Mistress Margaret, weeping both for herself and for the lonely queen, tells the older woman of her heartache: her beloved is fighting far away in Ireland, and she empathizes with the queen's loneliness, anger, and sorrow. The queen comforts her and promises to return Miss Margaret's soldier home. Alas, she learns that the fighting in Ireland has worsened, and Margaret's soldier is one of the casualties. "Poor child," the queen says of her soon-to-be grief-stricken lady-in-waiting. "Poor child."

Elizabeth may be considered myopic as a historical analysis of Elizabethan monarchy; very little attention is paid to statecraft or policy. Nevertheless, the film is a spellbinding example of the woman's film and the power of melodrama. Along with Dorothy Arzner (*Christopher Strong*, 1933), Josef von Sternberg (his films with Marlene Dietrich), George Cukor (*A Woman's Face*, 1941), George Stevens (*Alice Adams*, 1935), King Vidor (*Stella Dallas*, 1937), Edmund Goulding (*Dark Victory*, 1939), Irving Rapper (*Now, Voyager*, 1942), Alfred Hitchcock (*Rebecca*, 1940; *Suspicion*, 1941), and Curtis Bernhardt (*Possessed*, 1947), Curtiz is one of the major visionaries of the woman's film and female melodrama.[7] The scenes between Elizabeth and Essex crackle with sexual tension and contain deep levels of agonized, brutalized feeling. Much of this lies in Davis's peerless, career-defining ability to mine the act of erotic renunciation for all its pathos. (The Edmund Goulding–directed *The Old Maid* [1939] is a definitive example of such renunciation, as is *Now, Voyager*, that masterpiece of the woman's film genre.) Curtiz, however, brings his visual brilliance to the Davis-Flynn scenes, especially the climactic one.

Having gone to Ireland to put down Tyrone's rebellion, Essex fails to receive the letters, full of love and support, that Elizabeth sent him. Her men, aided by Lady Penelope, have sabotaged the letters and sent him false ones, and have made sure that the queen has not received his. So when Essex returns, he is infuriated at his apparently coldhearted and indifferent ruler, and she with him. Their makeup scene, once they have learned about the epistolary sabotage, is tender and intense. But the main rift between them remains, more damagingly than ever. Essex, aware that he is being once again acclaimed a hero, wants the power of a ruler. Elizabeth cannot relinquish her throne, and also fears that the narcissistic Essex would plunge England into endless war to fuel his ambition and appetite for fame (another overlap with *Front Page Woman*). She convinces him to dismiss his private army by fooling him into believing that she will split her rule, only to imprison him in the Tower and sentence him to death once he has fallen into her trap.

Yet before Essex left for Ireland, Elizabeth had given him a gift that emblematized their love, the ring her father once gave her. This ring, she tells Essex, allowed her to escape execution when her father was displeased with her; she showed him the ring, and he remembered his love for his daughter and spared her life (the ring was meant for precisely such a situation). Now, having given Essex the ring, she waits and waits for him to give it back to her, but to no avail. She sits alone, gravely waiting for his response in her apartment in the Tower. Finally, she summons him. She asks him why, since he is about to die, he has not sent her the ring and won his release. Essex tells her that even if freed, he would not be able to let go of his ambition to rule and would always be a threat to her. Though shattered by this decision, Elizabeth sends him to his death, even as she begs him to take her crown as he implacably departs.

Curtiz and his set designers make this entire last act one of his signature visual allegories. The queen's apartment is spare and stagelike, as if it were a shrine to her loneliness and isolation. A trapdoor mysteriously and suddenly opens to reveal a staircase, which Essex ascends for his audience with the queen and then descends on the way to his doom. The trapdoor is like the ring, a secret passageway to the ruler's love and desire. The queen's gaunt, completely bereft state and appearance are also a stylized effect. She has become a monument to, an icon of, the great sorrow she endures. Her deep emerald gown, like all of Orry-Kelly's superbly conceived costumes, symbolizes the emotional reality of the scene. If green represents both new life and enduring life, the costume's color can only ironize the aged queen's lost youth and her necessary decision to end her beloved's life.

In one of their intimate embraces, which Curtiz consistently films as versions of the *Pietà*, Elizabeth speaks to Essex of the "lovely, dreadful thing" between them, which brings them together and drives them apart with equal force. Davis and Curtiz disliked each other greatly—Curtiz would not direct *Now, Voyager*, because of his dislike of the star (Chandler 2006, 156). In some ways, however, their pairing was a similarly lovely, dreadful thing. Davis revealed that she approached her role in *Elizabeth* apprehensively. "I was secretly a bit tentative about playing Elizabeth at this time. I was only thirty years old. Elizabeth was sixty." And the star had also never been "photographed in color before" (Davis 1962, 166).[8] Given the antagonistic relationship between director and star, the star's ambivalence about her challenging role, and her frustrations with her co-star, *Elizabeth* could easily have been a disaster. But it endures as an impressive, moving work. Davis and Curtiz each helped the other to achieve a newfound grandeur in the woman's film genre.

Notes

1. "Compensatory" is the general view, at any rate, of her Oscar for *Dangerous*. Davis in fact gives a terrific performance in a role modeled on the career of Jeanne Eagels. She is especially good in the scenes in which she is a belligerent drunk.

2. Davis fought for realism in her portrayals. In a well-known effort to do so in the seething crime film *Marked Woman* (1937), she insisted on using lifelike makeup to show that her character, Mary, a prostitute who works in the mob-run Club Intime, had been brutally beaten by the mob boss's henchmen. Mary seeks justice for her younger sister, murdered by the boss, the gangster Johnny Vanning (Eduardo Ciannelli), memorably threatening, "I'll get you, even if I have to come back from the grave to do it."

3. A woman's transformation is an essential event of the woman's film narrative, as I argue in my book *Representations of Femininity in American Genre Cinema*. This transformation often occurs in the heroine's appearance, but this physical transformation is the result of, or an allegory for, numerous prior changes in the woman's emotional and economic circumstances. We see Mildred Pierce become "Mildred Pierce," her transition from workaday frump to the wearer of stylish and spectacular furs, which both diegetically and symbolically reveal her social ascendency.

4. Curtiz's penchant for female gender and sexual ambiguity is on display in *Front Page Woman*, and not just in the plot. In one notable shot, a lesbian reporter (as her mannish appearance codes her to be) has a drink with her fellow journalists, and the whole atmosphere seems quite comfortable.

5. Bethany Latham offers a surprisingly unsympathetic account of Davis's positions regarding Flynn and other matters during the making of the film (2011, 79). Latham essentially adopts Flynn's view of Davis as haughty and insecure.

6. I argue that this moment has lesbian overtones: the queen as the butch figure presiding over singing, scheming femmes.

7. David Thomson says some admiring things about Curtiz, but notes that none of his films "survives as art" (1994, 165).

8. Davis notes that she "studied the Holbein portrait of [Elizabeth] and was not a little amazed at the resemblance between us" (1962, 166).

Works Cited

Chandler, Charlotte. 2006. *The Girl Who Walked Home Alone: Bette Davis; A Personal Biography*. New York: Simon and Schuster.

Davis, Bette. 1962. *The Lonely Life: An Autobiography*. New York: Lancer.

Flynn, Errol. 1979. *My Wicked, Wicked Ways*. London: Pan.

Hark, Ina Rae. 2014. "Michael Curtiz." In *Fifty Hollywood Directors*, edited by Suzanne Leonard and Yvonne Tasker, 84–96. New York: Routledge.

Latham, Bethany. 2011. *Elizabeth I in Film and Television: A Study of the Major Portrayals*. Jefferson, NC: McFarland.

Pomerance, Murray. 2013. *The Eyes Have It: Cinema and the Reality Effect*. New Brunswick, NJ: Rutgers University Press.

Ray, Robert B. *A Certain Tendency of the Hollywood Cinema, 1930–1980*. Princeton, NJ: Princeton University Press, 1985.

Shingler, Martin. 1995. "Masquerade or Drag? Bette Davis and the Ambiguities of Gender." *Screen* 36, no. 3 (Autumn): 179–192.

Sikov, Ed. 2007. *Dark Victory: The Life of Bette Davis*. New York: Holt.

Thomson, David. 1994. *A Biographical Dictionary of Film*. 3rd ed. New York: Knopf.

CHAPTER 6

Double-Time in America: *Yankee Doodle Dandy*

JULIE GROSSMAN

Yankee Doodle Dandy opened on Memorial Day 1942. The film became Michael Curtiz's most profitable film and star James Cagney's "greatest grosser" to date. The film was a huge hit, earning $5 million in profit for Warner Bros. (Robertson 1993, 76). Of the eight films Curtiz made during World War II, five were patriotic films, playing a significant role in the studio's support for the government's newly formed Office of War Information (OWI). When *Yankee Doodle Dandy* was released, *Time* magazine described it as "the most genial screen biography ever made" (quoted in Dickens 1972, 170), aided by the "satin smoothness" of Michael Curtiz's direction (*Hollywood Reporter* 1942). Such anodyne language glosses over the film's contribution to the OWI's propaganda efforts, as well as Cagney's and Cohan's strong-willed authorial interventions in the making of the film.

Curtiz was instrumental in negotiating several challenges: studio pressures to be efficient and make the film jingoistic; Cagney's ambivalence about his contract and his desire to clear his name unequivocally after House Un-American Activities Committee chair Martin Dies implied that the actor was a communist; and George M. Cohan's determination to control the film's message about his personal and professional life. Curtiz was faced with the additional task of making a musical biopic during a time when both the musical and the biopic were out of fashion at Warner Bros. Despite these challenges, Curtiz not only directed a film that Bosley Crowther called "an exhilarating portrait of a spirited trouper and a warmly emotional man" (Crowther 1942) but also succeeded in "linking," according to *Variety*, "the assertive, energetic and sentimental America of George M. Cohan's heyday to these present days of critical test" (*Variety* 1942).

When the film premiered in New York, it sold $5.5 million worth of war bonds (*Hollywood Reporter* 1942). The evocation of World War II in the film's representation of America's entry into World War I provoked strong feelings in viewers, much as Laurence Olivier's *Henry V*, a play about another invasion of France, surely also did on the eve of D-Day, in June 1944. But it is a unique fact about this most patriotic American film that it emerged out of efforts on the part of the Cagney family to disabuse politicians, Hollywood moguls, and audiences of the idea that Cagney was affiliated with communism (Anderson 1997). Intent on solidifying Cagney's persona as a loyal American, James and his brother William lobbied Warner Bros. to make the film, with James in the lead role and William, alongside Jack Warner and Hal Wallis, as its producer. Cohan had previously pitched the idea of the biopic to Samuel Goldwyn, with Fred Astaire starring. Astaire refused.

Many have observed that the film omits darker elements of Cohan's character, such as his quick temper and his bitter opposition to unions, especially his "implacable enemy," Actors' Equity (Kenrick 2008, 155). In this he was decidedly unlike his "double," James Cagney. Cagney was a staunch liberal (the first vice president of the Screen Actors Guild when it was formed in 1933), active in protesting working conditions for field-workers and miners throughout the 1930s. In *Yankee Doodle Dandy*, Cohan's breakup with his longtime partner Sam Harris is treated as a lighthearted misunderstanding (neither man can remember why the two parted ways); in real life, Cohan dissolved the union "to spare his beloved friend any collateral damage" after his bitter battle with Actors' Equity following the actors' strike of 1919 (155).

Cohan was an important authorial presence in the making of *Yankee Doodle Dandy*. His interviews with Robert Buckner were the source of the original story (the script was co-written by Buckner and Edmund Joseph). Cohan retained the right of final approval of the film, a highly unusual concession that caused everyone involved in the production great anxiety, especially since, despite his illness at the time, Cohan was both controlling and dubious about the project from its inception. Early on in negotiations over a script he thought weak, Cagney used his leverage with Warner Bros.—his contract was about to expire, and the studio didn't want to risk losing the star—to insist on hiring Julius and Philip Epstein as script doctors. To appease Cagney, as James C. Robertson writes, "Jack Warner sanctioned the reshaping of the film to the Cagneys' specifications and gambled that Cohan would approve" (1993, 75).

As *Yankee Doodle Dandy*'s "shaky script" and its future remained uncertain, scenes continued to change repeatedly throughout the film's production. In addition to Cagney's improvised bits of "business," the Epstein brothers added humor to the script and shifted emphases, such as making Cohan's relationship with Mary (Joan Leslie), a "composite" of Cohan's wives Ethel and Agnes and his daughter Mary, who became a central figure in the story despite Cohan's earlier insistence that his private life stay out. Another example of these modifications, as Rudy Behlmer reports, was Curtiz's clever intercutting of unscripted shots of theater managers behind the scenes, done to avoid showing some of the duller moments of the Four Cohans performing "I Was Born in Virginia." These interventions prompted the unit manager Frank Madison to send a strong message to the production manager, Tenny Wright, on the threats these changes posed to Cohan's ultimate consent: "Curtiz must learn someday to stay within the regulations of a contract. We have a specific contract and agreement for this picture with George M. Cohan and we have violated it in many places. It is only with the aid of our legal department that we can hope to get this straightened out before the picture is released. This concerns not only music, but interpolated bits of plays and numbers, as well" (quoted in Behlmer 2005).

In the end, Cagney's portrait of "a lusty spontaneous character" (Crowther 1942) disarmed Cohan and his representatives. As George Custen notes, even the film's focus on the performer's marriage, which Cohan had vehemently opposed from the project's beginning, was outweighed by *Yankee Doodle Dandy*'s tone of adulation: "Mary venerates her husband, a fitting tribute, no doubt, that Cohan felt he deserved, but wildly at odds with the attitude of either of his real wives" (1992, 161). Signaling his approval of the finished *Yankee Doodle Dandy* when the film was about to premiere, Cohan wrote to Cagney, "How's my double?"

Yankee Doodle Dandy begins with another significant instance of doubling or imitation, in Cohan's performance of President Roosevelt in *I'd Rather Be Right*. Moss Hart and George Kaufman's Broadway show starred Cohan playing FDR and ran for 290 performances between 1937 and 1938. In *Yankee Doodle Dandy*, the president summons Cohan during the run of the show, the latter expecting to be chastised by FDR for caricaturing him in the musical. He is met, instead, with the phrase Cohan later quoted, "How's my double?" Cagney was more a "double" of FDR than Cohan was a double of either Cagney or FDR, Cohan having delayed his visit with the president to receive the Congressional Gold Medal because of the composer's adamant disagreements with FDR concerning unions (Behlmer 2005). In *Yankee Doodle Dandy*, the scene in which the two men meet gives the film its patriotic bona fides as Cagney's Cohan explains the idea of American democracy: "Where else in the world today could a plain guy like me come in and talk things over with the head man?" Curtiz positions the camera behind the "head man," adding to the aura of FDR while at the same time making it easier for audiences to imagine the president actually inhabiting the scene. *Yankee Doodle Dandy*'s patriotic idealism is grounded in this idea of the common man. The final scene features a rousing reprise of the World War I anthem "Over There," for which Cohan has just received the Congressional Gold Medal. He marches alongside the singing soldiers on a densely populated street, thus adopting, in Jennifer Jenkins's words about musical war films, "the perspective and the plight of ordinary viewers to rally support for the larger cause abroad and to maintain morale at home" (2001, 316).

At Jack Warner's behest, Warner Bros. had long established itself as an ally of FDR. As Grahame Daseler (2014) observes, "Today, no movie studio would dare propagandize so openly for a sitting president, but, during the '30s, Warners did it with the enthusiasm of a love-sick teenager, turning movies like *G Men* (1935) into advertisements for the efficiency of the new Federal Bureau of Investigation, using dance numbers to create pictograms of the NRA Eagle and the president's face in *Footlight Parade* (1933), and, in *Yankee Doodle Dandy*, turning F.D.R. into a character in the movie." Indeed, *Yankee Doodle Dandy* begins with Cagney imitating Cohan playing FDR, with his signature talk-singing of "Off the Record," a satiric litany of complaints about the president's political colleagues and contemporaries. In a film that aims on one level to establish the record of Cohan's life and work, the song further mythologizes FDR, since Cagney dances exuberantly on the stage while impersonating a sitting president immobilized by polio.[1]

The patriotic scaffolding of *Yankee Doodle Dandy* is indisputable—and clearly the source of today's viewers' association of it with "guilty pleasures," or outmoded flag-waving sentimentality. For Donald Lyons, the film is "a period artifact aglow with an immigrant's gratitude and a patriot's sincerity, but lacking wit or irony" (1996, 84). Certainly, *Yankee Doodle Dandy* pays tribute to melting-pot America, enhancing George M. Cohan's forceful individual personality with an homage to blended American communities: Irish Americans; family bonds (the story of the Four Cohans and the three Cagneys at work on the film); boardinghouse denizens; American soldiers and the military; vaudeville and Broadway theater worlds; and business partnerships, including deals made on the basis of a handshake.[2] These communities model for viewers a notion of the world as fully cohesive and wholly Americanized in its shared values. *Yankee Doodle Dandy*'s springboard, "Over There," presents a unified vision of "here" (America) in contrast with "over there"—that is, everywhere else. But "Over There" functions at the same time as an expansion of the "here" to the "over there." In this sense, American values (those associated with "here," home) are universally exportable—and virtuous. That notion is aptly demonstrated in the moving-postcard sequence of the film, during which a Chinese-inflected version of "Yankee Doodle Dandy" plays in the background as George and Mary travel abroad, suggesting their global dissemination of American culture and values.

There is hardly a better vehicle for promoting these nationalist myths about the supremacy of American values than the classic Hollywood biopic. But with the departure of the Warners biopic star Paul Muni and the musical choreographer and director Busby Berkeley before the war, the studio shifted focus away from these genres (Schatz 1997, 50). Though a musical biopic, *Yankee Doodle Dandy* relied for its success on the charismatic presence and star power of Cagney, and on its "strenuous patriotism" (Custen 1992, 3). The following year, Michael Curtiz directed another wartime musical, *This Is the Army* (1943), the product of further collaboration between the War Department and Warner Bros. Instead of stars, the ensemble cast featured actual soldiers, including army lieutenant Ronald Reagan. Uncredited, Captain Jack Young reprised his role as FDR from *Yankee Doodle Dandy*. For *Army*, Curtiz worked closely with the producer Hal Wallis to adapt Irving Berlin's stage musical for the screen, and both the stage show and the film were wildly successful morale boosters, playing throughout the war (Schatz 1997, 224).

While *This Is the Army* used cameos by Irving Berlin, Kate Smith, Frances Langford, and Joe Louis to enhance its authenticity, *Yankee Doodle Dandy* relied on the traditions of the Hollywood biopic to create the illusion of truthfulness and reality. Many celebrated biopics were released in the 1930s, and Warner Bros. and Fox were particularly effective in representing characters with strong motivations that audiences would identify with and champion. *Yankee Doodle Dandy*'s success at achieving such "rooting interest"[3] was made clear in a comment by Cohan's daughter Georgette, who said of Cagney's rendition that it was "the kind of life Daddy would have liked to have lived" (quoted in Dwyer-Ryan 2011, 58). Biopics often posit individual agency as a synecdoche for American achievement. There is a long tradition of this kind of metaphorical identification in American culture, from Benjamin Franklin being named by a *New York Times* reporter in 1856 "the incarnation of the true American character" (Huang 1994, 31); to Mark Twain's notebook entry "I am not *an* American, I am *the* American";[4] even to Maureen O'Hara's plea to Congress in 1971 to award a medal to John Wayne, whom she claimed *"is* the United States of America" (emphasis added). O'Hara went on to say, "And I feel that the medal should say just one thing: 'John Wayne, American'" (quoted in Roberts and Olson 1995, 641).

According to the film's title song, George M. Cohan was born on July 4 (in 1878). Contemporary reviews of the film repeated this hyper-American mythology, though in fact Cohan was born July 3. The film's flashback narration begins with an Independence Day parade coinciding with the birth of young Cohan, who is handed a flag by his excited father (Walter Huston). George M.'s voiceover establishes baby George's inaugurative act: "First thing I ever had in my fist was the American flag."

The film's infusion of personal biography with patriotic values extends outward to director Michael Curtiz's own story. The Hungarian-born Curtiz reinvented himself often: from Kaminer Manó to Mihaly Kertész to Michael Curtiz. In his autobiography *My First Hundred Years in Hollywood*, Jack Warner maintained that Curtiz "had a deep love for America and understood his adopted country better than many Americans" (1965, 288). It is perhaps for this reason that Warner claimed that Curtiz first arrived in the United States on, of all days, July 4. Other scholars have repeated the story, adding that Curtiz, a "natural show-off" from early on, thought the fireworks were for him (Marton 2006, 15, 21; on Curtiz's American arrival, see Paris 1991, 36, and *Michael Curtiz: Greatest Director*).[5] Especially because the fiction of Curtiz's arrival was fueled by Jack Warner, the myth stands interestingly alongside anecdotes chronicled in Neil Gabler's *An Empire of Their Own* about the strategies of the early Hollywood moguls who were born in eastern European shtetls to assimilate into American culture. Louis B. Mayer adopted July 4 as his birth date, for example, to erase suspicion that immigrant Jews were more European or Jewish than they were American. Curtiz's *This Is the Army* capitalized on the powerful cultural merger between popular music and patriotism, featuring songs by another Jewish immigrant, Irving Berlin, including "God Bless America," an anthem for assimilated Judeo-Christian values (Gabler 1989, 79).[6]

But *Yankee Doodle Dandy* presents other sources of gratification that have less to do with the film's unified patriotic front than with its performance of identities. Looking at this film nearly seventy-five years after its release may leave viewers with a sense of its datedness, but a fresh view of *Yankee Doodle Dandy* may also warrant appreciation for its exuberance, on display not only in Cagney's dancing but also in the film's whimsy at certain moments: Curtiz's rich mise-en-scène, and a pliable sense of the real and fictive that belies its ostensible status as simply a whitewashed record of the life and times of George M. Cohan. This iconic film seems invested in stable forces of personal and political forms of identity; yet at the same time, its fascination with alternating figures of sameness and difference points not only to melting-pot universality and can-do Yankee individualism but also to collaborative artistic creativity, eclecticism, and flexibility—all values at least partly in tension with an easy patriotism conveyed in that stable generic art form, the Hollywood biopic.

Cagney's performance, a major strength of this film, in some sense literalizes the point that Tom Brown and Belén Vidal recently made about the biopic, that it "trades on a sense of authenticity that stems from the actor's body itself" (2014, 11). Nowhere is the "actor's body" more emphatically present and dramatized than in Cagney's George M. Cohan, from the straight-legged impersonation in the signature "Yankee Doodle Dandy" number to Cagney's frenetic backstage old-man dance to his gymnastic dance "audition" for the military induction center.

Added to the Cagneys' desire to verify James's patriotic credentials was the movie star's wish to break away from gangster roles, a career shift he had tried to pull off in the two films he released the year before *Dandy* premiered: *The Strawberry Blonde* (Raoul Walsh) and *The Bride Came C.O.D.* (William Keighley). Owing to his huge success in playing gangsters in the 1930s, in films such as William Wellman's *Public Enemy* (1931) and Curtiz's *Angels with Dirty Faces* (1938), Cagney was typed as a tough guy, while he saw himself more as a song and dance man. Furthermore, he wanted more variety in his professional career. Mae Clarke once commented that even in his gangster roles Cagney "was a dancer, essentially." "Everything that James Cagney did was choreographed," Clarke continues, citing the sequence in *Lady Killers* (1933) in which he drags her by the hair, the physical choreography of the scene made symmetrical by her grabbing onto his wrist to counter the hair pulling (*James Cagney: Top of the World*). The actor Pat O'Brien called Cagney "just a dancer gone wrong" (Anderson 1997).

When in 1949 Cagney again played a memorable gangster, the sociopathic Cody Jarrett in Raoul Walsh's *White Heat*, the actor's rigorous physicality made the role remarkable but also established the grounds on which we sympathize with Jarrett's suffering: in the prison dining hall, Jarrett learns of his mother's death and pitches forward, on top of and across the table, then around the room, in a psychotic dance. So, too, in the film's finale, when Jarrett climbs a gas storage tank ("Made it, Ma! Top of the world!"), the seeming recklessness of Jarrett's movement is achieved by Cagney's grace and physical agility.

It is precisely this extreme physicality that Cagney brought to *Yankee Doodle Dandy*. But the film exhibits this trait more generally, a kind of gymnastic ethic. Countering its reputation as merely a period artifact, *Yankee Doodle Dandy* stands for values associated with flexibility, seen in the film's dispersed authorship; its preoccupation with mirrors and doubling; and the imbuing of every scene with a profound sense of the importance of imagination and adaptability.

Cagney's body art, to call it that, is complemented by Curtiz's emphasis on performance and nimbleness in the film's style. Such a tone seems out of keeping with a film directed by Michael Curtiz, long identified by his famously autocratic style. Those present during the filming of Jerry Cohan's death scene saw and heard no "Iron Mike" (Lyons 1996) at the helm, but a suggestible viewer, crying so loudly at the poignancy of the scene that one of the takes was reportedly ruined by the director's sobbing. This detail points to not only Curtiz's emotionality but also an extemporaneous spirit that characterized the production as a whole, a case of constantly shifting gears as Curtiz rewrote scenes and shared creative choices, with speed and finesse. Despite the *Los Angeles Times*' comment that Curtiz was at the time "identified with the thunderhoofs school of cinema" (Scheuer 1941), the director's energy and versatility were a perfect match for this film. At the time, the stage manager Sam Forrest described the world of Cohan specifically as "variety" rather than as the narrower "vaudeville"; as a "variety" director, Curtiz fit this bill, too, having worked on comedies, musicals, film noir, and adventure dramas. He was, according to Barry Paris, "the most consistent—he was certainly the most prolific—maker of top-flight entertainment films in all genres" (1991, 35).

Yankee Doodle Dandy thrived on the rampant energy and versatility of Cohan, Cagney, and Curtiz, but the film was also the product of Don Siegel's montage design, Johnny Boyle's choreography (strongly informed by Boyle's earlier work with Cohan), the dance directors Seymour Felix and LeRoy Prinz's work with the actors, and James Wong Howe's cinematography. Carl Jules Weyl's art direction was put to dramatic use in the 285 sets the studio undertook to build for the film (McGilligan 1981, 53). For example, working with Curtiz, Weyl developed the Broadway number "You're a Grand Old Flag" from the 1906 show *George Washington, Jr.* by using a moving treadmill, cutouts of soldiers (waved by stagehands behind the live action) to create depth on the stage, and the filmed projection of a flag on the theatrical stage (Behlmer 2005). Within the sequence, Curtiz deftly positioned the camera to create the illusion of battlegrounds and multitudes of marching people.

More importantly, beginning the film with "Off the Record" raises the issue of representation, suggesting the elusiveness of purporting to imitate the real. We see this idea as well in a particular doubling in which Eddie Foy Jr. plays his father, Eddie Foy, a rival of Cohan's. In the film, the two meet in front of a theater featuring Cohan's *George Washington Jr.*, and, in-cognito, flatter themselves and insult each other.[7] But the most intriguing instance of the film's self-consciousness about performance and authen-ticity is the scene in which Cohan meets Mary, who later becomes his wife. Mary goes backstage to ask Cohan for advice: "I'm 18, I can sing and dance, and I'm going to New York. Should I? . . . Oh, Mr. Cohan, you're so old." While she means by this that he has the experience to provide her with guidance, the comment provokes the scene's quirky reflection on the adaptability of experience via performance. Far from actors being "cast" as simply "so old," for example, they are nimble, transformable— as Cagney-Cohan, with the director's help, graphically demonstrates by shedding his dotage, to Mary's momentary astonishment. (Joan Leslie was seventeen during the filming, "aged" thanks to the makeup by Perc Westmore.)

Here Curtiz makes use of multiple mirrors: Cagney's bemused gaze at Mary is a reflection in the mirror, but he was looking at his makeup in a cosmetic mirror just before Mary's entrance. Cagney's tour-de-force dance routine follows, as if to resolve, in the exuberance of the actor's per-formance, the tension the scene displays between image and reality. He tries to show Mary how a performance must toggle between mimicry and innovation, a sly reference to the film's negotiation between document-ing a life and creating an entertaining film. "You don't want to be just an imitator, do you?" he asks Mary. "But on the other hand, you don't want to be too original either." The way the lines frame Cohan's performance philosophy mirrors Cagney's method. As the actor astutely summarized in the *Saturday Evening Post*, "[Cohan's] stage mannerisms were so marked and at times so flamboyant that I felt the offstage portrayal of [him] would have to be toned down. The idea was to show the Cohan the public knew without weakening the realism of his life story. I decided that the way to handle it was to do the obvious Cohan tricks only on the stage; offstage, I used just the slightest suggestion of his mannerisms" (Cagney 1948).

Cohan impersonates an old man (without being "too original") engag-ing in a frenetic dance, as seen in the top image at right (paired with an

James Cagney's gymnastic dancing as George M. Cohan in *Yankee Doodle Dandy* (Warner Bros., 1942). Digital frame enlargements.

image of one of Cagney's signature leaps in the "Yankee Doodle Dandy" number). He stuns Mary, who exclaims, "So fast! Such excitement!" Mary's growing insight that Cohan seems "different," "younger," is met with a provocative reply: "I'm always as young as the people I'm with." A metaphor for Hollywood cinema, which morphs to meet audience desire, the comment also reflects Cohan's, Cagney's, and Curtiz's creative and speedy adaptability. The scene ends with Mary's jumpy aversion to George's old-man prop wig. George drops it in her lap, Mary pushes it to the floor, and Cagney, improvising, imagines the wig to be a bug that he then mock-heroically stomps on.

Everything in this film is figured as performance. As the paternal Jerry appears in a variety show in Providence, his wife, Nellie (Rosemary DeCamp), "busy on a smaller production," gives birth to George M. When George proposes marriage to Mary, she asks to "see the script." The wedding march he will write for Mary, George tells his sister Josie (Jeanne Cagney), will "pack the pews." It should be noted, however, that Josie's exit from the family troupe in order to marry reveals the considerably less "gymnastic" reality of a female performer during that period, who was acculturated to abandon her career for marriage. Josie's tears may signal not just her sadness about leaving the Four Cohans but also her regret at having to choose between her life as a performer and marriage and family.

In 1942, George M. Cohan was said to be "the quickest theatrical mind of the century" (Forrest). But even in the film's scene construction, Cohan's improvisation is seen as a broader value. Twice, Curtiz blocks scenes with Cagney doing a double take, feigning an attitude in order to adapt to a domestic situation. First, at Madame Bartholdi's boardinghouse, Cohan overhears his family defend him, despite the troupe's unemployment and his having become a liability for the Four Cohans because of his arrogance. In the second instance, later in the film, George makes a similar double entrance when he overhears Mary playing "Grand Old Name." This is the song he promised to her, but he and Sam have just given it to Fay Templeton to entice her to work with Cohan. In an effort to console and appease Mary, a worried Cohan reenters the apartment with candy and flowers.

The mental and physical energy that Cagney embodies throughout, best captured in the spectacle of Cohan's frenetic old-man dance, stands in contrast to the farm scene late in the film, in which Cohan is foiled by a group of animated teens who don't recognize him. "Raised in a vacuum bottle," he murmurs. The newspaper article Cohan is reading when the teenagers happen on the scene, "Stix nix hix pix," is drawn from an actual *Variety* headline from July 17, 1935, "Sticks nix hick pix," about midwestern theaters (in the sticks) rejecting pictures about rural stories. A reference to the vibrant world of showbiz "slanguage," the headline is interpreted by Cohan for the young kids in their jalopy. But at the moment, in an intriguing reversal, Cohan, now actually old, is lying uncharacteristically at rest on a hammock, and the kids become the live-wire performers. They offer an improvised jive-swing version of "Stix Nix Hix Pix" before sharing the chorus of "Jeepers Creepers" (though the setting of the scene may in fact predate this 1938 popular song). In addition, the scene provides motivation for Cohan's return to Broadway in *I'd Rather Be Right*.

Yankee Doodle Dandy's songs and dance routines are "leaps" of faith based on the sovereignty of performance. A "Marie" can transform to "grand old Mary" when the passion is there ("For it is Mary, Mary / Plain as any name can be / But with propriety, society will say Marie"). By far the best example of the film's art deriving from the primacy of improvisation is Cagney's purportedly ad-libbed dance down the steps after his interview with FDR. Cagney fully adapted to what would normally be a forbidding space, the stairs of the White House. In one of Michael Curtiz's well-known mangled metaphors, the director called *Yankee Doodle Dandy* the "pinochle of my career" (McCabe 1997, 231). If language is somewhat unstable for the film's director, the film itself, for all its association with fixed notions of patriotism, endorses a freedom of the mind and body passionately expressed in the realm of performance.

Notes

I am grateful to Homer Pettey for his feedback on this essay.

1. This element of disjunction in FDR's presence in the film—represented as a dancing satirist—may be softened in light of recent journalistic reports that the secret of FDR's paralysis and the collaboration of the press was itself a sort of myth (Pressman 2013).

2. The handshake deal, which defines the relationship between Cohan and his partner Sam Harris in the film, was touted by Cohan's stage manager, Sam Forrest, in a 1942 editorial in the *New York Herald Tribune*: "There has never been a scrap of paper or formal contractual agreement between us. There has never been need for such a formality. [Cohan] has always tried to do business with his friends. With them, there has never been need for formalities, and he has more friends than anybody on Broadway." The Cagney family was a force in the making of *Yankee Doodle Dandy*. Jeanne Cagney played Cohan's sister Josie, and James's brother William Cagney co-produced the film with Hal Wallis and Jack Warner.

3. See Custen for his discussion of Darryl Zanuck's role in "the personalizing of history that made the great man, or woman, a figure to root for in some cosmic contest" (1992, 19). Zanuck began his career as a writer at Warner Bros., and this

philosophy also drove Hal Wallis and the studio in their heavy production and marketing of biopics.

4. The quote about Franklin's quintessential Americanness continues, "Franklin was the true type of the pure, noble, republican feeling of America" (quoted in Huang 1994, 31). The attribution to Mark Twain of "I am not *an* American. I am *the* American" has been contested by Twain scholars, who now believe that Twain was quoting his friend Frank Fuller (Cindy Lovell, "That's What He Said: Quoting Mark Twain," *Huffington Post*, November 18, 2013, huffingtonpost.com/cindy -lovell/thats-what-he-said-quotin_b_4282800.html). In any case, Twain wrote this phrase in his notebooks because it captured, for him, the idea that one exceptional American could stand in for the country. Twain certainly desired to be that person.

5. Robertson debunks the myth in *The Casablanca Man*, noting that Curtiz arrived in the States on June 6, 1926 (1993, 8). (In that same year, Cagney auditioned for Cohan, who didn't give him the part, because he thought the younger man was too similar to himself.)

6. Gabler observes that for the Jewish Hollywood moguls, "it was their citizenship rather than their religion that spurred them" (1989, 348). Irving Berlin wrote two other iconic popular songs representing religion as utterly assimilated into cultural politics, "Easter Parade" and "White Christmas," the latter featured in the 1954 film of the same name, also directed by Michael Curtiz.

7. Thirteen years after the release of *Yankee Doodle Dandy*, Cagney reprised his role as George M. Cohan, doing a tabletop dance with Bob Hope as Eddie Foy in *The Seven Little Foys*.

Archive

Margaret Herrick Library, Academy of Motion Picture Arts and Sciences, Beverly Hills (HER). Cited items from this archive were found in the *Yankee Doodle Dandy* Press Clippings file.

Works Cited

Anderson, Fred. 1997. "My God, What an Act to Follow." *American Heritage* 48, no. 4 (July–August): 66–77.

Behlmer, Rudy. 2005. Audio commentary on *Yankee Doodle Dandy*. Directed by Michael Curtiz. Warner Home Video.

Brown, Tom, and Belén Vidal, eds. 2014. *The Biopic in Contemporary Film Culture*. New York: Routledge.

Cagney, James. 1948. "The Role I Liked Best . . ." *Saturday Evening Post*, July 10. HER.

Crowther, Bosley. 1942. "Yankee Doodle Goes to Town." *New York Times*, June 7. HER.

Custen, George. 1992. *Bio/Pics: How Hollywood Constructed Public History*. New Brunswick, NJ: Rutgers University Press.

Daseler, Graham. 2014. "The Fall of the House of Warners: The Warner Brothers." *Bright Lights Film Journal*, January 25. www.brightlightsfilm.com /the-fall-of-the-house-of-warner-the-warner-brothers/#V0352JMrLow.

Dickens, Homer. 1972. *The Films of James Cagney*. Secaucus, NJ: Citadel.

Dwyer-Ryan, Meaghan. 2011. "'Yankee Doodle Paddy': Themes of Ethnic Acculturation in *Yankee Doodle Dandy*." *Journal of American Ethnic History* 30, no. 4 (Summer): 57–62.

Forrest, Sam. 1942. "Three Decades with George M. Cohan." *New York Herald Tribune*, May 24. HER.

Gabler, Neil. 1989. *An Empire of Their Own: How the Jews Invented Hollywood*. New York: Anchor.

Hollywood Reporter. 1942. "Cagney's Cohan Tops Superb Film." June 1. HER.

Huang, Nian-Sheng. 1994. *Benjamin Franklin in American Thought and Culture, 1790–1990*. Philadelphia: American Philosophical Society.

James Cagney: Top of the World. Turner Classic Movies. Documentary hosted by Michael J. Fox. Written by Bob Waldman and Carl H. Lindahl. Directed by Carl H. Lindahl. On the two-disc special edition of *Yankee Doodle Dandy*.

Jenkins, Jennifer R. 2001. "'Say It with Firecrackers': Defining the 'War Musical' of the 1940s." *American Music* 19, no. 3 (Autumn): 315–339.

Kenrick, John. 2008. *Musical Theatre: A History*. New York: Continuum.

Lyons, Donald. 1996. "Iron Mike: At Home with Michael Curtiz." *Film Comment* 32, no. 2 (March–April): 80–88.

Marton, Kati. 2006. *Nine Jews Who Fled Hitler and Changed the World*. New York: Simon and Shuster.

McCabe, John. 1997. *Cagney*. New York: Knopf.

McGilligan, Patrick. 1981. *Yankee Doodle Dandy*. Madison: University of Wisconsin Press.

Michael Curtiz: Greatest Director You Never Heard Of. Directed by Gary Leva. Leva FilmWorks, Warner Bros., 2012.

Paris, Barry. 1991. "The Little Tyrant Who Could." *American Film* 16, no. 1 (January): 34–37, 44–45.

Pressman, Matthew. 2013. "The Myth of FDR's Secret Disability." *Time*, July 12. http://ideas.time.com/2013/07/12/the-myth-of-fdrs-secret-disability.

Roberts, Randy, and James S. Olson. 1995. *John Wayne: American*. Lincoln: University of Nebraska Press.

Robertson, James C. 1993. *The Casablanca Man: The Cinema of Michael Curtiz*. London: Routledge.

Schatz, Thomas. 1997. *Boom and Bust: American Cinema in the 1940s*. Berkeley: University of California Press.

Scheuer, Philip K. 1941. "Town Called Hollywood." *Los Angeles Times*, December 28. HER.

Variety. 1942. "Review of *Yankee Doodle Dandy*." June 1. HER.

Warner, Jack L., and Dean Southern Jennings. 1965. *My First Hundred Years in Hollywood*. New York: Random House.

CHAPTER 7

Mildred Pierce: From Script to Screen

KRISTEN HATCH

The question of Michael Curtiz's status as an auteur has remained open ever since the director was dismissed by members of the *Cahiers du cinéma* as a *metteur en scène*, skilled at making commercial cinema, rather than an auteur capable of imprinting his personal vision on films made within the limitations of the studio system. Peter Wollen makes a compelling case for Curtiz's standing in his reassessment of the director's oeuvre and the auteur theory more generally. Wollen's evaluation, like that of the mid-century auteur theorists, rests on the belief that an auteur is identifiable by the consistency of his or her vision, a logical approach to the question of authorship in a collaborative art when the only evidence at hand is the films themselves. But in the case of *Mildred Pierce* (1945), the detailed production files provide an opportunity to trace the evolution of the project from book to film. It would be fruitless to try to parse the contributions of any single individual to the film. Nevertheless, these files and the published shooting script do offer a glimpse into the process by which *Mildred Pierce* made its dramatic transformation from book to screen, and into the role that Curtiz played in this process.

Mildred Pierce begins with a murder. Monte Beragon (Zachary Scott) is shot and left to die on the floor of his beach house. Mildred Pierce (Joan Crawford) walks, crying, along the Santa Monica pier. Her thoughts of suicide are interrupted by a beat cop, and she accepts an invitation from her old friend Wally (Jack Carson) to join him for a drink in a seedy bar. Mildred lures Wally to the beach house, where she locks him in with the dead man's body. Later, police detectives bring Mildred in for questioning. Through a series of flashbacks that recount Mildred's divorce from Bert (Bruce Bennett), her subsequent tremendous success in opening a chain of restaurants, and her marriage to the Pasadena playboy Monte, she eventually reveals the truth: that Monte was killed by her daughter Veda (Ann Blyth), an amoral viper who had been the apple of her mother's eye. Indeed, every decision Mildred made—throwing Bert out, opening her restaurant chain, and marrying Monte—was motivated by her desire to please the insatiable Veda. The film ends with Veda being led away to prison while Mildred and Bert reunite against the backdrop of a splendid sunrise.

In 1948, the year that Alexandre Astruc wrote "The Birth of a New Avant-Garde: La Caméra-stylo," which helped inspire debates in France about film authorship by arguing for an understanding of the director as author, *Harper's Magazine* put forward a different theory of authorship in Hollywood film. In a profile of Jerry Wald, the film's producer, *Harper's* explained: "Hollywood today, with rare exceptions, is a producers' medium. . . . The director is rarely more than a middleman between the script and the screen. He may, as Wald charitably defends him, 'do more to interpret and help transcribe to the screen what the author means than any one man,' but he has no part in staking out the boundaries of a film. . . . [The director] does not materially affect the film in terms of content and rarely in terms of style" (Goodman 1948, 420). The production files for *Mildred Pierce* certainly bear out the claim that the producer's was the central voice guiding the film. But as Wald asserted, this guidance was achieved not by suppressing the director's vision but by synthesizing it with his own and adapting it to the limitations of the Production Code and the imperatives of the star system.

The Producer

Mildred Pierce was Curtiz's first film with Jerry Wald. Then at the peak of his career, Wald was widely believed to have been the inspiration, years before, for Sammy Glick in Budd Schulberg's novel *What Makes Sammy Run?* (1941), though it was Schulberg's assertion that his character was meant to represent a type rather than an individual (Goodman 1948, 416). Born in Brooklyn, Wald began his career while he was a journalism student at New York University, having talked his way into a position as the radio columnist for the *New York Graphic* in 1932. His column there, "The Walds Have Ears," was canceled six months into his contract after his criticism of a fight broadcast met with objections from NBC ("Wald Will Maintain Salary Raises Offset Paper's 'Out' Clause," *Variety*, July 5, 1932, 43). Ever the fast talker, Wald was able to parlay his short stint as a radio columnist into a film career. In 1932 and 1933, he wrote and appeared in several short Vitaphone films that featured radio celebrities (*Ramblin' Round Radio Row*), and Warner Bros. hired him in 1934 on the basis of a magazine profile he had written of the crooner Russ Columbo. In 1940, the *Chicago Daily Tribune* described twenty-nine-year-old Wald, who had been with Warners for seven years, as "at once the youngest and the oldest writer on the Warner lot" (John Chapman, "Looking at Hollywood," *Chicago Daily Tribune*, December 25, 1940, 30). The following year, Wald became an associate producer, and he was promoted to full producer status in 1942. During the war, he made a name for himself by producing a series of battle films: *Air Force* (1943), *Destination Tokyo* (1943), *Action in the North Atlantic* (1943), *Objective, Burma!* (1945), and *Pride of the Marines* (1945). He was frustrated, however, at not being given the opportunity to develop a film from a Broadway play or an "important" novel ("Warner Settles Wald Peeve with Broadway Play," *Variety*, June 21, 1944, 3). *Mildred Pierce* represented a turning point for him: it was his first adaptation of an established property, and the first of many films he was to make with Joan Crawford.

Unlike James M. Cain's crime fiction (*Double Indemnity, The Postman Always Rings Twice*), the 1941 novel *Mildred Pierce* was not a tale of infidelity and murder recounted in the first person. It was the story of a mother's obsessive love for her grasping daughter, Veda, whose volatility and selfishness were attributed by Cain to her being a natural-born coloratura singer. Rather than killing her stepfather, as in the movie, Veda runs off with him and enjoys a successful radio career after ruining and publicly humiliating her mother. Given Mildred's healthy enjoyment of sex and Veda's reprehensible behavior, the novel did not seem a likely candidate for film adaptation under the Production Code. Nevertheless, when Val Lewton at Selznick International sent a treatment to the Production Code Administration (PCA) in 1941, the reply was promising. With the elimination of any indication of extramarital sex between Bert and his neighbor Mrs. Biederhoff, or between Mildred and Monte, and by having Mildred become engaged to Monte rather than marrying him, in order to avoid any indication of "legal incest" between Veda and her stepfather, Geoffrey M. Shurlock of the Production Code office assured Selznick in a memorandum (September 18, 1941) that the project would likely receive its approval. But Selznick did not purchase the rights, and the novel remained unfilmed.

In the summer of 1943, shortly after Cain's 1937 novella *Double Indemnity* was reprinted in the omnibus *Three of a Kind*, Jerry Wald met with

Cain and proposed that *Mildred Pierce* might be made more suspenseful by the addition of a murder and a flashback structure, which was then a somewhat fresh approach to film narrative (Wald's discussions with Cain were set out in a memo by Joseph Karp, of the Warner Bros. legal department, February 2, 1950). In January 1944, Warner Bros. sent a treatment to the PCA. Selznick had sent his studio's treatment to the PCA during the brief period when Joseph Breen took a hiatus from the administration, but by 1944 Breen was back at his PCA desk, and his response to the prospect of adapting Cain's novel was far less inviting than his assistant Geoffrey Shurlock's had earlier been. Breen found the story to be overrun by "sordid and repellent" elements and suggested that Warners "dismiss the story from any further consideration" (Breen to Warner, February 2, 1944). Wald met with Breen and agreed to eliminate the inference that Wally was merely "on the make" for Mildred; that Mildred and Monte were engaged in an extramarital affair; and that Monte married Mildred only with an eye toward seducing Veda. Further, "it was also agreed that a very definite effort would be made to raise the general all-over tone of the picture, and thus add to its general over-all acceptability" (Breen to Warner, February 22, 1944). Warner Bros. purchased the rights, which were assigned to the studio on March 14, and Wald began the process of translating the sprawling novel into a murder mystery.

The Warner Bros. Archives contain a detailed analysis of the film's adaptation from novel to script. In 1949, an aspiring screenwriter threatened suit against Cain and Warner Bros. for plagiarism, prompting the Warners lawyer Roy Obringer to work with one of the studio's story editors, Tom Chapman, to retrace the film's genesis.[1] The Obringer-Chapman analysis suggests that Wald played a central role in shaping the project. Catherine Turney was the first to work on adapting the initial treatment into a full script. When she resisted Wald's suggestion that the story be framed by a flashback (Karp memorandum), he turned to several other writers on his staff, including William Faulkner and Albert Maltz. According to the analysis that Obringer and Chapman compiled (dated November 8, 1949), "While [the screenwriters were] revising everybody else's work Wald was synthesizing everything." As Chapman put it in a memorandum to Obringer (also dated November 8, 1949), his was the central consciousness that shaped the film: "Changes develop informally, over a period of time, as the result of a highly complex dialectical relationship among writers, the producer, the basic material, the scripts, the Breen office, the director, actors, etc."

In addition to framing the narrative around a murder mystery and introducing the flashback structure, Wald sought to increase the dramatic appeal of Cain's novel by polarizing the personalities, "establishing a group of characters fighting for the good as against a group representing evil," with the result that Veda and Monte became more "villainous" and Mildred more virtuous (Chapman to Obringer, March 4, 1949). Veda no longer sang light opera but popular music; "Mr. Wald felt [against Catherine Turney's advice] that audience sympathy might be lost for Mildred if Veda had this much talent and ability, and he therefore insisted that she go into a low dive and become a night club singer" (Obringer and Chapman analysis). Monte's economic dependence on Mildred was emphasized, and their mutual sexual attraction downplayed. Interestingly, much as Veda's villainy was signaled by her singing in a "low" nightclub, Mildred was made more virtuous by playing down her working-class origins: "It is well known that in a successful motion picture the audience must be able to identify itself with the interests of certain good characters as against certain bad ones. . . . Since it was clear that Mildred must be the heroine of this story it was necessary to clean up her character. For this reason she was made a member of the upper middle class instead of the lower middle class; vulgarisms were dropped from her speech; she was made more the victim of circumstances than a sinner" (Chapman to Obringer, March 4, 1949). These changes in Mildred's character not only made her more appealing to audiences but also made the film more acceptable to the Production Code Administration: "The rise in moral tone . . . was accomplished [by] promoting Mildred to a higher bracket of the middle class and softening her behavior" (Chapman, memorandum to Obringer, February 13, 1950).

With these changes in place, Wald turned to Ranald MacDougall, a former writer for NBC radio, to finalize the script. Wald and Curtiz spent nights and weekends in conversation with MacDougall until production began in December 1944.

The Star

In May 1944, two months after Warner Bros. had purchased the rights to the Cain novel, Joan Crawford appeared at the top of the list of possibilities for the role of Mildred (according to an untitled document, dated May 15, 1944, in the Warner Bros. Archives). Six weeks later, in late June, the *New York Times* announced that she would star in the film ("Screen News Here and In Hollywood: Warners to Star Crawford in *Mildred Pierce*,"

New York Times, June 28, 1944, 21). Crawford's career was at a turning point. She had not starred in a film for nearly two years, since leaving MGM, where she had become a star in the silent era and had remained for eighteen years. Crawford signed a lucrative agreement with Warner Bros., which gave her the right to approve her scripts. But the studio was unable to come up with anything she found acceptable. After she turned down several promising stories, the studio renegotiated her contract to a three-picture deal rather than keeping her on salary. Both Crawford and the studio were invested not only in making a successful film but also in building her star image.

Contemporary sources report that Curtiz objected to working with Crawford, particularly when she insisted on wearing glamorous costumes for the scenes in which she is slaving in the kitchen. The press kit for *Mildred Pierce* includes stories of their clashes on the set, particularly over her wardrobe. Reporting on "the battle over her wardrobe" several years later, Hedda Hopper describes Crawford as being at the mercy of the director and producer: "Joan, who'd always been a fashion plate, insisted on stylish clothes. Both Wald and Mike Curtiz . . . put thumbs down. They wouldn't even let her wear shoulder padding. There was weeping on Joan's part. But the fellows were adamant. . . . In the end Joan wore plain dresses" (Hedda Hopper, "Actress, Woman, and Mother," *Salt Lake Tribune*, June 4, 1950, 36). When Crawford asked the studio to indulge her, it was to have Gertrude, her hairdresser from MGM, brought in for *Mildred Pierce*, a request that Warner Bros. was willing to accommodate (Wald to Steve Trilling [Jack Warner's lieutenant], November 11, 1944). The archival record tells a different story about the clothing. Glamour and fashion were important elements of Crawford's star image at MGM, where the costume designer Adrian had developed a distinctive look to camouflage her broad shoulders and emphasize her small waist. Part of the thrill of *Mildred Pierce* for her fans was to witness her transformation from a downtrodden housewife into the more familiar fashion plate in shoulder pads when Mildred's business becomes a success. Jack Warner exercised his right to oversee this aspect of the film, screening the many wardrobe tests that were made (Warner, memorandum to Wald, February 1, 1945).

Likewise, the necessity of lighting Crawford for glamour played an important role in the film's cinematography. With filming only a month away, Jerry Wald was anxious to find a cinematographer who would do justice to Crawford's face: "Curtiz and I are becoming [worried] about the cameraman. . . . Both Curtiz and I looked at the films she made at Metro and there is no doubt that men like Bob Plank and Ray June managed to capture on the screen what we are trying to get for Miss Crawford" (Wald, memorandum to Tenny Wright [Warners' head of production], November 8, 1944). They had conducted four tests, using Ernest Haller, Bert Glennon, Sol Polito, and Carl Cuthrie, and Peverell Marley was scheduled to make a fifth. There was strong interest in James Wong Howe, but ultimately they were unable to secure his services, since he had a vacation planned. Haller took the role.

While wardrobe and cinematography were in part dictated by Crawford's star image, Mildred was shaped by the star's offscreen persona. Mary Beth Haralovich (1992) has demonstrated that *Mildred Pierce* often echoed and reinforced Crawford's star image, at a crucial point in her career. Just as Mildred fought to turn her work as a waitress and her pie baking into a lucrative chain of restaurants, so Crawford fought for her career. Hedda Hopper's attribution of Crawford's comeback to her "waiting, fighting, and sheer luck" might also describe Mildred's fight to build her business (Hedda Hopper, "1945 To Be a 'Comeback Year' for Many Stars in Hollywood," *Washington Post*, February 4, 1945, S6). Indeed, several newspaper and magazine articles played up the similarities between Mildred and Crawford. When it was announced that Crawford would take the role, the *Los Angeles Times* remarked, "It is significant that *Mildred Pierce* is the story of a poor working girl, a waitress, who fought her way to the top. The particular problem involved is that of Veda, a— to put it politely—dancing daughter of this generation. Mildred, said Miss Crawford, with a fond glance at her own two adopted children . . . wants her daughter to have all the things SHE wanted and couldn't have" (Philip K. Scheuer, "Joan Crawford Prepares for Return to Screen," *Los Angeles Times*, October 29, 1944, B1).

Inevitably, the well-publicized similarities between Crawford and Mildred helped shape the film's meaning as well as Crawford's stardom. Crawford lent glamour to the character, who is a middle-aged frump in Cain's novel. Crawford's "indomitable will to get to the top" made Mildred's drive to build her business seem like something more than a desperate ploy to gain Veda's love (Scheuer, "Joan Crawford Prepares"). And Crawford's triumph in the film contributed to the optimism of the film's final image.

The Director

Michael Curtiz was not assigned to *Mildred Pierce* until October 1944, three months after it was announced that Crawford would star and six months after Warner Bros. acquired the rights. Initially, Wald suggested Curtis Bernhardt or Vincent Sherman to direct. But then, much as Wald had begged Warner Bros. for an opportunity to develop a Broadway play or important novel into a film, in July 1944 he began his campaign to work with Curtis, begging Steve Trilling, Jack Warner's second in command, "At least once I'd like to be able to have Curtiz do a picture for me" (Wald to Trilling, July 17, 1944). Having Curtiz on the film required not only Trilling's go-ahead but also Curtiz's acceptance of the project. As Wald waited for a decision, he continued to send halfhearted suggestions to Trilling, including Crawford's idea that George Cukor—with whom she had worked successfully in *The Women* (1939)—be brought in to direct. Curtiz had been scheduled to direct Cary Grant in *Night and Day* following production of *Roughly Speaking*. Because Grant delayed filming so that he could go on vacation, however, Curtiz was free to do *Mildred Pierce*.

Between October and mid-December, when shooting began, Curtiz and Wald were in close consultation about all aspects of the film, including the script and casting, as well as selecting the editor, dialogue director, and cinematographer. While Curtiz took a great deal of credit for developing the script, Tom Chapman was more circumspect about the director's contributions: "Curtiz informs us that he originated all the significant changes in the script, including the murder device, the flashback, the suicide impulse of Mildred, and scenes in the beach house, and that he contributed to raising the moral tone of the picture as well. He perhaps accomplished this last goal in direction, but the other assertions, except those relating to the beach house, are known to be hyperbolic" (Chapman to Obringer, November 8, 1949). One change Curtiz did make to the script was to relocate Monte's weekend home from Lake Arrowhead, eighty miles east of Los Angeles, to the beach in Santa Monica. He had been staying at Anatole Litvak's beach house in Malibu and thought this would be a "colorful" setting for Monte's death. The art director, Anton Grot, had portions of the house re-created on a Warner Bros. soundstage (ibid.).

Once Curtiz was committed to the project, Wald and the director worked closely as collaborators. Together they had dinner with Cain to talk about the script, and together they screened several films in the Warner Bros. screening room, seeking inspiration for the film's flashbacks in *Rebecca*, *Above Suspicion*, and *The Woman in the Window* (Wald to Curtiz, October 24, 1944; Wald to Curtiz, October 31, 1944; Wald to Wright, November 8, 1944).

It is difficult, likely impossible, to identify how any specific aspect of the film emerged during the final script development, when Wald, Curtiz, and MacDougall were meeting regularly on nights and weekends to complete revisions before shooting began in December. Curtiz's wife, the screenwriter Bess Meredyth, may have contributed ideas. And according to the Warner Bros. files, Curtiz worked with another writer, Louise Randall Pierson, to develop the script at the same time that MacDougall and William Faulkner were making revisions. Wald, it appears, had the final say. Pierson made this clear to Tom Chapman: "Curtiz had some ideas which he wished incorporated in the picture and she was supposed to do this. Wald, who differed with Curtiz on some of these points, had Ranald MacDougall trying to get Wald's ideas in the script. Mrs. Pierson said that Wald won out" (Obringer and Chapman analysis, 18).

Wald and Curtiz continued to collaborate during shooting, though Wald was not present on the set: "When shooting actually starts, Wald rarely appears on the set. . . . 'Too many producers,' he says, 'spend too much time interfering with creative people.' He keeps in touch with the director and the cast by watching the daily rushes, but he believes that on the set the director should be in complete control. Usually the director and Wald have gone over the entire script prior to shooting and there is not likely to be any basic difference of opinion" (Goodman 1948, 420). Despite Wald's assertion that he and the director shared a vision of the film by the time shooting began, the film's meanings did change subtly from script to screen. Wald had instructed the film's screenwriters that *Mildred Pierce* should focus on one central element: "[A mother who] sacrifices a great deal for a child she loves. The child turns out to be empty of real talent and a bitch who betrays her mother" (Albert Maltz, screenwriter, notes on *Mildred Pierce*, May 26, 1944). Certainly, the relationship between Mildred and Veda remained central to the film. But Curtiz's direction added weight to the murder mystery and produced the distinct impression that there was something psychologically wrong with Mildred.

Mildred Pierce is widely recognized as being indebted to two genres: the woman's picture and film noir. The earliest treatment for the film described Mildred as a "Stella Dallas," referring to one of the most popular narratives of mother love of the 1930s (Thames Williamson, memorandum to Wald, January 14, 1944). Tom Chapman explained that "*Mildred Pierce* was designed as a 'woman's picture,' and Wald wished to assign it to Catherine Turney, who at the time was one of our best developers of this type of material" (Chapman to Obringer, February 13, 1950, 7). And some reviewers defined the film as a "mother love melodrama," and "the type of sob story which carries a tremendous appeal to feminine patrons" ("Review of *Mildred Pierce*," *Picturegoer*, May 23, 1946, 13; "*Mildred Pierce*

Joan Crawford and Ann Blyth in *Mildred Pierce* (Warner Bros., 1945). Critics were more enthusiastic about the noir elements of *Mildred Pierce* than they were about its story of mother love gone amok. Digital frame enlargement.

Lurid Melodrama Is Meat for the Maids," *Monthly Film Bulletin*, March 1946). Publicity for the film described Mildred in terms that evoked the self-abnegating mothers associated with the woman's film. She was "virtuous and buffeted . . . anguished by the excesses of an unfaithful daughter and an unstable husband," as well as the "sacrificing, doubt-ridden, incorruptible Mildred Pierce, squaring off against the world, true to what she conceives to be a duty to her daughter, for whom she unflinchingly undergoes every privation" (Nelson Bell, "Tilting the Telescope across the Horizon," *Washington Post*, October 9, 1945, 5; "Joan Crawford in 'Oscar' Winning Picture," *Longview (TX) Daily News*, April 14, 1946).

Curtiz was not altogether successful at conveying the sentimental aspects of the script. For example, the death of Mildred's younger daughter, Kay, "lacked the poignancy that such a tragic happening might imply" (Edwin Schallert, "*Mildred Pierce* Luridly Effective Crawford Opus," *Los Angeles Times*, October 13, 1945, A5). One reviewer complained that "the doctor says, 'I'm sorry I couldn't save her' in the manner in which the grocer would say, 'I'm sorry we have no bananas'" (Jeanne Germane, "Review," *Eugene (OR) Guard*, January 18, 1945, 18). And Mildred's self-sacrifice was wont to produce laughter instead of tears, drawing "titters during several highly-theatrical scenes, notably as the hard-working, sacrificial mother proposes marriage to an utterly worthless playboy in order to lure her selfish, society-made daughter back to her—surely a situation straight out of the pages of *True Confessions*" (*Monthly Film Bulletin*, "Meat for the Maids").

While the focus on the relationship between a mother and her daughter may have led some reviewers to identify *Mildred Pierce* as the sort of woman's film that Jerry Wald had initially envisioned, others saw something different in the film. Rather than associating it with other films about self-sacrificing women, such as the Bette Davis tearjerkers *Dark Victory* (1939) and *Now Voyager* (1942), reviewers compared *Mildred Pierce* with darker, more suspenseful films: *The Maltese Falcon* (1941), *Murder My Sweet* (1944), *Scarlett Street* (1945), *Gilda* (1946), *The Blue Dahlia* (1946), *The Postman Always Rings Twice* (1946), and, especially, *Double Indemnity* (1944). Comparisons with the last two may have had to do with the fact that they too were adapted from James M. Cain novels. But much can also be attributed to Curtiz's experimentation with film style, which led many reviewers to see it as something other than a woman's film.

Today, the noir aspects of *Mildred Pierce* are easily identifiable in the expressionist lighting, the focus on crime, and the figure of the femme fatale, Veda, who coldly manipulates anyone who falls under her spell. However, the term "film noir" was not coined until a decade after the film's release. And while the genre of the woman's film was already well established, in overlaying the story with this dark style Curtiz helped invent a new genre. In the mid-1940s, reviewers strove to articulate what it was about *Mildred Pierce* that made it seem like those other films, whether it was its "hard-boiled" story, its "stark realism," its affinity for the "domestic gangster" genre, or its "psychological" aspects. Regardless of what this quality was called, it was often attributed to Curtiz's direction. *Sight and Sound*, for example, identified *Mildred Pierce* as one of several "domestic gangster pictures," and particularly admired its cinematic qualities, especially "the tipping body of the dead man which opens *Mildred Pierce*" (Manvell 1946, 62). The *Monthly Film Bulletin* described it as producing the "authentic Cain touch of brutal realism" and admired its direction, particularly such "effective tricks" as "the dropping blind to cut the sequence, the woman's shadow on the stair wall after the murder, the dance of the man and his shadow seeking escape through successive locked doors" ("Review," *Monthly Film Bulletin*, January 1, 1946, 13). And *Harrison's Reports* felt that the film failed as a woman's film but excelled as a suspenseful thriller: "The story, which revolves around a mother's sacrifices for an ungrateful, wayward daughter, lacks conviction. . . . [However], deft handling of the flashback technique gives the story considerable success" ("Review," *Harrison's Reports*, September 29, 1945, 155).

Ultimately, it is less important to understand who contributed to what aspect of the film than it is to recognize the complex interplay of influences that shaped *Mildred Pierce*. The film was the darling of its producer, who envisioned a film about a mother's troubled relationship with her daughter. Somewhere between script and screen, however, its emphasis shifted toward something darker and more compelling. After the film proved to be a tremendous box-office success, and after Joan Crawford won an Academy Award for her performance and Ann Blyth and Eve Arden received Oscar nominations, Wald wrote to Curtiz: "My working with you on *Pierce* taught me a lot of things, foremost being always try to do something better despite obstacles of all kinds. Both Warner's and the industry should be grateful to a man like yourself who is trying to lift pictures out of the 'great train robbery flickers' to an artistic level" (Wald to Curtiz, September 29, 1945).

Note

1. Warner Bros. eventually settled with the writer, Mae Caro, for $750 because she was unable to produce proof that she had submitted her manuscript before the publication of Cain's novel.

Archives

Margaret Herrick Library, Academy of Motion Picture Arts and Sciences, Beverly Hills. The letters from Joseph Breen and Geoffrey Shurlock were found in the Production Code Administration Records for *Mildred Pierce*.
Warner Bros. Archives, University of Southern California, Los Angeles. Files consulted included the *Mildred Pierce* Story File 2876 and the *Mildred Pierce* Story Memos File 2086.

Works Cited

Goodman, Ezra. 1948. "How to Be a Hollywood Producer." *Harper's Magazine*, May 1, 413–423.

Haralovich, Mary Beth. 1992. "Too Much Guilt Is Never Enough for Working Mothers: Joan Crawford, *Mildred Pierce*, and *Mommie Dearest*." *Velvet Light Trap* 29 (Spring): 43–52.

MacDougall, Ranald et al. 1980. *Mildred Pierce*. Edited by Albert J. LaValley. Madison: University of Wisconsin Press.

Manvell, Roger. 1946. "The Gangster Comes Home." *Sight and Sound*, Summer, 62–63.

Wollen, Peter. "The Auteur Theory: Michael Curtiz and *Casablanca*." In *Authorship and Film*, edited by David Gerstner and Janet Staiger, 61–76. New York: Routledge.

CHAPTER 8

Curtiz at Sea: *Captain Blood, The Sea Hawk, The Sea Wolf,* and *The Breaking Point*

NATHAN HOLMES

In 1935, Warner Bros., renowned for economically spinning stories out of contemporary urban America, announced that it would turn its energies toward a genre it had previously avoided: the historical adventure. The decision was part of the studio's broader plan to expand from its social-realist base into prestige pictures, a realm hitherto dominated by MGM, Paramount, and Fox (Schatz 2015, 34). After Warners' lavish production of *A Midsummer Night's Dream* (1935) met with success, it released the more action-oriented *Captain Blood* (1935). The film garnered critical praise and box-office success, cementing both the star appeal of Errol Flynn (the film was his first starring role) and the directorial acumen of Michael Curtiz. The successful pairing of Flynn and Olivia de Havilland with Curtiz (not to mention the production designer Anton Grot) would continue through the balance of the decade until America's entrance into World War II diminished the appeal of dreamy Europeanized period pictures.

Significant as it was for the studio and for Flynn, *Captain Blood* also represents a thread of Curtiz's career that is devoted to maritime exploit. The beginning of this thread stretches back to Curtiz's direction of the German-language version of Warners' *Moby Dick* (1930), *Dämon des Meeres* (1931), starring William Dieterle as Ahab. Bookending his historical adventure series with Flynn—which included *The Charge of the Light Brigade* (1936), *The Adventures of Robin Hood* (1938), and *The Private Lives of Elizabeth and Essex* (1939)—is *The Sea Hawk* (1940), another swashbuckler based, as was *Captain Blood* (but here in name only), on source material by the best-selling novelist Rafael Sabatini. One year after *The Sea Hawk*, Curtiz moved into more noirish waters, directing Robert Rossen's adaptation of Jack London's *The Sea Wolf* (1941). Throughout the 1940s, the sea pops up here and there on Curtiz's résumé, in romantic comedies such as *Romance on the High Seas* (1948) and *Lady Takes a Sailor* (1949). In 1947, Warner Bros. rereleased *The Sea Hawk* and *The Sea Wolf* as a double feature, touting "The *Sea Show* that must be *Seen!*" In 1950, he directed *The Breaking Point*, the second of three films based on Ernest Hemingway's *To Have and To Have Not*—and rarely mentioned in critical commentaries on Curtiz. Starring John Garfield, who also starred in *The Sea Wolf*, *The Breaking Point* marked the last time the ocean would be a significant setting in one of Curtiz's films.

Although not as significant a setting as the western frontier, the city, or even outer space, the high seas have played an important role in the American imagination. They can be seen, for example, in the work of James Fenimore Cooper, Herman Melville, Edgar Allan Poe, and Jack London; in the public mourning and outcry surrounding the sinking of the British ships *Titanic* (1912) and *Lusitania* (1915); in America's marine engagements in the Pacific theater of World War II; in the filmed voyages of Jacques Cousteau; as well as in the films *Jaws* (1975), *Titanic* (1997), and *Castaway* (2000), the television program *Deadliest Catch* (2005–present), the documentary *Leviathan* (2012), and the video game *Assassin's Creed IV: Black Flag* (Ubisoft, 2013). In contradistinction to the westwardly locked gaze of frontier myth, popular representations of seafaring in literature and visual media have functioned as ways of reflecting on the nation's dilating geopolitical perimeters and interests and of exploring the "edge zones" of modernity (Cohen 2012, 62).

Throughout the nineteenth century and into the twentieth, as the age of sail gave way to the age of steam, the bodies of water that divided continents and the seats of imperial power from their colonies became more heavily traveled and industrialized. Yet while advancing global capitalism rationalized the sea, seafaring itself remained tied to adventure and romance. As Michel Foucault observed, since the sixteenth century the boat has not only "been the great instrument of economic development . . . but simultaneously the greatest reserve of the imagination" (1986, 9). The boat exemplifies Foucault's concept of heterotopia, a space that, unlike utopia (and even, perhaps, its more contemporaneously fashionable inversion, dystopia) is a strange alteration of the everyday, an existing "counter-site": "[It is] a kind of effectively enacted utopia in which the real sites, all the other real sites that can be found within the culture, are simultaneously represented, contested, and inverted. Places of this kind are outside of all places, even though it may be possible to indicate their location in reality" (24). At sea, the boat is physically distant from the homes of its passengers, yet it is also called on to represent the identity and values of the home territory through flags, protocols, and missions. This distance, however, produces distortion and atrophy. Clung to through tokens and protocols, the outside world becomes inverted, contested, and re-formed. Thus, while the boat is a microcosm of nation, civilization, inhabitation, and culture, it is also where these categories begin to shift and, seen from an external point of view that is always "outside of all places," to be understood in new ways. "Where have you been these last few months?" an English lord asks Peter Blood. "I've been at sea, out of touch with the world." Curtiz's small corpus of maritime cinema takes us to sea to put us "out of touch with the world," if only to see it anew.

Captain Blood and *The Sea Hawk*

Curtiz's piratical swashbucklers are predicated on the idea of freedom lost and regained, Errol Flynn being in both cases the dashing masculine medium of this movement. Although these are enduring themes within American film, the sea as a locale allows for novel formations of this idea to play out. In *Captain Blood*, Flynn's Peter Blood is an Irish doctor who becomes unwittingly caught up in the Monmouth Rebellion of 1685 after coming to the aid of a wounded rebel. At the Bloody Assizes, Blood proclaims his innocence, and instead of being hanged is exiled to a British colony to be sold into slavery. When he lands in Port Royal, Jamaica, Blood's impudence toward the commander of a local plantation, Colonel Bishop (Lionel Atwill), during a slave auction almost lands him in the dreaded sulfur mines. He is saved from this fate by Bishop's daughter Arabella (de Havilland), who purchases Blood to work on her father's plantation.

A man of science, Curtiz's Blood embodies Enlightenment subjectivity and American pluck, facts underlined by his relentless pursuit of self-determination. Yet what constricts him is not, as in the case of the sea adventurer Odysseus, creatures of myth—who, for Max Horkheimer and Theodor Adorno, embodied the forces of nature that the Enlightenment thought to master (2002, 35–62)—but the more contemporary despotism of King James II's England, one that is abundantly registered in the administered barbarism of England's slave economy. In all the 1930s adventure films, Flynn "plays a man for whom moral and political decisions are unambiguous, and who is provided with a chance to put these decisions into practice through direct physical action" (Roddick 1983, 235). Blood's resistance to despotism is both physical and intellectual, visually expressed through bodily toil (all the better to showcase Flynn's physique), balletic evasion, and feats of cunning deception.

The first scene set at Bishop's plantation opens with a high-angle view of its waterwheel, an enormous structure drawing water from the ground via the power of men, who propel it by pushing a cog around and around, urged on by a whip. As with the slave galley scenes in *The Sea Hawk*, the brutal environment of the stockade is pervaded by types of torture, aspects that were viewed negatively by Hal Wallis and others in Warners' inter-departmental memos (Behlmer 1985, 25). In scenes pairing Blood with his closest friend, the young navigator Jeremy Pitt (Ross Alexander), surviving this cruelty occasions forms of intimacy—Blood tenderly bandaging Pitt's leg, for example—that Curtiz unreservedly codes as homoerotic.[1] Both the waterwheel and the scenes of individual suffering that surround it are sig-nificant in that they create an inverse image of the apparatus that will come to refocus the men's productive power and the course of the narrative itself: the pirate ship. On their newly hijacked Spanish ship, the escaped slaves cooperate to turn a crank, similar to the waterwheel, in order to raise its anchor. As they gaily sing together, Blood encouragingly shouts, "Round you go men, round! That's no waterwheel you're working!"

From the fetters of England and its colony, Blood and his crew establish a heterotopic zone of freedom on their ship, a mobile technology allow-ing them to embody productive equity rather than forced labor. The pirate code (*chasse partie*) they formulate distributes the booty to be plundered evenly and offers additional compensation for those who lose limbs in the process.[2] The act is sealed with the raising of a pirate flag, a skull above two crossed arms, each holding a cutlass. The somewhat idiosyncratic design of the flag hints at the film's collectivist themes. Although Curtiz was said to be apolitical (Robertson 1993, 149), it is difficult not to notice subtle allusions to contemporaneous leftist formations. "I noticed when the sailors cheer for any reason, that a great many of them use a clenched fist in what is really the Communist salute," Hal Wallis complained of Curtiz's dailies. "This is very noticeable, and I don't understand why you allow people to do it" (quoted in Behlmer 1982, 34). Perhaps the Hun-garian didn't direct political films, he just allowed them to happen.

As Curtiz continued to make swashbuckling pictures with Flynn and de Havilland, so too did Warner Bros. increase its investment in large-scale action spectaculars, particularly following the success of *The Adventures of Robin Hood*. A portion of this investment came in the form of the con-struction of a large soundstage dedicated to reproducing maritime envi-ronments. Unlike MGM, which shot most of *Mutiny on the Bounty* (1935)

Peter Blood (Errol Flynn) and his crew plunder a ship in *Captain Blood* (Warner Bros., 1935). Digital frame enlargement.

off the California coast, Warner Bros. preferred that natural conditions be re-created. To house their projected slate of nautical offerings, they elected to build a new marine facility, Stage 21, which was completed just in time to film *The Sea Hawk*. Rudy Behlmer reports that Stage 21 could be filled with water (entailing an extensive plumbing infrastructure) and featured two ships built to scale, a British man-o'-war and a Spanish galleass (165 feet and 135 feet, respectively). The ships were placed on steel platforms that used tracks to allow repositioning, and were connected to hydraulics that could rock them back and forth. A deep pit between the two ships (deeper than the rest of the stage) allowed actors to dive into the water from great heights. The naturalism of the Stage 21 environment was rounded out by a "ripple machine" developed by Grot, which could be modulated to effect a spectrum of oceanic conditions, and a muslin cyclorama that filled in the background horizon of sea and sky (Behlmer 1982, 26–27).

Stage 21 and a visual effects team headed up by Byron Haskin were put to good use in *The Sea Hawk*'s many action sequences, particularly the scene close to the film's opening in which Flynn's Geoffrey Thorpe and his crew skillfully seize a galleass. The sequence nicely illustrates that Curtiz's adeptness at staging action in large crowds and on multiple planes was not separate from his eye for composition; the dynamic action unfolds within a fully realized mise-en-scène. Threatened by Thorpe's approach, Spanish troops pour out from belowdecks and scale shrouds, the camera craning around the boat and cutting to multiple long-shot perspectives as they take battle positions. As Thorpe's infamous ship, the *Albatross*, is positively identified by Spanish lookouts, the accompaniment of a clarion trumpet from Erich Wolfgang Korngold's score initiates a long shot of the English vessel in full sail, Grot's manufactured waves breaking across its bow. In contrast to the anxiousness on the Spanish decks, the *Albatross*'s preparations for conflict are a model of efficiency and even irreverence, the crew splitting with laughter as the Spaniards' opening volley manages only to make a single small hole in one of the ship's sails.

As this scene continues, a style of command different from the democratic ethos of *Captain Blood* comes into view. The introduction of the *Albatross* is continued by the camera tracking laterally from the bow in a seemingly continuous shot (with only one, barely perceptible cut) to settle on a long shot of the bridge. In a manner befitting both Flynn's stardom and the diegetic notoriety of the character he plays, Thorpe is discussed by characters before he appears onscreen, first by the Spanish then by the *Albatross* crew, a directorial choice that also plays with the expectations of an audience primed for Flynn's return to pirate togs. In this long shot, Thorpe stands imperceptibly in the far background, behind and above his second in command, Pitt (Alan Hale). Curtiz further delays Flynn's entrance by having him respond as an offscreen voice to Pitt, in close-up, requesting to fire on the Spanish. After a beat, there is finally a cut to Flynn, customarily dressed in a fitted leather vest, a white shirt with rolled sleeves, and a sword at his hip. The series of views and cuts by which we are carried toward Thorpe is re-covered again as he issues the command to hail the Spanish ship, and again after he commands Pitt to "show them how to lower those colors." In medium close-up, Pitt turns excitedly from Thorpe, saying, "Aye, aye, sir. Scott, teach them some etiquette!" Another cut now to Scott (Julien Mitchell), in a slightly longer shot, who turns from the stern, putting hand to mouth to yell, "Ready men? Lay for the foremast and fire on the uproll." In turn, a cut to a gun port shows men standing behind a cannon barrel that pitches upward with the boat then fires as it reaches its highest point. The damage: the top of a Spanish mast cracked clean off, tumbling to the deck below. Here, the components of studio-based cinematography are masterfully brought

The scale of Warner Bros. Stage 21 illustrated in a long shot from a battle scene in *The Sea Hawk* (Warner Bros., 1940). Digital frame enlargement.

together: the breadth of Stage 21, allowing for both long shots of the deck and medium inserts to register its detail; the hydraulics pitching the boat up and down, reflexively referred to ("fire on the uproll") in the technique of warfare; and the spectacular realism of an exploding mast, likely from one of the miniature ships built by Haskin and filmed in slow motion. In this same strip of action, Curtiz cuts up this space to underscore the extensiveness and rhythm of Thorpe's chain of command, which organically ripples throughout the ship.[3]

The transformation in the management and organization of piracy from *Captain Blood* to *The Sea Hawk* is an expression of changing historical circumstance. In *Captain Blood*, the resistant energies of the slave rebellion become allied with Britain's aims only when the nation steers a course closer to its own ideals (after William of Orange replaces James II and pardons Blood and his crew), a politics of solidarity resonating with the leftist visions of the American Popular Front and the New Deal. In the Elizabethan era of the *Sea Hawk*, based on the exploits of the British "sea dogs," a paramilitary force that, with the blessing of Queen Elizabeth, plundered Spanish ships, Thorpe is a patriot friendly with the queen (Flora Robson) and informally aligned with national interests.[4] Whereas

Captain Blood visually foregrounds egalitarian principles against despotic capitalism, *The Sea Hawk* aligns its imperial antagonists with the rise of fascism, both explicitly (Franco's Spain) and indirectly (Nazi Germany). The film's opening scene of Philip II of Spain (Montagu Love) emphatically closes with his silhouette casting a dark shadow over a map of the world, his index finger pointing directly to Europe in a precise expressionist emblem of the aspirations of the Third Reich (McElhaney 2014). Queen Elizabeth's powerful concluding speech, originally included on only the British release, proclaims that "when the ruthless ambition of one man threatens to engulf the world" it is the duty of free men to stand up to him, portentously pledging to build a navy that will become the "foremost in the world, not only in our time, but for generations to come." In the British release, a flash-forward to the present shows warships being built in British navy yards (Behlmer 1982, 213n43).

Set safely "out of time," *Captain Blood* and *The Sea Hawk*, more than Warners' social-realist productions, cast an eye toward the spatial order of modern geopolitics. Yet because these films were also romances, they could question not just the normative arrangements of the nation but also the emotional self. In both pirate films, the ocean provides the physical separation necessary for the production of romantic longing as well as a space of chance encounter. Love offers opportunities to become, as Blood puts it, "out of touch with the world."

The Sea Wolf and *The Breaking Point*

In the studio-based swashbuckling films that Curtiz made with Flynn, the ocean is mostly flat, devoid of inclement weather, a good condition for spying on enemies and making speedy attacks, and for generally rendering a sun-drenched mise-en-scène of adventure. *The Sea Wolf*, made only a year after *The Sea Hawk* (again on Stage 21) registers a somber turn into murkier territory. The film's signature image, which appears behind the opening credits, is of a ship emerging out of deep fog. Fog, in fact, hangs over almost every scene: the desperate streets of San Francisco, where George Leach (John Garfield) is commissioned to join the crew of the *Ghost*; the nighttime waters in which a steamer carrying the writer Humphrey Van Weyden (Alexander Knox) and Ruth Brewster (Ida Lupino), an escaped convict, is demolished by an oncoming ship; and the directionless flight of Wolf Larsen's (Edward G. Robinson) *Ghost* from his pursuing brother, Death Larsen.

The vaporous milieu of *The Sea Wolf* reinforces the notion that to board the *Ghost* is to enter a circle of hell apart from the outside world, external to society. Everyday life on the ship is marked by morbidity, craven self-interest, and humiliation—a world specifically designed by Wolf. The brutality and cruelty seen on the *Ghost* is intended as a reflection of his studied philosophical perspective, developed from beliefs in social Darwinism and Nietzsche's conceptualization of the superman. Key to Larsen's undoing is the perspicacity of Van Weyden, who quickly diagnoses the man's eagerness to rule over others: "Since he has found it so difficult in the outside world to maintain [. . .] dignity, he creates a world for himself: a ship on which he alone can be master, on which he alone can rule." To emphasize this point, a passage from *Paradise Lost* that Larsen has underlined is reprised throughout the film: "Better to reign in hell than to serve in heaven."

Yet while the fog apparently seals the *Ghost* from the world, the ship remains everyday reality's strange extension rather than Larsen's truly sovereign dominion, a heterotopia rather than a dystopia. While Van Weyden unlocks Larsen's mind, Leach's insurrections are marked by the proletarian energy that Garfield later brought to parts in *Tortilla Flat* (1942), *Body and Soul* (1947), and *The Breaking Point*. Although Leach was a minor figure in Jack London's source novel, Robert Rossen's script amplifies the role by having the character resist Larsen's despotic rule. Wolf's haphazard assignment of duties (Leach as "ship puller," for example) and arbitrary promotion would likely have resonated with those who worked, or tried to, through the 1930s. Much like the ship's lumpen crew, Leach and Brewster, the prison escapee, who in London's book is a poet and romantic interest for Van Weyden rather than for him, signal affiliations with the working-class poor, for whom the conditions on the *Ghost* could hardly seem unique. As Leach relays his plans to escape the ship, Brewster wistfully replies in a soft close-up, "Inside or out, it's all the same. To be free, to be let alone, to live in peace even if only for a little while . . . like this. I don't expect that anymore." She is suggesting that freedom is linked with a temporary state of mind rather than a physical space. Even if they are saved from the "iron gate" that awaits them on land or at sea, freedom is a utopia, a nowhere. The *Ghost* is simply another of the world's many prisons.

In the years between *The Sea Wolf* and *The Breaking Point*, Curtiz directed some of his finest films, including *Casablanca* (1942) and *Mildred Pierce* (1945). *The Breaking Point* is the last of his films set at sea, and it sustains the existential-noir tendencies of *The Sea Wolf*, even though forgoing the expressionist design that marks Curtiz's 1930s work (and the

Wolf Larsen's ship, *The Ghost*, emerges from fog in *The Sea Wolf* (Warner Bros., 1941). Digital frame enlargement.

noir cycle more broadly). Set in the sunny harbors of Newport Beach and Mexico, *The Breaking Point* shares qualities with the "sunshine noir" of films like Orson Welles's *The Lady from Shanghai* (1947), likewise portraying what Michael O'Hara (Welles) calls in that film a "bright guilty world." Like the setting of *Mildred Pierce*, this world is a midcentury California beset by the frictions of class and economic precariousness. Ernest Hemingway's source novel, like James M. Cain's for *Mildred Pierce*, is set during the Depression, thus forming thematic connections with Curtiz's earlier sea adventures. But because *The Breaking Point* takes place in the present, it must more directly represent the contemporary spatial order.

The ocean in *The Breaking Point* largely features as conceptual space rather than natural entity. For Harry Morgan (John Garfield) and his charter business, the sea is a space of autonomous self-enterprise, but one that is increasingly strained by a flagging market. Nation-states in this film have passed from the just-unjust dichotomy seen in the historical adventure films to bureaucratic administration: the sea is not a place where moral battles are fought, but a completely settled domain of exploitation and law. In the form of the Coast Guard, the gaze of the law pervades the harbor and beyond. Harry ferries an apparently wealthy client to Mexico, but when the man skips out on him without paying, he is forced to accept a deal to smuggle Chinese immigrants back across the border in order to cover harbor fees and gas. The plan goes awry, and the Coast Guard investigates him, impounding his boat. Harry's Mexican itinerary overlaps with the discovery of another smuggler's body; thus he and his business are suspended.

Faced with increasing economic difficulty, Harry's wife, Lucy (Phyllis Thaxter), urges him to consider taking up work on her father's lettuce farm in Salinas. He angrily resists, seeing land-based work as a surrender of self-rule. Without customers, however, his boat ceases to become a means of production, becoming instead a financial burden. The looming impossibility of his sea-based enterprise is signaled by the narrative spaces within which he increasingly moves. Instead of shuttling between home and sea, Harry routinely detours through the bars and lounges that adjoin the marina.

In some ways, maritime drinking establishments are both an extension

Harry Morgan (John Garfield) and his first mate, Wesley Park (Juano Hernandez), in the Newport Beach marina, in *The Breaking Point* (Warner Bros., 1950). Digital frame enlargement.

of the heterotopia of the ship and a significant site for mediating the differences between land and sea. It is in maritime drinking spaces, decorated with nautical instruments and images—particularly those in *Captain Blood* and *The Sea Wolf*—that sailors spend their pay and are hired. These are spaces apart from the life of the sea, but that necessarily represent it in their patrons and décor. As Vivian Sobchack (1998) has shown, bars are recurrent locales in noir, significant for establishing the cycle's connection with everyday postwar life. The bar in noir cinema is a space of waiting and idleness that is neither home nor work, and thus helps bind the films to a historical moment marked by economic uncertainty and unhomeliness. An in-between space, the bar is a way to desynchronize oneself from the world.

In some ways, Curtiz's sea films evince noir sensibility. The three bars that Morgan visits in *The Breaking Point* are spaces distinct from the normative zones of work and family. At a Mexican cantina early in the film, he converses with Leona Charles (Patricia Neal), the traveling companion of his client, who unreservedly flirts with him. Leona pops up, by chance, at each of the other bars, too; Harry's growing attraction to her is increasingly entwined with his hard-boiled tendency to drink and undertake illicit ventures. As Sobchack points out, the bars, lounges, diners, and boarding-houses constituting the primary settings of noir are nonfamily spaces, the genre as a whole lacking in depictions of communal or domestic life (1998, 137–146). *The Breaking Point* is a fairly atypical noir in this sense; in sensitively mapping the intimate dynamics of the Morgans' waterfront bungalow, it shows him caring for and loving his wife and two children deeply.

A key moment in the film, however, plays out a family melodrama within a bar setting. The scene unfolds at a tiki lounge, Christian's Hut, where Morgan has decided to deal with the sting of his boat being impounded by "turning [himself] loose" with a bottle of rum. He is joined at a table by Leona, but their arch flirtation is interrupted by Lucy, who arrives abruptly (the bartender has called her) to take Harry home. Lucy is disturbed by the milieu in which she finds her husband, though both Leona and Harry persuade her of its innocence. In a generic sense, the lounge is punctured by Lucy's presence. The domestic and cultural commitments she represents unravel the bar's role as a counterdomestic world of its own. The fact that the bartender has called Lucy pulls the space out of the urban anonymity that marks most noir drinking establishments, placing it back in the realm of neighborly concern.

Harry's final scheme, involving a racetrack heist, goes sour, resulting in the death of his first mate, Wesley (Juano Hernandez, who stars in

Curtiz's *Young Man with a Horn*, also 1950). While Harry is Wesley's boss, the smallness of their operation encourages an egalitarian relationship. Harry's daughter and Wesley's son play together, offering the sense of a racially integrated community rare for 1950s cinema. The gangsters who kill Wesley are the men whom Harry has agreed to help escape from the racetrack. (The generic incongruence of gangsters, typically landlubbers, on a small seacraft offers another example of spatial disturbance, further suggesting the total domination of the sea by land.)[5] Knowing they will try to kill him, Harry plans to stage a counterattack. He manages to kill the gangsters, but is severely wounded, passing out on deck. The film ends with Harry's rescue and return to shore, an acknowledgment of his repeated line: "A man alone hasn't got a chance." The final crane shot shows Wesley's son waiting alone on the dock after a crowd has dispersed. With no one to tell him about the fate of his father, Curtiz intimates that other stories of Wesley being cast adrift stand behind the happy conclusion of the one we have just been told.

Through pirate ships and medieval castles, as much as through dynamic processes of editing and framing, Curtiz was employed by Warners to represent, amplify, and invert all existing spaces. For Curtiz, the techniques of narrative film and the studio spaces in which it was forged were also a heterotopia. His career came to an end just as Hollywood was facing the economic challenges that brought the studio system, in which he flourished, to an end. Stage 21 was razed by a fire in 1952. Through the 1950s, Warners' nautical films—for example *Captain Horatio Hornblower* (1951), *The Crimson Pirate* (1952), and *Moby Dick* (1956)—were all shot on actual ships at sea (Behlmer 1982, 27). Made on location and in studio, *The Breaking Point* photographically confronts its historical moment, but as it does, the sea becomes a reference point for the film rather a realized physical entity. Morgan is "underwater." He repeatedly tells people to "shove off." The sea becomes lingo. For most people, of course, the sea is only ever a reference point. Except, perhaps, when we are taken there by way of cinema.

Notes

1. In this scene, Pitt's leg is draped over Blood's lap as they discuss their escape plans. The sense of scandal is amplified when Colonel Bishop arrives on the scene and barks, "What the devil have you been up to!" to the secretive pair.

2. This is based, likely, on Sabatini's familiarity with a version of Alexandre Exquemelin's famous seventeenth-century text, *The History of the Bucaniers, Free-*

Booters, and Pyrates of America, and its descriptions of the adventures of Henry Morgan.

3. Curtiz preferred to leave little for editors to get creative with, stating: "A right director cuts on the set, instead of in the cutting room. His individuality should be on the film, not the individuality of a cutter" (quoted in Robertson 1993, 139–140).

4. The screenwriter, Howard Koch, based his characterization of Thorpe on a composite of actual British sea dogs, most significantly Sir Francis Drake (1540–1596; see Behlmer 1982, 21).

5. Another gangsters-at-sea plot from this era is in the conclusion of John Huston's *Key Largo* (1948).

Works Cited

Behlmer, Rudy. 1982. "Introduction: The Heroic Virtues." In *The Sea Hawk*, edited by Rudy Behlmer, 11–43. Madison: University of Wisconsin Press, 1982.

Behlmer, Rudy, ed. 1985. *Inside Warner Bros., 1935-1951*. New York: Viking.

Cohen, Margaret. 2012. *The Novel and the Sea*. Princeton, NJ: Princeton University Press.

Foucault, Michel. 1986. "Of Other Spaces: Utopias and Heterotopias." Translated by Jay Miskowiec. *Diacritics* 16 (Spring): 22–27.

Horkheimer, Max, and Theodor W. Adorno. 2002. *Dialectic of Enlightenment: Philosophical Fragments*. Translated by Edmund Jephcott. Stanford, CA: Stanford University Press. Originally published 1947.

McElhaney, Joe. 2014. "Survival Tactics: German Filmmakers in Hollywood, 1940-1960." *Lola* 5 (November). www.lolajournal.com/5/survival.html.

Robertson, James C. 1993. *The Casablanca Man: The Cinema of Michael Curtiz*. London: Routledge.

Roddick, Nick. 1983. *A New Deal in Entertainment: Warner Brothers in the 1930s*. London: BFI.

Schatz, Thomas. 2015. "Warner Bros.: Power Plays and Prestige (1988)." In *The American Film History Reader*, edited by Jon Lewis and Eric Smoodin, 29–48. New York: Routledge.

Sobchack, Vivian. 1998. "Lounge-time: Postwar Crises and the Chronotope of Film Noir." In *Refiguring American Film Genres*, edited by Nick Browne, 129–170. Berkeley: University of California Press.

CHAPTER 9
Curtiz in the White House

BILL KROHN

A great deal has been written about *Casablanca* (1942), all of it lauda-tory, from the 1943 reviews to the analyses of present-day critics, includ-ing Richard Corliss and Umberto Eco (see Koch 1973). In the process, it has become a cinematic classic: an enduring work of recognized value and an exemplar of classical American cinema.

But *Casablanca* is a film without a directorial auteur. Michael Curtiz signed notable films throughout a career that spanned five decades and two continents, many made for Warner Bros., the studio where he took up residence in 1933. *Casablanca*, however, was a group effort to which he affixed his name. The film's producer, Hal Wallis, purchased the property (an unproduced play, *Everyone Comes to Rick's*, by Murray Burnett and Joan Alison) and closely supervised every aspect of the production until the film premiered, on Thanksgiving Day 1943, in New York City. As Al-jean Harmetz informs us, thinking that his new vehicle would work well for either Humphrey Bogart or George Raft, Wallis suspected it could be "tailored into a piece along the lines of *Algiers*" (quoting a Warners memo-randum dated December 23, 1941), John Cromwell's 1938 American-style version of Julien Duvivier's *Pépé le Moko* (1937). This tale of exotic casbah intrigue and love "was obviously in Wallis's mind when, three days after he purchased *Everybody Comes to Rick's*, he changed the title to *Casablanca*," and "when he tried unsuccessfully to borrow Hedy Lamarr from M-G-M" (30). So Wallis (a friend and golfing buddy of the director) became the auteur of a text that is like a rock wall with no place to sink a piton because it is riddled with holes.

Wallis even wrote the famous last line, "I think this is the beginning of a beautiful friendship," which Corliss glosses with two theories: first, that *Casablanca* is a political allegory, with Rick (Humphrey Bogart) as Presi-dent Roosevelt (*casa blanca* being Spanish for "white house"), a man who

A MacGuffin in Morocco? Ugarte (Peter Lorre) showing Rick (Humphrey Bogart) the letters of transit around which the story of *Casablanca* revolves. We never see the letters themselves (Warner Bros., 1942). Digital frame enlargement.

gambles on the odds of going to war until his own submerged nobility forces him to close the casino (that is, overcome partisan politics) and commit himself, first by financing the Side of Right and then by fighting for it; second, that *Casablanca* is a repressed homosexual fantasy, in which Rick rejects his token mistress, Ilsa Lund (Ingrid Bergman), for an honest though furtive affair with Captain Louis Renault, prefect of police in Casablanca (Claude Rains).

Contrary to Hollywood practice, Rick puts Ilsa on the plane with her lover, the Resistance leader Victor Laszlo (Paul Henreid)—a bit of a Boy Scout, with a facial scar that could do with some glossing itself—and exits the film in the company of Renault, uttering Wallis's resonant punch line as the image fades to black.

As for Eco, he translates "classical" as "stereotypical":

When you don't know how to deal with a story, you put stereotyped situations in it because you know that they, at least, have already worked elsewhere. . . .

. . . Forced to improvise a plot, the authors mixed a little of everything, and everything they chose came from a repertoire that had stood the test of time.

A backhanded version of "classical," Eco's definition describes elements that "have stood the test of time" as clichés, which abound in *Casablanca*.

My own interpretation of the film steers between the Scylla of depth psychology and the Charybdis of semiotic platitudes by sketching an approach to a linguistic analysis of the film's screenplay, which is extraordinarily rich in the New Critical tropes of ambiguity and irony. For that reason, I refer to "writing" as one image among many others, and not as a deconstructive procedure.

Let's begin with a simple rhetorical example: occurrences of the word "impress." When the oily black marketer Ugarte (Peter Lorre) shows Rick the "letters of transit" that everyone is trying to get their hands on, he says, "Rick, I hope you are more impressed with me now, huh?" Rick replies that the German couriers carrying the letters were murdered, and Ugarte says that he "heard that rumor, too." Rick looks at Ugarte steadily and says slowly, "Yes, you're right, Ugarte. I am a little more *impressed* with you" (Bogart's stress).

When Renault tells Rick that Victor Laszlo will do anything to get his hands on the letters and the usually imperturbable saloon keeper reacts, Renault comments, "Rick, that is the first time I have ever seen you so impressed."

RICK (*casual again*): Well, he's succeeded in impressing half the world.
RENAULT: It is my duty to see that he doesn't impress the other half.

Renault's duty as a Vichy cat's-paw is to keep Laszlo from leaving Casablanca and flying to America. He violates that duty in the film's last scene, changing sides and joining Rick on the dangerous path to the Resistance. The enormous character arc from "It is my duty" to that change sums up Renault's character as defined by his acts, including his speech acts, from his first appearance to his final exit.

Let's follow a word-image, in the New Critical sense: rings. Two minutes into the film, a desperate upper-class woman bargains with a Moor:

She has a bracelet on her wrist, no other jewelry.
WOMAN: But can't you make it just a little more? Please.
MOOR: I'm sorry, Madame, but diamonds are a drug on the market.

Everybody sells diamonds. There are diamonds everywhere. Two thousand, four hundred.

WOMAN (*distressed*): All right.

A few seconds later, two conspirators are talking:

MAN: It's the fishing smack Santiago. It leaves at one tomorrow night, here from the end of La Medina. Third boat.

REFUGEE: Thank you, oh, thank you.

MAN: And bring fifteen thousand francs in cash. Remember, in cash.

The economy of the dialogue is breathtaking. Having learned in a few seconds that class relations, like monetary values, have been turned upside down by the Occupation; that the currency in which the Moor's paltry offer is denominated is the franc; and that escape from Casablanca is a cash-on-the-barrelhead business, we are prepared to decode the following, as a man named Berger appears when Laszlo and Ilsa enter the café:

BERGER: Excuse me, but you look like a couple who are on their way to America.

LASZLO: Well?

BERGER (*taking a ring from his finger*): You will find a market for this ring. I am forced to sell it at a great sacrifice. . . . Then perhaps for the lady. The ring is quite unique. *He holds it down for their view. Carefully lifting up the stone, he reveals, on a gold plate in the setting underneath, an impression of the Lorraine Cross of General de Gaulle.* (emphasis added)

Berger identifies himself as a member of the Norwegian Resistance.

LASZLO (*to Berger, in a low voice*): I'll meet you in a few minutes at the bar. (*In a louder voice, obviously for the benefit of someone off-scene*): I do not think I want to buy the ring. But thank you for showing it to us.

BERGER (*He takes the cue, sighs, and puts the ring away*): Such a bargain. But that is your decision?

LASZLO: I'm sorry. It is.

After the appearance of the main heavy, Major Heinrich Strasser (Conrad Veidt), Laszlo and Berger pursue their conversation at the bar, informing us that Laszlo has escaped from a concentration camp and has been reported killed on five occasions. Laszlo: "As you see, it was true every single time." He is informed that Ugarte, who was going to sell him the letters of transit, is under arrest for murder. But a meeting of the underground is scheduled for the following night at the Caverne du Roi.

RENAULT (*Coming up to where Berger and Laszlo are sitting*): How's the jewelry business, Berger?

BERGER: Er, not so good. (*To Sacha* [the bartender]): May I have my check, please?

We will never see Ugarte or Berger again, but we learn the next day in Renault's office, where Laszlo and Ilsa have promised to appear, that Ugarte has been killed by the Gestapo. Major Strasser is waiting for them when they get there. He informs them (and us) that Renault's signature is necessary on every exit visa. Renault expresses his regrets and informs them that they will not receive one.

The ring has done its work. Under its aegis, we were offered a range of treasures: exposition, character traits, linguistic nuances (connoted by Renault's *formules de politesse*), and the paradoxes of truth. It is true that Laszlo has been killed all five times, yet there he is. And Ugarte's death, which we are not inclined to mourn, deprives Laszlo and Ilsa of the letters of transit they came to the café to buy, setting in motion all the subsequent twists and turns of the plot. Like every inhabitant of Casablanca, the characters are two-faced: a shot of Ilsa next to her mirrored reflection makes the point. Carl (S. Z. Sakall), the cheerful headwaiter at Rick's, is a member of the underground; Renault may be for Vichy or for France; a sluttish collaborator can become a member of the Resistance in response to the singing of "La Marseillaise"; an angelic girl turns out to have prostituted herself to get papers for herself and her husband; Ilsa appears to be doing the same thing when she meets clandestinely with Rick, until she pulls a gun on him.

Throughout, the dialogue constantly plays on words: Ferrari (Sydney Greenstreet), a rival club owner commenting on Rick's refusal to play the black market: "My dear Rick. When will you realize that in the world today isolationism is no longer a practical policy?" Or Rick, when Renault warns him not to "put himself out" for Laszlo: "I stick my neck out for nobody," to which Renault rejoins, "A wise foreign policy." Or Rick, drinking as he waits for Ilsa to come:

RICK: Sam, it's December 1941 in Casablanca. What time is it in New York?

SAM [Dooley Wilson]: Uh, my watch stopped.

> RICK (*drunken nostalgia*): I bet they're asleep in New York. I bet they're
> asleep all over America.

America has not yet entered the war.

Language mirrors the chaos of Casablanca, connoted by a babel of foreign accents, all genuine because the refugees in the film are played by real
refugees from the Nazis. For example, a good German couple learning
English for their escape to America butcher the language:

> MR. LEUCHTAG: Liebchen, uh, sweetnessheart, what watch?
> MRS. LEUCHTAG (*glancing at her wristwatch*): Ten watch.
> MR. LEUCHTAG (*surprised*): Such much?
> CARL: Er, you will get along beautifully in America, huh.

Even proverbial expressions are played on. A flashback to happier days:

> ILSA: A franc for your thoughts.
> RICK: In America they'd bring only a penny. I guess that's about all
> they're worth.
> ILSA: I'm willing to be overcharged. Tell me.

And a proper name connotes a time:

> ILSA: Richard, I had to see you.
> RICK: You use "Richard" again? We're back in Paris.

This intricate web (and ring) of linguistic tropes is simply part of the
verbal texture of good dialogue circa 1943. We have grown unaccustomed
to such largesse, but 1943 audiences took it as their due.

Interlude: A Trailer

Here is my approximation of the 1942 trailer, created by Warners' one-
man trailer department, Arthur Silver, using every action scene in the
movie and the outtakes. A microcosm of the film, it employs twenty-two
wipes in a variety of shapes between segments (shattered image, wind-
shield wiper, teeth coming down, teeth coming up), as well as straight
cuts, dollies-in, and pullbacks between shots.

Title: IF YOU'RE LOOKING FOR ADVENTURE YOU'LL FIND IT IN
CASABLANCA

Segment: Fleeing man shot in the back, Petain poster in the background.

Narrator: Casablanca, city of hope and despair, located in French Morocco in North Africa. The meeting place of adventurers, fugitives, criminals, refugees lured into this danger-swept oasis by the hope of escape to the Americas. But they're all trapped, because there is no escape. Against this fascinating background is more than the story of an imperishable love and the saga of six desperate people, each in Casablanca to keep an appointment with destiny.

Title: THE WORLD'S MOST DANGEROUS MAN IN THE WORLD'S MOST DANGEROUS CITY

Segment: Rick shoves a German at the bar.

CUT to:

RICK: I was willing to shoot Captain Renault, and I'm willing to shoot you. (*The Major draws his gun.*) All right, major, you asked for it. . . . (*Rick shoots him.*)[1]

Title: FIGHTING THE STRANGE FASCINATION THAT DREW HER CLOSER AND CLOSER TO HIM

ILSA (*She advances and melts in his arms*): If you knew how much I love you, how much I still love you. (*They kiss.*)

Title: WHERE EVERY BURNING MOMENT BRINGS NEW DANGER / WHERE EVERY KISS MAY BE THE LAST

CUT to:

ILSA: I tried to reason with you, I tried to. . . . Now I want those letters. (*She draws a gun. He advances.*)

CUT to:

LASZLO: I know a great deal more about you than you suspect. . . . I know that you're in love with a woman. That's a strange circumstance that we're both in love with the same woman.

CUT to:

FERRARI: What do you want for Sam?

RICK: I don't buy and sell human beings.

FERRARI: That's too bad. That's Morocco's leading commodity.

The minifilm, lasting two minutes and nine seconds, is scored to a mix of "As Time Goes By" and Moroccan music. Editors at Warner Bros. studied Eisenstein and Slavko Vorkapich, and Eisenstein and Vorkapich studied them. Silver was an apt pupil. Every action shown and every line of dialogue in the trailer is a promise.

Warner Bros. was a small city with many streets and back alleys, not all of which were real. The flashback sequences in *Casablanca* used the French Street for the scenes in which the French learn that the Nazis are coming. Wartime restrictions curtailed location shooting out of fear that Hollywood was vulnerable to a Japanese attack (see, on this issue, Steven Spielberg's *1941* [1979]), so Curtiz directed *Casablanca* on several soundstages at Warner Bros., going out to locations in Van Nuys, Yuma, and Flagstaff for pickup shots. The concluding airport sequence was done at the Metropolitan Airport in Van Nuys, with the runway on Waterman Drive.

Warners was also a kind of home for the people who worked there. Another Wallis protégé, Don Siegel, directed the montage sequence that opens *Casablanca*. In 1958 he directed *The Gun Runners* (filmed entirely on practical locations), and a remake of Curtiz's *The Breaking Point* (1950), filmed on soundstages and practical locations on the coast. *The Breaking Point* was a remake of Howard Hawks's *To Have and Have Not* (1944), filmed on two Warner Bros. soundstages. By the time Curtiz made *The Adventures of Huckleberry Finn* (1960), he could film exteriors at the Warner Bros. Ranch and on practical locations in Stockton and the Sacramento River Valley. In Hungary, he had gotten his first taste of location shooting when he directed a second unit on August Blom's *Atlantis* (1913), a film made entirely on practical locations in Berlin, Denmark, Norway, and New York City.

Actors were another matter. For Bogart, Lorre, and Greenstreet, Warners was home base. James Cagney, who starred in *Yankee Doodle Dandy* (1942), the film Curtiz made before *Casablanca*, was another native. But Bergman was on loan from David O. Selznick. When Curtiz made the sequel to *Casablanca*, *Passage to Marseille* (1944), Bogart played a Frenchman who had escaped from Devil's Island to join the Resistance, and Bergman was replaced by Michèle Morgan, who had initially been cast as Ilsa. Wallis got the cameraman he would have liked for *Casablanca*, James Wong Howe. Greenstreet was transformed into a major in the French Army; Philip Dorn played the new Renault; Lorre became Marius, a Resistance fighter; and George Tobias and Helmut Dantine, settling in at Warners after hopping between Fox and MGM, played his comrades in arms. Dantine inherited Henreid's scar.

All this was strictly par for the course. "LAST YEAR *WARNER BROS.* ELECTRIFIED THE WORLD WITH *CASABLANCA*," the titles trumpeted, with no sense of incongruity or shame. "THIS YEAR WARNER BROS. AN- NOUNCE 'PASSAGE TO MARSEILLE'. HUMPHREY BOGART THE STRONG MAN OF CASABLANCA SETS HIS COURSE FOR MARSEILLE. TO LIVE HIS *MOST DANGEROUS* ADVENTURE TO FIND HIS *MOST BREATHLESS* RO- MANCE." Again, this is an approximate description, not only because of the barrage of wipes, but also because animation makes the titles zoom out of the screen, and a circular wipe frames Bogart, who was being built up from supporting player to a star with the attendant compensation: he became the highest-paid actor in the world.

Curtiz's salary took a bounce, too, proportionate to his place in the studio system. People buy tickets to see stars, not mise-en-scène, and this situation, which dates back to the days of the pharaohs, with exceptions recorded on tablets of stone (see Frank Capra's *The Name above the Title* [1971]), hasn't noticeably improved, despite the efforts of critics and the Directors Guild. (A researcher polling people coming out of a screening of *Jurassic Park* in 1993 found that none of them had heard of Steven Spiel- berg.) Curtiz, whose English was famously bad ("poodle" for "puddle"; "Bring on the empty horses"), thought in images and was a master of all the forms of cinematic syntax. "Curtiz signed each film in the 1930s," says Aljean Harmetz, "with coherent and exciting action within a scene that masked the fact that the heavy cameras could only move slowly and pon- derously. And if something worked in one film, it might pop up in the director's other films" (1992, 75–76). She cites Julius Epstein to confirm that Curtiz had "tics and obsessions" like any auteur: "We had a very suc- cessful birthday scene in *Four Daughters*, so Mike wanted a birthday scene in every picture we wrote. So on one picture—I forget the name of it—we said, 'Forget it. It doesn't belong.' We went to the preview and there was the birthday scene" (ibid.).

Harmetz repeats the twice-told tale of Curtiz's sadism in forcing cast and crew to go without lunch. What makes this example particularly hor- rible is the unwritten tradition that he had a sandwich concealed in a large viewfinder, which he nipped on while pretending to scope out shots. Giving the devil his due, she notes: "His films had three things in common. They were brought in on time, they rarely went over budget, and they al- most always made money" (1992, 63). She credits Curtiz with two striking visual touches in *Casablanca*: the plume of cigarette smoke that leads into the Paris flashback, and the glass of wine that Ilsa knocks over when Rick kisses her, "as if it were the last time," to conclude the sequence. Arguably, these metaphors are more effective and less ponderous than the scripted touches that serve the same function, which they complement: *From the steps, he looks off into the distance, he crumbles* [sic] *the letter and tosses it away as the steam from the engine clouds over the scene. There is a close-up of a glass on the table in the café. Rick's hand reaches for it and knocks it over.* Imperfect mastery of the spoken language generated visual supplements that live on the screen, not on the page.

Successive layers of interpretation have enhanced the auteurist reading of the film. Take Harmetz's observation (offered to correct or supplement the "repressed homosexuality" business) that the relation between Rick and Renault is like those of the Beatrice-and-Benedick couples in the director's historical romances, although it is highly unlikely that the master dispenser of Hungarian goulash ever read *Much Ado About Nothing*, a play whose intricate and largely outdated puns drive the hardiest native speakers to the footnote section several times per page.

But a glance at the trailer of Curtiz's 1934 *The Key* shows that even in a film pitting the very British Edna Best and Colin Clive against William Powell ("IN HIS MOST DYNAMIC CHARACTERIZATION"), Curtiz retained a sense of his employers' shtick addiction, which he shared (Julius Epstein: "If you were good at a particular thing, you would do that kind of thing on one picture and another and another" [Harmetz 1992, 56]): "BUT MORE STIRRING THAN REBELLION OF A NATION, IS THE STRUGGLE OF TWO MEN AND A WOMAN, FIGHTING TO FREE THEMSELVES FROM THE PASSIONS THAT THREATEN TO DESTROY THEM."

> BILL [William Powell]: I'm sorry it had to happen like this, but when two men are in love with the same woman, someone is always hurt.
> NORAH [Edna Best] (*who couldn't resist the man who came out of her past*): It was like a fire that I thought had gone out, but suddenly it flared up again! For fifteen years I'd been telling myself it was finished. And then in a split second, time ceased to exist!

Max Steiner's recycling of music lifted Curtiz's repetition compulsion to a higher plane, mixing and transforming the native theme from Curtiz's *Charge of the Light Brigade* (1936) and a complementary theme from John Ford and Dudley Nichols's *The Lost Patrol* (1934). "The song 'As Time Goes By,' recycled along with the scene of dueling anthems from the play, is a main character, not mere music," Harmetz quotes the spokesman for a group of students from the Yale School of Music, who examined a videocassette of *Casablanca* over a banquet of pizzas and beer. "It functions in the plot. It ushers in the past. And, to some extent, it implies humanity in a world thrown out of kilter" (1992, 255).

Drawing on her notes from that highly technical conversation, Harmetz reports: "Steiner may not have liked the song, but he gave Herman Hupfield [the composer] a gift. During one minute and forty-six seconds of underscoring, when Rick is saying goodbye to Ilsa, 'As Time Goes By' is transformed emotionally from a tone of tragic loss to romantic love to bittersweet resignation to a tragic and final climax as Ilsa and Laszlo turn their backs and walk to the Lisbon plane" (1992, 255). And as the composer of the underscore for David O. Selznick's *Gone with the Wind*, Steiner foregrounded the analogy between Rhett Butler and Rick Blaine, to the immense satisfaction of Joan Alison, co-author of *Everyone Comes to Rick's*, who hated Bogart and had always seen Gable in the part of Rick (55).

Casablanca sprang from personal experiences that remained ciphers until Harmetz's book supplied the code: Jack Warner's masseur lending his name to Abdul, the doorman at Rick's (1992, 26); Rick's chess game, which was a real game that Bogart was playing by mail during the shoot (73); the scene in which Rick tells the young chump to keep playing "22," which came from an experience of Philip Epstein's wife: "Phil's wife Lilian had played 25-cent roulette in Palm Springs and lost. 'She was moaning and complaining about losing,' says Julie. 'Finally the croupier told her to put her chips on 22. She won, and he told her to get out and never come back'" (58–59).

The film has generated a dense array of intertexts, to borrow a concept from Eco. Allegories (Renault as Europe, Rick as America); Warners versus the other studios in the arc of Rick's transformation; sexual metaphors in the form of shots and cuts that replaced the implied sex between the principals, nixed by the Breen Office (Harmetz 1992, 166); and high-hat psychoanalytic interpretations that are best summed up by Richard Schickel, who describes Rick's arc as his journey out of childhood (331). The Marx Brothers' *A Night in Casablanca* (330) was yet another spoof. There was also a sequel, *Brazzick*, that never got made, which Harmetz recounts in chilling detail (228, 339). And New Critical analyses: all those instances of thefts, all those pieces of paper, all those shadows, all those mirrors, all those 1940s pop tunes cleverly worked into Steiner's score. And Hitchcockian observations: the letters of transit, which never existed in reality, and would have gotten the bearers shot dead if they had, are the film's MacGuffin.

And meta-derivatives: Woody Allen's *Play It Again, Sam*, which I had the pleasure of seeing on stage and on film. That line is never spoken in *Casablanca*, but therein lies another story.

Note

1. Reshot after the film wrapped, according to instructions from Hal Wallis.

Works Cited

Corliss, Richard. 1992. "*Casablanca*: An Analysis of the Film." In *Casablanca: Script and Legend*, edited by Howard Koch, 233–247. Woodstock, NY: Overlook.

Eco, Umberto. 1985. "*Casablanca*: Cult Movies and Intertextual Collage." *SubStance* 14, no. 2: 3–12.

Harmetz, Aljean. 1992. *Round Up the Usual Suspects: The Making of "Casablanca"; Bogart, Bergman, and World War II*. New York: Hyperion.

Koch, Howard. 1973. *Casablanca: Script and Film*. Woodstock, NY: Overlook.

CHAPTER 10

The Spectacle of the Ages: *Noah's Ark*

KATHARINA LOEW

Noah's Ark (1928) represents an important junction in Michael Curtiz's career. The film was meant to introduce him as a director of distinction to the American public. Not coincidentally, the film had recourse to the Austrian epics that had been instrumental in establishing his fame in Europe. *Noah's Ark* was Warner Bros.' first big-budget production, signaling the studio's readiness to enter Hollywood's major league. It was "made to top any picture ever made" ("*Noah's Ark* Made to Top Any Film Ever Made," *Variety*, April 25, 1928, 1), and above all it aimed for audience appeal. In a popular silent-era format, this allegorical episodic film embeds the story of the biblical deluge within a frame narrative set in World War I France. It draws on several of the most successful epics of the 1920s and assembles crowd-pleasing motifs such as a spectacular natural disaster, a train crash, trench warfare, mass pageants, two melodramatic love stories, a male-male relationship, and an uplifting allegory. The talking sequences of the modern story anticipated the sound era, and the silent biblical episode reminded critics of a type of "lavish pictorial entertainment" that was becoming rare (Edwin Schallert, "Spectacle Remains Supreme," *Los Angeles Times*, October 28, 1928, 1). In fact, *Noah's Ark* was one of Hollywood's final epics with an ancient-world setting before the genre's 1950s revival, to which Curtiz and Twentieth Century–Fox's Darryl F. Zanuck contributed *The Egyptian* (1954).[1]

When Michael Curtiz (still known as Kertész or Courtice at the time) arrived in Hollywood on June 21, 1926, he was a prominent European filmmaker with over sixty directorial credits to his name. But none of his films had caused a stir in the American film industry comparable to that of Ernst Lubitsch's *Madame Dubarry* (*Passion*, 1919), F. W. Murnau's *Der letzte Mann* (*The Last Laugh*, 1924), or E. A. Dupont's *Varieté* (*Jealousy*,

1925), all films whose directors had recently been hired by major Hollywood studios. Instead, Kertész had attracted attention with a film that for the time being was not being shown in the United States. His spectacular epic *Die Sklavenkönigin* (*The Moon of Israel*, 1924) showed the potential to rival Cecil B. DeMille's *The Ten Commandments* (1923), one of the most profitable films of the silent era. Indeed, *Variety* reported from London, where both films opened almost simultaneously in January 1925: "In direction and production *Moon of Israel* is strong enough to enter into competition with *The Ten Commandments* anywhere in the world, even in the United States" (Jolo., "Moon of Israel," *Variety*, February 4, 1925, 39). Consequently, Paramount, which owned both pictures, made certain that *Moon of Israel* was not released in America until 1927.

In November 1925, Harry M. Warner met Kertész in Paris, and by May 1926 a contract had been finalized. It was announced that Kertész would join Warner Bros. to direct the studio's first superproduction, an adaptation of *Noah's Ark* ("Viennese Director Coming," *Motion Picture News*, June 19, 1926, 2845). Jack Warner made clear what was expected from Kertész: he was to replicate (or even surpass) what had impressed the Warners about his Austrian epics: "*Noah's Ark* will be the greatest spectacle ever seen on the screen. The sets will be among the most gigantic ever constructed for a picture. You can appreciate the opportunity for spectacular and for great mob scenes" (quoted in "Warners to Start Work on Noah's Ark," *Motion Picture News*, October 23, 1926, 1579).

In the mid-1920s, spectacular epics set in the ancient world were in vogue. Jan-Christopher Horak has called the time between 1922 and 1926 the "second heyday of the epic film" (2002, 63). The genre's first prime, between 1912 and 1914, produced films such as Enrico Guazzoni's *Quo Vadis* (1913) and Giovanni Pastrone's *Cabiria* (1914); its golden age, between 1955 and 1965, generated such films as William Wyler's *Ben-Hur* (1959) and Stanley Kubrick's *Spartacus* (1960). In the silent era, the making of films with ancient-world settings partly coincided with another filmmaking trend: episodic narration. Starting in the 1910s, films that tied multiple, historically diverse narratives together by means of a common theme became popular. This narrative structure offered an array of unfamiliar and picturesque settings that, like short film programs, satisfied the audience's wish for variety; thematic unity and the use of the same actors in multiple episodes provided a sense of coherence characteristic of feature-length films. One of the earliest examples of this kind of film is Luigi Maggi's Italian production *Satana* (1912, considered lost), which portrays Satan tempting people throughout the ages.[2]

Critics often automatically assume that the fashion of episodic films during the silent era was modeled on Griffith's immensely influential *Intolerance* (1916), doubtless the best-known example of the type. But the early reception of *Intolerance* in Europe cannot be taken for granted: the film was not shown there until after the war, and it did not premiere in Germany until 1924 (Rother 1998, 385). While the direct influence of *Intolerance* on German and Austrian episodic films of the late 1910s and early 1920s—including Kertész's *Sodom und Gomorrha* (1922)—cannot be ruled out, Italian prewar epics and contemporary European films were likely more influential role models.

Noah's Ark displays extensive similarities with *Sodom und Gomorrha*, which suggests that Curtiz had considerable bearing on the *Noah's Ark* script.[3] Framed by contemporary narratives, *Noah's Ark* and *Sodom und Gomorrha* narrate two of the most awe-inspiring events in the book of Genesis, the annihilation of a world of sin by means of primordial elements: fiery brimstone in *Sodom und Gomorrha* and a deluge in *Noah's Ark*. Both films establish a strong melodramatic polarity of virtue versus vice. The divine punishment is preceded by a spectacular procession to honor an idol, the attempted sacrificial murder of the pure and innocent—an angel in *Sodom und Gomorrha*, a virgin in *Noah's Ark*—in front of a colossal idol statue, which is subsequently destroyed by a vengeful God. The biblical heroes, Lot and Noah's son Japheth, rescue their companions from the collapsing idol's temple.[4]

Sodom und Gomorrha and *Noah's Ark* rely on the same strategies for harmonizing a biblical tale and a contemporary frame narrative. Both motivate the biblical episode as a lesson from a priest. Actors are cast in multiple roles, and certain narrative situations are repeated in both modern and biblical episodes. For instance, in *Sodom und Gomorrha*, Mary (Lucy Doraine) attempts to seduce a priest as a modern vamp and to charm an angel as Lot's naughty wife, Sarah; both the priest and angel are played by Victor Varconi. As a pillar of salt, Sarah appears like the young sculptor's statue of Mary. Mary's orgiastic engagement party is echoed in the festivities honoring the fertility goddess Astarte, which are led by Lot's wife. Similarly, in *Noah's Ark*, the biblical deluge is prefigured in a washed-out bridge that causes a dramatic train wreck. The villainous Russian agent Nickoloff and the wicked Akkadian King Nephilim (both portrayed by Noah Beery) receive the same hand injury, and Marie and Miriam (Dolores Costello in each case) are both rescued from execution squads—one equipped with rifles and one with bows and arrows.

Originally, *Sodom und Gomorrha* and *Noah's Ark* both featured an allegorical prologue. The prologue of *Sodom und Gomorrha* is considered lost,[5] but plot summaries, reviews, and censorship reports suggest it was remarkably similar to that of *Noah's Ark*. It castigated "the depravity and sensuality of modern society" and rendered "historical events that led to today's moral corruption," which were contrasted with an image of Jesus.[6] *Noah's Ark* begins by associating the Tower of Babel and the golden calf with contemporary greed and hedonism, depicting a corrupt human race indifferent to God's voice, which is visualized by a close-up of a Jesus statue. As in *Sodom und Gomorrha*, the beginning of *Noah's Ark* shows an investor frantically confronting the unscrupulous broker who has beggared him. Both films call rather banally for the moral betterment of men. *Sodom und Gomorrha* draws an analogy between modern excesses of the superrich and the biblical cities of impenitent sin. *Noah's Ark* equates World War I with the biblical deluge, a parallel that critics found preposterous, the attempted exegesis in the intertitles notwithstanding: "The Flood—it was a Deluge of Water drowning a World of Lust! . . . The War— it is a Deluge of Blood drowning a World of Hate. . . . The Flood and the War—God Almighty's Parallel of the Ages."

Even more so than *Sodom und Gomorrha*, *Noah's Ark* incorporates familiar tropes from other biblical stories, such as the burning bush, the conveyance of the Decalogue, the blinded Samson, Moses confronting pharaoh, and the Passion of Christ. In addition, it appropriates motifs from visual culture, most notably Gustave Doré's tremendously influential Bible illustrations. The film's prologue, for instance, features close copies of Doré's engravings of the ark on Mount Ararat and the Tower of Babel, which were re-created as spectacular glass matte paintings.

Not only the biblical episode attests to the effort to assemble as many guarantors of success as possible. It is likely that the frame narrative was situated during World War I because three epic dramas set in France during the war were among the highest-grossing recent releases. The love story between an American soldier and a European girl in *Noah's Ark* evokes King Vidor's *The Big Parade* (1925) and Raoul Walsh's *What Price Glory?* (1926), and the soldier's tragic killing of his best friend in combat recalls William Wellman's *Wings* (1927). Curtiz's spectacular train wreck may have been inspired by DeMille's *The Road to Yesterday* (1925), and his staging of it recalls the notoriously costly one in *The General* (1926), in which a real locomotive was crashed through a bridge into a river. The numerous borrowings in *Noah's Ark* did not go unnoticed; critics pointed to "touches reminiscent of *Ten Commandments*, *King of Kings*, *Wings*, *The Big Parade* and quite a few other screen epics that have been leaders and money getters in their class" ("Noah's Ark," *Variety*, November 7, 1928, 15).

Noah's sacrifice after the flood, in *Noah's Ark* (Warner Bros., 1928). Glass painting by Paul Grimm. Digital frame enlargement.

In the fall of 1926, Warner Bros. announced that *Noah's Ark* was about to go into production ("Warners to Start Work on Noah's Ark," *Motion Picture News*, October 23, 1926, 1579), which turned out not to be the case. According to James Robertson, the reason for the delay was that "by mid-1926 [Warner Bros.'] deep financial commitment to expansion had become a policy in which prestige features were to be kept to a bare minimum for the indefinite future" (1993, 12). Robertson argues that only after the record-setting cash infusion from *The Jazz Singer* (1927) did the Warners feel in a position to take on a prestige project like *Noah's Ark* (14). Meanwhile, Curtiz directed five mostly routine films, three of which are considered lost.

Principal photography on *Noah's Ark* began on April 4, 1928, at the old Vitagraph lot in Los Feliz. As was customary with epic pictures, the studio boasted of its expenditures. Allegedly, five thousand extras, sixty assistant directors, twenty-three motion picture cameras, and seven still cameras were used (Herbert Cruikshank, "Art for Art's Sake," *Motion Picture Magazine*, August 1928, 94). While these numbers are possibly exaggerated, there is no doubt that *Noah's Ark* was Warners' most lavish production to date. As Mark Glancy (1995) points out, its cost, $1,005,000, was nearly double that of any previous Warner Bros. film. At the same time, budgets over one million dollars were no longer a rarity in Hollywood. In 1927, as a film magazine reported, "nearly every big company is releasing at least one feature which has cost somewhere up in seven figures" (Edwin Schallert and Elza Schallert, "Hollywood High Lights," *Picture-Play*, June 4, 1927, 63). In fact, recent large-scale productions such as *King of Kings* (at $2,000,000) and *Wings* (at $3,000,000) were considerably more expensive than *Noah's Ark*. What is more, Curtiz reportedly brought in the film under budget and completed principal (silent) photography ahead of schedule in early June 1928 ("Curtiz Completes Noah's Ark Cutting Budget and Schedule," *Exhibitors Herald and Moving Picture World*, June 16, 1928, 55). He managed to deliver to the famously frugal Warner Bros. a rather reasonably priced "spectacle of the ages."

Noah's Ark is best remembered for its epic flood sequence. Every account of it reiterates an anecdote that is often used to denounce Curtiz as a reckless director with a callous disregard for human life. On closer inspection, however, its relevance for assessing Curtiz's director persona seems questionable. The story traces back to the cinematographer Hal Mohr, who, according to his own account, resigned from *Noah's Ark* (his fourth collaboration with Curtiz) because he considered shooting conditions during the flood sequence unsafe. Rather than blaming Curtiz for the situation on the set, Mohr singled out the producer Darryl Zanuck:

> I stayed with Warners' until I got into trouble over *Noah's Ark*, a big biblical epic. Zanuck and I didn't see eye to eye on a few things. *Noah's Ark* needed an enormous flood with plenty of sets collapsing at once. On Sunday we were rehearsing a scene that had to be photographed the following day. . . . The trick specialist, the producers, the director, and I were all there. They started talking about how to do it, and I objected, not as a cameraman, but as a human being, for Christ sake, because it seemed to me, and I could have been mistaken, although at the time I didn't think so, that they were going to kill a few people with these tons of water and huge set falling on them. I knew the stuntmen could guard themselves to some degree. But what about the others? So I walked off the picture. I wouldn't have any part of it. They were trifling with lives—and did modify their plan somewhat. But some stuntmen were seriously hurt. I don't know whether they left just the stuntmen and took the others out or not. (1970, 364–365)

The perilous shooting conditions that Mohr describes are rumored to have caused up to three deaths. Although this tale has been reiterated many times, it cannot be substantiated from contemporary sources. Mohr, for one, mentions injuries rather than deaths. Nevertheless, the rumor was circulating in 1931 when the fan magazine *Silver Screen* mentioned that "the story has been told of the lives lost during the making of *Noah's Ark*" (Allan Jordan, "The Price of Realism—Human Life: The Heroes of Hollywood Are the Unknown Extras," *Silver Screen*, January 3, 1931, 36).

The twenty-minute flood sequence not only presents a spectacle of extraordinary proportions but also exhibits a skillfully constructed dramatic arc. The first half shows the preparations for Miriam's sacrifice in the splendid Temple of Jaghuth, which are accompanied by the rising tempest, the gathering of the animals, and the Akkadians' flight from the torrential downpour. In the second half, incessant flood waves and cascades of water crush everybody and everything while the blind Japheth carries Miriam to safety in the ark and his vision is miraculously restored. The sequence is particularly noteworthy for its expertly built-up and gradual transition from a dazzling, exotic pageant to ferocious scenes of mass destruction.

It begins with shots of the huge temple set, which was reportedly three hundred feet long and seventy-five feet wide (Cruikshank, "Art for Ark's Sake," 33). The temple consists of a long rectangular hall with two opposing flights of stairs. One leads to Nephilim's throne, and the other to a colossal statue of Jaghuth at the opposite end of the hall; they are flanked by massive pseudo-Mesopotamian columns. The space is jam-packed with groups of warriors, cymbal players, dancing girls, pagan priests, ladies-in-waiting, and worshippers in glittering garments. Spatially disjointed, static extra-long shots from a variety of angles display the imposing space and the sparkling multitude, but prevent the viewer from becoming fully oriented. Interspersed are closer shots of King Nephilim and his victim, Miriam, accentuating the melodramatic opposition of virtue and vice. Miriam is chained in front of the Jaghuth statue, and Nephilim's archers set out to shoot her. In what follows, the atmosphere grows gradually tenser and gloomier. Winds spring up. Noah enters to call upon the Akkadians to repent; he is ridiculed and—ironically—doused. An archer is struck by lightning as he targets Miriam. Gusts of wind make it impossible for the others to take aim. The elements, first wind, then lightning, and eventually rain, increasingly determine the events inside the temple.

Initially, the rising storm is illustrated by means of wind machines and cutaways to a windswept miniature cityscape, which constituted the centerpiece of the film's special-effects efforts. Supervised by Ned Mann, 125 men are reported to have worked for four months on the 300-by-250-foot model, which cost a staggering $40,000 (Dunning 1929, 301). Preparations for the flood were comprehensive: "Water flumes were laid underground, emerging at the proper points. Perforated pipes were installed overhead for the rain. Then every house was removed, broken apart and reset with clay in the broken joints in order that the flood would break them up realistically. As a precaution wires were tied to pull them apart if the water failed and as a second precaution, dynamite caps were wired to a remote control" (ibid.).

Overall, the flood sequence consists of roughly 15 percent special-effects shots, which become increasingly frequent. In addition to elaborate miniature work, which was photographed by Vernon Walker, the film made use of physical and electrical effects (by J. Gibbons and Frank N. Murphy); color separation, traveling mattes, and optical effects (by Hans Koenekamp and William Butler); and glass paintings (by Paul Grimm and Ellis "Bud" Thackery). *Noah's Ark* established the reputation of the Warner Bros. Scientific Research Department (as the studio's special-effects unit was known at the time) as "one of the wonders of the picture business" (Haskin 1995, 108). Between 1925 and 1937, the department was headed by its founder, the former Keystone cinematographer Fred W. Jackman. Jackman was credited as "technical director" on *Noah's Ark* and celebrated as the film's "hero" (Donald Beaton, "As They Appeal to a Youth," *Film Spectator*, November 17, 1928, 10). Jackman's achievements in establishing and running the special effects department are undisputed. But his contribution to special effects production, generally speaking, has been called into question, most notably by his successor, Byron Haskin, who recognized Hans Koenekamp, "the greatest trick cameraman of them all," as the department's guiding spirit (Haskin 1995, 89, 107).

In *Noah's Ark*, Koenekamp demonstrated his mastery, for instance, in depicting the gathering of the animals. For the most part, the scene takes a low-cost approach, simply intercutting footage of moving animals at the San Diego Zoo ("Director Curtiz Starts *Noah's Ark*," *Exhibitors Herald and Moving Picture World*, April 14, 1928, 27). But one shot—one of Koenekamp's split-screen composites—shows them all together, simultaneously proceeding up a mountainside. The rocky slope resembles a maze of sorts, which helped conceal the transitions between the successively exposed portions of the frame. In the foreground, small groups of live animals, which were used multiple times in different parts of the frame, move into the maze. In the middle and background, model animals of various sizes are drawn uphill on wheels. The live animals in the foreground effectively distract from the models in the back. The clever use of relative size and the concealed matte lines further contribute to a compelling overall impression.

Following the high winds and torrential rain in the first half of the sequence, the floodgates open in the second half. In marked contrast with the hitherto mostly static camera work, increasingly fluid shots echo the gushing waters. From a 600,000-gallon tank installed in the hills above the lot, water was dumped onto actors and extras below. Multiple cameras captured the resulting cataracts. Central to depicting the epic destruction of Akkad was the flooding of the vast miniature cityscape. Since the destruction of the model could be photographed only once, a complicated setup was necessary to facilitate the recording of two types of footage at the same time. Actors were recorded at normal speed, with the flooding miniature behind them in forced perspective; footage of the miniature was also recorded at high speed, for subsequent use in traveling matte composites and cutaway shots: "Three hundred actors were on the life size set in the foreground. One hundred and five skilled men were at the various stations controlling wind machines, rain, flood water, lightning and other effects. Eleven high speed cameras with various focal length lenses were hidden between the foreground set and the miniature. Four normal speed cameras were on the foreground action. The high speeds picked up the individual details. . . . It took nerve to flash the starting signal for there could be no retakes" (Dunning 1929, 301). The higher-than-normal frame rates captured at high speed make it possible to slow down the movement when projecting it at normal speed. This makes the miniature flood look more realistic. The footage of collapsing model buildings and miniature waves was later combined with live action by means of color-separation traveling mattes.[7] The same technique was employed to depict the toppling of the Jaghuth statue behind Miriam earlier in the sequence. As the deluge reaches its destructive climax, special effects shots were employed with increased frequency.

Another special effect was sound. *Noah's Ark* was produced in two renditions: one for theaters wired for sound and one for the over 80 percent of film venues that were not (*Noah's Ark* advertisement, *Film Daily*, May 16, 1929, 4–5).[8] The Vitaphone release has a synchronized musical score and sound effects. In addition, the modern story includes several talking sequences, which, in the surviving 108-minute version, add up to no more than 15 minutes. Although *Noah's Ark* had been planned with Vitaphone accompaniment in mind since the summer of 1926 ("Vitaphone Plans," *Film Daily*, August 29, 1926, 1), the dialogue scenes were likely added in response to the tremendous success of *The Jazz Singer*. Critics were impressed by the sound effects, but not convinced by the dialogue sequences, which were widely perceived as stilted and ultimately dispensable. A reviewer remarked, "The fascinating role played by Vitaphone is in the effects through the flood and the scenes preceding it" (*"Noah's Ark,* Vitaphone Film, Coming to the Majestic," *Boston Sunday Globe*, April 7, 1929, 58). The talking sequences, which stand out formally for their tight framing, frontal composition, and long static takes, were shot after principal photography had been completed. It is unclear to what extent Curtiz was involved with them: in July 1928, he was reportedly hospitalized, and Roy Del Ruth directed the remaining scenes ("Curtiz' Illness," *Variety*, July 25, 1928, 5).

Noah's Ark premiered on November 1, 1928, at Grauman's Chinese Theatre in Hollywood. Initial reviews were friendly, but reserved. Most critics agreed that the film was a "mammoth show" (Edwin Schallert, *"Noah's Ark* Grips Throng," *Los Angeles Times*, November 3, 1928), "notable for its lavishness of production, for its 'stupendous' sets, for its massed humanity" (*"Noah's Ark,"* *Motion Picture Magazine*, January 1929, 68). Curtiz was widely commended for his handling of the crowd scenes and the deluge. Even commentators who disliked the film were unequivocally impressed by the flood sequence, which presented "as terrific a climax as has been seen in ages and the scope of the entire Biblical portion is pictorially tremendous" (Schallert, *"Noah's Ark*: Exclusive Review of Warner Production," *Motion Picture News*, October 27, 1928, 1272-B). Many, however, found fault with "the inconsistencies of the construction of the plot" (*"Noah's Ark* (PT)," *Harrison's Reports*, March 23, 1929, n.p.), and it was generally felt that the film was "far too long and padded" (*"Noah's Ark,"* *Variety*, November 7, 1928, 15). Reservations regarding the film's artistic merits notwithstanding, critics were certain that *Noah's Ark* would be "enormously popular with the public" (Norbert Lusk, *"The Letter* Is Sensation," *Los Angeles Times*, March 17, 1929). In fact *Noah's Ark* made a solid profit, earning more than $2,000,000 (Glancy 1995). The film did particularly well abroad. In Germany, it was the most successful production of the 1929–1930 season (Garncarz 2013, 187).

Despite immense marketing efforts, however, American revenues tapered off far more quickly than predicted. The film's run at Grauman's was canceled prematurely after nine weeks. *Noah's Ark* was subsequently cut from 13,500 feet (135 minutes), to 9,500 feet (108 minutes); the original-release version is considered lost. Starting in March 1929, the shortened version was exhibited as a road show presentation, which in many cases involved state-of-the-art visual and audio effects. For instance, in venues such as the Winter Garden in New York and the Majestic in Boston, a Magna-scope screen was used to facilitate the enlarged projection of the prologue and the flood sequence (*"Noah's Ark* Fine Screen Spectacle," *Boston Globe*,

April 16, 1929, 36; Rubin 1928). Sounds not only emanated from the screen but were reportedly also "made in various sections of the theater" (Mordaunt Hall, *"The Letter* as a Film," *New York Times*, March 17, 1929, 7).

Neither aggressive publicity nor recourse to the latest exhibition technologies produced the anticipated results at the box office. Even though the film earned $2 million, receipts were generally considered inadequate. The film has even been taunted as one of the "most expensive flops in movie history" (Medved and Medved, 1984, 29–34). While the perceived failure at the box office might have had more to do with exaggerated expectations than with actual losses, epics like *Noah's Ark* were evidently no longer in vogue. The blockbuster hits of 1928–1929 in the United States were films like *The Singing Fool* (1928), *Broadway Melody* (1929), and *Sunny Side Up* (1929), which all belonged to a new genre: the feature-length musical. In the context of the musical craze of 1929, *Noah's Ark* must have appeared to be the culmination of a bygone era.

In their effort to deliver the box-office hit that Warner Bros. was expecting, Curtiz and Zanuck assembled an array of material with great audience appeal, yet the result was perceived as muddled and unoriginal. *Noah's Ark* allowed Curtiz to once again demonstrate his talent for spectacular action and crowd scenes. But it did not markedly advance his position at the studio, and he continued to engage in routine productions. Although *Noah's Ark* is an uneven film, individual episodes, including the imposing flood sequence, the train wreck, and God's instructions to Noah, testify to Curtiz's visual mastery and remain noteworthy today.

Notes

Many thanks to David Degras and Ariel Rogers for their generous support.

1. Only three epics with ancient-world settings were made by a major Hollywood studio between 1928 and 1948: Cecil B. DeMille's *The Sign of the Cross* (1932) and *Cleopatra* (1934), and Ernest B. Schoedsack and Merian C. Cooper's *The Last Days of Pompeii* (1935).

2. The film was allegedly adapted from John Milton's *Paradise Lost* (1667), yet the more immediate source may have been the Hungarian play *The Tragedy of Man* (1861), by Imre Medách, which depicts Satan's temptations of Adam and Eve across ten historical periods.

3. The script was written by Anthony Coldeway, based on a story by the producer, Darryl Zanuck.

4. Incidentally, some of these tropes are also present in *Die Sklavenkönigin*, in particular the sacrificial murder of the innocent heroine, God's destruction of a colossal idol statue, and a spectacular procession (during the pharaoh's coronation ceremony).

5. About eighty minutes of *Sodom und Gomorrha* are considered lost. At its pre-

miere, the film was shown in two parts and was 3,945 meters long. The most recent restoration (2002) is 2,320 meters (ninety-eight minutes) long.

6. See the plot summary and cue sheet reprinted in Loacker and Steiner (2002, 426, 436).

7. Numerous traveling-matte processes were devised during the 1910s and 1920s. In the color separation, or "self-matting," process, complementary colored light is used to combine two independently recorded (by way of color filtration) images.

8. For the number of cinemas wired for sound in 1928–1929, see Belton (1999, 235).

Works Cited

Belton, John. 1999. "Awkward Transitions: Hitchcock's Blackmail and the Dynamics of Early Film Sound." *Musical Quarterly* 2 (Summer): 227–246.

Dunning, Carroll. 1929. "Typical Problems in Process Photography." *Transactions of the SMPE* 38:298–302.

Garncarz, Joseph. 2013. *Hollywood in Deutschland: Zur Internationalisierung der Kinokultur 1925–1990*. Frankfurt am Main: Stroemfeld.

Glancy, Mark. 1995. "Warner Bros Film Grosses, 1921–51: The William Schaefer Ledger." *Historical Journal of Film, Radio and Television* 15, no. 1: 55–73.

Haskin, Byron. 1995. *Byron Haskin*. Directors Guild of America Oral History 1. Interview by Joe Adamson. Lanham, MD: Scarecrow.

Horak, Jan-Christopher. 2002. "Österreichische Monumentalfilme in Amerika." In *Imaginierte Antike: Österreichische Monumental-Stummfilme; Historienbilder und Geschichtskonstruktionen in Sodom und Gomorrha, Samson und Delila, Die Sklavenkönigin und Salammbô*, edited by Armin Loacker and Ines Steiner, 63–76. Vienna: Filmarchiv Austria.

Loacker, Armin, and Ines Steiner, eds. 2002. *Imaginierte Antike: Österreichische Monumental-Stummfilme. Historienbilder und Geschichtskonstruktionen in Sodom und Gomorrha, Samson und Delila, Die Sklavenkönigin und Salammbô*. Vienna: Filmarchiv Austria.

Medved, Harry, and Michael Medved. 1984. *The Hollywood Hall of Shame: The Most Expensive Flops in Movie History*. London: Penguin.

Mohr, Hal. 1970. "The Cameraman." In *The Real Tinsel*, edited by Bernard Rosenberg and Harry Silverstein, 351–370. New York: Macmillan.

Robertson, James C. 1993. *The Casablanca Man: The Cinema of Michael Curtiz*. London: Routledge.

Rother, Rainer. 1998. "Monumentalkino: Zum Entstehen des 'Großfilms' in Deutschland." In *Die Modellierung des Kinofilms: Zur Geschichte des Kinoprogramms zwischen Kurzfilm und Langfilm (1905/06–1918)*, edited by Corinna Müller, 375–396. Munich: Wilhelm Fink Verlag.

Rubin, Harry. 1928. "The Magnascope." *Transactions of the SMPE* 34:403–405.

CHAPTER 11

Jazz Me Blues: Lo-Fi, Fantasy, Audiovisuality in *Young Man with a Horn*

ROBERT MIKLITSCH

One of the best, most succinct synopses of Michael Curtiz's style describes it as "distinguished by aggressive visual compositions, . . . quick fluid movements, shadow play, location inserts, . . . and the kind of speed that results from keeping a story on track and free of distraction" (Giddins 2010, 91). I cite Gary Giddins on Curtiz not simply because he is a respected jazz critic, but also because his précis concentrates on the graphic as opposed to the sonic aspects of the director's style. This is noteworthy, since the extant criticism on the film style of *Young Man with a Horn* (1950) has focused on the picture's soundtrack and, in particular, on the score (co-composed by Ray Heindorf and Max Steiner) and source music (for example, the protagonist's Harry James–ghosted solos). What is striking about the latter critical tack is how it raises the whole question of musical fidelity, a question that has historically plagued questions about adaptation, as in, is Curtiz's film faithful to Dorothy Baker's *Young Man with a Horn* (1938)? Hence, my recourse in what follows to a lo- as opposed to hi-sense of fidelity and, in my coda, the notion of fantasy.

Shadow Play: The Bottle

The note that precedes the prologue of Baker's novel reads: "The inspiration for the writing of this book has been the music, not the life, of . . . 'Bix' Beiderbecke" (9). While this note can be read as a prototypical legal disclaimer, I take Baker at her word, since except in its most general contours, the novel's narrative does not reflect Bix's life. Giddins dutifully notes a number of parallels: the bandleader Phil Morrison's Paul Whiteman–esque band, Harry Cromwell as a dead ringer for Harry

"Bing" Crosby, and, of course, the fact that "the young man with a horn," Rick Martin, like Bix, "takes to drink and dies obscenely young" (Giddins 1993, 178). The resemblance, however, ends there. Giddins: "It may all sound like a *clef*, but Rick's upbringing, character, and dilemma are largely antithetical to that of Bix" (178–179). Giddins's take on the relation between the novel and the film is particularly tonic because it effectively defuses the issue of fidelity at play in the notion of a roman à clef, introducing as it does a caesura between the roman and the clef.

Consider, to begin with, the opening scene of Curtiz's *Young Man with a Horn*, the flashback that, like another one at the conclusion, frames the body of the picture. Willie "Smoke" Willoughby (Hoagy Carmichael) is sitting at a piano, an ever-present cigarette in one hand, musing on the past: "I play piano in a run-of-the-mill dance band. . . . But there were times when . . . I palled around with Rick Martin, famous trumpet player." Although *Young Man with a Horn* is not the "story of Bix's life" (Carmichael 1999, 115), Carmichael was nevertheless an intimate of Bix's, and their relationship, which haunts his first autobiography, *The Stardust Road* (1946), invests his narration with a peculiar pathos: "People ask me about [Rick Martin] and those times. Ordinarily, I don't talk much about it, but I think about it a lot." Dissolve to a wide shot of young Rick (Orley Lindgren) and his sister departing the cemetery where his mother has just been buried. It is a simple but evocative image: Rick and his sister are about to pass under an arched gate that reads "CEMETERY," and when he turns around, there is the suggestion he already has one foot in the other world.

Earlier, to highlight Giddins's emphasis on Curtiz's visual style, I elided a number of elements, one of which is the director's "shameless mastery of emotional manipulation" (Giddins 2010, 90). A classic example of this mastery occurs when Curtiz punctuates the opening flashback with a straight cut to a close-up of Rick's face, riven with tears, framed in the receding rear window of a car. Then to "keep [the] story on track," Curtiz picks up the pace and the film speeds up, the camera tilting down to a license plate "856 MISSOURI," a close-up succeeded by a montage of license plates: "TEXAS," "OKLAHOMA," "CALIFORNIA."

In his appreciation of Curtiz, Giddins submits that "if one theme animates Curtiz's work, suggesting a stronger thematic hand than is usually credited to a studio pro who didn't generate his own projects, it is the plight of the outsider" (2010, 92). This theme is vividly conveyed in the dissolve to a wide shot of school-age Rick exiting a playground through a narrow opening between two fenced gates. In the ensuing lap dissolve, Rick restlessly turns in bed, entrapped by the fence's black diamond mesh.

His sister is preparing to go out for the night, and an empty bottle looms in the foreground of the frame as she lays down the law: "Either you gotta go back to school or you gotta get a job.'"

The music assumes a meditative, blues cast as Rick desultorily makes his way down a city street crowded with signs ("CRED —," "SAV—"). In the distance a train can be heard chugging, an offscreen sound that acts as a sonic transition to a high wide shot of a train yard where a locomotive is departing. The mise-en-scène, though stark, is salient: in addition to the stationary train cars and electrical rigging overhead, a container building whose diamonded façade recollects the playground fence dominates the setting. The train imagery foreshadows Rick's eventual career as a professional musician for a big band—a life that, by necessity, involves a lot of time on the road—but it is as if Rick, still mourning his mother's death, is trapped within himself and unable to find any direction.

The introductory passages of *Young Man with a Horn* represent a loose translation of Baker's novel, but the remainder of the first act more closely hews to the book's trajectory. In Curtiz's film, Rick is aimlessly walking down another, more densely urban part of the city when he hears the sound of men singing at the Midnight Mission. The mise-en-scène is again understated but eloquent: a triple-paned stained-glass window, in front of which the preacher stands, hymnal in hand. Dissolve to an angled medium shot of Rick lit by an overhead light like an angel, picking out notes on a piano. Rick was lost but now he is found. The infernal or, at least, noirish aspect of Baker's heaven-and-hell imagery materializes after Rick, having seen a trumpet in a pawnshop window (on the window imagery, see Rosenzweig 1982, 149–150), works as a pin boy at a bowling alley and hears a trumpet that is too hot to be Gabriel's horn. The window this time is not stained glass, but neon lit, and the letters spell "CLUB." The subsequent shot—a straight cut to a back alley where Rick is momentarily poised between a sign for the bowling alley and one for "Art Hazard and His DIXIE PICKERS"—is a marvel of location chiaroscuro, the alley space slashed by the deep shadow cast by the late Southern California sunlight.

The shot marks a momentous transition for Rick: from the workaday world of the bowling alley to the intoxicating life of a nightclub. The noirish lighting continues in a lower, darker key in the next shot as Rick, one hand on a trash barrel, looks up at an open window where shadows play on the ceiling inside. Noticing a fire-escape ladder, Rick climbs up to the window, where, perched on the ledge, he can see couples dancing to a black, tuxedo-clad band. As opposed to the description in Baker's novel, of the Beaux Arts Ball murals in the Cotton Club, which gave the "impression that they had something to do with Hell" (1938, 55), the initial interior scenes of the Club Dixie in Curtiz's film are relatively high key and, except for the passing shot of a female lush alone at the bar, upbeat.

In the next scene, Art's band is jamming after hours to "I Gotta Right to Sing the Blues." Rick, who is getting sleepy, falls off his perch and lands feetfirst in the now-open doorway. In the reverse shot, he stands in the dead center of the doorframe, the shadow of a large bottle to his left, a picture of a trumpet player, horn raised, to his right, a pitcher of milk sitting on a table in the middle ground. The picture of the trumpet player heralds Rick's future career as a horn player, and the shadows portend Rick's eventual switch to the bottle. The sequence ends on an ominous note: Rick is looking up at Art Hazzard (Juano Hernandez) fingering the valves of his horn (the band is playing Ralph Rainger's "Moanin' Low") when the camera cranes down, and the shadow of a trumpet falls over him. The shot is as subtly expressive as it is ambiguous. Is Rick's later fall from grace due to his having gotten himself—as Baker's narrator wonders at the very beginning of book one—"mixed up with negroes" (1938, 9)? Or is Rick doomed because, unlike Art, his drink of choice is not milk but booze? Or is it because the "art" of jazz is somehow a "hazard"?

No Jive: A Killer Note

The second act of Curtiz's film extends from Rick's time with Jack Chandler's (Walter Reed) band to becoming a featured performer with Phil Morrison's (Jerome Cowan) Orchestra. The switch point is a match shot of Rick tapping his foot as Art listens, admiringly, to a much older Rick (Kirk Douglas), dressed in a "circus" uniform, playing "Pretty Baby" next to a hula dancer. Narration again by Smoke: "It was about then that he started playing two ways, one way for money . . . and one way for himself." Cut to an exterior, open-curtain shot of Rick woodshedding in his hotel room.[1] Out of the blue, Art's shadow appears on the wall: he is off to New York City with his Pickers for a new, better gig at Galba's. But before Pops leaves, he casts a long, metaphorical shadow over Rick's bright vision of the future, warning him about how hard the life is: "Look at me. What have I got after twenty years of it: wife, kids, money in the bank? No."

Rick gives Pops a cigar, and as a shadow passes over him like a cloud, the film cuts to a long exterior shot of Lick Pier in Santa Monica. As soon as Rick steps inside the Aragon Ball Room, he pauses, his ear pricked by the sound of a piano reverberating in the enormous, hangar-like space:

Smoke, smoke billowing from his ubiquitous cigarette, is playing "Rick's theme," "Melancholy Rhapsody" (composed by Sammy Cahn and Ray Heindorf). Startled by Rick's spirited fluency on "The Japanese Sandman," Smoke briefly plays under him, and then they are off to the races until Smoke spies Jack Chandler and Jo Jordan (Doris Day) in the distance and stops midphrase; Rick, lost in the music, continues for a few more bars. Rick's musical faux pas is only the first in a series of gaffes that he makes with Chandler, who says, instructing the assembled band members for their June opening, "We're a dance orchestra, and our main job is to play a tempo they can dance to. No blues and no low-down jive."

The rehearsal for the Aragon engagement starts with one of Jo's numbers, Ray Noble's "The Very Thought of You," and she doesn't get through the first verse before Rick starts blowing as if picking up where he and Smoke left off:

JACK: What's the matter, Martin? Can't you read music?
RICK: You want every number played the way it's written?

Although this answer gets a laugh from the band, Rick isn't trying to be smart; he really can't understand how anyone with any musical wits would pay good money for such insipid arrangements or would want to play every song the exact same way it is written.

The match cut, from the band rehearsing "The Very Thought of You" with Rick blending in to Jo performing in front of an audience and Rick in the very rear of the frame, renders him virtually indistinguishable from the other sidemen. When the film finally cuts away to Rick, he is faithfully nodding to the music, though he is obviously itching to take a solo. In a high wide-angle shot of the now-deserted ballroom, Jo is about to leave for the night when she hears the sound of a trumpet ricocheting in the cavernous space. Cut to a chiaroscuro-rich shot of Jo descending a staircase to the locker room, a veritable "underworld" where she discovers Rick playing by himself. The abrupt cut to a close-up of the bell of the trumpet, a black hole that blots the screen like a stain, is unusually expressive: though ambiguous, like the shadow that fell on Rick when he met Art for the first time, it intimates that, as Pops admonished him, there is something missing in his life. Cue Jo.

A number of critics have observed that Jo is a white double of Josephine Jordan, Smoke's sister in Baker's novel, who, like Art and the pianist-bandleader Jeff Williams, is a metonym for the kind of music, whether the blues or jazz, defined by its directness and "full-throated ease" (Baker

1938, 9). But whereas Baker's Josephine Jordan appears to be modeled on the blues singer Ethel Waters, in Curtiz's film Jo is a big-band singer (Day toured twice with Les Brown and his Band of Renown before making her film début in Curtiz's *Romance on the High Seas*, in 1948) and, unlike Jordan, a potential love interest.[2]

Cut to a point-of-view shot of Jo gazing at Rick, who is alone and walking down the lamp-lit pier like Mildred Pierce in Curtiz's picture of the same name. When Jo joins him on a bench, Rick confesses, "Someday . . . I'm going to hit a high note that nobody's ever heard before." In Baker's novel, this "impossible-to-hit, never-heard-before high note" signifies the "difference between the demands of expression" and the "demands of life here below" (Baker 1938, 135–136). The expressive impulse surfaces when Rick gets some like-minded members of Chandler's band to jam to Harold Arlen's "Get Happy." The audience crowds around the bandstand, not dancing but—and this is anathema to Jack—listening. At the end of the song, the kids enthusiastically applaud. Jack, however, is not happy and fires Rick on the spot. The ensuing scene, in which Jo valiantly tries to talk Rick into asking for his job back, is initially played in the light of his hotel room; it ends in shadowy darkness when, frustrated, she calls Rick a "young man with a horn, a crazy young man with a horn."

Although Jo walks out on Rick, hiding behind a plant in the hallway is Smoke, a plot twist in the film that establishes the primacy of the relation "between men," which pervades the first three books of Baker's novel. In this homosocial context, Jo is something of an anomaly, as female singers were in big bands at the time, an outsider in an all-male world where the fraternity between players trumps the lure of femininity. The scene in which Rick and Smoke play Ben Bernie and Maceo Pinkard's "Sweet Georgia Brown" (in the pit orchestra of just the sort of dive that Jo warned Rick about) is the first in an extended sequence—comprising the two of them singing Milton Ager and Jack Yellen's "Lovin' Sam (The Sheik of Alabam)" in an open-air jalopy, then being threatened by a mobster in a bar on Christmas Eve—that represents their flight from civilization and the responsibilities associated not merely with the bourgeois respectability that Bix rebelled against, like Huck and Jim in Mark Twain's *Huckleberry Finn*, but also with domesticity.[3]

While the music on the soundtrack segues from a brief Gershwin-inflected passage to a bright, blaring rendition of Rick's theme, the sudden fade from the wintry darkness of Chicago to a windy summer day in New York City is bracing. Is the low-angle shot of Rick passing under an enormous "CAMEL" billboard an allusion to Bix's disastrous, career-ending performance on *The Camel Pleasure Hour*? (Lion 2005, 256). A window shot of Rick pausing in front of a record store, his horn crooked in his arm, resumes the heterosexual romance narrative even as it extends the play of windows in Curtiz's film, a stratagem that, like the use of shadows, delineates Rick's "emotional alienation" and his simultaneous determination to overcome his sense of isolation (Rosenzweig 1992, 145–146). In this window shot, Rick is stationed between two standees of Jo on the left and a saxophone on the right. The symbolism is as clear as the tone of Jo's voice on the record playing inside: Rick must choose between romance and music.

Dissolve to a proscenium shot of Jo performing Richard Whiting and Johnny Mercer's "Too Marvelous for Words," in which the screen is split along a diagonal axis with Jo, radiant in a white corset, illuminated in a cone of smoke-hazed light. Rick, it seems, has chosen Jo, but when she rushes offstage and asks whether he would like to take her out for a sandwich, he asks instead about Art. At Galba's, Rick greets his mentor by giving him another two-bit cigar, and Art, in turn, asks him to sit in with the band. In a provocative reading of the cigar exchange in Curtiz's film, a phallic one that recalls the black cigar that Rick gives Smoke in Baker's novel, Krin Gabbard explains that "Rick appears to be on the verge of *possessing* the brass phallus" (1996, 71). In the racial political-libidinal economy of *Young Man with a Horn*, Rick's mastery comes at the direct expense of Art's career, a development that has no correlative in the novel and has the determinate effect of minimizing the black blues and jazz tradition to which, as the film attests, Rick's music is manifestly indebted.

Mirror Play: Bad, Bad Girl

The montage of Rick's triumphant return to the world of big-band music represents the apex of his career as a trumpet player, and act three of Curtiz's *Young Man with a Horn* charts Rick's roller-coaster relationship with Amy North (Lauren Bacall), a "society girl"—her surname is indicative—who is alternately cool, then hot, but ultimately cold as ice. When Rick joins Jo and Amy at Galba's, Jo declares that Amy, who is studying to be a psychiatrist, "likes to analyze everything":

AMY: Tell me about jazz. Do you think it's purely African?
RICK: I dunno. I don't do too much thinking about it. I just like to play it.
    If you listen to it enough . . .

AMY: I didn't come here to listen to it. I came to study the people. . . .
There's something about jazz that releases inhibitions, sort of a cheap
mass-produced narcotic.
RICK: I gather you don't like jazz.
AMY: Not particularly. Oh, I know it's supposed to be our native art: cot-
ton fields, the levees, old New Orleans, and blues in the night . . .

Besides alluding to Warner Bros.' *Blues in the Night* (1941), Amy's super-
cilious criticism of jazz as a "cheap, mass produced narcotic" is reminiscent of the high-culture, Adornian critique of jazz (Miklitsch 2006,
63–66). At the same time, Rick characterizes jazz mainly as emotive rather
than intellectual, despite the fact that the film takes pains to show that
"Rick gets to be as good a trumpeter as he is only after years of intense
practice" (Butler 2012, 84).

Amy's willful behavior notwithstanding, Rick goes home with her,
the expensive "sweater girl" who writes "white-hot" poems inspired by
Baudelaire's *Les Pièces condamnées* (Baker 1938, 180) and whose palatial
apartment is decorated with a Steinway and French impressionist paintings, a fireplace set off by a dramatic ornamental arch and capacious mirror, and a white cockatoo. The cockatoo is an odd objet, but, together
with the junglelike foliage, it suggests that Amy has a predilection for the
exotic, or even for *Citizen Kane*. Cut to Rick packing his treasured collection of Art Hazzard records. Despite Jo's advice ("Inside, way inside,
[Amy's] all mixed up. She's wrong for you, Rick, she'll hurt you"), he has
decided to move in with her. In the following Central Park carriage scene,
however, he already looks distracted, the offscreen sound (in Rick's head)
of a trumpet playing "With a Song in My Heart" a sign of his disaffection
with Amy.

The cut to a deep-focus shot of Amy's apartment with Rick in the left
foreground, holding one of Art's records, and Amy in the far right background, listlessly smoking on the couch, evinces the growing distance
between the two, as does the shot of Rick on a stepladder, picking out
another one of Art's recordings to play for her. He is enthusing about a
disc—"Wait until you hear what Art does with this"—when, as she did
the first time that she brought him back to her apartment, she gets up
and walks out. Rick tracks her to the bathroom, where, having emerged
from the shower ("symbol of discipline, emblem of the great reformation"
[Baker 1938, 197]), she informs him she is returning to school: "I'm afraid
it's going to be early to bed and early to rise." Amy leaves for bed and is
baroquely framed in a mirror—a recurrent figure of her duplicity and nar-

cissism—while Rick, silhouetted, puts on another one of Art's records. And then, since the record is in the run-out groove, she asks him to take it off. He doesn't turn down the volume.

Rick retreats to Grady's bar, where he is sullenly drinking by himself when Art arrives and unsuccessfully tries to comfort him. In fact, Rick is so oblivious that it isn't until later that night, when the orchestra is about to go on, that he realizes Art was hit by a taxi while he sat morosely at the bar. At the funeral, Rick picks up Art's trumpet from the top of the flower-covered casket as light streams through a stained-glass window. A deep-focus shot, one of Curtiz's signature visual devices in *Young Man with a Horn*, indicates that Art's and Rick's positions have switched once again: while Rick, together with members of Art's band, plays "Nobody Knows the Trouble I've Seen," the "coffin lies in the foreground" so that the "dead man dominates the image as he dominated Rick's life" (Rosenzweig 1982, 149).

When Rick finally returns home, Amy appears with a young woman in tow, whom she introduces as Miss Carson (Katharine Kurasch). The relationship between Amy and Miss Carson, as opposed to Rick and Smoke's "honeymoon kick," is overtly coded as homosexual (and, in the very next scene, "sick"). Once Rick and Amy are alone together, she screams, "Get these records out of here!" and starts pulling his records out of the wall cabinet onto the floor, the shellac discs shattering like glass.[4] She never wants to hear a trumpet, nor Rick to touch her, again, a double negative that, in a melo-noir-musical like *Young Man with a Horn*, marks her as a bad, bad girl.

This said, one of the performative contradictions of Curtiz's picture is that whereas Amy is the "dark woman," she is also metaphorically associated with Europe, elite art (i.e., classical as opposed to jazz music), and intellectuality. In other words, paradoxical as it may seem, this femme's fatality can be read as a buried, twisted trope of bebop, which was associated with intellectual aspiration, avant-garde (read "serious") European art, and militant post-Dixie blackness.

Rick Lives!

Dissolve to a close-up of Rick sweating on the bandstand, missing a cue on "Someone to Watch Over Me." Dissolve to a dressing room where Phil Morrison berates him for drinking on the job: "What do you think this is, a spasm band like Art Hazzard's?" Rick lets Morrison have it right between the ears: "If that tin ear of yours could hear the kind of music Art Hazzard played, you'd go out and shoot yourself." No one is laughing this time. Although Smoke, standing between Morrison and Rick in a three-shot, tries to pacify him, Rick quits on the spot. The sight of Douglas's naked, finely chiseled torso reiterates the primacy of the relation between men in Curtiz's film (compare the celebrated conclusion to *Casablanca*), in which Morrison's "sweet" orchestra and the sort of commercial music he fronts is a displaced figure of femininity and domesticity. It is no surprise, then, that the scene concludes with Rick and Smoke agreeing to get "together that night with some of the guys" at one of the Jersey joints to jam.

As the morning light slants through a transom, only Rick, Smoke, and a saxophonist are still jamming. "We've got a recording date at ten o'clock," Smoke says, "and I'm dead before I'll begin." Rick, wild-eyed, is still raring to go when he suddenly collapses. While Smoke pours him a cup of coffee, Rick pours himself another shot from the bottle on the table. (It is here that all the alcohol imagery in the film begins to assume its full, ruinous implications.) As the flame on the candle stubble flickers (Rick, by implication, is burning it at both ends), he waxes about making records the way they want to. Smoke, though, has already read the tea leaves: "You know who buys records? High school girls."

The dissolve to a studio where Jo is recording a new song is, in this commercial context, not without a certain ambiguity. On one hand, she is the good, sweet (heterosexual) antithesis to Amy, her normalcy and altruism an antidote to the latter's poisonous narcissism and vapid intellectualism. On the other hand, as a pop singer Jo represents the ascendance of the vocalist in the postwar period, a trend that was accelerated by the 1942–1943 American Federation of Musicians' strike-inspired recording ban on instrumental music, which eventually sealed the "fate of big bands and drove a permanent wedge between [swing] and jazz" (Schuller 1989, 847). Indeed, the recording sequence is so thematically overdetermined that it can be said to constitute an aporia. The camera pulls back from a close-up of a 78 rpm disc being recorded, the engineer's face reflected in the black, glass-like surface as, offscreen, the musicians play the opening bars of "With a Song in My Heart." The difference between the spontaneity of the previous jam session and the rehearsed formality of the recording date couldn't be clearer.

Jo begins to sing, and as the camera pulls back for a wide shot, Rick, his face tense with anticipation, steals up behind her and starts to solo. Surprised, Jo turns around, and Rick fluffs a high note. Before she can talk to the conductor, he fluffs another one. The silence is deafening. When Jo walks out on Rick again ("That note you were looking for . . . there's no

Washed up: Rick Martin (Kirk Douglas) fluffs a high note in *Young Man with a Horn* (Warner Bros., 1950), as Jo Jordan (Doris Day) stands at the microphone and "Smoke" (Hoagy Carmichael) watches from the sidelines. Digital frame enlargement.

such thing"), he picks up his trumpet and smashes it against a desk before breaking down. The camera cranes up and away, with Rick all alone among the encroaching shadows cast by the music stands and the now-vacant chairs.

The low-angle shot of Rick walking alone and without his trumpet beneath the Brooklyn Bridge, an enormous sign with the word "WASTE" prominent in the upper-right quadrant of the screen, bookends the earlier, blithe sequence of him first arriving in the city. The lateral tracking shot as he walks in Harlem recalls an even earlier period in his life: standing outside a window listening to men singing. The flashback to the old woman playing "In the Sweet By-and-By" at the Midnight Mission—a flashback within a flashback—mirrors Rick's psychic regression and increasing isolation from the outside world. The location footage that follows, mood infused, all sterling silvers and ink-stained blacks, is the most expressive in a film everywhere graced by Ted McCord's stunning cinematography: it is early evening, and a subway train, its windows lit like squares of light, travels in a semicircle across the rear of the frame. Rick stumbles toward the camera and pitches into the street as a taxi, headlights blazing, pulls up and runs over the battered, paper-bagged horn he just purchased from a pawnshop for seventy-five cents.

Cut to the Weaver Alcoholic Sanitarium, where Rick, not unlike Bix at the end of his life, has been diagnosed with pneumonia. Delirious, he rhapsodizes about Jo and Smoke playing just for themselves—"Some of the old ones, the good ones." The sound of an ambulance siren grows closer and closer. "Hear it," Rick pleads, "Hear that note—clear and sweet." The dissolve to Smoke sitting at a piano suggests that this is the end where, if only in fantasy (and as in Carl Foreman's first draft), Rick tries "*and hits* that incredible, impossible note" (quoted in Butler 2012, 75). Smoke's concluding voiceover implies, however, that Rick survives his dark night of the soul: "A man doesn't destroy himself just because he can't hit some high note that he dreamed up." A trumpet suddenly blares offscreen, and the camera pans to the right, where Rick is in the recording studio again, standing out front and blowing his horn. While Jo croons the last verse of "With a Song in My Heart," he completes his solo without fluffing a single note.

Coda: Rick Dies

The happy-ever-after ending of Curtiz's *Young Man with a Horn* feels totally tacked on, as, in fact, it is. In response to the first draft of Foreman's script, Jack Warner asked for a revision with a "hefty reduction in the negro material" and with an eye to a "happy ending" (Robertson 1993, 7). For anyone familiar with the conventions of classical Hollywood cinema, this is not only *not* surprising, it suggests a tacit, subterranean link between the complex racial politics of the period and the sort of compensatory (audio-)visual pleasures associated with the classic realist narrative. In the latter, Art, the black jazzman who is both a "Pop" and "mammy" figure, must die so that Rick, the white antihero, can live.

Of course, one of the historical ironies of this raced economy is that the celebrated refrain "Bix lives!" makes sense only in the context of the cornetist's early, tragic, and, in retrospect, canonical death, in which Bix's life rather than, say, Buddy Bolden's or James "Bubber" Miley's, becomes "the story" (on Bolden and Miley, see Gabbard 2008, 158–160; 163–165). As an avowed, unapologetic aficionado of classical Hollywood cinema, I read the "happy ending" of Curtiz's *Young Man with a Horn* as a cultural fantasy. In my inveterate counter-fantasy, *Young Man with a Horn* is a "black film," Art Hazzard lives a long, artistically illustrious life like Louis Armstrong, and Rick Martin, true at least to the dark dénouement of Baker's novel, destroys himself because he can't hit that killer note. Hence, my adulterated, more than "kind of blue" ending: Rick dies!

Notes

1. In *Really the Blues*, Milton "Mezz" Mezzrow defines "woodshed" as "to practise or study alone" (380). Woodshedding is not simply a way for Rick to hone his musical chops, but also something of a survivalist ethos, since he can't play "hot" in "sweet" bands like Jack Chandler's.

2. Interestingly, Doris Day portrays another singer named Jo in Alfred Hitchcock's *The Man Who Knew Too Much* (1956).

3. On the "Huck/Jim template," a trope repeated in *Casablanca* (Rick [Humphrey Bogart]/Sam [Dooley Wilson]), see Giddins (1993, 179).

4. Richard Brooks re-created a moment reminiscent of this in his *Blackboard Jungle* (1955).

Works Cited

Baker, Dorothy. 1938. *Young Man with a Horn*. New York: Press of the Readers Club.

Butler, David. 2012. *Jazz Noir: Listening to Music from "Phantom Lady" to "The Last Seduction."* Westport, CT: Praeger.

Carmichael, Hoagy. 1999. *"The Stardust Road" and "Sometimes I Wonder": The Autobiographies of Hoagy Carmichael*. New York: Da Capo, 1999.

Gabbard, Krin. 1996. *Jammin' at the Margins: Jazz and the American Cinema*. Chicago: University of Chicago Press.

———. 2008. *Hotter than That: The Trumpet, Jazz, and American Culture*. New York: Faber and Faber.

Giddins, Gary. 1993. Afterword to *Young Man with a Horn*, by Dorothy Baker. New York: New York Review Books.

———. 2010. *Storm Warnings: Home Alone with Classic Cinema*. New York: Norton.

Lion, Jean-Pierre. 2005. *Bix*. New York: Continuum.

Mezzrow, Milton. 1946. *Really the Blues*. New York: Citadel.

Miklitsch, Robert. 2006. "Reprise: Beethoven's Hair." In *Roll over Adorno: Critical Theory, Popular Culture, Audiovisual Media*, 63–66. Albany: SUNY Press.

Robertson, James. 1993. *The Casablanca Man: The Cinema of Michael Curtiz*. New York: Routledge.

Rosenzweig, Sidney. 1982. *"Casablanca" and Other Major Films of Michael Curtiz*. Ann Arbor, MI: UMI Research Press.

Schuller, Gunther. 1989. *The Swing Era: The Development of Jazz, 1930–1945*. New York: Oxford University Press.

CHAPTER 12

A Setting Sun: *The Egyptian*

DERON OVERPECK

By the time Michael Curtiz made *The Egyptian* (1954), he was at an uncertain time in his career. He had come to Hollywood during the studio system era, perhaps the zenith of the film industry's cultural power, and established himself as one of the top directors at Warner Bros. But the industrial changes wrought by political turmoil, and broader socioeconomic changes of the post–World War II years, had led to him leaving that studio on less-than-happy terms. In *The Casablanca Man: The Cinema of Michael Curtiz*, James Robertson refers to Curtiz as a "Hollywood nomad" during his final eight years, moving from studio to studio to helm for-hire projects.[1]

The Egyptian is informed by the decline of the studio system. Although the film contains Curtiz's traditional thematic concerns about the abuses of power, it is also marked by a sense of decline that is uncommon in the director's works. Adapted from the best-selling Finnish novel of the same name by Mika Waltari, itself based on an Egyptian Middle Kingdom literary work, the film follows an idealistic young physician, Sinuhe (Edmund Purdom), as he becomes disillusioned with a political system that outwardly reflects cultural glory but is marked by petty vanities and selfish motivations. This chapter begins with an overview of the production context of the film before situating the film within Curtiz's cinematic style and the direction of the industry in the mid-1950s.

Curtiz and Warner Bros.

The early 1950s were a difficult time for the American film industry. According to Ben Hecht, the producer David O. Selznick likened it to the decline of an earlier empire: "Hollywood's like Egypt," Selznick told him. "Full of crumbled pyramids" (Hecht 1995, 31). Unlike ancient Egypt, undone through conquest by other regional powers, Hollywood was hamstrung by political and economic shifts within society. A sharp decline at the box office, exacerbated by the popularity of television and coupled with the US Supreme Court decision in *Paramount v. the United States* (1948), which ended the vertical integration of the film industry, prompted the studios to drastically scale back production. These industrial changes caught Curtiz at an awkward time in his career. Like other top directors, including John Ford and Howard Hawks, Curtiz in 1947 had sought to benefit from this trend by forming his own production company; Warners would distribute the films and split the profits with him. But after only four films—*The Unsuspected* (1947), *Romance on the High Seas* (1948), *My Dream Is Yours* (1949), and *Flamingo Road* (1949)—Curtiz re-signed with Warners, transforming his production company into a semiautonomous production unit within the studio in a 1950 contract that still awarded him a share of his films' profits.

As this was occurring, Curtiz seemed to hit a professional lull. None of his films had been nominated for a major Academy Award since William Powell's Best Actor nod for *Life with Father* (1947).[2] Of greater concern to Warners, the films had not been as profitable as his earlier work for the studio (Robertson 1993, 110–116). In 1953, the studio asked him to take a 50 percent reduction in salary; Curtiz refused and left the studio ("Curtiz, WB End Pact over 50% Salary Cut," *Variety*, April 15, 1953, 24). According to Curtiz, Warner Bros.' practice of charging overhead costs against a film's profits meant that he had lost money over the course of his final contract at the studio ("Good Properties Shelved by Dearth of Names, Sez Curtiz; Blames Public," *Variety*, August 25, 1954, 4). For the first time in nearly thirty years in the American film industry, Curtiz was no longer a company man. Although he soon began a five-picture deal with Paramount, Curtiz spent the rest of his career as a director for hire, moving from one project to the next without the stability and leverage that had marked the majority of his time at Warners.

"The Tale of Sinuhe"

His first film after leaving Warner Bros., *The Egyptian* exemplified another response to the industry's postwar economic downturn—the widescreen historical epic. Although the industry had made epics since the silent era, high costs had curtailed their production in the 1930s and 1940s. But by the 1950s, seeking ways to recapture audiences that had turned their attention to television, Hollywood revived the epic format, pairing it with new widescreen technologies inspired by the success of Cinerama. *The Egyptian* was produced in CinemaScope, Fox's anamorphic widescreen technology. The first CinemaScope film, Henry Koster's *The Robe* (1953), was a smash hit, and Fox was eager to exploit its new technology. Darryl Zanuck had optioned the Waltari novel in 1952, before the success of *The Robe*, but soon identified it as a suitable project for widescreen treatment and assigned Corey Robinson, who had written an earlier epic adaptation for Zanuck, *The Snows of Kilimanjaro* (1952), to pen the screenplay ("Zanuck Wraps Rights to Best-Selling 'Egyptian,'" *Variety*, September 17, 1952, 3). Zanuck knew that Curtiz was experienced at directing epic films, particularly since the two of them had worked together on *Noah's Ark* (1928) during Zanuck's time as a Warner Bros. writer. He hired Curtiz to direct *The Egyptian* a few weeks after his departure from Warners (Robertson 1993, 118).

Curtiz joined a production already in difficulty. Zanuck, dissatisfied with Robinson's screenplay, had secured Philip Dunne for rewrites (Robertson 1993, 118). Casting likewise proved problematic, and one contemporary press account claims that 21,000 feet of film were shot for screen tests alone—twice as much as required for a standard two-hour feature ("'Egyptian' Starts Late," *Variety*, March 10, 1954, 4). Marlon Brando signed on to play Sinuhe; indeed, he departed New York immediately after completing *On the Waterfront* (1954) for Elia Kazan in order to begin shooting *The Egyptian* in January 1954 ("Marlon Brando to Coast," *Variety*, January 20, 1954, 7). But just as quickly he returned to New York, stating that he needed to see his therapist ("Marlon Brando's Therapist Excuse Not Acceptable, 20th Will Sue Actor," *Variety*, February 10, 1954, 16). Fox balked at the actor's excuse and sued for breach of contract; as it happened, Brando was dissatisfied with both Curtiz's approach to the material and the casting of Zanuck's mistress, Bella Darvi, as Nefer, the object of Sinuhe's lust. He refused to return (Robertson 1993, 118–119; Richards 2008, 142).[3] Zanuck approached Dirk Bogarde, but negotiations faltered on financial terms ("20th-Rank Tiff Continues," *Variety*, February 17, 1954, 2). The role at last went to Edmund Purdom, an MGM contract player whose first starring role, in *The Student Prince* (1954), was to be released in mid-June. Production finally began in March, two months behind schedule, but was completed in time for a late-August debut.

Waltari's novel deviates from its source material, creating the themes of regret that animate the Curtiz film. It is thus worthwhile to provide an overview of "The Tale of Sinuhe," which was probably composed sometime in the twentieth century BCE. Told in the first person, it relates the story of an official during the reign of Pharaoh Amenemhet I (ruled 1991–1962 BCE) who flees to Canaan when he overhears that the monarch has died.[4] In Canaan, Sinuhe flourishes in the retinue of a local chieftain, marrying a woman and having children who become powerful tribal leaders. But as an old man, Sinuhe prays to the gods to be able to return to Egypt before he dies: "Be gracious and bring me home! Surely you will let me see the place where my heart still stays! / What matters more than being buried in the land where I was born?" ("Tale of Sinuhe" 1997, 34). They hear his entreaties: he receives an invitation to come home from Pharaoh Senusret, Amenemhet's son and heir, and back in Egypt finds that a lavish pyramid has been erected to house his body when he dies. The original tale, then, does not have the same sense of faded glory we find in *The Egyptian*; though exiled, Sinuhe is called home before his death and returns to find the kingdom as magnificent as he left it and his reputation secure.

The Egyptian, novel and film, transplants Sinuhe to the reign of Akhenaton, approximately four hundred years after the time period of the ancient text. This transforms the story from one of continuity into one of turmoil. The historical Akhenaton is notable for having disrupted polytheistic Egyptian religious practices in order to institute a monotheistic faith organized around the worship of Aten, the sun god.[5] After Akhenaton's death, the traditional observances were resumed under his successor, Tutankhamen, and Akhenaton's rule became anathematized. Waltari's Sinuhe is present for these events, but is ultimately sickened by the violence used to suppress Atenism; when he persists in loudly criticizing his nation's violent militarism, his former friend, now Pharaoh Horemheb, banishes him from Egypt. The novel is thus presented as the mournful memoir of an exile who has learned that political upheaval results in lasting breaks not only in cultural identity but also in personal relationships. It is this sense of loss that informs Curtiz's cinematic adaptation.

The Egyptian

The Egyptian opens with two sequences invoking a decayed past. The first makes use of the CinemaScope format to present spectacular travelogue-style images of the ruins of ancient Egypt, including the Great Sphinx of

Giza, the Temple of Karnak, and the Colossi of Memnon. In voiceover, a narrator emphasizes the tension between the still-impressive scale of these monuments and the frail humans who created them, noting that they were created by "the rulers of the world," "a civilization never surpassed for beauty and splendor" that is now "ruins and dust," "a thing of darkness and mystery." But, he adds reassuringly, the ancient Egyptian masters were in truth "human beings, no different from ourselves." A contemporary shot of the weathered Sphinx and its surrounding pyramids dissolves to an image of them glistening in the hot sun (effected with mattes); this shifts the film back some three thousand years in one neat edit.

This image, in turn, dissolves into the second sequence and incorporates the memoir structure of the Waltari novel. The titular Egyptian, aged Sinuhe, sits in front of a nondescript hut near the shores of the Red Sea. The bland but sturdy walls offer a stark counterpart to the monuments of the first sequence. As vultures circle overhead, the old man muses on his life and invites the reader (and viewers of the film) to judge him. He admits to having lived deeply and encountered passion and tenderness, and to have committed murder. Then, for the third time in less than four minutes, the film again shifts in time, via a dissolve, to an earlier period as Sinuhe narrates his convoluted life story.

As an infant, Sinuhe is found floating in a small boat made of reeds by a family that lives in a modest home along the Nile in Thebes; his adoptive father is a doctor serving the poor and downtrodden. Following a standard education from the temple priests, Sinuhe intends to follow his father's path as a healer of the impoverished. He befriends Horemheb (Victor Mature), an exceptional swordsman who wants to be part of the palace guard but has been passed over because of his lowly birth.[6] Sinuhe attracts the attention of a pretty servant, Merit (Jean Simmons), and procures the services of a crafty slave, Kaptah (Peter Ustinov). While on a lion hunt with Horemheb, Sinuhe unwittingly treats the epileptic Pharaoh Akhnaton (Michael Wilding), who has come to the desert to meditate before his ascent to the throne.[7] Sinuhe and Horemheb are arrested because it is illegal for a commoner to touch the monarch. Once he has recovered, the grateful pharaoh pardons them. A peaceful, gentle man, Akhnaton names Horemheb to the palace guard and offers Sinuhe a position as palace physician. Although Sinuhe initially declines in order to devote himself to caring for the poor, he soon becomes fascinated by the Babylonian courtesan Nefer (Bella Darvi). Forsaking both Merit and his own sense of duty, Sinuhe bankrupts his family to win Nefer's affection. She rejects him, and in a fit of blind rage he nearly drowns her. After his par-

Although he has won the love of the moral Merit (Jean Simmons), Sinuhe (Edmond Purdom) still finds himself torn between his calling to serve the poor and the decadent allure of the royal palace, in *The Egyptian* (Twentieth Century–Fox, 1954). Digital frame enlargement.

ents kill themselves in shame, Sinuhe leaves Thebes to bury them. In his absence, one of Akhnaton's daughters dies, and Sinuhe is blamed for not being there to attend to her; when the pharaoh issues a death sentence against him, Sinuhe flees Egypt with Kaptah.

For a decade, they travel throughout Canaan, eventually settling with the Hittites, who are planning to invade Egypt. Still loyal to his native land, Sinuhe travels to Thebes to warn Horemheb about the Hittites' superior weaponry. Pardoned yet again by Akhnaton, Sinuhe learns he has a son by Merit, who has become a devotee of the pharaoh's Atenistic religion. Horemheb and the pharaoh's sister Baketamun (Gene Tierney) believe that the new faith is responsible for both the unrest throughout the nation and the Hittite threat on its borders, and they try to lure Sinuhe into a plot to assassinate Akhnaton. Sinuhe refuses, even after Baketamun reveals that Sinuhe could rule Egypt himself, since he is in fact a member of the royal family. The son of the previous pharaoh by a concubine, he had been cast adrift as a child by his grandmother, who was eager to preserve Akhenaton's claim to the throne. But when Merit is killed during an attack on worshipping Atenists, Sinuhe blames Akhnaton for introducing a new religion and poisons him—an act he regrets once he witnesses the pharaoh's humane, introspective approach to death. Horemheb and Ba-ketamun succeed Akhnaton and rule with an iron fist. Sinuhe criticizes their violent regime, forcing Horemheb to banish his former friend to the Red Sea. The narrative then returns to the elderly Sinuhe as he finishes his memoir—which he hopes will be read by his long-lost son—and sadly but contentedly goes to sleep in the setting sun.

Politics and Plot

Curtiz and his screenwriters altered Waltari's plot, as would be expected in the process of adapting a talky five-hundred-page novel for the screen. Subplots involving the future King Tutankhamen and other actual royal personages were excised to tell a more straightforward story of personal redemption. Changes in characterization made Sinuhe and the supporting cast more appealing to modern audiences, demonstrating that they were indeed "human beings, no different than ourselves." In the book, Sinuhe's father treats the poor because he is a physician of modest talents, and Sinuhe must learn cranial surgery from a wizened priest; in the film, Si-nuhe's father works among the poor even though "from the rich he could have commanded princely fees, for he alone in Thebes was a master of the art of opening skulls," and he inculcates in his son a sense of duty to the less fortunate. In the book, Sinuhe quickly takes a liking to the nightlife in Thebes, enjoys diverse sexual encounters, and buys Kaptah shortly after joining the royal household's medical staff; in the film, Sinuhe initially rejects pharaoh's offer of a palace job in order to continue his mission to the disadvantaged, and feels shame for betraying Merit to pursue Nefer—Kaptah more or less forces Sinuhe to accept him as his slave. In his later years, the filmic Sinuhe is a gentle man, regretful of the violence he com-mitted but also wiser for it, whereas the novel's Sinuhe remains proud of his past and boasts that "slaves still fear my rod" (Waltari 1949, 3).

The efforts to soften Sinuhe bring the character closer to the kind of protagonist for which Curtiz is known: a man who must find the moral courage to confront the injustice and oppression embodied in political and legal systems (Hark 2014, 85). According to James Robertson, many of these characters find themselves "function[ing] in an alien environment," which resonated with Curtiz's own experiences of shifting from the film industries in Europe to those in the United States (Robertson 1993, 150). Sinuhe thus exemplifies both the Curtizian protagonist and Curtiz himself. Like Bradford in *Virginia City* (1940) or Rick in *Casablanca* (1942), he is forced to recognize the difference between right and wrong regardless of the personal consequences. He must reject his royal heritage when his half sister Baketamun tries to lure him into the plot to assassinate Akhnaton, and then accept exile rather than condone his former friend Horemheb's oppressive rule. And like Thorpe in *The Sea Hawk* (1940) or the three convicts in *We're No Angels* (1955), Sinuhe finds himself within a strange land whose customs he must learn to exploit. Indeed, Sinuhe's life is predicated on being such a stranger: he spends his childhood in a situation beneath his birth, learning to minister to those who are exploited by his natural class; as an adult, these values are challenged as he lusts for the self-centered, hedonistic Nefer. His two exiles come from his need to right the wrongs that he has committed: he flees Egypt first to rededicate himself to the selfless ideals that he betrayed during his dalliance with Nefer, and finally accepts banishment when he rejects the political cynicism that brought Horemheb to the throne.

Along with Sinuhe, many of the other characters reflect the mistrust of political systems that is typically seen in Curtiz's films. The high priests are pompous and beholden to ceremony; studying with them as a young man, Sinuhe vows never to humble his inquisitive spirit even as he begrudgingly bows his body before them. The slave Kaptah voices a healthy disregard for authority when he tells Sinuhe how he lost his eye—a punishment for urinating in his previous master's beer jar—and at times openly disregards Sinuhe's orders. When Akhnaton learns that Sinuhe and Horemheb are to be put to death because they touched the royal body when saving him from an epileptic attack, he irritates his vizier Mekere (a dauntingly bald Henry Daniell) by immediately pardoning the men and rescinding the law that threatened their lives. On the other hand, the schemes and open covetousness of power displayed by the film's main antagonists, Horemheb and Baketamun, underscore the venal calculations that are rife within any political system, even one guided by a man as apparently beneficent as Akhnaton.

Theology and *The Egyptian*

The film's treatment of Atenism—Akhnaton's monotheistic belief system—is striking. The biblical parallels in the film are unmistakable: Sinuhe's life story draws on traditions about both Moses (being set adrift on the Nile in a boat of reeds) and Joseph (being exiled in a foreign land where he rises to prominence, a parallel also found in "The Tale of Sinuhe"), and like Jesus, Akhnaton accepts death, in his case as a means of reunifying the nation. It would be easy to see Akhnaton's religious beliefs as a reference to Judeo-Christian monotheism, especially given the theory linking the historical Akhenaton to Moses.[8] But the film takes a somewhat cynical attitude toward this new faith. Although Curtiz apparently held no particular disdain for religious faith, in *The Egyptian* religion is but another social structure that lends itself to abuse. Atenism spurs a civil unrest that makes Egypt seem weak to its enemies abroad and that can be ameliorated only through the death of the pharaoh. Akhnaton seems to recognize the incorrectness of his religious movement when he admits that his beloved sun was merely a symbol of a higher power that a future prophet would reveal — a fitting message for a film produced by the conservative Zanuck. In the end, however, *The Egyptian* reasserts Judeo-Christian thought even as it casts a skeptical eye on religion. When Sinuhe condemns Horemheb's warmongering and denigration of the memory of Akhnaton, he uses language that recalls both the book of Ecclesiastes in its reminder that humans and all they do will eventually crumble to dust, and the Gospel of John's logos in its invocation of a "great truth" created by God to unite the world and its peoples. The film's concluding scrawl — "These things happened thirteen centuries before the birth of Jesus Christ" — makes clear exactly who Akhnaton's future religious leader will be and of which God Sinuhe speaks.

This theologically tinged message notwithstanding, *The Egyptian* ends with the notes of regret and decay on which it began. As Sinuhe leaves Horemheb and Baketamun in the opulent royal palace, we dissolve to Sinuhe at his simple mud hut, a visual echo of the transition from the gleaming Sphinx to Sinuhe's home at the beginning of the film. The warm red glow of the setting sun is more attractive than the vultures and hyenas invoked at the beginning of the film, but it still punctuates Sinuhe's tale of betrayal and ruin. Not only is Sinuhe exiled from his homeland, he is estranged from his son; Kaptah took Thoth (Tommy Rettig) to safety during the purge of the Atenists, and Sinuhe apparently has not seen him since. And the true religion of which Akhnaton and Sinuhe speak before their departures from Egypt is still more than a millennium distant, suggesting that it will be quite some time before things improve in Egypt and the ancient world beyond. Curtiz's earlier works generally featured protagonists triumphing in their efforts. Perhaps only *20,000 Years in Sing Sing* (1932) and

The Private Lives of Elizabeth and Essex (1939) have endings as downbeat as that of *The Egyptian*.

The Curtiz Style

Despite the sense of regret that permeates *The Egyptian*, it seems to point to a resurgence in Michael Curtiz's career. As Curtiz's first experience with widescreen composition, it bears the signs of a director feeling out how to adapt his style to the new technology. Sidney Rosenzweig describes this style as featuring high-angle establishing shots, complex composi- tions, expressionistic lighting, and a highly mobile camera (1982, 6–7); Ina Rae Hark notes that Curtiz frequently gave his actors close-ups to allow "their performances to carry the story" (2014, 87). The widescreen format provides plenty of opportunities for Curtiz's trademark high-angle establishing shots, which situate characters within expansive and detailed sets. Indeed, *The Egyptian* has many cinematically striking moments. A long tracking shot that takes us into Nefer's salon as pairs of revelers cross in front of the camera; an underwater shot of Nefer struggling as Sinuhe strangles her; and the slaughter of the worshippers of Aten during the cli- mactic rebellion would all stand with the best of Curtiz's output. All the same, there is a certain generic feeling to the cinematography. The film is brightly lit; even scenes of intrigue and violence—such as Sinuhe's near murder of Nefer and his poisoning of Akhnaton—make no use of the moodier lighting that Curtiz traditionally employed for such sequences. Perhaps because of the need to feature spectacular sets, or perhaps be- cause of the technical limitations of the anamorphic lens,[9] Curtiz relied primarily on long shots and medium-long shots, and the actors never re- ceive anything more than a medium close-up.[10] Thus, although *The Egyp- tian* looks like a Curtiz film, it seems impersonal when compared with what the director had been able to accomplish on even his action films for Warners.

The Egyptian was at best a modest critical and box-office success. Re- views for the film were mixed. *Variety* offered a rave, praising its spectacu- lar CinemaScope visuals and Curtiz's balanced direction, and enthusing about its strong box-office potential ("The Egyptian," *Variety*, August 25, 1954, 6). On the other hand, Bosley Crowther found it bloated, inconsis- tent in tone, and poorly acted ("'The Egyptian' at the Roxy Is Based on the Novel," *New York Times*, August 25, 1954, 23). Splitting the difference, *Time* mocked the film's pretensions to historical accuracy before deciding that "for moviegoers who feel hardier than Brando and can stand up to the broadsides of grandeur, *The Egyptian* has kind of a blurby, big-adjective poetry about it" ("The Egyptian," *Time*, August 30, 1954, 76). Initial box-office returns seemed to support the *Variety* critic's enthusiasm, and by the end of the year *The Egyptian* had grossed $6 million, good enough for fourth place on the list of the year's top box-office performers (Gene Arneel, "'54 Dream Pic: 'White Xmas,'" *Variety*, January 5, 1955, 5).[11] But the film cost approximately $4 million and returned only $4.25 million in rentals (Solomon 1989, 248; "The Top Box Office Hits of 1954," *Variety*, January 5, 1955, 59).[12] In addition to the film's production cost, Fox spent $1 million on advertising that included television spots; a traveling exhibition of "items from the film and . . . lion and leopard cubs"; and lavish premieres in New York and Los Angeles ("Splashiest Preem since 'Robe' for N.Y.'s 'Egyptian,'" *Variety*, August 25, 1954; Edwin Schallert, "'Egyptian' Gives Lavish Start to New Premieres," *Los Angeles Times*, September 2, 1954, B8). *The Egyptian* probably at best broke even. This marginal performance did not stop Fox and other studios from continuing to pursue widescreen historical epics, however, as the subsequent success of films like Cecil B. DeMille's *The Ten Commandments* (1956), William Wyler's *Ben-Hur* (1959), and Anthony Mann's *El Cid* (1961) demonstrated. Thus, the Curtiz film surely showed the viability of the format and genre.

All things considered, *The Egyptian* must have felt like a success for Curtiz in the wake of his recent unhappy experiences with Warner Bros. It demonstrated both that he could still handle epic subject matter and that he could work with widescreen formats. This ability to adapt his visual style to a broader compositional palette would serve Curtiz well over the next two years: all of his Paramount films were shot in VistaVision, and he worked in CinemaScope again for the Fox musical *The Best Things in Life Are Free* (1956). *The Egyptian* signified a promising future for Curtiz. Unlike Sinuhe's banishment from his native land, Curtiz's departure from Warner Bros., which he had called home for nearly three decades, did not result in exile from the industry itself, and he remained an active filmmaker until his death in 1962. Yet perhaps Curtiz resembled Sinuhe more than might be immediately apparent. Like the Egyptian, Curtiz was fairly close to the end of his life, the peak of his career behind him. With the exceptions of *White Christmas*, *We're No Angels*, and, perhaps, the Elvis Presley vehicle *Kid Creole* (1958), none of the remaining titles in his filmography are particularly well remembered. Even if the vultures were not yet circling overhead, the sun was beginning to set.

Notes

1. "Hollywood Nomad, 1953–1962" is the title of the seventh chapter of the book.

2. Indeed, that was the last Curtiz-directed performance to receive an Oscar nomination. A few later films received nominations in musical categories, and *The Egyptian* was nominated for Best Cinematography. After his win for *Casablanca* (1942), Curtiz never received another nod for Best Director.

3. When Brando agreed to appear as Napoleon in *Désirée* (1954), Zanuck dropped the suit (see James Bacon, "What Is Marlon Brando? The Greatest Living Actor? A Crazy Mixed-Up Kid? World's Highest Paid Geek?," *Los Angeles Times*, April 11, 1954, D8).

4. The extant manuscripts of "Sinuhe" are unclear, but it is possible that he overhears people discussing the conspiracy to assassinate Amenemhet (Baines 1982).

5. There is some debate about whether Akhenaton's reforms constituted a true monotheistic religion or one in which Aten was elevated above all other gods and the pharaoh was identified with him.

6. While Horemheb may not have been the son of a cheesemaker, he does appear to have been of common birth. After serving as Tutankhamen's commander in chief of the army, he became pharaoh around 1306 BCE.

7. "Akhenaton" is the preferred spelling of the name of the historical figure, but the film uses this variation.

8. The idea was first introduced into popular consciousness by Sigmund Freud in *Moses and Monotheism* (1939). The theory that Moses and Akhenaton were connected is not accepted today. Moses is probably a mythical figure (Dever 1993); but had he existed and led an exodus out of Egypt, it would have been during the reign of Ramesses II, which was approximately a century after that of Akhenaton. Since Atenism was abandoned within five or six years of Akhenaton's death (and his reign was officially expunged from records at some point during Horemheb's reign, which began about fifteen years after Akhenaton's death), it is fair to say that the Akhenaton-Moses link is nonexistent (see Wilkinson 2013, 275–277, 290).

9. According to Sheldon Hall and Steve Neale, the distorting effects of the anamorphic format were not overcome by the new and improved lens used to shoot *The Egyptian* (2010, 148).

10. Ronald Neame, who directed *The Man Who Never Was* in CinemaScope for Fox in 1955, recalled in June 2000 that Zanuck wanted his directors not to use close-ups because they were "unnecessary"—in short, didn't ideally feature the new process. He recalled a "No Close Shots Necessary" edict at the studio.

11. The number one film that year was *White Christmas*, which Curtiz directed for Paramount immediately after finishing *The Egyptian*. Even though it was released two months later, *White Christmas* grossed twice as much as the biblical epic did.

12. Aubrey Solomon lists the cost at $3.9 million (1989, 248). At the time, *Variety* listed its cost at $4.2 million ("The Egyptian," *Variety*, August 25, 1954, 6).

Archive

Margaret Herrick Library, Academy of Motion Picture Arts and Sciences, Beverly Hills. Files consulted include the Barbara Roisman Cooper Collection of Ronald Neame Research Interviews, file 53 (Ronald Neame, notes of June 13, 2000).

Works Cited

Baines, John. 1982. "Interpreting Sinuhe." *Journal of Egyptian Archaeology* 68: 31–44.

Dever, William G. 1993. "What Remains of the House That Albright Built?" *Biblical Archaeologist* 56, no. 1 (March): 25–35.

Hall, Sheldon, and Steve Neale. 2010. *Epics, Spectacles, and Blockbusters: A Hollywood History*. Detroit: Wayne State University Press.

Hark, Ina Rae. 2014. "Michael Curtiz." In *Fifty Hollywood Directors*, edited by Suzanne Leonard and Yvonne Tasker, 84–96. New York: Routledge.

Hecht, Ben. 1995. "Artist, Friend, and Money-maker." In *West of the West: Imagining California*, edited by Leonard Michaels, David Reid, and Raquel Scherr, 30–38. Berkeley: University of California Press.

Richards, Jeffrey. 2008. *Hollywood's Ancient Worlds*. London: Continuum.

Robertson, James C. 1993. *The Casablanca Man: The Cinema of Michael Curtiz*. London: Routledge.

Rosenzweig, Sidney. 1982. Casablanca *and Other Major Films of Michael Curtiz*. Ann Arbor: University of Michigan Press.

Solomon, Aubrey. 1989. *Twentieth Century-Fox: A Corporate and Financial History*. Methuchen, NJ: Scarecrow.

"Tale of Sinuhe, The." 1997. In *The Tale of Sinuhe, and Other Egyptian Poems, 1940–1640 BC*, translated by R. B. Parkinson, 21–53. Oxford: Oxford University Press.

Waltari, Mika. 1949. *The Egyptian*. Translated by Naomi Walford. New York: G. P. Putnam's Sons.

Wilkinson, Toby. 2013. *The Rise and Fall of Ancient Egypt*. New York: Random House.

CHAPTER 13

King Creole: Michael Curtiz and the Great Elvis Presley Industry

LANDON PALMER

Alongside Richard Thorpe's *Jailhouse Rock* (1957), *King Creole* (1958) is widely considered by critics, scholars, and biographers as one of the best parts—perhaps *the* best part—of Elvis Presley's prolific but largely un-celebrated film career. Upon its release, Howard Thompson of the *New York Times* observed with wry amusement, "Elvis Presley can act," and contrasted the film with Presley's previous features by stating, "Acting is his assignment in this shrewdly upholstered showcase, and he does it, so help us over a picket fence" ("Actor with Guitar," July 4, 1958). *Billboard* and *Variety* echoed such qualified expressions of praise (Bob Bernstein, "Elvis Acts, Songs Are Solid in King Creole," *Billboard*, May 26, 1958, 7; Victor 2008, 287). Presley later cited his work in *King Creole* as his favorite among his screen performances, and the dramatic potential he displayed in it likely informed his continued goal "to progress as an actor" beyond musicals into the early 1960s (James 2016, 84, 93).

In tune with these rare lauds for a Presley screen role, Michael Curtiz holds a uniquely prominent place as one of few distinctive filmmakers who directed the rock 'n' roll star. Thompson's review describes Curtiz as "a shrewd director" and credits him with "snugly drap[ing the narra-tive] around Mr. Presley's shoulders" in a New Orleans setting "beguil-ingly drenched with atmosphere." Even pans of *King Creole* recognized Curtiz's talent, as indicated by Phillip Hartung's review in *Commonweal*: "It must be said in favor of Director Michael Curtiz that he does succeed in getting Presley to act every now and then" (1958, 68). Reflecting on Presley's film career as a whole, the biographer Peter Guralnick credits Curtiz with manifesting a Presley "full of jauntiness, assurance, an ease and melodiousness of nuanced approach" that is missing from Presley's later filmography (1999, 87). The historian Mark Feeney pointedly cites

Curtiz as one of few especially talented filmmakers with whom Presley worked (2001, 55).

While Curtiz is credited with developing Presley's most celebrated film performance, *King Creole*'s exceptional place within its star's filmography has hardly extended to its director's reputation. Sidney Rosenzweig's book surveying Curtiz's career through his work across genres is tellingly titled *Casablanca and Other Major Films of Michael Curtiz*. *King Creole* is not listed as one of the director's "major films," and the author mentions only briefly that the film "retain[s] the distinctive Curtiz look and atmosphere" (1982, 160). The first published accounts of Curtiz's career demonstrate critics' struggle to place the director's impressive filmography within the auteurist terms that dominated 1960s film criticism of studio-era directing, and scholars have instead favored understanding Curtiz as a consummate and prolific professional who thrived within the norms of the studio system. Finding in him a "contract director's mentality," James C. Robertson argues that Curtiz's "individualism was hidden from public view and he could not be associated with any one genre" of the many within which he worked (1993, 2–3). Within this framework for evaluating Curtiz's body of work, his late-career period, accompanying the disintegration of the studio system, becomes understandably marginalized as less representative of his contributions to film culture as a whole. Robertson notably places *King Creole* in Curtiz's post-studio-era "nomadic period," wherein his declining health coincided with a time in which "the Hollywood studio system was under strain" (117–118). In this respect, it is easy to understand why *King Creole* is a standout in the rock 'n' roll star's otherwise less-than-venerated film career, while the film does not hold a similar place within the overall reputation of its director. A closer examination of *King Creole*, however, illuminates how Curtiz functioned within the post-studio era. Curtiz played an instrumental role in developing the screen persona of a star who portended a new industrial design of Hollywood performance, an "electronic age" star whose screen image united media commodities and cultural industries.[1]

This essay considers Curtiz's reputation as an adaptive creative laborer contributing to *King Creole*'s important role in structuring the industrial formula that came to define Presley's screen career. Although *King Creole* is now commonly considered a rare work of prestige drama within Presley's otherwise interchangeable output of candy-colored stake-free musicals, the film was hardly a departure from the greater industrial design of Presley's film career. By "greater industrial design," I refer to the collaboration between the recording and film industries that brought about

King Creole **173**

the integrated production of feature films and soundtrack records, a design that helped form what the *Look* journalist Chester Morrison termed "the Great Elvis Presley Industry," namely, the lucrative network of music, films, and merchandise that manager Colonel Tom Parker extended from Presley's star image (1956, 98). By examining the production history of *King Creole* in the context of both Curtiz's longtime professional relationship with the producer Hal Wallis and its role in buttressing the emergent industrial formula that shaped Presley's subsequent films, this essay demonstrates how *King Creole* constituted both a rare prestige Presley vehicle and an important pretext for the commercial concerns that governed the rest of Presley's cinematic career. *King Creole* is not a venerable outlier in its star's otherwise disreputable filmography but a drama that was instrumental in fostering the musical screen career of its star—an aspect of the film's history that is overlooked in a critical reputation characterized by its distinction from Presley's other films.

In this respect, *King Creole* exhibits how Curtiz's capacities as a skilled dramatist and a reliable worker within the greater Hollywood system continued in the post-studio era. Curtiz is best known for his work within the Hollywood studio system—indeed, his most celebrated film, *Casablanca* (1942), is now widely considered an exemplary work of the studio era (Robertson 1993, 1, 79–80). Curtiz's post-studio-era work has thus been regarded as less representative of his career in general. As Robertson notes, *King Creole* was produced during Curtiz's "nomadic," "freelance" period (117). And Kingsley Canham (1973) does not mention the film at all in his early monograph on Curtiz's career. Yet *King Creole* speaks profoundly to how the gatekeepers of a former studio system adapted to a Hollywood characterized by wider screens and growing competition from other forms of media leisure. Curtiz's longtime producer Hal Wallis mobilized his studio-era star-making practices to draw Presley's youth audience to movie theaters. This effort not only meant eventually pursuing "a Bing Crosby picture starring Elvis Presley" (Guralnick 1999, 100) but also organizing promotion through the integrated production of feature films and soundtrack LP records, which by the end of the 1950s had become the dominant consumer format for commercial music consumption (Sanjek 1988, 333–356). Wallis's integrated approach to the Great Elvis Presley Industry has drawn ire from critics and historians who consider the cinematic period of Presley's greater career to represent the nadir of his cultural output (Guralnick 1999, xi, 87; Feeney 2001, 56–60). Yet Wallis was also the producer of this most celebrated film in Presley's filmography, for which he hired an accomplished colleague with whom he had shared a long history in the former studio system. Despite these seeming contradictions, the production of *King Creole* cultivated a dramatic Presley while serving an instrumental role in the eventual standardization of the Presley formula.

Following several nascent collaborations at Warner Bros. during the early 1930s, Wallis played some role in producing every Curtiz feature at the studio from 1937 until 1943. Later reflecting on Curtiz as his "favorite director then and always," Wallis admired what he considered Curtiz's "command of lighting, mood, and action" and his ability to "handle any kind of picture" (Wallis and Higham 1980, 24–25). Wallis's self-described reputation, as indicated by the title of his 1980 autobiography, was that of "starmaker," and many of Wallis and Curtiz's projects served to develop the careers and realize some of the most celebrated performances of several of Warners' best-known stars, including James Cagney in the musical biopic *Yankee Doodle Dandy* (1942) and Humphrey Bogart in *Casablanca*. In 1944, Wallis departed Warner Bros. to become an independent producer, shepherding stars primarily at Paramount for the rest of his career. Following his development of the Dean Martin–Jerry Lewis comedy cycle of the 1950s, Wallis sought to cultivate, in the biographer Bernard F. Dick's terms, "a 1950s equivalent of a 1930s radio star" (2004, 158). After watching Presley perform on CBS's *Stage Show* in March 1956, Wallis scheduled a screen test and then quickly contracted his newest star project. But since Paramount delayed in finding a suitable initial starring role for Elvis, his screen debut arrived via Twentieth Century–Fox's western-musical *Love Me Tender* (1956). Paramount followed shortly with Presley's first top-billed role, in the musical biopic *Loving You* (1957). Although Paramount's contract with Parker and Presley allowed the emerging film star to be cast in a limited number of "outside" pictures (Joseph Hazen [Wallis's frequent producing partner], memorandum to Sidney Justin [Paramount's legal counsel], October 30, 1958), Wallis endeavored to define Presley's screen image and set out to develop his second Paramount project before the star's March 1958 induction into the US Army (Wallis, memorandum to Hazen, September 6, 1957).

When Curtiz's contract with Warner Bros. expired in 1954, the director worked freelance in a rapidly changing postwar Hollywood. Under a "seven year contract" that "allowed him considerable latitude to direct films for other studios," Curtiz conducted most of his post-Warners career at Paramount, beginning with the Bing Crosby– and Danny Kaye–starring musical *White Christmas* (1954) (Robertson 1993, 117). Curtiz did not reunite with his mainstay producer from his studio-era heyday until *King Creole*.

As with prior Presley films such as *Love Me Tender* and Metro-Goldwyn-Mayer's *Jailhouse Rock*, the project that became *King Creole* originated as a studio property that preceded Presley's stardom and was adapted to his persona. Paramount initially pursued an adaptation of Harold Robbins's 1952 novel *A Stone for Danny Fisher*—about a young Brooklynite who takes up boxing in order to help his family through the Great Depression—as a starring vehicle for the Actors Studio graduate Ben Gazzara and the New York–based film and teleplay director Sidney Lumet. But by 1954, Paul Nathan, Wallis's associate producer, grew skeptical of the property's viability as a feature, claiming that the source material "seems to be such a sordid, down-hill, depressing story that I cannot believe it would be a box-office picture" (Nathan, memorandum to Hazen, December 18, 1954). Yet Nathan acknowledged that the project could serve as a viable means of "turn[ing] the Paramount star-making machine in the direction of Gazzara," and he connected this possibility with Wallis's history of developing male city-boy-type star images at Warner Bros. (Nathan, memorandum to Wallis, December 17, 1954),[2] stating, "I suppose Eddie Robinson, Cagney, etc., are shining examples of what Wallis has in mind for Gazzara" (Nathan to Hazen).

The potential for Wallis to adapt his star-making history of 1930s city-boy types for the Actors Studio generation of Method performers could explain why Wallis reunited with Curtiz, the director of Robinson and Cagney features such as *The Sea Wolf* (1941) and *Angels with Dirty Faces* (1938), respectively. According to Robertson, Curtiz read a screenplay adaptation of the Robbins novel "as early as May 1955" and "approved the film in principle," despite some reservations. Taking the property in a different direction, Wallis found his commercial draw by transforming *Danny Fisher* into Presley's second starring role for the studio, "with Curtiz's agreement" and the director's involvement with the rest of the film's casting (Robertson 1993, 123). The 1930s Brooklyn setting was updated to present-day New Orleans (where filming took place on location), and Paramount recharacterized the protagonist as a nightclub singer, thereby allowing the production to integrate several jazz-infused rock 'n' roll and blues numbers, which served to attract Presley's core audience and cross-promote soundtrack materials.

King Creole portrays Presley as Danny Fisher, a teen who struggles to graduate from high school while moonlighting as a busboy in the seedy underworld of a New Orleans nightclub owned by the Bourbon Street kingpin Maxie Fields (Walter Matthau). A loner and middle-class nomad, Danny bears a clenched fist and evident street smarts to compensate for the failures of his listless father (Dean Jagger), a pharmacist who struggles to find work following the death of Danny's mother. Once members of Maxie's nightclub realize that Danny can sing, a territorial war ensues between the straitlaced owner of The King Creole nightclub, Charlie LeGrand (Paul Stewart), and Fields, who, after seeing how popular Danny becomes, goes to violent lengths to trap Danny in a contract. Similarly, Danny's love life is caught between darkness and light as he wavers in his affection between Maxie's mistress Ronnie (Carolyn Jones) and the angelic Nellie (Dolores Hart). Ronnie and Maxie are killed in Maxie's failed attempt to murder Danny, and Danny returns to The King Creole, melancholic but triumphant, with the promise of middle-class income, virtuous love, and a restored family life in his future.

King Creole is one of several Presley films between 1956 and 1961 to feature its performer embodying the "rebel" type, what Richard Dyer describes as an "alternative or subversive" category of postwar male Hollywood stardom (1998, 52–54). In his history of midcentury rebel identity, Leerom Medovoi compares *King Creole* to Nicholas Ray's *Rebel Without a Cause* (1955), referring to the former as a proper "rebel youth movie" in the tradition of the latter, particularly in the shared disdain that Danny and James Dean's Jim Stark bear toward their impotent middle-class fathers (2005, 191–214). *King Creole*'s status as Presley's favorite movie in which he acted further contributes to his biographical veneration of James Dean, and *Rebel* in particular, a film that Presley told Wallis he could recite word for word (James 2016, 73).[3] Although Curtiz was reportedly nervous about Presley's limitations as a screen actor, informing Wallis that he wanted his formally untrained headliner to avoid "excess acting" (perhaps in reference to the Method's popularity among young male stars at the time) (79), the director developed Presley's performance for a film that Peter Guralnick describes as "written more for an experienced actor," principally by mobilizing Presley's anger (1994, 456; Dick 2004, 163). Thanks to Curtiz's direction, *King Creole* stands among the most potent cinematic translations of Presley's 1950s rebel musical identity.

Curtiz had worked with numerous musicians turned actors within the framework of the dramatic musical, most notably in *Young Man with a Horn* (1950).[4] A noirish biopic inspired by the life of Bix Beiderbecke that chronicles the rise and fall of the obsessive trumpet player Rick Martin (Kirk Douglas), *Young Man with a Horn* is bookended by direct-address narration from Rick's accompanist Smoke, played by the jazz pianist Hoagy Carmichael. Carmichael's character serves as—in the words of the Carmichael biographer Richard M. Sudhalter—a "sounding board and

Elvis Presley performs as Danny Fisher in the rebel mode for *King Creole* (opposite Dolores Hart as Nellie, *left*) (Wallis-Hazen, 1958). Digital frame enlargement.

foil for the leading man" and "a casual outsider commenting on the main action," much like Dooley Wilson's Sam in *Casablanca* (2003, 269–270). Curtiz employed actors as screen musicians and musicians as screen stars in several capacities: supporting characters like Smoke and Sam, the movie stars who led his composer biopics, and his comparatively lightweight comedy and musical work with multiplatform stars such as Al Jolson, Bing Crosby, Danny Thomas, and Danny Kaye. *King Creole*, by contrast, inherited *Young Man with a Horn*'s dramatic biopic skeleton but presented new challenges for Curtiz in showcasing a lead musician turned movie star as a simultaneously dramatic and musical performer. Curtiz reportedly sought to decrease the film's musical numbers in service of the film's drama (Robertson 1993,123), a tactic that would have reflected *King Creole*'s source material with greater fidelity. But the musical elements were essential to Wallis's commercial pursuits.

   Song placement and integration held a prominent place among Paul Nathan and Hal Wallis's concerns during the development of *King Creole*. Nathan's shepherding of the project indicates his eagerness to integrate music into the film with corporate ease, even if not necessarily narrative cogency. In October 1956, he proposed "Sing, You Sinners" as a prospective title for the film, after a 1930 song by W. Franke Harling and Sam Coslow, to which Paramount held the rights. The song had been used to title the studio's 1938 Bing Crosby film (although the song is not featured in the film's final cut) and had been performed, as well, in Paramount's pre-Code comedy *Honey* (1930). Nathan wanted to capitalize on musical properties already owned by Paramount to advertise both the film's title and a prospective single (memorandum to Wallis, October 15, 1956). When "King Creole" was ultimately chosen for this purpose, Wallis stressed that the title number had to be placed prominently in the narrative (Wallis, memorandum to Charles O'Curran [choreographer], December 26, 1957), thus Presley performs the song at the height of Danny's fame in the titular nightclub. This continued practice of titling Presley's films in union with a hit single demonstrates the larger cross-industrial and cross-promotional aims of Presley movies as containers for soundtrack releases and vice versa.

Despite Paramount's inability to envision a project as dramatic as *King Creole* without Presley singing, Wallis prioritized the use of music as a dramatic device, not exclusively a commercial one. During preproduction, he described Herbert Baker and Michael V. Gazzo's screenplay as "a very strong drama" but expressed skepticism about the film's justifications for musical performance: "I thought at first it was only because I was aware that the script had been changed for Elvis Presley, but on a very careful second reading, I feel several of these situations are artificial" (Wallis, memorandum to Nathan, November 27, 1957). Wallis's concern is leveled at an early scene in which, working as a busboy at Maxie's nightclub, Danny is harassed by several drunk patrons. An inebriated bar goer asks him to entertain them with a song after the club's official entertainment has long closed, to which Danny answers with a rendition of his school's fight song. This scene sets in motion the narrative of the rest of *King Creole*, since Danny's ability to sing opens a path out of stagnant delinquency and initiates the film's central conflict, which puts him at the center of a nightclub rivalry. Wallis saw contrivance in the script's assumption that the drunk customer "should take it for granted that busboy can sing," suggesting a desire to find a cogent means for *King Creole*'s narrative to navigate the gap between Elvis Presley the screen performer and his embodiment of a diegetic character (memorandum to Nathan). Such reservations recognize that *King Creole*'s audiences would be familiar with—and drawn in by—Presley the singer, and would almost certainly enter his films assuming that he would perform music at some point. But Wallis sought the means to realize Presley as "Danny Fisher," an ordinary-boy character who would not provoke the same set of preexisting assumptions regarding a capacity for musical performance within the world of the film.

Wallis's priorities reverberated in Curtiz's skilled integration of music and narrative. During the film's initial development into a Presley vehicle, Curtiz "feared that turning the young hero into a singer would adversely influence his characterization," but eventually "integrated the Presley tunes into the main plot" (Robertson 1993, 123). Within this narrative integration of music, *King Creole* is the only Presley film to explicitly illustrate African American cultural influence on Presley's music and star image. As summarized by David E. James, rather than suppressing "African American music and [Presley's] biracial attraction," *King Creole* constituted "the only dramatization of Elvis's musical indebtedness to the black working class" (2016, 84, 90–91). Such representation is particularly evident in the "Crawfish" musical sequence. *King Creole*'s opening minutes focus on African American vendors on Bourbon Street, before the film's opening credits and Presley's introduction. Featured are three (uncredited) vendors advertising their goods through song: turtles, berries, and gumbo. Because they sing to minimal nondiegetic orchestral accompaniment and because these vendors are portrayed within wide establishing shots of early morning in New Orleans, Curtiz situates the film's music within a realist, location-shot portrayal of a city within which, famously, music echoes through everyday urban life.

After the film's opening titles, Danny wakes and approaches his balcony, singing "Crawfish" alongside the African American jazz vocalist Kitty White, portrayed as a fishmonger (credited on the soundtrack but not in the film). This opening sequence establishes Danny's authentic ties to the culture of Bourbon Street, despite his white middle-class origins, in a way that echoes Presley's cultural power during the 1950s as a figure who embodied racial hybridity and, as noted by Michael T. Bertrand, thereby "challenged . . . notions and images [of African Americans that] earlier groups had taken for granted" (2000, 4–5). While these African American characters are given no significant narrative agency—they exist in service of characterizing Danny, a fact emphasized by his literal position on a balcony above the vendors on Bourbon Street—that they are given any representation at all in a Presley film extends from Curtiz's previous practices of representing music cultures. During the production of *Young Man with a Horn*, Curtiz fought with Warner Bros. for Juano Hernandez's prominent supporting role as Art Hazzard, Rick's mentor, despite the studio's demands that "the film devote less attention to black city life and black musicians" (Sudhalter 2003, 394). Moreover, the "Crawfish" sequence displays Curtiz's priorities in combining Presley's musical and dramatic capacities by staging music in a way that does not interfere with atmospheric or narrative verisimilitude. This approach unified *King Creole*'s commercial impetus with its narrative drive.

Film soundtracks served as a vital source for cross-industrial promotion and ancillary revenue in postwar Hollywood (Smith 1998). But the matter of release formats for commercial soundtracks had not been settled by 1958. While the soundtrack for Presley's first Paramount film, *Loving You*, was released as both a 45 rpm single and an LP (long-playing) record, the soundtracks for *Love Me Tender* and *Jailhouse Rock* were released as single and EP (extended play) records. Wallis and Parker stipulated which format would be best to release the *King Creole* soundtrack, and the result of such correspondence standardized the promotional soundtrack arrangement governing Presley's later screen career. Instead of an LP soundtrack, Wallis and Parker initially planned to release "two EPs and a single" in order to maximally profit from promotional commodities that, individually, would cost consumers less but could together sell in greater numbers and thereby augment revenue for Colonel Parker and promotion for Wallis (Parker to Wallis, April 9, 1958). Parker was skeptical of the gradually popularizing LP record format's marketability, and Wallis saw multitiered promotional possibilities in the staggered release of soundtrack commodities: "Not only is the cost factor important, as more kids will be able to afford them, but the idea of getting three plugs by staggering the releases is even more important" (Wallis, memorandum to Parker, April 11, 1958). Despite these initial plans, RCA released the *King Creole* soundtrack as a 45 rpm single of "Hard Headed Woman" on June 10, 1958, several weeks before the film's opening, on July 2, followed by a ten-track LP released on September 19. As the LP format became the music industry's standard recorded commodity by the end of the 1950s, advance (rather than delayed) releases of LP soundtracks accompanied the seven films in which Presley subsequently starred for Paramount and the majority of films in which he starred throughout the 1960s. The Great Elvis Presley Industry persisted via a continued cycle of mutually promotional LP records and feature films.

Between Curtiz's development of a musical and dramatic Presley and the solidification of the LP format as the primary vehicle for packaging the complete music of Presley's films, *King Creole* seems to represent an apotheosis of the Great Elvis Presley Industry, a stable establishment of narrative and commercial priorities. But *King Creole* in several ways represented a distinct break in the production practices of Presley's films. Perhaps as a result of *King Creole*'s rushed production during the military deferment granted Presley so that he could complete the film, Jerry Leiber and Mike Stoller—Presley's regular songwriters, who created numerous hits for his previous soundtracks, including the title songs "Loving You" and "Jailhouse Rock"—grew discouraged by Parker's transactional focus on soundtrack production (Guralnick 1994, 449), and were reportedly shunned by Parker after suggesting that Presley continue pursuing dramatic film roles by starring in a prospective adaptation of Nelson Algren's New Orleans–set novel *A Walk on the Wild Side* (1956), which they would score under Elia Kazan's direction (Guralnick 1992, 46–48). The songwriters did not collaborate on any future Presley soundtracks, paving the way for a variety of contracted songwriters to create a prolific output of film songs in the service of LP soundtracks.

Such changes extended to Presley's film persona. Presley's eventual abandonment of dramatic roles was ensured by his first two post-army musicals for Paramount, Norman Taurog's *G.I. Blues* (1960) and *Blue Hawaii* (1961), both produced by Wallis, the success of which, as films and as soundtracks, eclipsed his two Fox dramas released during the same two years, Don Siegel's *Flaming Star* (1960) and Philip Dunne's *Wild in the Country* (1961). Like *King Creole*, these two Paramount films used their settings (West Germany and Hawaii) as part of the filmic spectacle, whether in studio or on location. But they abandoned *King Creole*'s rebel mode of typifying Presley in favor of colorful, largely conflict-free platforms for musical performance. Gone were Wallis's concerns about whether music in Presley's films made sense narratively. The producer's ensuing approach instead relied on a durable combination of exotic locations, young women, and music, a formula practiced well beyond Presley's Paramount films (Feeney 2001, 58; James 2016, 92–122). This pattern became so standardized that one Paramount producer pitched a treatment for what would become *Fun in Acapulco* (1963) by attaching a brief synopsis of an Acapulco tourist brochure (Dick Sokolove, May 1, 1962). Yet Wallis relied on Curtiz's counsel in his continuing development of Presley's screen stardom. According to Guralnick, Curtiz "read the script" for what would become *G.I. Blues* "and agreed that with certain minor changes this could be the best Presley picture yet" (1999, 28). As far as the film's service to the Great Elvis Presley Industry was concerned, Curtiz was right.

In the early 1960s, the Great Elvis Presley Industry intersected with Curtiz's Warner Bros. filmography. Presley's former producer at Fox, David Weisbart, cast the rock 'n' roll star as the lead in a Phil Karlson remake of Curtiz's Wallis-produced 1937 boxing drama *Kid Galahad* (1962), set up as a musical for United Artists. During the years shortly before Presley ascended to screen stardom, the three Warners regulars who starred in Curtiz's *Kid Galahad* had been forced to adapt to the new obstacles of 1950s Hollywood. Edward G. Robinson had broken a streak of employment marginalization by testifying before the House Un-American Activities Committee, Humphrey Bogart established Santana Productions in order to gain autonomy over his film roles, and Bette Davis navigated the roller coaster of a new freelance career. Curtiz, too, faced the unique challenges and opportunities of a new Hollywood. *King Creole* constitutes a bridge between old and new star practices, wherein a veteran producer-director team partook in developing a star image fit for a changing Hollywood no longer structured by a vertically organized, assembly-line studio system, and wherein narrative had to meet the extratextual commercial requirements of promotional commodities. More than simply part of Curtiz's post-Warners nomadic period, *King Creole* demonstrates how Curtiz and Wallis adapted to a changing popular culture defined by emergent rebel personae, new music genres, a growing teen demographic, and a Hollywood that both competed and sought collaboration with other media—changes that the old guard endeavored to address via a rock star whom Paramount cultivated from a television appearance toward the double duties of film acting and soundtrack recording in the same breath.

Notes

1. "Electronic age" is a contemporaneous term that was widely employed to describe the expansion of midcentury media formats and industries, principally around new popular music culture (Curtis 1984). "Electronic Age" was also the name of RCA-Victor's corporate promotional magazine, which often featured articles about Presley. The songbook of Presley's first film soundtrack for *Love Me Tender* described him as an ideal figure of "today's slick electronic age" (Presley 1956).

2. In a detailed examination of the formation of star images within the Hollywood studio system, Robert Sklar examines the "performance type" of the city boy, which was developed at Warners as an idealized figure rooted in urban male street life within "the teeming polyglot of the modern industrial city" (1994, xii–xiii). The city boy is one of many gendered star or performance categories of Hollywood history, including the post-studio-system rebel type explored by Dyer.

3. In contrast to Wallis's eventual formation of Presley's star image against the rebel type, David Weisbart at Fox, the producer of *Rebel Without a Cause*, pointedly sought to integrate Presley into a mode similar to Dean's in *Love Me Tender* and *Flaming Star*, and saw Presley's untutored acting skills as an asset that would bring a raw energy to his roles (Guralnick 1994, 327, 332).

4. Krin Gabbard situates *Young Man with a Horn* within a formulaic history of tragic biopics of jazz musicians (1996, 66–67), and *King Creole* adapts and inte-

grates rock 'n' roll into this prototype of the dramatic musical biopic (James 2016, 88–89).

Archive

Margaret Herrick Library, Academy of Motion Picture Arts and Sciences, Beverly Hills. All letters and memoranda cited in the text are found in the Hal Wallis Collection.

Works Cited

Bertrand, Michael T. 2000. *Race, Rock, and Elvis.* Urbana: University of Illinois Press.

Canham, Kinglsey. 1973. *Michael Curtiz, Raoul Walsh, Henry Hathaway.* Hollywood Professionals, vol. 1. London: Tantivy.

Curtis, James M. 1984. "Towards a Sociotechnological Interpretation of Popular Music in the Electronic Age." *Technology and Culture* 25, no. 1: 91–102.

Dick, Bernard F. 2004. *Hal Wallis: Producer to the Stars.* Lexington: University Press of Kentucky.

Dyer, Richard. *Stars.* 1998. New ed. London: BFI.

Feeney, Mark. 2001. "Elvis Movies." *American Scholar* 70, no. 1 (Winter): 53–60.

Gabbard, Krin. 1996. *Jammin' at the Margins: Jazz and the American Cinema.* Chicago: University of Chicago Press.

Guralnick, Peter. 1992. *The King of Rock 'n' Roll: The Complete 50s Masters.* Boxset insert booklet. RCA.

———. 1994. *Last Train to Memphis: The Rise of Elvis Presley.* Boston: Little, Brown.

———. 1999. *Careless Love: The Unmaking of Elvis Presley.* Boston: Little, Brown.

Hartung, Phillip. 1958. "King Creole." *Commonweal*, August 1, 68.

James, David E. 2016. *Rock 'n' Film: Cinema's Dance with Popular Music.* New York: Oxford University Press.

Medovoi, Leerom. 2005. *Rebels: Youth and the Cold War Origins of Identity.* Durham, NC: Duke University Press, 2005.

Morrison, Chester. 1956. "The Great Elvis Presley Industry." *Look*, November 13, 98–103.

Presley, Elvis. 1956. *Love Me Tender: Song Folio with Pictures.* New York: Elvis Presley Music.

Robertson, James C. 1993. *The Casablanca Man: The Cinema of Michael Curtiz.* London: Routledge.

Rosenzweig, Sidney. 1982. *"Casablanca" and Other Major Films of Michael Curtiz.* Ann Arbor, MI: UMI Research Press.

Sanjek, Russell. 1988. *American Popular Music and Its Business: The First Four Hundred Years; Volume III, From 1900 to 1984.* New York: Oxford University Press.

Sklar, Robert. 1994. *City Boys: Cagney, Bogart, Garfield.* Princeton, NJ: Princeton University Press.

Smith, Jeff. 1998. *The Sounds of Commerce: Marketing Popular Film Music*. New York: Columbia University Press.

Sudhalter, Richard M. 2003. *Stardust Melody: The Life and Music of Hoagy Carmichael*. New York: Oxford University Press.

Victor, Adam. 2008. *The Elvis Encyclopedia*. New York: Overlook.

Wallis, Hal, and Charles Higham. 1980. *Starmaker: The Autobiography of Hal Wallis*. New York: Macmillan.

CHAPTER 14

Michael Curtiz's Political Cinema of Sorts

R. BARTON PALMER

During the 1930s, with everyone on one-year renewable contracts, and cost-effectiveness the watchword at financially strapped Warner Bros., directors who could not meet extraordinary demands for productivity simply did not thrive. It was lucky for Curtiz that directing for a studio determined to put itself securely in the black through the production of a steady stream of products suited his extraordinary work ethic (Nolan 1970). He welcomed an absorption in the technical issues of filmmaking, often down to the smallest detail, but was untroubled by tight schedules and thin margins for error. On the contrary, the pressure of constant work allowed Curtiz to take full advantage of and refine his exceptional managerial skills; he was quite the multitasker *avant la lettre*, according to the reports of co-workers, and his value to the studio, which grew substantially during the 1930s and 1940s, was as dependent on his "productivity" as on his "artistry."

But that artistry had nothing to do with an aspect of personal *mentalité* that the *Cahiers* critics in the 1950s identified, with neoromantic exaggeration, as "obsessive." Curtiz's particular brand of excellence in fact deconstructs the auteurist opposition of competence (craftsmanship) to individual vision (the supposed province of the true artist). He was perhaps unrivaled by his colleagues of the era in his apparently effortless talent for telling a story with speed and grace. This *sprezzatura* should be seen as crucial to both his productivity and also the pleasure his films provided viewers. His artistry should thus not be considered as some consistent add-on to unchosen assignments (not a "signature," to use the term popularized by auteurism). Nor did it consist of a set repertoire of themes, developed in depth and variety through the diachronic unfolding of an oeuvre consisting of vehicles that the director played some role in choosing. Curtiz instead supplied what the industry required and audiences found engaging: a flexible sensibility adaptable to what would enhance their enjoyment, insofar as a desire for formal excellence might meld with his need to work quickly and with minimal waste. Often with only a few days for anything more than perfunctory preproduction planning, Curtiz proved able during the 1930s to conceive effective visual programs for the disparate scripts handed him, saving both time and money. This was an ability that was more instinctive than calculating, defying articulation but manifesting itself in practice, and thus suiting rushed conditions of production in which improvisation was often required. Consider, for example, what one of the actors who worked with Curtiz, Paul Henreid, had to say about him on the set: "He had an instinctual visual flair . . . quite different from the way actors visualise. Every now and again he would stop the camera and say 'There's something wrong here, I don't know what it is.' By and large he'd realise what it was, and we'd begin the scene again" (quoted in Canham 1973, 52). Henreid is speaking here about what, lacking a better term, we might call presentation. The "something wrong" was identified and resolved by intuition, not intellection. Were it possible to compose such a chronicle, Curtiz's authorship would emerge as the sum total of on-the-spot decisions such as these, which were collectively responsible for the consistent success that his films achieved.

Unlike many of his later releases, the typical Curtiz film from this period was in fact rather spare, driving its narrative forward at a rapid pace. He never slighted storytelling clarity or failed to showcase effectively the studio's stars when the project was a performance vehicle. His disciplined style of filmmaking matched the Taylorized approach of the production chief, Darryl F. Zanuck, who, as some who worked with him remarked, had made himself into

> a filmmaking machine running the studio like an assembly line. He had a huge chart the size of his desk divided up into the fifty-two weeks of the year. In the left-hand column of the chart he'd list fifty-two stories and on the right side the major stars at the studio. (Sperling and Millner 1998, 166)

The contract directors were then "matched up" with projects in accordance with some sense of their demonstrated competences and success in the marketplace, as measured by box office. There was a pecking order among this group, and Curtiz's long career at Warners was marked by his continuing rise up the ladder, fueled by box-office success. By the mid-

1930s, he was on the verge of becoming a star player in this tightly organized system, a status he had secured by the early years of the next decade.

Though he was often relied on as a screenwriter or script doctor, Darryl
Zanuck was never all-determining when it came to production decisions;
the studio boss Harry Warner hardly refrained from making his views
known. And sometimes it was the studio's major stars, such as William
Powell or Paul Muni, who chose or sponsored a property. At least in this
period, Curtiz seems never to have enjoyed creative freedom of this kind,
though being trusted with important star vehicles indicated the faith that
management had in his ability. Muni, Powell, and others were able to play
the role of expressive artists at least occasionally, that is, if the selection
of narrative and dramatic material meant to suit one's performance style
and acting persona could be thought of as an expressive gesture. A-list
actors, whose participation was crucial to box-office success, disposed of
the power of the marketplace; contract directors like Curtiz, invisible to
the paying public, did not.

Politics and Romance

Four of Curtiz's films from the early 1930s have routinely been understood as "political," even though, given their conditions of production as
outlined above, they did not bring to the screen events and issues, historical or contemporary, that their director thought significant. And for the
same reason, he would have been unable to promote his own views in the
stories he did not choose but so ably brought to the screen, even had he
been so inclined. But to judge from his lack of interest in writing about
himself and his career, he was not inclined. Curtiz could not have been
a commentator on the domestic and international political scene in the
latter-day mold of Oliver Stone, and he showed no sign of such ambitions,
even though the wide-ranging and sometime tumultuous experiences of
his early professional life might well have pushed him in that direction.
His was not a voice stifled by industrial constraints, which was just as
well. Working for Warners, he could not even match his contemporary
Frank Capra for a personally expressive engagement with politics, even
though two of the films considered here, *Sing Sing* and *Black Fury*, because
they take up issues of social class, offer critiques of the American system
that resonate with Capra's films of the period, including *Lady for a Day*
(1933) and *Mr. Deeds Goes to Town* (1936). There is no revelation of self
or personal political values to be found in the quartet of productions that

are a focus of this chapter, along with a later, wartime release, *Mission to Moscow* (1943), which is preeminently a studio project whose most important authors were Joseph E. Davies, who wrote the film's source book, and Jack Warner. So why label these films "political," when for their director they were anything but?

There is good reason beyond convenience to consider these five films as a thematically defined group. The 1930s releases were not produced intentionally as part of a cycle or in response to some larger studio strategy. Yet in addition to their (generally) shared themes, *20,000 Years in Sing Sing* (1932), *The Key* (1934), *British Agent* (1934), and *Black Fury* (1935) constitute remarkably similar exceptions, at least in part, to typical Warners production protocols. They point the way toward the much greater success that both Curtiz and his employers enjoyed by the end of the decade. All four are based on presold properties whose filming rights cost the studio considerable money to acquire. This approach was not one that the notoriously tightfisted brothers were inclined often to adopt, especially so soon after the studio's brush with disaster during the first three years of the Depression. In fact, it may well be true that Warners spent more to acquire the rights to the sensational international best seller on which *British Agent* was based than on any other literary property it ever purchased.[1] These four films, moreover, were star vehicles, disposing of more generous budgets because they were intended to showcase the charisma and acting talents of the most important contract players at Warners (or, in the case of *Sing Sing*, of Spencer Tracy, on loan from Fox as a replacement for the suspended James Cagney, who was protesting being overworked and underpaid). Warners promoted quality with these films, distinguishing them from Curtiz's most pedestrian projects of the period such as *Doctor X* (1932) and *Goodbye Again* (1933).

Most important, in all four films, the "problem" posed to Curtiz was how to manage an effective balance between the politically charged backgrounds, whose action scenes were meant to provide viewers with topical interest and visual pleasure, and the love relationship between the male and female leads in the foreground, where star power and the erotic were meant to offer irresistible hooks. The ups and downs of passion were designed to prompt and satisfy the flow of emotions on which audience satisfaction was known to depend. A decade later, Curtiz faced a similar problem with *Mission to Moscow*, whose pro-Soviet screed—heavy, like all propaganda, with the conveying of often detailed information—needed to be made effectively cinematic by a central focus on the character of Ambassador Joseph E. Davies (Walter Huston), whose personal story reso-

Curtiz begins *Mission to Moscow* (Warner Bros., 1943) with a tastefully done interview with the former ambassador Joseph Davies, whose book was the film's main source. This sequence, in which Davies mentions that he will be "played" by Walter Huston, anticipates the later use of documentary footage to heighten the supposed truth-telling of the film. Digital frame enlargement.

nates with a narrative of global scale in which for a time he played a central role. Here, too, the material posed a problem of presentation, and once again Curtiz proved masterly in solving it while taking a backseat to the studio's promotion of Davies, who appears in the trailer and in the film's prologue to vouch for the veracity and importance of the story that Warners had chosen to tell and of which he claims onscreen ownership.

In these political films, spectacle and scope mattered, as reflected in the authenticity and energy that Curtiz was able to impart to larger-scale public scenes, often remarked on by reviewers. The artful confection of backgrounds in these films was enhanced by the director's cost-conscious deployment of what the industry called "production values." An engagement with the political, broadly conceived, thus served Warners as an important marker of quality. The trailer for *The Key*, offering a global judgment on its appeal, proclaims, "This actually happened!" In regard to the melodrama at the film's center, such a comment is disingenuous at best. As a plea of sorts for the appreciation of Curtiz's success in evoking, on studio soundstages and exteriors, the atmosphere of a bitter civil war fought in Ireland, it proclaims that *The Key* is no ordinary picture. And acknowledging the importance of the film's portrayal of an important international event, the

1917 revolutions in Russia, the trailer for *British Agent* nonetheless declares that its center is romance: "More stirring than the rebellion of a nation is the struggle of two men and one woman, fighting to free themselves from the passions that threaten to destroy them."

Similarly, the trailer for *British Agent* makes an especially strong argument for prestige. It first announces that the film is an adaptation of one of the period's most admired accounts of recent history, but then quickly moves to the many, often lighthearted, romantic scenes between Leslie Howard and Kay Francis, which mark a strange tonal contrast with the deadly seriousness of the political setting. At the same time, the trailer does not neglect how *British Agent* evokes the history of which its well-known source is a primary document. Clips from the impressive public and crowd scenes figure prominently, and they advance the claim that this is a serious production, not ordinary entertainment. Though large-scale scenes are a particular mark of Curtiz's approach, his name is of course never mentioned in advertising; the film's literary source, the memoirs of R. H. Bruce Lockhart, receive the central focus. Telling the tale of the October Revolution and the subsequent withdrawal of Russia from the war with the Central Powers is certainly not the subject of the film per se. In the end, of course, love triumphs over the twin threats of death and separation. With cheerless irresolution, the political recedes into the background. Such a focus on the personal was well received. The critic W. E. Oliver, for example, observed: "For such a large canvas, the picture strikes a very intimate response. . . . This is due of course to the love story of Miss Francis and Leslie Howard being made important" (quoted in O'Brien 2007, 136). Romance dominates the trailer copy for the other two films of the group as well, with quality filmmaking (visual and narrative) ballyhooed as part of the background for conflicted love affairs.

"Violence, savagery, and terror" are said to have erupted into the "black fury" of the miners' dissatisfaction in *Black Fury*, explaining the film's title, but this community-threatening uproar occurs because "a faithless woman couldn't be true." A hot topic at the time, prison reform provides the subject of *Sing Sing*, which is based on the best-selling memoir of the famous prison's long-serving warden, Lewis E. Lawes. Incarceration should teach the lesson of radical social equality to a successful gangster, Tommy Connors (Spencer Tracy), who has grown used to the finer things in life and making one and all do his bidding. He becomes forced to accept that he is just one prisoner among many, no better but no worse than any of his fellows. But the test of his newly found humanity is that with a false confession he saves the love of his life, Fay (Bette Davis), from prose-

Curtiz was often able to endow his crowd scenes with the painterly qualities of the great masters of political messaging. In *British Agent* (First National, 1934), the resemblance to the giant canvases of Jacques-Louis David (1748–1825) is especially striking. Digital frame enlargement.

cution for murder. "Only one man," proclaims the trailer, as an image of Lawes and his book flashes across the screen, "could condense the sensationally dramatic lives of a thousand men into a single evening's entertainment." Perhaps, but it is the masses of similarly uniformed men, walking in lockstep through the grim set designed by Anton Grot, that provide *Sing Sing* with its most memorable images, and these were choreographed by Curtiz, as were the action-packed scenes of the inevitable prison break, expertly and suspensefully staged. Though their relationship becomes central to the narrative only in its final stages, the pairing of Spencer and Davis was emphasized in marketing. "One day of freedom, one day in the arms of his girl" is how the trailer outlines the goal of the narrative: love, not the triumphally progressive demonstration that Lawes's reformist agenda worked even with the most hardened criminal, who had made a fortune in the rackets.

   The Key and *British Agent* reconstruct international events that were very much in the news a decade earlier and remained objects of vague public interest. *British Agent* dramatizes failed British diplomatic and military initiatives launched during 1917 in Moscow and St. Petersburg, as well as the subsequent debate in the newly installed Soviet government about signing a separate peace treaty with the Central Powers. One unfortunate result was the outbreak of civil war, in which British forces participated on the doomed side of the anti-Bolshevik "Whites." The historical setting for *The Key* is the early stage of the Irish War of Independence (1919–1921), in which British police and military units, especially the notorious Black and Tans, clashed in the crowded residential neighborhoods of Dublin with the urban irregulars of the Irish Republican Army, who, in a somewhat unusual move for Hollywood treatments of the "Troubles," figure as the villains of the piece.

Despite these representations of world-shaking events, however, *The Key* and *British Agent* focus not on political questions, but rather on individuals, drawn together by love, who find themselves trapped by conflicts in loyalties, following a familiar Hollywood pattern that Curtiz most famously exploited in *Casablanca* (1942). In that more famous later film, as in these earlier romantic thrillers (if we might call them that), Curtiz shows his talent in quickly and effectively staging the many talky interior set-ups needed to portray both the romantic relationships and the relevant political themes (in simplified form, of course). Consider what Mordaunt Hall, reviewing the film in the *New York Times*, has to say about *The Key*: "The picture is finished in an adroit fashion and it is so good that it seems to have taken only half the time it has" ("William Powell, Edna Best, and Colin Clive in a Story of the Black and Tans," *New York Times*, May 30, 1934). The chief qualities of these literary properties were their evident authenticity as well as the opportunities for complex, intriguing drama; the authors had been central participants in the events they recount. Viewers and critics were quick to notice and approve of how Curtiz and company had confected atmospheres in each case that were understood as realistic. As André Sennwald enthused in the *New York Times*, for example, "a situation richly veined with striking dramatic values has been utilized with considerable vitality in 'The British Agent'" ("'British Agent' with Leslie Howard Dramatizes an Incident from the Lockhart Book at the Strand," *New York Times*, September 20, 1934, 20). Hall was similarly impressed with the scope of *The Key* and its transference to the screen: "It is a story which gains much from its background, for the director, Michael Curtiz, has gone about his task with consummate artistry."

The Key screens a stage melodrama whose principal author was Jocelyn Lee Hardy, a retired army major who worked as an intelligence officer for the Royal Irish Constabulary, a unit that played an important role in confronting IRA gunmen. The previous year, the play that served as the source text had enjoyed a successful run in London's West End. *British Agent* drew on an international best seller, the quite sensational memoirs of the diplomat R. H. Bruce Lockhart, who first served in 1917 as the acting consul general in Moscow. Conveniently for the scriptwriter Laird Doyle, Lockhart's somewhat rambling account of his experiences in Russia includes a scandalous romance, his relationship with Moura Budberg, widow of a tsarist diplomat, that, as Lockhart frankly and in some detail relates, results in him being sent home in disgrace for some time before he returns in ever-deteriorating circumstances and with a slightly changed portfolio as the UK's first envoy to the Bolshevik government. The erstwhile political operative, exceeding his authority, then fails to prevent Russia's withdrawal from the war, arguing in vain for British support of the vulnerable regime.

In adapting Lockhart's confessional narrative, Doyle put a Hollywood spin on the material. The adventuresome Duchess Budberg (who worked, it seems, for the Bolshevik security chief, Genrikh Yagoda) became an even more exotic secret agent renamed Elena Moura. Incarnated by Kay Francis, then one of the studio's hottest female performers and reportedly Hollywood's most highly paid actress, Elena cannot resist the charming and somewhat frolicsome Englishman (Howard) and finds herself prepared to give up everything in order to run away from a Russia convulsed by violent change. The trailer promises that "glamorous" Francis is involved in a story that will "reveal every secret of the world's most beautiful spy," teaming her "for the first time with Leslie Howard." She was a perfect choice for this role if a sense of authenticity was desirable. Francis's career, onstage and then onscreen, was likely enhanced by her somewhat notorious personal life. By the time she made *British Agent* at age twenty-eight, Francis was twice divorced and married to her third husband, while several other amorous relationships, including one with Maurice Chevalier, had been making tabloid headlines (LaSalle 2000; O'Brien 2007). The former noblewoman whom Francis impersonated, having turned down a marriage proposal from fellow émigré Maxim Gorky, was living in England as the sometime mistress of H. G. Wells and the hostess of a literary salon whose frequent guests included such luminaries as Laurence Olivier, Graham Greene, and Martha Gellhorn.

When the film was released, the two celebrities at its center, still very much alive, had a certain notoriety that likely enhanced box-office appeal. *British Agent* seems to have been the first major screen biography to deal with contemporary public figures, and that gave the film a certain buzz.

194 R. Barton Palmer

The original screenplay called for the lovers to be killed by artillery as they shelter together in an abandoned building, but the inescapable fact that both protagonists survived the revolution in which they played interesting roles obviated this tragic finale, which *Variety* opined would have made it "a much finer picture"(quoted in O'Brien 2007, 136). To be sure, the passionate romance that develops between Lockhart (Locke in the film) and Moura is foregrounded as a counterpoint to the ever-shifting relations between the erstwhile allies that they separately represent; the story adopts a *multum in parvo* (much in a little) approach common in stories of this kind, as was later seen in David Lean's *Doctor Zhivago* (1965). The momentous changes that follow the fall of the Kerensky government conflict with Locke and Moura's desire to be together, which is satisfied in the story's hard to credit but mostly true finale, when the two are united after Locke escapes execution through an exchange of prisoners.

The Key conforms to Hollywood conventions slightly differently. The rakish Captain Bill Tennant (William Powell) in a penitential gesture sacrifices his military career in order to save the life of his friend Captain Andrew Kerr (Colin Clive). This somewhat hackneyed plot is entirely fictional, based only indirectly on authorial experience. Tennant in the past carried on with Kerr's wife, Nora (Edna Best), a passionate affair that, it seems, is about to resume; when Kerr discovers Edna's deception, he deliberately puts himself in harm's way and is abducted by the IRA. The disconsolate officer is slated for death unless the Sinn Fein leader Peadar Conlon (Donald Crisp), captured earlier by Kerr in a daring raid and now scheduled to face a firing squad for treason, is set free. Eager to save the friend whom he betrayed, Tennant forges an order for the rebel's release, knowing that he will be cashiered and imprisoned in consequence. The deception works. The film ends with Kerr set free and Tennant under arrest and on his way to prison, but still very much the bon vivant, unfazed by the bleak future that awaits him.

Class Politics, More or Less

In an era when criminality on a vast and highly profitable scale had become a fact of national life because of Prohibition, the much-publicized views of Warden Lewis Lawes on reformation created a storm of controversy that was increased by the publication of his memoir in 1932. Lawes advocated for the harsh but fair treatment of inmates, with a view toward preventing them from returning to crime after their release; controversially, he instituted a program of temporary furloughs, on the theory that maintaining family and social relationships during incarceration decreased the chances of recidivism upon release. Taking full advantage of Lawes's fame and the popularity of his memoir, Curtiz's 20,000 *Years in Sing Sing* showcases these ideas, but Brown Holmes's screenplay (one of many crime stories that he wrote for the studio in the decade) is hackneyed at best and mediocre at worst. In the tradition established by George Hill's *The Big House* (1930), the inevitable escape sequence does not focus on the main character, because Tommy Connors, convinced by the advice of Warden Lawes to "keep his nose clean," remains in his cell and for the most part out of range of Curtiz's camera. Surely, this is a violation of screenplay-writing rule number one, but there is nothing that a director can do to remedy such a fundamental problem.

Lawes rewards this demonstration of a changed heart by allowing Connors to visit Fay—even though this goes against then-existing policy—who is thought to be dying. But their reunion is disrupted when one of Tommy's former partners shows up. In the fight that follows, Fay shoots the man, who falsely accuses Connors (who has fled the scene) before dying. So powerful is the bond established between Lawes and Connors that the criminal returns to Sing Sing, even though it means he will likely face the death penalty. He pleads guilty in order to shield Fay, and is condemned despite Fay's confession. The state ends up executing an innocent man, but *Sing Sing* is no indictment of a system that, in punishing an innocent victim, can hardly be blamed when he cooperates in the error. Tommy dies for love, and his selflessness seems to have nothing to do with the radical egalitarianism at the heart of the warden's message. Lawes enjoyed script approval, and it seems no accident that much of the first half of the film is devoted to the comeuppance that the nouveau riche and arrogant Connors is made to endure in solitary confinement under the warden's careful management, which, after some weeks pass, makes the erstwhile "swell" eager to rejoin his fellows.

And so the film's ending is hopelessly contradictory. After the furlough, Connors returns to the prison and thus validates the warden's positive view of a malleable human nature. But this victory, which belongs to them both, is overshadowed by Connors's fall, however unwilling, into renewed criminality when, as the cliché puts it, his past catches up to him. An unfortunate turn of events costs him his life, making an unintentional mockery of the claim of the system to shield the innocent as well as punish the guilty. Curtiz was given access to the prison through Lawes, but the documentary sequences stunningly incorporated into the finished film do not

Warner Bros. marketed *The Key* (1934) as a true story, even though its political themes were only slightly developed. Digital frame enlargement.

indict a failing or inhumane system. *Sing Sing* was intended as a sequel of sorts to the studio's immensely popular *I Am a Fugitive from a Chain Gang* (Mervyn LeRoy, 1932), which showed the practice of chain-gang incarceration to be barbaric and inhumane and raised a national outcry against it. Curtiz's film, however, depicts a basically just penitentiary establishment needing only the minor adjustments that an enlightened manager like Lawes might implement, but these refinements, as the execution of Connors bears out, cannot eliminate the possibility of an irremediable subversion of justice.

Treating labor unrest in the Pennsylvania coalfields, *Black Fury* raises one of the principal economic issues that had roiled American society for decades. Conflicts between labor and management had been a constant, usually worrying aspect of the national experience, ever since the Industrial Revolution transformed the American economy in the second half of the nineteenth century. Simply by virtue of its subject matter, then, *Black Fury* can hardly be classified as other than a political film; it had a considerable impact on American culture even though it delivered no clear message about the problems it depicted. There were particular reasons why this subject was calculated, correctly, to be of particular interest at the time; once again, Warners was responding to current events in ways that were becoming a mark of the studio's engagement with the national culture. As the labor historians Robert H. Zieger and Gilbert J. Gall report, "union membership mushroomed" in the early 1930s, sweeping up "workers in every geographical area and in every trade and industry"; this was an unsurprising reflection of the increased "determination of working people to resist the victimization and distress that the depression had brought" (2002, 67). The result was not only increased government regulation of industries, like mining, that posed significant risks to workers. During this period, the advocacy of union membership through collective bargaining was legalized and institutionalized by the National Labor Relations Act (1935), which was, in the view of Zieger and Gall, "one of the seminal enactments in American history" because it established "basic machinery in the realm of labor relations" (80). In fact, the proposed legislation was being passionately discussed while the project that would become *Black Fury* was in development.

It is not too much to claim that *Black Fury* helped focus the nation's attention on labor unrest in the mining industry and the sometimes murderous strikebreaking efforts of private police forces, notably the notorious Pinkertons, hired by management. To be sure, Curtiz's film takes no position in regard to these transformative national developments, but it is certainly true, as Rudy Behlmer points out, that *Black Fury* "touched movie critics and fans on a nerve . . . the nerve that quickens to serious social issues," even though those at the studio were quick to protest that their only interest was a "harmless passion for gold" (Behlmer 1985, 55). Even more so than in *British Agent* and *The Key*, this was a story grabbed from the headlines, its script sourced from the "true" account of a sensational event provided by one of the participants, who became a celebrity as a result. In 1929, the murder of a miner named John Barkowski in Imperial, Pennsylvania, by operatives of the Coal and Iron Police force outraged the public, including the state legislator Mike Musmanno, who introduced a bill that would have banned the company from continuing to operate in the state. Although the bill passed, the Republican governor, advocating for the industry, vetoed it, prompting Musmanno to resign. Soon afterward, he published a story that lightly fictionalized the events in question; it eventually served as the basis for the screenplay that he was contracted to write for Warners, and decades later he turned it into a novel (Musmanno 1924).

Warners had another reason for its interest in coal mining. Hal Wallis and Harry Warner knew that the role of an uneducated but charismatic and sympathetic Slovakian miner would be perfect for Paul Muni, who had shown remarkable skill in creating exotic characters during his stage and screen career. In his second film, Berthold Viertel's *Seven Faces* (1929), he played all seven protagonists. In 1933, after his sensational performance in *Chain Gang*, one of the studio's biggest hits of the era, Muni was signed to a contract. As it turned out, he was eager to make a film about a mining industry troubled by widespread unrest, since the subject was, like *Chain Gang*'s prison conditions in the South, yet another one grabbed from the headlines. At the time the project was being developed, John L. Lewis, president of the United Mine Workers, was using his influence to unionize other industries under a new umbrella organization called the Congress of Industrial Organizations (Bernstein 1969). But the treatment developed by Musmanno offered Muni little opportunity to develop his character. To provide more material, he purchased an unproduced play (or perhaps an unpublished story—it is uncertain) called *The Bohunk*, which had been sent to him by the George McCall Agency. He then resold the property to the studio, and it proved to be of much use to Musmanno and the industry professionals Abem Finkel and Carl Erickson, with whom he collaborated and who functioned as his "beard" while work progressed (see Herzberg 2011, 42–48, for further details; these challenge Robertson's account [1993, 31–32] at certain important points). That the film belongs to Muni is beyond any doubt. To please his many admirers, *Black Fury* features a number of rather lengthy performance scenes meant to display the actor's considerable talents in creating with broad, stagy strokes a character fundamentally different from his sophisticated and urbane self. That the narrative otherwise moves along at an exciting pace is a tribute to Curtiz's always economical storytelling expertise.

Because it portrayed, with some sympathy, the dissatisfaction of miners with their working conditions, as well as management's intransigency in addressing them, the script encountered difficulty with studio bosses and Production Code Administration (PCA) censors. The approach taken by the writers, however, provided an acceptable way beyond promoting what might otherwise have seemed a primitive Marxist analysis of the conflict. Joe Radek (Muni) accidentally does the work of the detectives, who have infiltrated the union. While on a bender after his fiancée throws him over, he barges full of anger and bitterness into a meeting where the agitators are promoting a wildcat strike. With Joe's uncomprehending support, the proposal succeeds, and the union is split. The resulting strike bitterly divides the town as scabs are brought in to keep the mine operating. Joe ignores efforts to effect a reconciliation supported by the union president, his good friend Mike Shemanski (John Qualen). Shemanski is later mur-

As its trailer suggests, *Black Fury* (First National, 1935) was built up around sensationalized scenes of violence designed to provoke feelings of fear and terror. Curtiz delivered on this promise of engaging affect. Digital frame enlargement.

dered by the detectives, including their boss, McGee (Barton MacLane), who seriously injure Joe when he tries to save Mike.

Realizing as he recovers that he has put his community at risk, Joe barricades himself in the mineshaft, which he rigs with dynamite, threatening to blow it up if the company does not open negotiations with the union. A confrontation with McGee ends with the detective taken hostage. Joe manages to effect a peaceful resolution after the company is brought to the negotiating table and forced to admit responsibility of a sort. A federal investigation provides evidence that the dispute with the union was caused by the hired detectives, the leader of whom has skipped town; no matter, their organization has been discredited. In a strangely sideways engagement with the matter of the exploitation suffered by miners, Joe's drunkenness makes him the protagonist *malgré lui* in the escalating labor dispute. And it is Shemanski's death, as well as the attack on Joe by company goons, that "radicalize" him, so to speak, not some sudden insight into the real nature of the exploitation that shapes his life. As Thomas Doherty correctly observes, "preachment yarns" of this era such as *Black Fury* express the anguish of "the dispossessed and fearful" but fail to imagine what might relieve it (Doherty 1999, 53).

Black Fury, then, is no social realist tract. The film exculpates a management that might have been presented as more indifferent to the suffering of their employees. It is not because of the detectives that the owners short-change the miners on safety equipment while enforcing an unfair system of payment for each day's yield. Yet the villain of the piece becomes a third party with less skin in the industrial game than the owners or miners. As the project developed, the owners became less culpable in bringing about the dispute meant to wreck the union. In fact, as Bob Herzberg points out, it was Joseph Breen at the PCA who suggested to Warners that mine man-agement be shown opposing the strong-arm tactics of the contract detec-tives. As a result, in a significant alteration to the script, a scene was added in which the mine owner, John Hendricks (Henry O'Neill), directly orders his erstwhile employees (of whose schemes to incite trouble he is shown to be ignorant) to avoid violence and ensure the safety of the miners' fami-lies. As PCA records show, Breen was representing the interests of the National Coal Association, which was eager to avoid bad publicity during an especially volatile era; only a bit more than a decade had passed since the industry had endured in 1921 the so-called Battle of Blair Mountain, a deadly firefight between Pinkertons and striking West Virginia miners that left over 150 killed and saw nearly 1,000 miners subsequently brought to trial in the deadliest outbreak of labor unrest in the nation's history (Herz-berg 2011, 47; Shogan 2006).

Black Fury was appreciated at the time—not inappropriately—as shed-ding light on the kind of workplace trouble that the Progressive movement had pushed to the fore of American politics in the first decades of the twen-tieth century. As Claude A. LaBelle of the *San Francisco News* observed, Warners had failed "to come out and say what it really is, a conflict be-tween labor and capital." And yet the critic enthused that it was "the first film to . . . deal with something that is truly a part of our present social upheaval" (quoted in Herzberg 2011, 48). That political message had little to do with Curtiz, but much more with Muni (proud to be known as a lib-eral), Musmanno, and Warners (each enjoying similar reputations), and, of course, Breen. What redounds to Curtiz's credit is that *Black Fury* offers a well-paced and compelling narrative, replete with carefully staged crowd and action sequences. Among the many marks of Curtiz's brand of excel-lence is that footage shot on soundstages and in studio exteriors is care-fully given the same gloomy, dust-covered look as that of sequences shot in the authentically replicated "mine" constructed at Warners' Calabasas Ranch.

Mission to Moscow: **Message Delivered**

An interesting contrast with these early films featuring political atmospheres and themes is provided by *Mission to Moscow*, one of the five wartime morale boosters that Curtiz directed for Warner Bros. nearly a decade
later.[2] *Mission* treats events in which the Soviet Union figures most prominently, inviting comparison to *British Agent*; in fact, both films dramatize
the experiences of Western ambassadors sent to a Russia roiled by threat,
and both are based on presold literary properties. In 1933, the events of the
Bolshevik Revolution and its consequences must have seemed more than
a little exotic and distant to US moviegoers. Ten years later, however, the
United States and the film industry, which had become central to American life, found themselves in a very different place. What was happening
in Russia had become of vital national concern, and Hollywood could not
remain uninvolved (Koppes and Black 1987).

On December 7, 1941, a Japanese naval task force attacked US military installations on the Hawaiian island of Oahu. Four days later, an
unprovoked but supremely confident Hitler declared war against the
United States. Because in such circumstances the enemy of my enemy is
my friend, the United States immediately became an ally of the Soviet
Union, at war with Germany and its European allies since June. At the
end of 1941, America's new ally found itself in desperate straits, locked in
a titanic struggle upon which American hopes for victory were completely
dependent. A vast German army had invaded the Soviet Union in June in
what was the largest-scale military operation in world history, advancing
steadily across the vastness of western Russian territories. By late October,
it had destroyed much of the Red Army.

If there was to be any chance of preserving British independence and
wresting Western Europe from Hitler's grasp, then the Soviet military, as
President Roosevelt recognized, had, at any cost, to be kept in the fight
against the vast German-led multinational forces. Until a second front
could be opened, via invasion from southern England, Russia required
substantial material support from the United States, and that meant ap-
propriations from a Congress that was generally unsympathetic to the
Soviet Union, its institutions, and its values. These anti-Soviet views were,
unsurprisingly, shared by most ordinary Americans. A more favorable
opinion of America's new ally was necessary. And Hollywood enlisted in
this effort to change hearts and minds by producing a series of pro-Russia
films, of which *Mission* provided the most extensive portrait of Soviet
culture, emphasizing its strengths and downplaying its significant differ-

ences from the United States. As additional support for the Roosevelt administration, the film detailed the president's prescient preparations for a European war, from which the United States could hardly stand aside, in the process ridiculing the isolationism of many in the American political establishment. In delivering these messages, the film stayed largely faithful to its source, *Mission to Moscow*, the memoir of Roosevelt's ambassador to the Soviet Union, Joseph E. Davies, and one of the era's best-selling non-fiction books, first published in 1941.

Warners undertook this project with great seriousness, assigning the newly hired Robert Buckner to Curtiz as his producer. After a false start, the talented and experienced Howard Koch was signed on to do the screenplay. It was an astute choice; Buckner had just written the screenplay for *Yankee Doodle Dandy* (1942), the jingoistic biopic of the entertainment personality George M. Cohan, also directed by Curtiz, which Warners had just released with great success. As a British newspaper correspondent, he had, like Joseph Davies, spent time in Moscow. Buckner understood that his assignment was to produce propaganda, though he was knowledgeable enough to realize that much of the film's content would bend the truth and often break it. *Mission* is no political romance featuring a love affair between two of the studio's most glamorous stars. Its narrative can be best described as historical reconstruction, with studio players impersonating world figures such as Winston Churchill; Hitler's economics czar, Hjalmar Schacht; the Japanese diplomat Mamoru Shigemitsu; Joseph Stalin; and Franklin Roosevelt, among many others. The film has little to do with entertainment in the usual sense, though Curtiz and company made sure that *Mission* was not unpleasant to watch. Koch's script traces the gradual conversion of the initially skeptical Davies, a self-described "capitalist," to an admiration of sorts for what he believes are the substantial accomplishments of the Soviet regime. Returning to the United States in the summer of 1939, Davies fails to convince many in the Washington establishment that war in Europe and the Pacific is imminent, and that Germany and Japan pose a serious threat to US security and economic well-being. The principal concern of *Mission* is to cast a favorable light on the Soviet system, its people, and their determination to fight until victory is achieved, and it does much the same for Roosevelt's leadership. The president's prescient efforts to strengthen the American military and to secure lend-lease aid for Britain are shown to be indispensable to preventing an early collapse of the Allied cause.

The book anthologizes the numerous memos sent by Ambassador Davies to the president, who had charged him to "set forth objectively and dispassionately the facts connected with this extraordinary situation"; Davies's report was addressed "to my fellow Americans" (Davies 1941, xix). He concluded that the Russian leaders were "devoted to the cause of peace for both ideological and practical purposes" (xix). Davies found himself "disagreeing with them in many respects" and yet still "gave them credit for honest convictions and integrity of purpose" (xix). The film's positive portrayal of the Soviet Union, and of recent events in that country, including the so-called Great Purge (1936–1938), drew outraged comment from some quarters upon its release. Notably, a letter to Warners signed by a number of prominent political and intellectual figures, including Sidney Hook, Alfred Kazin, and A. Philip Randolph, protested that *Mission* "raises a most serious issue: it transplants to the American scene the kind of historical falsifications which have hitherto been characteristic of totalitarian propaganda" (printed in Culbert 1980, 257).

But the book and film found supporters as well, particularly among those who realized that a resilient Soviet Union would be central to America's winning its European war. The Broadway director Herman Shumlin thought criticisms of the property's pro-Soviet line not only irrelevant but also dangerous at a time of profound international danger; he wrote to the NAACP's director, Walter White, that the film "is an instrument for understanding and friendship between the allies, but it is being attacked by some whose hatred of the Soviet Union is greater than their desire to win the war" (printed in Culbert 1980, 258). It seems only somewhat true, as the critic David Culbert writes, that "all of Hollywood's skills were used to subvert an entertainment medium to sell a message in a risky and controversial fashion" (12). If, by subversion, Culbert means that during the war Hollywood made films like *Mission* that were short on truth-value in order to advance the national interest, he is absolutely correct. And yet many might agree with Shumlin that it hardly mattered whether this relentlessly positive account of Soviet history, politics, and culture was in many respects fantasy (as if, in any case, Hollywood films, in times of war or peace, should be judged by the truth-value of their representations).

Over the years, *Mission* has found more detractors than supporters, becoming, as Todd Bennett opines, "among the most infamous movies in American history" (2001, 490). That is no doubt true, but the question relevant to an assessment of Curtiz's participation in the project is whether the making of *Mission*, as Culbert suggests, was in fact "a tale of zeal gone awry, of misplaced enthusiasm" (11). The evidence suggests otherwise, and Curtiz's efforts in support of this important project should enhance, not detract from, his reputation. The director was asked to take on a motion picture fundamentally different from anything he had worked on before. *Mission to Moscow*, as *Variety* observed, was "truly a documentary; Hollywood's initial effort at living history," or what the industry would later term "pictorial journalism" or "films of fact." *Mission* was designed, in fact, to convey something like journalistic truth: "Every character is the counterpart of an actual person . . . The jolting realism of the likenesses is far from the least of the picture's interesting aspects" (review of *Mission to Moscow*, *Variety*, December 31, 1942). The film was not exactly Hollywood's "initial effort" at transcending the boundary between the fictional and the factual; Louis de Rochemont had introduced the docudrama form to American filmgoers in *The Ramparts We Watch* (1940), which was also designed to shape public opinion as the war in Europe became more threatening.

But pictorial journalism remained an unusual approach until the end of the war in 1945 (Palmer 2016). The other pro-Russia films of the period, such as Lewis Milestone's *Armored Attack* (1943) and Gregory Ratoff's *Song of Russia* (1944), were ordinary Hollywood fare, offering engaging fiction. Curtiz and Warners were presenting something as distinct from these war dramas as it was from the morale-boosting documentaries sponsored by the Office of War Information and supervised by Hollywood notables, including Frank Capra, John Huston, and John Ford. Unlike the "Why We Fight" series, for example, *Mission* made substantial demands on the viewer, for its material was, to quote the *Variety* review again, "of a highly intellectual nature, requiring constant attention and thought." The narrative involves constant changes of scene as the story moves from Europe to America and back again, depending upon a huge gallery of characters and consisting largely of nonstop dialogue about such topics as Soviet reaction to the appeasement of Hitler's aggression, the failure of the League of Nations to condemn Italian aggression against Ethiopia, the signing of the Molotov-Ribbentrop Pact as a prologue to the invasion of Poland, and the replacement of the Neutrality Act of 1939 by the Lend-Lease Act in 1941, which allowed the United States to help Britain substantially. What did Curtiz think of all this?

The film's producer, Robert Buckner, was something of an intellectual snob, but his account of the production and the particular challenges it posed for Curtiz seems particularly revealing, especially considering the discussion in this chapter of the director's so-called political films: "Curtiz, a Hungarian and totally unpolitically educated, had a great talent for graphic effects, but lacked any real understanding of the issues involved in *Mission to Moscow* (the book). Even after the script was finally written and approved, Curtiz had to be reminded almost daily of the meaning of the events he was directing. The fact that he succeeded in making the film fairly clear to the average person is a tribute to Curtiz's instinctive abilities as a director" (quoted in Culbert 1980, 252–253). Curtiz was nobody's fool, of course. He had been born into a well-off bourgeois family and given the finest education obtainable in his native Budapest, then one of Europe's cultural centers, dominated by a Jewish intelligentsia to which he had a ready entrée. After leaving Hungary to pursue his filmmaking career, he became a sophisticated citizen of the world, and like many of Hollywood's émigrés, he cultivated a certain commanding hauteur that put off many of those in the industry with whom he was to work. But he simply was not political.

Buckner's phrase "unpolitically educated" seems a particularly apt description of Curtiz's sensibility. If he had to be constantly reminded about the meaning of the events whose reconstruction he effected in *Mission*, it was only because he found them supremely unintriguing. Instead, he was interested in—and talented in—providing what Buckner terms "graphic effects," meaning the design of images that would be a source of considerable pleasure. *Mission* certainly repays close attention to Curtiz's blocking and composition, which in this film, as in others of this period, notably *Casablanca*, is beyond excellent, pleasing to the eye and always semiotically rich. But the greatest compliment that Buckner pays to his director is that he succeeded in making "the film fairly clear to the average person," no mean feat given the material to be screened; and we should observe that this is about as succinct a formulation of the primary goal of Hollywood filmmaking as one could hope for. *Mission* is a vehicle for the presentation of Davies's experiences and ideas; the film's prologue makes this clear by featuring the ambassador himself before his fictional avatar takes over the role. But Curtiz, as throughout his career, was responsible for the property's presentation, and it was in this that his true talents, what Buckner accurately identifies as his "instinctive abilities," made their compositional weight felt.

Notes

1. In his introduction to one of the many reprintings of *Memoirs of a Secret Agent*, R. H. Lockhart's son Robert claims that "Warners spent more money on *British Agent* than on any film they had previously produced," a large part of those expenses being the fee paid to Lockhart (Lockhart 1932, xi).

2. The others are *Yankee Doodle Dandy* and *Casablanca* (both 1942), and *This Is the Army* and *Passage to Marseille* (both 1943).

Works Cited

Behlmer, Rudy, ed. 1985. *Inside Warner Bros., 1935–1951*. New York: Viking.

Bennett, Todd. 2001. "Culture, Power, and *Mission to Moscow*: Film and Soviet-American Relations during World War Two." *Journal of American History* 88, no. 2 (September): 489–519.

Bernstein, Irving. 1969. *The Turbulent Years: A History of the American Worker, 1933–1940*. Boston: Houghton Mifflin.

Canham, Kingsley. 1973. *Michael Curtiz, Raoul Walsh, Henry Hathaway*. Hollywood Professionals, vol. 1. New York: Barnes.

Culbert, David, ed. 1980. *Mission to Moscow*. Madison: University of Wisconsin Press.

Davies, Joseph E. 1941. *Mission to Moscow*. New York: Simon & Schuster.

Doherty, Thomas. 1999. *Pre-Code Hollywood: Sex, Immorality, and Insurrection in American Cinema, 1930–1934*. New York: Columbia University Press.

Herzberg, Bob. 2011. *The Left Side of the Screen: Communist and Left-Wing Ideology in Hollywood, 1929–2009*. Jefferson, NC: McFarland.

Koppes, Clayton R., and Gregory D. Black. 1987. *Hollywood Goes to War*. London: Macmillan.

LaSalle, Mike. 2000. *Complicated Women: Sex and Power in Pre-Code Hollywood*. New York: St. Martin's.

Lockhart, R. H. Bruce. 1932. *Memoirs of a British Agent*. London: Putnam.

Musmanno, Michael. 1924. *Black Fury*. New York: Fountainhead.

Nolan, J. E. 1970. "Michael Curtiz: Thought Living to Work Is Better than Working to Live." *Films in Review* 21, no. 9: 525–548.

O'Brien, Scott. 2007. *Kay Francis: I Can't Wait to Be Forgotten*. Albany, GA: BearManor Media.

Palmer, R. Barton. 2016. *Shot on Location: Postwar Hollywood's Exploration of Real Place*. New Brunswick, NJ: Rutgers University Press.

Robertson, James C. 1993. *The Casablanca Man: The Cinema of Michael Curtiz*. London: Routledge.

Shogan, Robert. 2006. *The Battle of Blair Mountain*. Boulder, CO: Westview.

Sperling, Cass Warner, and Cork Millner. 1998. *Hollywood Be Thy Name: The Warner Bros. Story*. Lexington: University Press of Kentucky.

Zieger, Robert H., and Gilbert J. Gall. 2002. *American Workers, American Unions*. 3rd ed. Baltimore: Johns Hopkins University Press.

CHAPTER 15

Curtiz's New Western Aesthetic

HOMER B. PETTEY

Michael Curtiz's early westerns do not attempt to re-create nineteenth-century photographic or artistic aesthetics, and they offer more than just star vehicles for George Brent, Errol Flynn, and Olivia de Havilland. Instead, they represent profound cinematic experiments with color and sound, indicative of Curtiz's willingness to exploit the latest technologies available for filmmaking. *Under a Texas Moon* (1930), for example, was the first talkie western shot entirely in two-color dye-transfer Technicolor. Even in the surge years of 1929–1930, when an astonishing number of films used this new imbibition print process, *Under a Texas Moon* stood out for its attempt to set a series of firsts. While *Gold Is Where You Find It* (1938) was shot in Technicolor, too (the first western to use the newer, three-strip process), Curtiz's *The Adventures of Robin Hood*, of that same year, overshadows it in critical discussions of the history of cinema. Subtleties, strategies, and variations of color technique remain overlooked for *Gold Is Where You Find It*. *Dodge City* (1939) continued Curtiz's experiments with early Technicolor, especially in using color as a means to allow creative camerawork in action sequences. *Santa Fe Trail* (1940) was one of only two films shot using Vitasound, an experimental process developed by Warner Bros.

These westerns transformed cinema because their innovations created visual-aural spectacles that set generic expectations for the theatergoing public. In many respects, Curtiz ushered in the great age of the feature-length western, convincing studio executives that audience interest would result in sustainable profits. Moreover, John Ford's westerns owed their popularity to the tone and experimentation set by Curtiz during this period. Curtiz's western aesthetic, then, fits squarely within the advancements, both technical and commercial, of his new Hollywood.

Under a Texas Moon

The annus mirabilis for Technicolor was 1930, which saw over thirty feature-length productions and films containing sequences or inserts done in the process. Certainly for Warner Bros., even if not for the industry as a whole, Michael Curtiz dominated the field of Technicolor. *Under a Texas Moon* (1930) stands out as the first musical, talkie western to be shot entirely outdoors and to use two-strip (Process 3 [1928] in the development of Technicolor by Herbert Kalmus, Daniel Comstock, and W. Burton Wescott). The plot involves a Mexican womanizer, Don Carlos (Frank Fay), who initially becomes embroiled in a Texas border town's cattle-rustling troubles but then spends much of his time pitching musical woo and a passel of lies to as many señoritas as possible. In the end, he recovers the stolen cattle and rides back southward across the border with his newly acquired reward and his latest, blindly enamored señorita. Filming began in late July 1929 in several high-desert locations, in Red Rock Canyon, and in Palm Springs. All these caused color problems, as James Layton and David Pierce point out: "Late afternoon filming added a red tinge to the photography, requiring a shift to artificial light . . . Color balance changed and shadows shifted continuously as the sun moved across the sky" (2015, 223). This type of filmmaking lacked a full-color spectrum and exaggerated some colors too much. Placing the enormous Technicolor camera in a soundproof bungalow and having music blaring from a large horn posed logistical problems, too, for Curtiz, even though Ray Perkins's title song became a very popular hit and worked perfectly for Frank Fay's Mexican–cum–mock gaucho–cum–true lothario guitar serenades, which occur several times in the film and are set to a late-twenties croon rather than a south-of-the-border rhythm.

Even though both song and film were popular, they had detractors, especially in the Latin sections of New York City, where, according to the Cuban cineaste J. M. Valdés Rodríguez, the film was found "openly offensive to Mexican women," primarily in the numerous seduction scenes (quoted in Chanan 2004, 100). In snarky, derisive, and racist comments, the *New Yorker* found *Under a Texas Moon* entirely unsatisfactory, particularly in its use of Technicolor: "It is very Spanish, with *hombres* and *señoritas* and mandolins, all washed in especially ghoulish shades from the Technicolor palette. For one reason, though, the picture marks a step forward in the history of the cinema: it shows the first appearance on the screen of the Mexican jumping bean in a full-fledged role" (April 12, 1930, 111–112). That same week, however, *Variety* reported that the box-office gross of *Under a Texas Moon* "ran ahead of seasonal average," and that the "out of ordinary feature clicked," since "Technicolor pleased" the audience ("Texas Moon, $8,000 Balto.—Good Wk," *Variety*, April 16, 1930, 9). Since the film cost an estimated $500,000, Creighton Peet wanted more numerous romps with the ladies by the gay caballero, and in particular more shots of Myrna Loy, an actress whose "red hair and green eyes" were made for two-strip Technicolor, and who was the "only substitute for Greta Garbo" ("The Movies," *Outlook*, April 16, 1930, 632). Curtiz's initial setbacks with color did not deter him from continuing to experiment with this technical form in the western.

Gold Is Where You Find It

Hollywood's shift to three-strip Technicolor intrigued Curtiz further. He employed it for *Gold Is Where You Find It* (1938), the first western shot in this process. The film's early environmentalist plot pits gold-strike opportunists of 1877 against established wheat farmers. A new California gold-mining company, supervised by Jared Whitney (George Brent), exploits the region through hydraulic-cannon blasting. The company's leached runoff contaminates the wheat harvest of the valley's dynastic patriarch, Colonel Ferris (Claude Rains). His daughter Serena (Olivia de Havilland), who dreams of expanding her own orchards, falls for Whitney, and the plot becomes a series of complicated love-legal-familial showdowns. The dam-bursting finale in "glorious Technicolor," as *Billboard* contended, "washes the mine out and saves the fruitful California land for oranges, lemons, and Hollywood" (Dean Owen, *"Gold Is Where You Find It," Billboard*, March 5, 1938, 12). *Variety* found the film's color "swell," applauded the combination of pigmentation and pan shots, which evoked "gasps[,] so brilliant are they," and predicted that the film's business would be "blaze-bright in the sticks and subsequenters" (*"Gold Is Where You Find It," Variety*, February 16, 1938, 17). Warner Bros. launched a campaign for the film's George Washington's Birthday release by emphasizing the "new Multiplane Technicolor" and letting exhibitors know that a "story in pictures" was planned, as a three-week newspaper serialization and a "six-month build-up" of Clements Ripley's story in *Cosmopolitan* (*Gold Is Where You Find It* advertisement, *Variety*, February 2, 1939, 28). One week later, the studio announced that "all tracks are cleared for next week's exciting transcontinental premieres" for this "Miracle Technicolor" feature, "the supreme triumph of the color camera" ("The Great 'Gold' Shipment Has Started!," *Variety*, February 9, 1938, 20).

These spectacular results, however, were achieved by the cinematographer, Sol Polito, only with considerable artistic and technical skill. The Technicolor camera was much wider than conventional studio cameras. Three-strip Technicolor divided the aperture to split prismatic light, at ninety degrees, onto bipacked strips of black-and-white negative behind a magenta filter to allow for one sensitive to blue light and the other to red light; a third black-and-white negative sat behind a green filter in direct alignment with the lens. Significantly, this color-filtering system allowed film to capture a great range of the spectrum, especially yellows and golds, which visually enhanced the thematic content of *Gold Is Where You Find It*. The three-strip process required considerably more light than conventional studio photography. Additionally, eye focusing could not be readily exploited; rather, focus was determined entirely on the scale of the lens itself, which had to be specially designed: "Because of the prism block between the back element of the lens and the film gates, ordinary lenses could not be used in the Technicolor camera, and a special set was designed and made by Taylor-Hobson Ltd., but it included no wide angle or, very long focal length lenses . . . This weight and bulk militated against using the larger number of camera set-ups that were required by the shorter end of the Hollywood A.S.L. [average shot length] range" (Salt 1976, 31–32). Technicolor expanded the number of lenses of focal lengths from 25 mm to 140 mm, which then required a pair of "selsyn motors" to aid in calibration: "One is attached to the lens mount, and the controlling motor is held in the technician's hand" (Hoch 1942, 102). When developed, the new positives were black-and-white, each recording the presence of a single primary. These were transferred to three strips of matrix stock, dyed, and then pressed into a single print.

These specifications required inventive preproduction outlines for scenes, camerawork, shot selection, and coordination of lighting for set design, costume, and décor. Moreover, to diminish motor sounds, the entire camera had to be placed in a heavy soundproof metal container, known as a blimp, which greatly limited mobility. Shooting much of *Gold Is Where You Find It* outdoors meant that Curtiz had to invent new methods of filmmaking to accommodate the new process, including shifting from painted backdrops to actual locations while maintaining the same color palette. In many ways, Curtiz's gift as a director was his ability to keep in step with advancing technology and still achieve the high standards of Hollywood studio filmmaking. So good was Curtiz with the new methods that this film turned a respectable profit at the box office.

Long has this Curtiz western been overshadowed by his swashbuckler of the same year, *The Adventures of Robin Hood* (1938), even though

Warner Bros. conceived of the two million-dollar productions as a pair. In fact, it was Curtiz's ability to control Technicolor in his western that led Jack Warner to oust William Keighley in favor of him for *Robin Hood* (Robertson 1993, 43). Emphasizing numerous visual signals involving the color gold, Scott Higgins's admirable analysis of the technical and aesthetic design of color in *Robin Hood* aptly suggests new strategies adopted by Curtiz in *Gold Is Where You Find It*: Sir Guy of Gisbourne's costumes are "saturated with Flame Scarlet and Rich Gold"; interiors often "feature relatively strong contrasts of red, blue, and gold"; and, décor also employs "gold tones," from tableware to "yellow apples" (2007, 144, 146, 147). Because the older two-strip Technicolor often washed out, limited, or exaggerated color, this new, expansive process made chromatic aesthetics part of cinema conversation. L. O. Huggins, in "The Language of Color" (1934), proffered that emotions could be achieved through the "judicious use of colour," which would also grant colors abstract associations, for example: "Gold is ostentatious, proud. The 'language' it speaks is very definite. It always reminds us of money, riches, palaces" (quoted in Higgins 2007, 363). Natalie Kalmus, the wife of Technicolor's founder, served as color adviser for most early productions employing this new process, including *Gold*. In 1935, Kalmus wrote "Color Consciousness," her manifesto on the use of cinematic color, and asserted that the new color range offered the chance to express "dramatic moods" by the harmonizing effect of color. She lists these new colors, giving ample attention to yellow and gold, which "symbolize wisdom, light, fruition, harvest, reward, riches, gaiety; but, yellow also symbolizes deceit, jealousy, inconstancy in its darker shades" (2006, 26). In this film, golden hues represent Americans' fetishistic obsession with gold and the sadistic violence needed to acquire it.

Gold was literally everywhere one looked in Curtiz's new Technicolor western, from the opening credits to THE END. The film begins with a montage of gold strikes in the nineteenth-century West, as well as the "new gold, flowing yellow gold of wheat." To accentuate the diegetic environmental problem associated with the hydro-erosion process of using pressurized water cannons, Curtiz's first shots tint the water golden, add a gold hue to the earth and mud, and sustain that red-gold color in the runoff from the sluices. When Jared Whitney first meets seventeen-year-old Serena Ferris, she shyly offers him an apple—a golden delicious, of course—that matches the highlights in her hair. Throughout the first half of the film, the gold palette visually associates the mountainside gold mining with the destruction of golden wheat fields in the Sacramento Valley.

Olivia de Havilland's costumes often include patterned yellows, bright yellow candles illuminate dinner and hotel scenes, and in the final dam-bursting scene, earth and water maintain the red-gold hues of the opening sequence. The triumph of the farmers over the evil gold-mining capitalists culminates in a "New Eden" shot of Jared and Serena in the lower left of the frame, looking out over the valley awash in the golden rays of the California sun.

Dodge City

Curtiz's next western, *Dodge City* (1939), was also shot in the three-strip format. The film focuses on the degeneration of Dodge City from a capitalist dream of free enterprise and new cattle markets into a site of mob violence and hooliganism. Wade Hatton (Errol Flynn), a former Confederate scout who helped the film's Colonel Dodge bring the railroad to Kansas after the war, leads a wagon train of new settlers to Dodge City, but discovers to his dismay a town in anarchy. Of course, Wade is asked to be the new sheriff by the uncle of his prairie love interest, Abbie Irving (Olivia de Havilland), and of course he declines, only to put on the badge after cattle baron Jeff Surrett's (Bruce Cabot) men kill a young, feckless lad. The plot shifts from white-hat/black-hat conflict to the just man against mob rule as Wade has to protect one of Surrett's henchmen from would-be lynchers. What makes this western unique is the sophisticated use of Technicolor for extreme long shots of locomotives, wagon trains, and panoramas of the western landscape, with its blue skies and golden prairie, as well as for elaborate camerawork in shots of saloon scenes and of runaway horses in town.

In the *Film Daily*, Warner Bros. ran a six-page spread for an event billed as "The Dodge City Roundup" to promote "The Most Sensational Outdoor Drama Ever Put On Celluloid": "Broadcast over 193 stations—half-hour programs on both Blue and Red networks of NBC and MBS [Mutual Broadcast System]! . . . Simultaneous premieres in every theatre in Dodge City covered by 185 newspaper reporters from major cities!" ("*Dodge City*," *Film Daily*, April 4, 1939, 8–9, 10). The next week, *Variety* reported that Warners "set 327 dates . . . to immediately follow the premiere in Dodge City, Kan" ("WB's 327 'Dodge' Dates," *Variety*, March 29, 1939, 10), which would include "a rodeo, music festival and street parade," along with the stars of the film as well as "Marlene Dietrich, Hugh Herbert, Leo Carillo" and invitations from Kansas governor Payne

Ratner to the "governors of Texas, Oklahoma, Colorado, Nebraska, and Missouri" ("Dodge City Fetes Awaited by 125,000 With Film's Preem," *Variety*, March 29, 1939, 10, 8). Arthur Ungar reported that Hollywood stars and executives arrived in a train of fourteen cars, with two Eastern sleepers added, and had "an aerial escort of 25 planes and a fleet of motor vehicles" ("Hollywood Players Capture Dodge City at Record Premiere," *Variety*, April 5, 1939, 8). At the end of May, *Variety* reported that Curtiz's *Dodge City* had grossed an average of $100,000 each week since the Kansas premiere and forecast that this "Technicolor western is pointed to better than $2,000,000 domestic return, with the prospect of $1,500,000 from the foreign market" ("'Dodge City' Grossing at the Rate of $100,000 Weekly; Sears to Coast," *Variety*, May 31, 1939, 6). In fact, its grosses in the first week topped those for *Robin Hood*. The front page of the *Film Daily* contended that the popular appeal of the film was as much due to the "breathtakingly beautiful" Technicolor photography as to its "brilliantly directed and superbly acted" qualities ("'Dodge' Sensational," *Film Daily*, April 3, 1939, 1). *Variety*'s mid-April review of *Dodge City* recognized its "superbly lensed" Technicolor, noting that Michael Curtiz's "forceful direction" lifted this "badman-and-honest sheriff saga" into the "big leagues" and ensured that the film would be a "rough, tough meller, socko for b.o. results" ("Dodge City," *Variety*, April 12, 1939, 18; "meller" was *Variety* slang for "melodrama"). The nearly $1.5 million profit garnered by *Dodge City* assuaged Jack Warner's anxiety and reluctance to invest in Technicolor films (Robertson 1993, 50).

With the exception of the fiery saloon destruction in William S. Hart's *Hell's Hinges* (1916), no western had concentrated so much footage on the action of a bar brawl as did *Dodge City*. Curtiz's elaborately choreographed saloon fight was imitated in Sam Peckinpah's *Junior Bonner* (1972) and parodied in Mel Brooks's *Blazing Saddles* (1974). The scene begins as a comedy: Rusty (Alan Hale) inadvertently enters the Pure Prairie League, a women's temperance union, where he receives a bright gold flower button as his initiation into the new flock. Rusty stands before the women and proclaims his transgressions: "I reckon I was a pretty bad sinner before I saw the Light." "With tears in his eyes," specifies Robert Buckner's script, "he drops his voice to a tremolo note" and acknowledges his newly embraced passivity: "When I seen the Light—it just come to me all at oncet—An' now there ain't a more peaceful, a more quiet, law-abidin' man on Earth than me" (2007, *Dodge City*, 66, 68). All the while, next door in the Gay Lady Saloon, the chorus gal Ruby (Ann Sheridan) leads lawless inebriates in a rendition of "Marching through Georgia," to which the upright cowpokes counter with a raucous version of "Dixie." As expected, the combat of songs turns into a massive barroom brawl. (In 1942, Curtiz employed a song battle in *Casablanca*, with the French national anthem, "La Marseillaise," soundly defeating the Nazi rendition of "Die Wacht am Rhein" in Rick's Café Américain.) As is typical in Curtiz's westerns, the North-South moral division sympathizes with the southern cause, at least by not denigrating its proponents or former Confederate soldiers. As the barroom enactment of the Civil War rages, Rusty's "gentle as a lamb" confession comically recedes; he enters the fray when "all Hell breaks loose. . . . A ferocious series of rebel yells, gunfire, shouting, screams, all explode in one long terrific blast" (Buckner 2007, *Dodge City*, 69).

In the midst of the fracas, the camera easily follows Rusty because his bright gold flower button stands out. The shot selections consist of several overhead sequences interspersed with medium shots of fisticuffs and chair breaking, and close-ups, in match-on-action editing, of thrown and landed punches and bodies tossed through windows. In a revealing blue-and-red-trimmed chorus outfit, Ruby ascends a table and screams for everyone to stop, but finds herself among the fallen. The brawl escalates into full-blown destruction: the bar's giant mirror is smashed, and wranglers rope the large oak liquor case in order to topple it and the bar to the floor. In a wide shot of the ruined saloon, Rusty's pal Tex Baird (Guinn "Big Boy" Williams) victoriously announces, as former Rebels point guns at wounded former Union soldiers: "All right, you Yanks— there's *one* battle you didn't win!" (Buckner 2007, *Dodge City*, 71). The entire drunken skirmish lasts a full five minutes, and Curtiz employed no fewer than ninety edits, foregrounding color for the prominent characters. As the gun-firing, whooping Texas Rebs depart, Surrett's men discover a semiconscious Rusty behind the bar. The comedy turns deadly as they seize Rusty and haul him to the livery stable to be hanged in retribution for the brawl. In this mob, Rusty again stands out in both long and medium shots because of his gold flower. Wade saves Rusty from the noose, as he will save Dodge City from the hands of these nefarious western baddies. The climactic shootout and rescue takes place not on Main Street but aboard a blazing mail car on the Atchison, Topeka and Santa Fe train. Like Rusty's badge, yellow streaks of fire dominate both the long shots in location shooting and the studio setups. Curtiz's eye for color detail transformed a somewhat confused and hackneyed plot into a series of visual vignettes that became western clichés in the decades to come.

Santa Fe Trail

According to the *Film Daily*'s front-page announcement about *Santa Fe Trail* (1940), the film's success was due to its "grandiose scale" and "skillful direction, opulent production value" ("'Santa Fe Trail' Entertainment Hit," *Film Daily*, December 16, 1940, 1). *Variety*'s mid-December review applauded Curtiz's direction and those sonic elements that contributed to Vitasound: "Superb cameraing of Sol Polito, with special effects by Byron Haskin and H. F. Koenekamp, plus the excellent Max Steiner score, add much to production values" ("*Santa Fe Trail*," *Variety*, December 18, 1940, 16). In mid-November, *BoxOffice* reported that Warner Bros.' "Vitasound" would be "a new control system which, it is claimed, represents improvements in both recording and projection techniques" and would be first employed on *Santa Fe Trail* ("Warner Sound Engineers Announce New System," *BoxOffice*, November 16, 1940, 24). Ten days later, *Variety* covered the first press preview of this new sound projection system, which had been developed by Warners and RCA at the Burbank studio. For the project, Warners' sound department "turned the new development on an old picture, 'The Sister,' which featured an earthquake (fire) and gave the scribes an idea of what a real temblor is"; the trade publication noted that it would cost around $2,500 to reequip theaters with this new system ("WB Vitasound Improved By RCA," *Variety*, November 27, 1940, 5). Vitasound, according to Kenneth MacGowan, operated through three speakers "behind the screen"; dialogue came through the center speaker, and the musical score was "spread" by means of a "control pattern to bring in the side speakers" (1957, 385–386). As its inventors, Nathan Levinson and L. T. Goldsmith, describe this revolution in almost-stereophonic sound projection, the "control-track" on the film did not affect dialogue but rather increased the role of music and sound effects: "A control-track printed in the sprocket-hole area of standard release prints is employed to operate a variable-gain amplifier to secure the increased effective volume range and to operate a loud speaker switching relay for extending the source of sound to loud speakers beyond the screen" (1941, 148). Along the left side of the film, a separate photocell printed these "control-track" directions, which did not interfere with soundtracks or impede projection in theaters that were not newly equipped for Vitasound, "provided the film is threaded over the control lamp to miss the control-track attachment" (152). The inventors regarded the experiments at Warner Bros.' Hollywood Theatre in Los Angeles and the Strand Theatre in New York City as "effective, reliable, and trouble-free in operation," which turned out to be

Shot, cannon blast, wall crumbling sequence from *Santa Fe Trail* (Warner Bros., 1940). Digital frame enlargements.

hardly the case during the commercial release of *Santa Fe Trail* in theaters unequipped with the system (152). Vitasound's multispeaker system surrounded audiences with sound in order "to heighten the *spectacle* of film" (Kerins 2011, 23). As with the use of early Technicolor, Curtiz envisioned cinematic possibilities for this new intensification of sound, particularly in the many battle scenes he arranged for this film.

Because of the additional costs associated with Vitasound, Curtiz shot *Santa Fe Trail* in black-and-white. Bloody Kansas serves as the backdrop for this peculiar, ahistorical treatment of John Brown's (Raymond Massey) conflicts. Fresh from their recent West Point graduation, Jeb Stuart (Errol Flynn) and his classmate George Custer (Ronald Reagan) are sent by Commandant Robert E. Lee (Moroni Olsen) to Kansas to punish them for fighting in the barracks with the abolitionist infiltrator and agent provocateur Carl Rader (Van Heflin), whom Lee expels with a dishonorable discharge. (Custer graduated eight years after Stuart, but this is Hollywood-style history.) The first great battle occurs when Brown's abolitionists raid the wagon train bearing Beecher's "Bibles" (concealed rifles). When Stuart and Custer chase the abolitionists, the resulting mul-

tiple camera angles, rough horse falls, and runaway wagons are filmed in a montage combining long shots, medium shots, and close-ups, not unlike what can be seen in John Ford's choreography of the now-famous Apache attack a year later in *Stagecoach* (1939).

The culminating battle at Harpers Ferry remains one of Curtiz's most enduring sequences. In just over twelve and a half minutes, Curtiz renders Brown's takeover of the armory, the arrival of Lee's brigade, the battle, and the recapture of the armory by the US troops in 220 shots, an exhilarating pace of nearly a shot every three and a half seconds on average. Robert Buckner's script reveals the cinematic plan for this quick pacing of shots:

> MONTAGE
> THE BATTLE OF HARPERS FERRY
> These shots, building excitedly and in rapid succession, should be as short and fast as was the actual final attack on the Arsenal, which was ended only fifteen minutes after Stuart gave his signal. (2007, *Santa Fe Trail*, 154)

Curtiz coordinates these edits to correspond to close-ups of gunshots, medium shots of rifle reports, and long shots of cannon blasts, which, along with Max Steiner's military score, create a new cinematic soundscape. Horses tumbling, bodies hitting the ground, walls exploding from cannon fire: all contribute to this film's groundbreaking visual and aural action sequences. In theaters, Vitasound raised the decibels to accompany weapon fire echoing from the peripheral speakers, allowing shouts and commands to reverberate from the central speaker. The daybreak execution of John Brown likewise uses the split-sound technique as Brown delivers his famous courtroom address on the scaffold: "Crimes of this guilty land will never be purged away, but with blood" (Buckner 2007, *Santa Fe Trail*, 159). His hanging is recorded on the faces of the witnesses as "softly, gently, like the first far-off rumble of an onrushing storm, comes the yet-unwritten MUSIC of 'John Brown's Body,' the powerful hymn to which five million Americans were soon to chant marching into Civil War" (160). Curtiz reverses this sound strategy of human speech segueing into dramatic music in the final scene, which provides a "FULL DOLLY SHOT" of a train car with the wedding between Jeb and Kit (Olivia de Havilland), which commences as "gradually the haunting music of 'John Brown's Body' gives way to Mendelssohn's 'Wedding March'" (160) before fading to the preacher's words countermanding Brown's curse: "whose shining paths shall run together from this day hence, unto Eternity" (161).

Late Westerns

In his final decade, Curtiz continued his experiments with the relatively new, two-year old WarnerColor, the studio trademark tag for Eastmancolor, for *The Boy from Oklahoma* (1954), starring Will Rogers Jr. WarnerColor superseded the cumbersome three-strip Technicolor by employing a single-strip negative. The process used cyan, yellow, and magenta dye couplers on a single emulsion support. These reacted "simultaneously during development to produce a separate dye image in each layer," thereby mimicking the Technicolor process (Ryan 1977, 151). Moreover, Eastmancolor's "integral tripack camera films" did not require a special camera but could be "used in a standard black-and-white camera" (Craig 1953, 149). This new way of color filming was more portable and flexible than other color processes, and reduced studio costs considerably. In response, Technicolor contractually agreed with the Eastman Kodak Company to process its negative stock and sometimes dye-transfer print from it, thereby retaining its trademark on films (Andrew 1979, 49). Curtiz's *The Proud Rebel* (1958), with Alan Ladd and Olivia de Havilland, was an example of this rich color technique, which used a very mobile camera and an exceptional color process. Economic factors in the marketplace certainly affected studio decisions to employ color, especially since an increased share of viewers were staying home to watch television. WarnerColor was a cost-effective means of remaining competitive in the early to mid-1950s, when over half of all films were shot in Technicolor, whereas by 1958 only 25 percent of features were made in color (Kindem 1979, 35).

Curtiz's experimental aesthetic, then, can be viewed also as an economic experiment, one that did not always pan out for him. Evidence for this can be seen in the modest success of his career after leaving Warner Bros. in 1953: "According to Warner Brothers [*sic*] only one of the eleven Curtiz Production Company films made a profit" (Peterson 2005, 149). Such a crass, self-serving statement does not do justice to Curtiz's final years. As an independent director, he achieved notable success aesthetically, especially with *The Proud Rebel* and at the box office with his final work, *The Comancheros* (1961), printed in Deluxe Technicolor and in CinemaScope. Michael Curtiz died from cancer shortly after the premiere of *The Comancheros*. To the end, he maintained an aesthetic vision of the possibilities for innovative technologies in filmmaking, which may well be his legacy to the art of cinema.

Works Cited

Andrew, Dudley. 1979. "The Postwar Struggle for Color." *Cinema Journal* 18, no. 2: 41–52.

Buckner, Robert. 2007. *Dodge City*. Screenplay, October 14, 1938. Alexandria, VA: Alexander Street Press.

———. 2007. *Santa Fe Trail*. Part I. Revised final screenplay, July 2, 1940, Alexandria, VA: Alexander Street Press.

Chanan, Michael. 2004. *Cuban Cinema*. Minneapolis: University of Minnesota Press.

Craig, G. J. 1953. "Eastman Colour Films for Professional Motion Picture Work." *British Kinematography* 22, no. 5: 146–158.

Higgins, Scott. 2000. "Demonstrating Three-Colour Technicolor: Early Three-Color Aesthetics and Design." *Film History* 12, no. 4: 358–383.

———. 2007. *Harnessing the Technicolor Rainbow: Color Design in the 1930s*. Austin: University of Texas Press.

Hoch, Winton. 1942. "Technicolor Cinematography." *Journal of the Society of Motion Picture Engineers* 39, no. 8 (August): 96–108.

Kalmus, Natalie M. 2006. "Color Consciousness" [1935]. In *Color: The Film Reader*, edited by Angela Dalle Vacche and Brian Price, 24–29. New York: Routledge, 2006.

Kerins, Mark. 2011. *Cinema in the Digital Sound Age*. Bloomington: Indiana University Press.

Kindem, Gorham A. 1979. "Hollywood's Conversion to Color: The Technological, Economic, and Aesthetic Factors." *Journal of the University Film Association* 31, no. 2 (Spring): 29–36.

Layton, James, and David Pierce. 2015. *The Dawn of Technicolor, 1915-1935*. Rochester, NY: George Eastman House.

Levinson, Nathan, and L. T. Goldsmith. 1941. "Vitasound." *SMPE Journal* 37 (August): 147–153.

MacGowan, Kenneth. 1957. "Screen Wonders of the Past: And to Come?" *Quarterly of Film, Radio, and Television* 11, no. 4 (Summer): 381–393.

Peterson, Paul. 2005. "Michael Curtiz: The Mystery-Man Director of *Casablanca*." In *Political Philosophy Comes to Rick's: "Casablanca" and American Civic Culture*, edited by James F. Pontuso, 135–152. Lanham, MD: Lexington.

Robertson, James C. 1993. *The Casablanca Man: The Cinema of Michael Curtiz*. London: Routledge.

Ryan, Roderick T. 1977. *A History of Motion Picture Color Technology*. London: Focal Press.

Salt, Barry. 1976. "Film Style and Technology in the Thirties." *Film Quarterly* 30, no. 1 (Autumn): 19–32.

CHAPTER 16

Michael Curtiz's Gamble for Christmas

MURRAY POMERANCE

While rhapsodizing about generally recognized artistic "genius," it can be difficult to find room for discussion of basic technical principles and operations. Thus may we detect in the many deprecating discussions of Michael Curtiz as a film artist—for instance, Andrew Sarris's labeling him "lightly likeable" or "the most amiable of Warners' technicians": "If many of the early Curtiz films are hardly worth remembering, none of the later ones are even worth seeing" (1996, 175-176); or Todd McCarthy's casual notation that by the mid-1950s, Howard Hawks had been "relegated to the *second tier* of Hollywood filmmakers" such as Curtiz (and William Wellman) (1997, 565; emphasis added)[1]—a distinct lapse of attention to what it is that directors do on set, how a director "directs," and how the challenges besetting any particular production might render such work more or less "heroic."

The Hack Auteur

While preparing for a shoot, directors are involved with screenwriters, intensively (as was Hitchcock) or at a relative distance; and wrapped in discussions with designers, costumers, and cinematographers about aesthetic issues. Once principal photography begins, a signal aspect of the director's work is the management of setups, almost always undertaken in collaboration with the assistant director(s). Where on the studio stage or at a location will action take place? Where will the camera be placed to "see" it, and will the photography be stationary or moving? Who is where in the shot (which performer gets the most light)? The intended composition will have much to do with such arrangements, and the ongoing flow of a narrative action, broken into a mere fragment in the shot, will be similarly dictatorial. Yet there are many ways to make a beautiful picture in which special attention is focused on a movement, a phrase, an expression, a gesture, or a collection. Which way shall be chosen? What are the implications of such a choice?

One interesting and illustrative case: Ronald Neame was confronted with special opportunities for picture construction as he shot his first CinemaScope feature (and one of the earliest produced) for Fox, *The Man Who Never Was* (1956). In 1999 he recollected to Barbara Roisman Cooper:

> Beauty of the wide screen is that you can get 2 more characters into the picture whilst not having to move the camera back. If I'm on the old shape [the Academy ratio of 1.33:1], I can put you and somebody else, and that fills the screen at waist figure. If I want 2 more people, I've got to go back to knee figure, which means I have to pull back; you lose the intimacy. With the wide screen, you have those 2 wings, as it were, to add to. A lot of people shoot on wide screen but don't use the width. They still put the characters in the middle. . . . Up 'til then, the thought was; because we have a wide screen, we won't have to go in for closeups and we'll save money by the number of setups. That was very foolish because you don't go into close shots in order to see better but to emphasize and use choreography, really, a sequence that you start back and gradually work forward as the drama works forward. (Neame 1999)

Even if the emphatic close-up adds expense by multiplying the number of setups required on the soundstage, the master shot and the action shot are insufficient, and close-up angles are occasionally needed.

More urgently for Neame in Culver City, however, and very much equally so for Curtiz working on *White Christmas* on Melrose Avenue at the same time, the pressure to economize on setups was a principal— perhaps *the* principal—factor in shaping directorial work on set. Assistant directors measured their success in significant part by the number of setups they could accomplish for the director in a working day (Rubin 2015). The director's need was to tell a story visually in the most economical way possible, and given the exigencies of studio production, in which stars varied in their personal styles of expressing commitment to a collective endeavor and in which technical complexities were always a threat, no matter the skill and experience of the crew, efficient narration finally meant getting forces together to make a shot, dismantling afterward, and getting forces ready for another shot, without undue delay. The successful filmmaker (in studio terms, one who brings in his project on or below budget and not late) has learned a repertory of setups that work expressively for him and for audiences, and knows, with his particular cast and crew, how challenging it will be to use any one of them. This managerial role—it is essentially an aggregation under one personality of the responsibility for mobilizing, organizing, and marshaling the work of a highly trained multitude—was of primary importance to the studio, as was shown, in the case of *White Christmas*, by Curtiz receiving a salary of $186,000, whereas the famous (and somewhat eccentric) Bing Crosby, whose voice had been associated with Irving Berlin's signature tune since 1942's *Holiday Inn*, earned $36,000 less.[2]

As with other forms of collaborative factory labor, producing and maintaining efficiency on a set involve flexibility of choice and a certain freedom of attitude, notwithstanding an overall imperative to work to the clock. Quirks of personality or demeanor are tolerated until and unless (as in the celebrated case of Judy Garland on *The Barkleys of Broadway* or the painful case of Marilyn Monroe on *Some Like It Hot*) they threaten or act to block production altogether. In the case of *White Christmas*, Curtiz had to live with movie-star "personalities," a normal cost of doing business in Hollywood: Danny Kaye had a bent for impetuous improvising—"whapping" Crosby with a "big blue feather fan" repeatedly during the males' takeoff of "Sisters" (Clooney 1989, 110), for example—and Crosby would not relinquish his sense of control: "Even though Curtiz was a celebrated director . . . and even though Danny Kaye had his own agenda and a very strong ego, Bing was always in charge. Sometimes he'd just disappear. He'd say, 'I'm going over the wall.' Nobody would know where he went, and nobody would ask" (111).

Sometimes the problematic personalities are above one's head. In his long years of serving the interests of Jack Warner, Curtiz had learned the limits of his directorial control. Warner signaled to Hal Wallis on January 11, 1935, for example, "I think it is a shame to let people like Curtiz . . . even think of opposing an order coming from you or myself" (Behlmer 1985, 19). The lack of respect coming from the top down was undeniable: "I had a general conversation with Mike Curtiz in the usual Curtiz manner in the dining room at noon, and all he talked about were the sets and that he wants to build a fort somewhere else, and all a lot of hooey. I didn't hear him say anything about the story. In other words, he's still the same old Curtiz—as he will always be!" (Warner to Wallis, in ibid., 29). The same old Curtiz, interested, with a visual mind hard at work, in how things might be made to look onscreen rather than on a page.

With Crosby sometimes skipping rehearsals for *White Christmas*'s musical numbers, on the success of which the production signally banked, it fell to Curtiz to work out his coverage with stand-ins and to forgo opportunities for improvising adjustments. For Curtiz, on this as on all his pictures, the placement and movement of the camera trumped actors and their foibles, since more than what any star was spectacularly doing in a story, Curtiz's camera was spectacularly revealing it.[3] With *Captain Blood* (1935), as Thomas Schatz observes, "Curtiz learned to rely less on [Errol] Flynn's acting skills than on his mere screen presence" (1988, 209). According to James Cagney, who worked with the filmmaker five times: "Mike was a pompous bastard who didn't know how to treat actors, but he sure as hell knew how to treat a camera. He was one of those few directors who could, at need, place a camera where it would do the most good" (McCabe 1997, 119). Ronald Davis supports this view: "[Curtiz] worked fast and was at his finest moving masses of people. . . . His expertise was with the camera; he was concerned always with the panoramic effect, and he had little to say on intimate scenes, assuming actors knew what they were doing" (1993, 76).[4] Curtiz's brusque quality may have lent his soundstage an unfriendly quality; he certainly operated on the side of management, not labor, as could have been seen by his joining Walt Disney, Ginger Rogers, John Wayne, and others on February 7, 1944, at the Beverly Wilshire Hotel's ballroom (familiar to readers, no doubt, as the site of the annual Golden Globe Awards) to form the Motion Picture Alliance for the Preservation of American Ideals (Eyman 2010, 397).

About the quirkiness of performers and the subtlety of their technique, Curtiz was far from uninformed, having himself worked as an actor in the Hungarian and German theater. Cagney—not only one of the most disciplined screen presences that Curtiz ever filmed but also, in *Yankee Doodle Dandy* (1942), a brave harbinger of the musical performers he would come to frame comfortably in *White Christmas*—offers a revealing (and charming) anecdote:

> He arrived one day on the set with a very specific idea of how a particular scene should be played. I said, "Go ahead, Mike. Show me how you want it." He went in and played it with all the old fancy European techniques—brushing off the cuffs with a flick of the finger, reaching fussily for a cigarette and lighting it with a flourish, then putting his foot up on a bench, and proceeding to talk with one hand on the hip.
>
> "All right, Mike," I said, "now I'm going to do just as you suggested. I want you to watch closely." I'm a fairly good mimic, so I got before the

camera and did it exactly as Mike had worked it out. When I finished, I asked him what he thought.

"I guess I'm a pretty lousy actor, huh, Jimmy." (Cagney 2005, 150)

"Increased-Size" Motion Pictures

Curtiz's break from Warner Bros. came in 1953, after he completed *The Boy from Oklahoma*. He made a single film, *The Egyptian*, for Darryl F. Zanuck—who had protested strongly to Warners that Curtiz was a free agent and that he had done nothing to lure him to Fox: "If you fail to sign him, then he is on the open market, and I will do my utmost to convince him to come with us" (Behlmer 1993, 79)—moving in the fall to Paramount for his maiden voyage, *White Christmas*. At Paramount, the timing was particularly auspicious for "setting sail," with *Rear Window* shortly to begin shooting on Stage 18. Exciting technical developments were in the wind, as well. Since the success of Cinerama in 1952, Herbert T. Kalmus's Technicolor Corporation had been thinking through possibilities for "increased size motion pictures" (*Independent Film Journal* 1954), undertaking close work with Paramount's technical head, Loren Ryder.[5] With Curtiz on the books—at least on paper—since the end of April, prerecording and rehearsals for *Christmas* could begin on September 14, 1953, with cameras turning the following week.

But work paused shortly thereafter because Paramount made a significant decision. Patrons attending the gala premiere on October 14, 1954, were to learn, by way of the sumptuous program—printed on cream card stock with red and green covers—that "Although only one VistaVision camera was in existence, Paramount, as a test, decided to shoot initial scenes of 'White Christmas' in this process, side by side with the conventional camera. The results were magnificent, and after the third day of shooting, the studio made the final decision—to gamble on filming the most costly and biggest musical in Paramount's history entirely in the new process." Some ten or twelve days into shooting, an internal memorandum verifies that the "'horizontal' camera or, as it has been nicknamed, the 'Chinese' or 'C' camera" was being used "alongside our regular cameras" on the picture (Frank Caffey [production manager] to Eugene Frank [of Paramount's legal department], September 24, 1953).

VistaVision became industry news early in 1954. On March 15, Kalmus issued a press release to state that his company was in the process of producing "six eight-perforation, horizontal-movement cameras used in

the Paramount-developed process"; Kalmus was "lavish in his praise of
VistaVision and unstintingly enthusiastic regarding its future and what it
is equipped to contribute to the betterment of the production and exhibition of motion pictures" (*BoxOffice* 1954). Further, he disclosed, "Paramount Pictures, VistaVision pioneer, will make all its color films this year
in VistaVision with Technicolor" (*Independent Film Journal* 1954).

White Christmas was photographed until the first week in December
1953, using a modified Mitchell camera, now with horizontal feed, from
Technicolor. The film stock was Kodak's Eastmancolor Negative. While
by this point the bulky Technicolor three-strip camera was not yet on the
way out (it would be mothballed about a year later, in large part because
Kodak ceased production of the black-and-white recording film it used),
the call was made for a smaller camera and for Technicolor to process
the film. Often in Hollywood in the early 1950s, a camera was loaded
with an emulsion-coated Kodak negative stock, from which the Technicolor laboratory could strike red, green, and blue matrices by a technique
of filtered contact printing; thence, the normal imbibition process could
be undertaken to make a standard Technicolor print. As an expert in the
history of Technicolor puts it, "No other multihued process was able to
match the ultrasharp appearance, vibrant color or grain free image. For
standard flat and scope releases, the competing labs like WarnerColor and
DeLuxe continued to send their top features to Technicolor for dye transfer printing" (Haines 1993, 119). With VistaVision, the camera negative
had a frame size two and a half times what it had been, since two typical
35 mm frames were joined laterally to make each frame. Matrices had to
be struck through projection rather than contact printing, but once the
frames were shrunk to "normal" size on regular 35 mm matrix stock, an
image could result that had so radical a decrease in grain that the final
projection—especially if theaters were able to use the large screens that
Paramount enthusiastically encouraged—would be not only enormous beyond comparison but virtually grain-free to the human eye. Coupled with
the potent saturation and rich blacks of Technicolor's imbibition printing,
the picture would be a stunner. "We have never before seen pictures on so
large a screen with such clarity, smoothness, visibility and freedom from
grain and with full preservation of magnificent color values," wrote the
New York Times (1954) after a test run.

There were increasing costs for moving ahead with VistaVision, even
beyond the production of the hardware. Technicolor possessed only one
printer capable of handling the horizontal negative, for instance, and this
limitation resulted in the lab taking more time to return color dailies than

black-and-white ones. It fell to Curtiz to decide which particular shots and scenes should be ordered in color, and which, for time savings, could be seen without (Charles F. West [head of the editing department], memorandum to Robert Emmett Dolan [producer of *White Christmas*] and Michael Curtiz, October 1, 1953). Eager to benefit from the expansion of Vista-Vision cinematography, Technicolor was still careful to protect itself. In a letter of contract to Paramount, whereby the corporation agreed to make four release prints of the film for screening at New York's Radio City Music Hall on October 14, 1954, Technicolor stipulated: that it would have to make changes in one of their printers to do the work, and that Paramount would have to reimburse the company for the cost involved in the change and in restoring the machine to its original condition afterward; that no firm guarantee could be given that the prints would be ready, but that Paramount could have as many as twenty-one further release prints within sixty days, at 11.25 cents per linear foot; that while printing was happening, the machine would be unavailable for Paramount orders on other pictures; and that all the work contemplated was to be considered experimental (David S. Shattuck [Technicolor executive] to Paramount, September 17, 1954)—which is to say, some difficulties and glitches were to be tolerated.

Curtiz's first trip out at Paramount was thus to be a major investment and a major gamble. The company's plans were to compete with Fox's proprietary CinemaScope and to use VistaVision for the next several years on all color features.[6] If *White Christmas* failed to impress, Paramount stood to lose in a big way. Then, ten days before the premiere, the company announced that for theaters with screens 50–100 feet in width, it could offer a lateral-feed projector, built by the Century Projector Corp., that would take film that had been specially contact-printed directly from the enormous VistaVision negative. This large-frame positive image would be "the largest ever photographed and projected from 35 mm. film" (Paramount, studio memorandum on VistaVision projection, October 5, 1954).

A Highly Creative Inventive

I do not put forward the argument that in helming *White Christmas*, Michael Curtiz contributed signally to the mythic structure of our culture or played in fascinating new ways with important sociological or psychological themes. The film is in every sense a matter-of-fact, businesslike, and clean-cut illustration of its story, and that story, told many times before through countless variations, has two loyal boys falling in love with two charming girls, caught in a chain of circumstantial traps (typically produced by incomplete or false understanding), patiently braving their way forward, and finally coming upon the reward of marriages that promise a happy future, all finally in the context of a snowy, gift-larded Christmas celebration with nostalgic bromantic undertones. Backgrounding the principal quartet is an aging former army general, Tom Waverly (Dean Jagger), who has put all his savings into a Vermont Inn that now, nearing Christmas, is without visitors and in danger of closure because there has been no snow. As Bob (Crosby), Phil (Kaye), Betty (Rosemary Clooney), and Judy (Vera-Ellen) make their way to this locale, where they are contracted to perform, they become caught up in the old man's predicament: the two boys were in his unit in the war, and the girls are hooked into romantic attachments with them. Through a blitzkrieg of warm bondings, angry partings, miscommunicated devotions, and complicated pullings of strings, it turns out that Bob is able to use (the still-new popular medium of) television to "secretly" call all the men of the army unit to come up to the inn in support of the old man. Hundreds of soldiers arrive with their wives, a gala concert performance is held—in which our heroes, dressed as Santa Clauses, belt out "White Christmas"—and in the final moments, redeeming snow begins to fall.[7]

In the best of Hollywood's musical traditions, the finale is arranged as a show within the show, curtains at the inn parting as an orchestra ramps up to the anthemic title song and the quartet glides onto the stage in Technicolor-red Santa outfits while an angelic little ballerina in sparkling silver emerges from behind the giant tree at center stage. Curtiz cuts to two-shots, offering first Clooney and Crosby, their eyes atwinkle, grey-blue and grey-green, informing us they are dreaming of a white Christmas; then cutting to Ellen and Kaye (like Curtiz, Jewish) singing, "Just like the ones I used to know." As "treetops glisten and children listen," still more little ballerinas emerge, now in radiant red, along with sweet little boys got up as junior Santas. An angled long shot (a Curtiz trademark) reveals this is all "only" a stage set, with gelled spots shining from the wings. It could hardly seem more constructed—we must really take the constructedness *as* the construction—with the spangles shining in the costumes, the fluffy fake ermine in the hats, the cardboard trees in the background, the off-scene chorus's white-bread harmony swelling like the snowy hillocks in *Citizen Kane*. Grain-free VistaVision shows even the delicacies of colored light reflecting from individual strands of tinsel on the tree! The two couples hide momentarily behind the *Tannenbaum* for some requisite plot-resolving smooching as the choir harps on in front of the barn full of eager soldiers. But as Crosby signals with his arm, the backdrop is suddenly raised, the tree slides abruptly away, and through the picture window that backs the stage we see a "real reality": a Vermont evening in the snow. Bing and Danny signal to the audience to sing along. The camera pulls back, past the lip of the stage, past the orchestra, past the tables, past the singing guests, to old Tom. And then—on Stage 16, Saturday, December 7, the twelfth anniversary of Pearl Harbor—back, back, back we go, away from Vermont, away from the now-lost vista of love and generosity, as the last chord of "White Christmas" resounds and dissolves in those irrevocable words, "The End."[8]

Working under Pressure

More important about *White Christmas* than its anodyne content (the high points seem designed to resemble Hallmark cards), and more revealing about the film as a part of Curtiz's remarkable career, is the simple fact of its existence, given the unprecedented pressures under which it was made. Curtiz's company included not only the relative ingénue Rosemary Clooney, terrified at the prospect of dancing with the veteran Vera-Ellen and the thought of duetting with the great crooner Bing Crosby, but also the terrifyingly spontaneous Danny Kaye. A Paramount production memo scathingly read:

> Mike Curtiz is a highly creative inventive Director with a reputation for creating and adding "business" on the set that is not spelled out in the script. He shot Scs. 84 and 85 as a test the other day with two pages of dialogue involved, running approximately 227 ft.
>
> Our timing of approx. 180' takes into consideration the fact that this was apparently a slow-tempoed scene. If this is any clue to Mike's inventiveness it is obvious that our timing of the picture at 6,999 ft. for an average of 76 ft. per page would be considerably off.
>
> It should not be forgotten that both Bing Crosby and Danny Kaye themselves, by ad libs and pieces of business, tend to, both in dramatic scenes as well as in musicals, string them out.
>
> Our past experience on this type of picture indicates always that with a creative group such as is connected with this production, everything tends to run longer. (Frank Caffey to Don Hartman [executive producer of *White Christmas*], September 14, 1953)

To make the implicit explicit: "Everything tends to run longer" means "We are going to have trouble curtailing the costs of this production." "'Business' on the set that is not spelled out in the script" means that at the studio, the airtight budgetary prediction and control typically provided by the use of the continuity script as a kind of interdepartmental blueprint would most likely evaporate. While in general practice, producers and their teams could carefully monitor in advance, and budget down to the penny, every action that audiences would later see onscreen, with this film, the fear apparently was that things could, and probably would, go haywire. Readers need no guide to help them sniff the aroma attached to the phrase "highly creative inventive" as a modifier of Curtiz, or sense the panic in the phrase "creative group such as is connected with this production"—with whom, as is claimed on the basis of the company's past experience, "everything tends to run longer." Paramount surely did have past experience. It had recently produced *The Caddy* (1953) and *Living It Up* (1954) with Martin and Lewis, "highly creative inventives" to the hilt.

A second pressure was the enormous publicity apparatus set in motion by Paramount, which spent "a staggering $800,000 promoting the film, including purchasing tie-ins on popular television programs" (Rhodes 2006, 296). If the film succeeded thanks to this onslaught, the success would be impressive and important for future earnings: if it failed, gloom would gather many players in its shadows. In the course of the exploitation, no salient aspect of the film's production failed to find coverage— even magnification—through advertising.[9] The pressbook was explosive in its celebration. The technical process came first, being the studio's "new baby" (and one so charming it was elucidated in gleefully dangling prose): "Filmed in the rich hues of Technicolor and in the revolutionary new Vista-Vision film process the viewer is able to see images on the screen with such clarity that it defies the imagination. 'White Christmas' was the perfect selection to be the first such film to be filmed in the electrifyingly stunning process." VistaVision permitted viewers "to see large-screen projection with complete, vivid, razor-sharp clarity" and assured exhibitors of the "strikingly attractive" production stills, "with exceptional eye-appeal and sell," that, thanks to VistaVision, the studio would make available: "When you see them you will recognize their tremendous merchandising value for window displays, lobby and tie-up displays" (Paramount pressbook for the 1954–1955 release season).

Did Curtiz feel an electrifying stun to see his work touted in advance as electrifyingly stunning? Or did he realize instead how little he mattered to Paramount beyond the success of VistaVision on this picture? In effect, he had little to do but to ensure the story told itself and to stand back to let the optical process shine. The pressbook could hardly have put the matter more bluntly than by demeaning even the picture's headliners in order to boast about the process: "In addition to its human stars, Bing Crosby, Danny Kaye, Rosemary Clooney and Vera-Ellen, Paramount's lavishly produced presentation of Irving Berlin's 'White Christmas,' . . . has *a fifth star*—VistaVision. This is the name given to the revolutionary new filming process which, when projected on the theater screen, gives such a clear image that even the background shots look as if they were only a few feet away from the viewer" (Paramount pressbook; emphasis added).[10] As a professional, Curtiz always composed shots so that the protagonists stood out against the background: that is, he gave the background a proportionate and considered place in the architecture of the shot. Here was the studio now warring with him on the most delicate and intimate artistic level, since VistaVision would pronounce the backgrounds, and to diminish this pronunciation would mean shortening focus and thus throwing the background much too distinctively out of focus. The alternative was what in fact resulted: shots in which everything onscreen became just what the studio predicted: so clear that the imagination was defied. The film looked real. Which is to say: it looked like a film. Many critics politely wondered whether VistaVision mightn't look better with exterior locations than with studio sets.

Curtiz received considerable hype in the publicity, being proclaimed "one of Hollywood's most colorful directors" ("colorful" meaning sensitive to Technicolor?) as well as "one of the most versatile." Since he had "megaphoned" biopics of "some of the world's most famous" and "had his talented hand in the filming of" numerous genres, including mysteries, modern dramas, historical films, and romantic comedies, it could be with nothing but assurance and deft skill that he now "held the reins over such stars as" Crosby and the others. Was Curtiz's ability to shift from genre to genre and brilliantly succeed with so many types of pictures merely, one author asked, "an intelligent adaptation to the studio system"? Writing soon after the film's release in the *British Film Academy Quarterly*, Oscar Rimoldi protested, "Anyone scanning his Hollywood films will find that despite its variety of genres, most of them have a common source: the American scene. Mike loved America from the moment he docked at a New York pier and thought a Fourth of July celebration was the reception the people of the United States were giving him."

There can be no doubt of proud Curtiz's directorial efficiencies. For just one example of his pacing: on October 19 he directed five pages of

A finale shot from *White Christmas* (Paramount, 1954), with, *from left*, Danny Kaye, Vera-Ellen, Rosemary Clooney, and Bing Crosby. Digital frame enlargement.

script in six setups; on the 20th, seven pages of script in seven setups; and on the 21st, seven more pages of script in eleven setups, as well as one page of music, "Count Your Blessings," in a single setup (*White Christmas* Production Reports). The producer reported numerous sacrifices made by Curtiz to shave expenses or increase production speed: "In order to eliminate the expense of shooting the scene showing [Crosby and Kaye] climbing on the observation platform of the train as it leaves Florida [early in the film, as they begin to follow the girls], Mike has found an interesting solution. Since we are going to shoot a sequence showing the boys getting off the train in Vermont, that same day Mike will shoot the boys getting on the steps of the train. This can be done in such a way as not to contain any surrounding Florida countryside obviating the necessity for plates, etc." (Dolan to Hartman, September 4, 1953).

I think it instructive in watching and considering *White Christmas*—with, for example, the astute analysis of content found in the work of David Rhodes (2006)—to keep in mind that the flow of action in this film (of whatever importance when examined philosophically), all the character tension pictured with perfect aptness and preparation, indeed all the tenderly warbled Berlin melodies—"Count Your Blessings Instead of Sheep," "Heat Wave," "White Christmas"—were arranged for the camera by a man with not only remarkable expertise in the varieties of studio genre filmmaking, and not only a sensitive aesthetic personality, but also an uninterrupted awareness of working with a filming process that was the gleam in his bosses' eyes, *and that neither he nor any other filmmaker had ever used.* All this at a studio that had invested so heavily in the success of that process—

> *White Christmas* became one of the highest-grossing films in Paramount's history, as well as the highest grossing film of 1954, earning gross receipts of twelve million dollars. The studio's gamble on VistaVision and *White Christmas* would seem to have been far- and clear-sighted. (Rhodes 296)

—that this major production, never less than lavish and always officially only "entertainment," was in truth an advertisement. *White Christmas* had story value only incidentally. Its deeper purpose was to show off Vista-Vision, creating for other filmmakers dreams of what they might do[11] and charging up audiences' anticipation of VistaVision pleasures to come—at least until 1963, when, with Curtiz and Kalmus recently deceased and Patrick Frawley in charge at Technicolor, the process was abruptly discontinued and Michael Curtiz's service to the industry more or less forgotten.

Notes

1. This notwithstanding Hawks's evaluation: "There are . . . directors who made perfectly good pictures—like Mike Curtiz, and he didn't stamp his pictures at all" (quoted in Bogdanovich 1997, 375).

2. Crosby's picture charge was $150,000. Donald O'Connor had been contracted to appear, but fell ill, and obtaining Danny Kaye as a replacement cost $200,000.

3. Don Siegel observed that Curtiz found Humphrey Bogart "impossibly difficult" (Bogdanovich 1997, 728); yet his framing and observation of Bogart in *Casablanca* are nonpareil.

4. Sarris glibly calls him a "first-take speedster" (1998, 348).

5. Robert Carr and R. M. Hayes make it clear that "a double frame 35mm wide screen system in which the film was exposed horizontally in the camera and projected in a like manner" had been conceived by George Hill and Filoteo Albertini in 1928, but when hawked in London and Hollywood, was rejected. Developed later by Lorenzo del Riccio, the "butterfly" camera system was adopted, renamed, and refined by Loren Ryder, John R. Bishop, and others at Paramount (1998, 144).

6. A decision possibly imbricated with Technicolor's warning that non-VistaVision printing for the studio would be impossible while VistaVision films were in process.

7. A chilling and deeply devoted homage to this moment is provided in the final frames of François Truffaut's *Fahrenheit 451* (1966).

8. Curtiz had wanted a miniature shot for the conclusion, but it was eliminated.

The producer felt they "could not, in all honesty, spend forty or fifty thousand dollars on a shot that we had no assurance the audience would still be in the theatre to see. [Curtiz] agreed that it was too expensive a risk. He thought perhaps we might consider a glass shot of the exterior of the inn. I, for one, do not think it is necessary. I feel very sure we can get a good end title with the footage we now have" (Dolan, memorandum ["Remaining Work to Be Done"], January 4, 1954).

9. At the time, print advertising typically meant the use of artists' drawings or photolithographic reproductions as well as considerable manipulations of typeface, arranged in compositions that were published in newspapers and, to a lesser extent, magazines in either black-and-white or black and one color. The pressbook for *White Christmas* was highlighted in red to pick up the "Santa Claus" theme, which is flagged in the film only in the musical finale.

10. Jerry Mosher has speculated to me that "VistaVision" derived from the company's mountaintop logo image, that it subtly dubbed the process with the studio's family name.

11. See *Variety*'s prediction from August 27, 1954: "VV's impact, while giving a full-stage effect to this musical, should be even greater when applied to outdoor and action-drama stories."

Archive

Margaret Herrick Library, Academy of Motion Picture Arts and Sciences, Beverly Hills (HER). Files consulted included Paramount Pictures Production Records (*White Christmas*, files 236.f.8 and 236.f.9), Paramount Pictures VistaVision Material, and the Technicolor Collection.

Works Cited

Behlmer, Rudy. 1985. *Inside Warner Bros., 1935-1951.* New York: Viking.
———, ed. 1993. *Memo from Darryl F. Zanuck: The Golden Years at Twentieth Century-Fox.* New York: Grove.
Bogdanovich, Peter. 1997. *Who the Devil Made It.* New York: Knopf.
BoxOffice. "Technicolor Corp. to Build Six Vista Vision Cameras." March 20, 1954. Clipping in Technicolor Collection, *The Man Who Never Was*, box 1, folder 8, HER.
Cagney, James. 2005. *Cagney by Cagney.* Garden City, NY: Doubleday.
Carr, Robert E., and R. M. Hayes. 1998. *Wide Screen Movies: A History and Filmography of Wide Gauge Filmmaking.* Jefferson, NC: McFarland.
Clooney, Rosemary. 1989. *Girl Singer: A Memoir of the Girl Next Door.* With Joan Barthel. New York: Doubleday.
Davis, Ronald L. 1993. *The Glamour Factory: Inside Hollywood's Big Studio System.* Dallas: Southern Methodist University Press.
Eyman, Scott. 2010. *Empire of Dreams: The Epic Life of Cecil B. DeMille.* New York: Simon and Schuster.
Haines, Richard W. 1993. *Technicolor Movies: The History of Dye Transfer Printing.* Jefferson, NC: McFarland.

Independent Film Journal. 1954. "Design Cameras for VistaVision." March 20. Clipping in Technicolor Collection, Clippings 1954 file, HER.

McCabe, John. 1997. *Cagney.* New York: Knopf.

McCarthy, Todd. 1997. *Howard Hawks: The Grey Fox of Hollywood.* New York: Grove.

Neame, Ronald. 1999. "Interview April–May 1999." Barbara Roisman Cooper Collection of Ronald Neame Research Interviews, file 51, HER.

New York Times. 1954. "New Color Techniques." March 16. Clipping in Technicolor Collection, file 1.f.8, HER.

Rhodes, David. 2006. "*White Christmas,* or Modernism." *Modernism/Modernity* 13, no. 2 (April): 291–308.

Rimoldi, Oscar. 1955. "Michael Curtiz: Colorful Character and Phenomenal Director." *British Film Academy Quarterly* 3 (Spring). Reprint, *Hollywood Studio Magazine* 17, no. 2 (March 1984), n.p.

Rubin, Bob. 2015. Interview by the author. December.

Sarris, Andrew. 1996. *The American Cinema: Directors and Directions, 1929-1968.* New York: Da Capo.

———. 1998. *"You Ain't Heard Nothin' Yet": The American Talking Film; History and Memory, 1927-1949.* New York: Oxford University Press.

Schatz, Thomas. 1988. *The Genius of the System: Hollywood Filmmaking in the Studio Era.* New York: Holt.

CHAPTER 17

Film Performance before and after the Code: *Mandalay* and *Stolen Holiday*

STEVEN RYBIN

Repeated collaborations between directors and stars were part of the day-to-day business of the classical Hollywood studio system. The prolific Michael Curtiz was one such director who, while under the employ of Warner Bros. in the thirties, worked recurrently with several actors—Dolores Costello, Bette Davis, and Errol Flynn, for example—across a variety of films. The work of one such collaboration is the subject here: two of the films that Curtiz made with the Warner Bros. star Kay Francis, *Mandalay* (1934) and *Stolen Holiday* (1937). These films, in themselves worthy additions to any discussion of Curtiz as a masterly filmmaker, are also notable case studies for exploring how a director and a performer work together to creatively negotiate the strictures of studio censorship and repression.

As employees of a major studio, Curtiz and Francis worked together four times (in addition to the films I discuss here, they also made *The Key-hole* [1933] and *British Agent* (1934]). There is no evidence that their repeated collaborations for Warners were the result of any particular friendship or intimate attachment; Curtiz and Francis were under contractual obligation to work on the projects assigned to them. Their work together was often a matter of creatively and suggestively circumventing, in their collaborative realization of onscreen performance, a set of rules governing the content of motion pictures. They did this through a contrapuntal style that emphasized Curtiz's economical, quick-moving narrative strategies while displaying Francis's more leisurely performative persona.

Performing before and after the Code

The second of the four Curtiz-Francis collaborations, *Mandalay*—part of the 1930s cycle of "fallen women" films—was made during what is now known as the pre-Code era of classical Hollywood cinema. This four-year stretch, from roughly March 1930 to July 1934, marks a period when the studios did not actively enforce the Production Code, which had been designed to regulate the content of films through a set of dictates. In his study of this period, Thomas Doherty describes pre-Code films as ones in which "the fissures crack open with rougher edges and sharper points" (1999, 3)—resulting in films that lay "bare what Hollywood under the code did its best to cover up and push off screen" (2). But the pre-Code years were not free of industry regulation of content. As Lea Jacobs has shown, an industry body known as the Studio Relations Committee wielded an underappreciated degree of power regarding what could and could not be shown on film before 1934 (1999, 90). Industry self-regulation during both eras focused on the film itself; in other words, rather than police the exhibition of motion pictures after a film was completed, studios policed the content during production. According to Jacobs, one of the primary jobs of any filmmaker or studio head was thus to ensure that a film did not pose a threat to either the political or the economic stability of the studio system as an industry (92). Questions of content and freedom of expressivity perpetually had to be renegotiated with the making of every film, both before and after 1934. It was not a question of making a film and seeing whether it "passed" a censorship board, but rather of negotiating and finding creative solutions in anticipation of what any particular body of censors might find objectionable (92).

What separates the films made before July 1934 (such as *Mandalay*) from the films made thereafter (including *Stolen Holiday*) is not a question of relative "freedom" in the expression of film content, then, but rather a question of what textual methods the studios used to police themselves. Before 1934, as Jacobs has observed, filmmakers negotiated potential objections to sexually frank material primarily through use of the ellipsis, creating a gap in the filmic narrative that enabled audiences to infer events and actions not explicitly shown. After the Code's enforcement began in 1934, however, industry censors moved to more actively regulate—through intensive script reading and demands for rewriting—the use of ellipsis, resulting in films that became less openly suggestive in their visual form and more contradictory in narrative meaning. Jacobs argues that pervasive textual censorship after 1934 resulted in the use of narrative ambiguity and contradiction as methods of regulating films. A sequence or image might suggest a naughty idea or action, but the film could later contradict this, demonstrating that no such salacious activity had occurred (Jacobs 1999, 94–95, 97). Arguably, this strategy allowed for an even greater degree of freedom in audience interpretation, requiring as it did more imagination in the face of greater textual ambiguity. Jacobs's example is George Cukor's *Camille* (1936), which suggests, in the ellipsis at the end of one scene, an affair between Greta Garbo's and Robert Taylor's characters, only to later contradict this implication with the blunt suggestion that nothing happened between the two of them (98).

What is perhaps underappreciated in this discussion of pre-Code and Production Code cinema, but relevant to the collaboration between Curtiz and Francis, is the effect of regulation on the performing body. Discussions of the Code by Jacobs and Doherty (see also Leff and Simmons 2001) focus mostly on the narrative regulation of filmic texts and, thus, the implications of censorship for writers. What consequence this kind of regulation has on the performer in cinema has gone mostly unremarked on. In a sense, what distinguishes a pre-Code from a Code performance is obvious: if prostitution (or a clever elision or visual symbolism suggesting prostitution) cannot be used as a narrative device in Production Code cinema, then no performer will be placed in any sort of context in which she might be called on to elaborate what it means to live a life of prostitution through a developed series of gestures, movements, and expressions. But this example remains tethered to an abstract consideration of narrative as such and focuses only secondarily on performers' actual onscreen work.

Ana Salzberg is one of the few scholars to carefully consider at any length the distinction of the pre-Code performing body and its impact on the spectator. Her ideas inform how I approach the creative strategies that Curtiz and Francis used, both before and after the Code, in *Mandalay* and *Stolen Holiday*. Salzberg employs a phenomenological approach to discuss the relationship between the performing body and the film spectator in pre-Code cinema. She argues that Laura Mulvey's conception of "possessive spectatorship," developed initially in Mulvey's consideration of the viewer's ability to "possess" the image by using the time-shifting and pause features of DVD technology, has parallels with pre-Code modes of spectatorship. Just as DVDs encourage a close and intimate relationship with film texts—the "pause" feature offering the promise of possessing an image that, in fact, remains always elusive and inevitably past—so too do pre-Code films offer an erotic and perpetual lure of sexual consummation in their flirtations with salacious content. Notably, Salzberg places a point of emphasis not only on the performers but also on the "filmic body" as a whole: that is, on the sensual work created through the collaboration of director, cinematographer, performer, and other personnel in the making of a film that could not explicitly show salacious acts but could suggest or imply them through the material form of the film itself. For Salzberg, not only the performing body in pre-Code cinema but also an entire range of cinematic devices that are potentially erotic in their relation to the performer work together to lure viewers toward an experience of "implicit carnality" (2012, 50).

Notably, this "implicit carnality" is achieved not through the work of performance by itself or by film technique alone but through their erotic fusion, resulting in a material, filmic charge that compels the imagination to conjure what censorship represses. Salzberg points to an example from Jack Conway's *Red-Headed Woman* (1932) to illustrate how the "filmic body" and the "performing body" collaborate to imply, rather than explicitly narrate, sensuality. She describes a moment when the virtuous Bill (Chester Morris) confronts the gold digger Lil (Jean Harlow) near the end of the film: "As Lil lies prone in medium close-up and slides the key down her blouse, the radiance of the lighting—imbuing her hair, skin, and clothing with a near-pearlescent quality—gradually cedes to dusky gray as Bill's shadow heralds his approach. Finally the dark mass of Bill's back is visible to the right of the frame, its darkness moving to the left and ultimately concealing Lil as he literally blacks-out the shot to access her body" (2012, 50). The performer here flirtatiously dances with a number of choices in cinematic technique: framing, camera movement, lighting, shadow, off-screen space, blocking, fading, dissolving, and other strategies of mise-en-scène and editing. Of course, this relationship between actorial technique and other film techniques is present in all narrative films, both before and after Code implementation. But in films made under censorship strictures, this dance between actor and film technique generates an erotic charge that cannot otherwise be displayed or conveyed on the screen. Salzberg demonstrates this effect in the passage quoted above, showing how, in *Red-Headed Woman*, an erotic charge is generated between measured revelation (the radiant close-up of Lil slipping a key down her blouse) and stark concealment (the arrival of a shadow that erects a temporary visual barrier between a viewer and her figure of desire).

Following Salzberg, my focus on the collaboration between Curtiz and Francis offers another valuable opportunity to explore how the creation of films as potentially sensual works intersected with industry regulations of the form such sensuality could take. In what follows, I avoid setting the "liberated" pre-Code aesthetics of *Mandalay* up against the "repressed" Production Code strategies used in *Stolen Holiday*. My argument is that both films developed methods of implication instead of statement, regulated as they were by the anticipation of objections from a variety of social groups during the pre-Code and Code periods. In the pre-Code *Mandalay*, Curtiz and Francis worked together to imply carnality in pronounced ways. In the Code-era *Stolen Holiday*, implicit carnality is exchanged for what we might call implicit sensuality, a subtler but equally material sensibility with connotations, in this particular film, of homoeroticism. In both films, and through an intriguingly contrapuntal style, Curtiz and Francis employ filmic strategies that tantalize the viewer with implications created not solely through narrative ellipses but more primarily through material, cinematic, and suggestive figurations of the performing body.

Mandalay

Kay Francis was a major star for Warner Bros. during the 1930s, reaching heights of popularity early in the decade. She is remembered today primarily for her performance in Ernst Lubitsch's *Trouble in Paradise* (1932, made for Paramount while she was under contract to Warners) and for the parade of Orry-Kelly gowns she wears in a number of films, including Tay Garnett's *One Way Passage* (1932). Beyond these career touchstones, she was a reliable box-office draw for most of the decade, and one of the studio's biggest stars before 1937. Her early-1930s films, in particular, remain favorites today on Turner Classic Movies and through distribution on DVD by Warner Archive.

Mandalay is exemplary of the kind of pre-Code film for which Francis is best known: salacious melodrama, with a plot that links it closely with the fallen woman genre. Francis plays Tanya Borodorff, the girlfriend of a black-market gun merchant named Tony Evans (Ricardo Cortez). Although she is in love with Tony, Tanya is not innocent: she is vaguely aware of Tony's criminality, but the knowledge does not stem the tide of the pleasure she takes in him. Tony loves her, too, but because this is a pre-Code film, he is not above selling her into slavish prostitution in exchange for guns. Thus, Tanya becomes "Spot White," ostensibly a hostess at a nightclub owned by the slimy Nick (Warner Oland). She manages to escape from this veritable brothel by blackmailing an official who has occasionally visited her there. In an effort to make a life as a new woman, Tanya, posing as "Marjorie Lang," makes her way toward Mandalay on a cruise ship. There, she meets another character looking for redemption, the tortured and alcoholic doctor Gregory Burton (Lyle Talbot). She soon realizes that Tony is stowed away on the ship, too, setting up the narrative's concluding confrontation between the two ex-lovers.

Curtiz's style in the picture is characteristic of the quick rhythms and narrative economy of his early work with Warners. James C. Robertson, in his book on Curtiz, suggests that the "cracking pace" (1993, 28) of Curtiz's work during this period was, in part, the inevitable result of working in the Warner Bros. house style, which in the early thirties emphasized both onscreen and offscreen narrative economy and efficiency (21). What is interesting about Curtiz's quicksilver filmmaking approach is the contrapuntal style it creates in tandem with Kay Francis's performance style. *Mandalay* is a model of narrative efficiency: in just over seventy minutes, it covers a wide terrain of plot information. Francis, however, is a performer of languor. She achieves her most striking effects when standing still: sipping a martini, smoking a cigarette, showing off a dress. In such moments, her character internally reflects upon a melodramatic plot point while her audience admires the way a gorgeous dress embraces her. The sheer kinesis of Curtiz's technique, in conjunction with Francis's unhurried postures, works to create a singularly cinematic eros: while the director rushes ahead to keep the melodrama moving, the performer lingers upon the feeling at play in the moment. Curtiz wants to finish the viewer off; Francis wants to linger a while longer. The result is a film that rushes toward consummation even as it lures us to tarry, and enjoy the physicality it takes to get us there.

The most notorious scene in *Mandalay* comes early. Tony arrives at his boat after a discussion about gunrunning with Nick. As Tony is motored from the dock to his ship, a tracking shot glides him along to Tanya, who stands posed on the side of the ship, one arm holding a parasol, to greet her lover, the wind whipping through a blouse hanging off her right shoulder. (In the matching reverse-angle shot, which shows us Tony getting onto the ship, there is a minor continuity error: the white blouse now hangs off her left shoulder, an early sign of the tension between Curtiz's quick, economic style and Francis's way of posing.) "Now hurry and put on your grandest," Tony tells her: they are to journey to Rangoon, where Tony will exchange his lover for the guns he needs to make his next deal. Tanya knows none of this, yet: she is being directed within the diegesis to perform not as a narrative agent but rather as a clotheshorse, a word used in one Francis biography to describe her fashionable appearances in her films (Kear and Rossman 2006, 46).

The next part of the scene, in which Francis undresses and "puts on her grandest," drew the ire of Curtiz's producer, Hal Wallis, because it presents the spectacle of an unmarried couple enjoying the possibility of sex. "When you show Kay Francis . . . stepping out of the tub and going into Cortez's arms . . . stick to the script . . . For God's sake, Mike, you have been making pictures long enough to know that it is impossible to show a man and woman who are not married in a scene of this kind" (quoted in O'Brien 2007, 125). "Stick to the script" here is likely code for "rely on ellipsis": that is, show Francis arriving fully dressed, with any suggestion of sex kept safely offscreen. But instead of entirely eliding the event, Curtiz's camera and its quick tracking movements, in tandem with Francis's moving figure, imply carnality through the conjunction of directorial style and actorial performance.

Tanya descends to the bottom level of the boat. The camera follows her as she drops the needle on a record, and tracks to the right as she begins to undress for her bath. As she begins to slip her blouse off, the shot cuts to Tony, lifting the door to the room from above to seize a look at her, the lilting music still playing offscreen. After a moment, the camera rejoins Tanya, now playfully aware that she is the subject of Tony's gaze. The film cuts back to her just as she wraps a towel around her torso and tracks leftward until she arrives at Tony. She steps up and gazes adoringly at her lover, her right hand on him, her left clinging to her towel. "I'll never get dressed, never!" Tanya exclaims—a perfect expression of Francis's tendency, as a performer, to soak up the viewer in a suspended moment of leisurely sensuality. She lifts her left arm and they embrace. The towel, hanging for a moment on the left side of Francis's body, drops out of frame. After they kiss, a brief exchange of loving words proceeds in a shot/reaction shot. Curtiz then punctuates the sequence with a shot of Francis's legs, softly lit and adorned with gleaming beads of water, as she steps up on a chair to greet her lover. The towel, which somehow had been lingering in midair, in the offscreen space between Francis's torso and her feet, now falls completely and finally to the ground. A wipe transitions to the next scene.

This sequence is a textbook case of pre-Code cinema's strategies of material implication, and an example of Curtiz and Francis's collaborative inflection of those strategies. Curtiz's camera swiftly and laterally moves across the interior of the ship as Francis plays her record and runs her bath. The narrative momentum of the scene is already at odds with Tanya's enjoyment of the moment: she wants to slip into the water and stay there for a while rather than speed through it like a boat. Curtiz, though,

Kay Francis and Ricardo Cortez embrace during a moment of leisurely
sensuality in *Mandalay* (Warner Bros., 1934). Digital frame enlargement.

cuts quickly away from Francis just as she takes off her blouse, and cuts
back to her just as she finishes the act of wrapping a towel around her
body. The impact of these cuts is twofold. On the one hand, they move the
plot quickly along, as Curtiz tended to do during this period of his work
with Warner Bros. But on the other, they deny full visual possession—in
this case, the viewer's possession of Francis as erotic subject—through
clever cinematic strategies: the film cuts before Francis is bare to the extra-
diegetic eye. Nevertheless, there is an erotic charge to the very cinematic
act of denying full visual possession. The moment of consummation, materially elided through a cut, remains implied through that same materi-
ality, inscribed in the viewer's desiring imagination.

These strategies are in keeping with a general tendency of pre-Code
cinema. What makes the scene exemplary of the particular nuances of the
Curtiz-Francis collaboration is the intriguing pitch struck between the director's efforts of narrative economy and Francis's tendency to languidly
pose. When Francis moves to the other side of the room to kiss Cortez,
and lifts her arms up to him, Curtiz works to move through the moment
swiftly: less than thirty seconds is enough for a bit of flirtatious dialogue

and a kiss. Yet a strange effect of the quick cutting and the teasing framing of the performers, as described above, is the implication that Francis's
towel has fallen from the side of her body not once but twice: once when
she lifts her right arm, the one that was clinging to the towel, to kiss him;
and then again, after a cut to the punctuating shot of her legs, when it
falls mysteriously once more. By quickly moving through the narrative
sequence, the cutting and its creation of an odd temporal repetition in
this sequence of *Mandalay* impress upon us the importance of Francis as
a filmic figure, a body so important to the sensual work of the film that
the clinging towel drops from her twice. This is again an example of the
pre-Code tendency to materially imply: the repeated falling of the towel
inscribes a kind of poetic sensuality, a repeated verse of fabric falling from
flesh. But it is also a material inscription of Francis as a performing body
whose powers of stillness and poise act in counterpoint to Curtiz's desire
to be in motion.

Stolen Holiday

The very title of the next Curtiz-Francis collaboration under discussion
here, *Stolen Holiday*, suggests the flavor of a pre-Code picture: the trans-
gression of theft and an escape, a holiday, from workaday morality. And as
with *Mandalay*, it works to materially imply things it cannot show. Yet this
is not a pre-Code film. Made after enforcement of the Production Code
began in July 1934, *Stolen Holiday* does not contain any scene as suggestive
as the one from *Mandalay* described above. Instead of implying carnality, I
suggest that this film, restricted by Code enforcement, implies a relatively
vague sensuality or sensibility, which here takes the form of a homoeroticism displayed by performance even as it is contradicted by narrative momentum. *Stolen Holiday*'s relatively subtle material implications work in
tandem with the narrative ambiguities and contradictions that became the
norm during the Production Code period of Hollywood cinema, even as
the Curtiz-Francis tension between speed and languidness continues to
operate in intriguing moments in the film.

   The film's narrative is very loosely inspired by real-life events involving
the fashion designer Gabrielle "Coco" Chanel and the embezzler Alexandre Stavisky, who owned a number of pawnshops as a front for illegal
financial activities. In the fictionalized version of these events, Kay Francis
plays a model named Nicole Picot. Tired of functioning as a "clotheshorse" for others and harboring a desire to become a fashion designer,

Nicole finds opportunity in Stefan Orloff (Claude Rains), who offers to help her open a dress salon. This business, unbeknownst to Nicole, will be a cover for Stefan's deceitful financial gambits. From that point, the plot develops along parallel lines. Nicole's business grows, and she is courted by a diplomat named Anthony Wayne (Ian Hunter) in a romantic subplot. Meanwhile, Orloff's embezzlement schemes fall apart, and he compels Nicole to marry him in an effort to provide further legitimate social cover for his activities. This plan eventually fails when Nicole unwittingly leads authorities to Orloff's hideout in the final act of the film.

The first sequences introduce a pronounced narrative ambiguity, produced, in part, through the film's reflexive presentation of Francis's star persona. In the opening sequence, set in 1931 Paris, Curtiz's camera dollies in on a glamorous fashion show as models display the latest couture. After a moment, Francis makes her first distinguished appearance, dressed in black, with her hair short and slicked back, in contrast to the white dresses and feminine appearance of the other models. Two of the chattering spectators comment upon the radical promise that Nicole Picot embodies for the future of fashion. She is something more than a mere model, they remark; she clearly has "ideas," and this is in part because of the "shocking" nature of her "mannish" appearance. Francis's star persona has been read for its lesbian and bisexual connotations (Mann 2001, 84), and her appearance in the first act of *Stolen Holiday* recalls the sexually ambiguous characters she played in her earliest films, in which a mannish haircut was often enough to suggest a subtextual queer identity (see, for example, *Gentlemen of the Press* [1929]). *Stolen Holiday* provides enough textual evidence to read Nicole Picot as lesbian before contradicting this narrative information in the film's second-act romantic subplot involving Wayne. In the second sequence in the film, Francis, backstage at the fashion show, converses with a former model, Suzanne (Alison Skipworth), declaring her exhaustion at being a clotheshorse but, at the same time, her refusal to hitch her financial future to a man—"any man." The narrative drive of the film will hitch the Francis character to not one man but two, and as the narrative jumps ahead to the present tense (1936), Francis becomes more conventionally feminine in appearance, wearing her hair down and flirting with Wayne. But the film works nevertheless to narratively imply that this heterosexual romance represses a homosexual identity hinted at in the film's first act.

The film's second-act contradiction of narrative ambiguities introduced in the first twenty minutes serves as an example of the sort of narrative conundrum that films made under the Production Code often introduce as a

Kay Francis, as Nicole Picot, enjoys a cigarette in *Stolen Holiday* (Warner Bros., 1937). Digital frame enlargement.

way to imply, rather than show, suggestive material. But the film continues to use material implications of sensuality and sensibility as a strategy to forcefully inscribe certain ambiguities through performance rather than only through narrative ellipsis. And it does so in ways that continue the Curtiz-Francis project of counterpointing languorous, delectable poses and gestures with swift-moving narrative momentum. As Curtiz's cinematic strategies again work to move quickly through the first act (and thus past the stretch of the film that works most strongly to inscribe Francis's queer identity), the star's gestures and expressions prefer to linger in the atmosphere of a suggestive moment.

The film's first backstage scene offers an example. Nicole's work as a model is done for the day. She sits at a table with Suzanne, who is passing the time with tarot cards. Nicole is casually curious about what the tarot cards portend—Suzanne's readings are a motif in the film, repeatedly signaling Nicole's narrative future—wanting them to tell what she might be fated to do in this world. The film's narrative answers that her talent is to become a fashion magnate, and that she might best do this alongside a man, indeed alongside two men, her choice of whom will mean more to the narrative's resolution of her happiness than her realization of a career.

Yet, unfolding before all this narrative works to qualify our sense of it, the scene suggests Francis does something else quite better than wear clothes: light and puff on a cigarette as a way to deflect the demands of the narrative (in this case, the heterosexual reality toward which Suzanne's cards seem to be pulling her). As Suzanne reads the cards, which point to Nicole's future with a dastardly man, Nicole asserts her lack of interest in "any man." What speaks more powerfully than the dialogue, or even the slicked-back, mannish haircut the star sports, is Francis's act of lighting, puffing, and handling a cigarette (all framed by Curtiz in a close medium shot as Francis leans back casually in her chair). These gestures seem to signal an intention to enjoy the pleasures of the unhurried moment, keeping narrative momentum at bay. Further emphasizing the importance of moment over narrative, and the toil that narrative might cause, is Skipworth's participation in the scene. For she is the figure who shows us the physical costs of becoming inscribed in a plot: Suzanne, a former model who once hitched her fate to a man, reminds Nicole (as Curtiz's camera moves vertically beneath the table) that her "rheumatic stumps" were once "insured for a million dollars." This is the physical fate of narrative: exhausted legs, a death knell for any model. This is the future that Francis's happily lazy Nicole is prepared to sit down and resist for the stretch of this scene.

As in *Mandalay*, in *Stolen Holiday* the star body (with the help of a supporting performer) materially inscribes a gestural, bodily resistance to the forward movement of narrative. But the presence of the tarot cards as a motif reminds us this is a classical Hollywood movie that believes in things like fate, destiny, and conclusion. So it will be Nicole's destiny to fall into a romantic and fully heterosexual clinch by the final scene. Francis's gestures and expressions in the film are a reminder that after the enforcement of the Production Code, narrative ambiguity still relied on material implication. If a queer reality lies dormant within the second and third acts of the film, it is largely because the film's first act inscribes material gestures that resist foretold consequences of narrative momentum. Curtiz was a master of that kind of momentum, so even as *Stolen Holiday* takes Francis where perhaps her devoted viewer doesn't wish to see her go, there is still a certain kind of pleasure in seeing this director take her there.

Works Cited

Doherty, Thomas. 1999. *Pre-Code Hollywood: Sex, Immorality, and Insurrection in American Cinema, 1930–1934*. New York: Columbia University Press.
Jacobs, Lea. 1999. "Industry Self-Regulation and the Problem of Textual Deter-

mination." In *Controlling Hollywood: Censorship and Regulation in the Studio Era*, edited by Matthew Bernstein, 87–101. New Brunswick, NJ: Rutgers University Press.

Kear, Lynn, and John Rossman. 2006. *Kay Francis: A Passionate Life and Career.* Jefferson, NC: McFarland.

Leff, Leonard J., and Jerold Simmons. 2001. *The Dame in the Kimono: Hollywood, Censorship, and the Production Code.* Lexington: University Press of Kentucky.

Mann, William J. 2001. *Behind the Screen: How Gays and Lesbians Shaped Hollywood.* New York: Viking.

O'Brien, Scott. 2007. *Kay Francis: I Can't Wait to be Forgotten.* Albany, GA: BearManor Media.

Robertson, James C. 1993. *The Casablanca Man: The Cinema of Michael Curtiz.* London: Routledge.

Salzberg, Ana. 2012. "Seduction Incarnate: Pre-Production Code Hollywood and Possessive Spectatorship." *Cinema: Journal of Philosophy and the Moving Image* 3 (January): 39–61. Accessed June 1, 2016. http://static1.1.sqspcdn.com/static /f/906805/21523955/1357328017777/3+Salzberg.pdf.

CHAPTER 18

"A Mass of Contradictions": Michael Curtiz and the Women's Film

MICHELE SCHREIBER

Michael Curtiz cannot be associated with a single genre. Like many directors under studio contract during the classical period, he made a broad
range of films that included musicals, swashbucklers, biopics, and westerns. He also worked extensively in the women's film genre, but is not
necessarily thought of as a woman's director, despite the fact that he made
Mildred Pierce (1945), perhaps the exemplar 1940s women's picture. *Positif*'s Eithne O'Neill, one of the few critics to discuss women in Curtiz's
films, argues that in his female characters, a "pattern emerges between
submission and defiance," and that we "see the representation of transgressive women" showing a "contradictory attitude": "Angel or demon?:
Two souls inhabit the same character" (2014, 103–105). Two Curtiz films
that O'Neill discusses, *Female* (1933) and *Flamingo Road* (1949), are particularly illuminating for how their plots, production histories, marketing,
and reviews reflect this deeply contradictory attitude about women. Inspired by salacious novels, both films were subject to extensive censorship
by the Production Code Administration, which targeted their depiction of
female protagonists—Alison (Ruth Chatterton) in *Female* and Lane (Joan
Crawford) in *Flamingo Road*—falling outside the boundaries of conventional femininity.

Under censorial pressure, both Alison and Lane—sexual women in their
source novels—were necessarily reworked in script revisions, becoming
"domesticated" through heterosexual romance narratives. The contradictions that O'Neill discusses arise from the incompatibility of the original
characters and their more palatable film versions. Both films suggest the
possibility of one woman housing contradictory selves, to move at will
between "types" and to try on different femininities. Alison's and Lane's
performances are deeply embedded in class discourses in which "disguise"

and "display" are crucial to social mobility. This fluidity allows the films to appeal at the same time to one audience that interprets them as genuine "happy ever after" stories and another that sees them as tales of audacious women whose transgressions eclipse their domestication. The films demonstrate Curtiz's valuable contribution to the success of the woman's film at Warner Bros. during his multidecade tenure with the studio. His consistent style and approach to the genre spans the eras of the "fallen woman" film (Jacobs 1995) and the 1940s woman's film (Doane 1987).

Female and *Flamingo Road* were made during notable periods in Curtiz's career and in Hollywood history more generally. *Female* came at the beginning of what Roy Kinnard and R. J. Vitone consider Curtiz's "peak years" at Warner Bros. (1986, 17). Warners put him under contract in 1926, and had enough confidence in Curtiz by 1933 to bring him in for polishing *Female* after the original director, William Dieterle, fell ill and his replacement, William Wellman, was fired. Curtiz's substantial reshoots altered the film enough for him to persuade the studio that he should be the only director credited (Robertson 1993, 29). The year 1933 was also the end of what is considered the pre-Code Hollywood period, a time when, as Thomas Doherty puts it, "compliance with the code was a verbal agreement that, as producer Samuel Goldwyn might have said, wasn't worth the paper it was written on" (1999, 2). Although Warner Bros. followed the PCA recommendations, *Female* retained a suggestive tone and was among the films banned by the Catholic Legion of Decency in 1934.

Flamingo Road was made in 1949, the year after the Supreme Court's Paramount decision forced studio divestiture of theater chains. With the rise of television and an influx of European art films, divestiture threatened Hollywood's livelihood. Marcia Landy writes that in 1949 "major studios took measures to stem the financial bloodletting through the radical cutting of production and personnel costs, the termination of star and producer contracts and the farming out of productions to independent companies" (2006, 223). Curtiz was a victim of this trend. After establishing his own production company at Warners in 1947, his failure to produce top box-office draws forced him to sell his 51 percent stake in Michael Curtiz Productions back to the studio two years later, ceding full creative control and returning to his earlier status as director under studio contract. *Flamingo Road* was the last film made by Michael Curtiz Productions.

Along with *The Strange Love of Molly Louvain* (1932), *The Private Lives of Elizabeth and Essex* (1938), and *Mildred Pierce*, Curtiz also made female-centered films such as *Four Daughters* (1938) and *Daughters Courageous*

(1939), in which the protagonists possess what would be considered traditionally feminine traits and are ultimately rendered wholesome and appealing despite the plots' twists and turns. The *Daughters* films, the first two of a series (a third, Curtiz's *Four Wives* [1939], were followed by William Keighley's *Four Mothers* [1941]) focus on four sisters (played by Priscilla Lane, Rosemary Lane, Lola Lane, and Gale Page) seeking or living in the midst of romantic relationships. As one reviewer put it, the four films focus on the "domestic life, romances, joys and sorrows" of a family (John Scott, "New Picture Acclaimed in Preview," *Los Angeles Times*, August 9, 1938, 8). The two early Curtiz films feature John Garfield as a romantic interest for Priscilla Lane, and Claude Rains as the girls' father. But the characters are different in the two films (while *Four Wives* returns to the women found in *Four Daughters*). *Four Daughters* focuses on the loving Lemp family, with Rains, dean of the Briarwood Music Foundation, instilling a love of music into his family. The jovial dynamic is disrupted by two male visitors: Felix (Jeffrey Lynn), the son of an old friend of the father's, and Felix's composer friend Mickey (Garfield). The two of them pique the romantic interest of daughters Ann (Priscilla Lane) and Emma (Gale Page). *Daughters Courageous* has Rains playing the estranged patriarch of the Masters family, returning home twenty years after abandoning his wife and daughters. He tries to win his daughters' affection while they engage in romantic relationships of their own. Again, the character played by Garfield is romantically pursuing one of the daughters, played by Lane.

Four Daughters* and *Daughters Courageous* were marketed as family films, not women's films. For instance, the campaign for *Four Daughters* pivots around the sacrifice that Ann makes when she discovers that she and her sister Emma are both in love with Felix. Although she and he have been carrying on a flirtation, she decides to marry Mickey in order to avoid getting in the way of her sister's crush. This leads her into a financially unstable and very unhappy marriage, and Mickey eventually commits suicide in his car. The somewhat bleak plot twist in which Ann loves two men at the same time did not lead to the type of marketing campaign one might have seen for a woman's film with this narrative. The taglines for *Four Daughters* glorify Ann's sacrifice and intertwine romantic love, familial love, and loyalty: "Any Woman Can Love a Man. . . . Only One in a Million Can Give Up a Man She Loves." And "Can family devotion send a girl into a ruinous marriage?" (*Four Daughters* pressbook 1988). Marrying a man you don't love is rendered heroic and unselfish, rather than calculated or ill advised. Family comes before the woman's happiness. The pressbook suggests that theater managers might do family theme nights: "Sure, it's a family affair! Make it a big affair in your theatre." Included is a statement by Jack Warner, enthusiastically extolling the film and recommending that his endorsement be used as part of the marketing campaign. In short, the *Daughters* films depict Curtiz women whose decisions are guided by a strong moral compass and whose sexuality goes unspoken. This puts them in striking contrast with the kind of autonomous, bold, libidinous Curtiz women seen in *Female* and *Flamingo Road*.

Female

Inspired by a 1933 Donald Henderson novel, *Female* portrays Alison Drake, the head of a car company with a staff made up primarily of men. She is organized, decisive, and unapologetic in business, and respected by her employees. Her pastime is to invite eager male employees to her house for dinner and then seduce them. After these one-night stands, she discontinues interactions with the men, and as "compensation" for their trouble either gives them a bonus or transfers them to another branch of her company. When an old friend asks Alison whether she feels she is missing out on something by not being married, she responds, "A long time ago, I decided to travel the same open road that men travel. So I treat men the same way they've always treated women."

At one of her lavish parties, Alison becomes impatient with the overtures of men who are interested in her only because of her power. She leaves, changes from her beautiful evening gown to an ordinary outfit, hops into her car, and goes out searching for a man. She sees Jim Thorne (George Brent) at a shooting gallery and pursues him. He reluctantly takes her dancing and for dinner, but leaves her at the end of the evening, saying that he "doesn't take pickups home." The next day, Alison learns that Jim is the Drake Company's new engineer. She continues to pursue him, but he resists her advances. She eventually asks her trusted assistant for advice, and he tells her that a man like Jim "wants a woman who will look up to him: gentle, feminine, someone he can protect." Alison decides to play the role of "gentle and feminine," all while rolling her eyes at her own performance behind Jim's back. He finally gives in to her pursuits and, in a precoital moment, tells her, "Do you realize that I know you as four entirely different people? The girl at the shooting gallery—she was amusing. Then the girl at the factory, she's a very efficient, capable sort of thinking machine. Then the girl at your house that night for dinner: I didn't like her

. . . perhaps because I'm a man and I prefer to do my own hunting. Then the girl you are here tonight." After they spend the night together, Jim proposes. Alison initially finds this preposterous, but accepts after much hemming and hawing and a very dramatic overnight car pursuit. The last scene of the film sees her telling Jim that she "never wants to see the factory again" and is "going to have nine children."

Alison's shift in characterization from a "superwoman" who would "rather have a canary than a man" to a "gentle and feminine" woman who wants to have nine kids is dramatic, as is the tone of the film itself, which begins as a refreshing ode to female professional and sexual independence and ends like a conventional love story, an about-face that reflects the PCA's intervention. When Joseph Breen reviewed the script in development on July 17, 1933, he wrote a damning interoffice memorandum arguing that the material was in clear violation of the code because "the irregular sexual practices of the leading character are presented *alluringly* and there is a patent effort on the part of the writers of the script to *justify* this conduct" (original emphasis). Breen objected to the comedic tone with which "sexual immorality" was treated, considered the whole project "cheap, mean and tawdry," and found "nauseating" the "extraordinary indulgences of the leading character." He suggested that Warners change the script so that Alison would go incognito as an everyday woman to see whether all these men still liked her. Furthermore, any revision had to "remove the idea that she uses her position to satisfy a sex hunger which, in its present proportions approaches nymphomania" (History of Cinema, *Female*, 1933). Many of these suggestions ended up in the finished film but didn't necessarily have the intended effect. One could argue that, just as Jim says there are many Alisons, there are two *Female*s—the first half and the second.

The first half of the film shows Alison in power, in both the boardroom and the bedroom, and the dialogue focuses on how happy she is with her life. There is no indication that she cares whether her male conquests are interested in her true self. Her interactions are purely sexual. She doesn't express an interest in finding a man who likes her for more than her power until midway through the film when she leaves the party and pursues Jim as an "ordinary" woman. But even in the first interaction with him, she expects to have sex at the end of the evening, and when he gives in and does have sex with her, she does not interpret their coupling as leading to a permanent commitment. Only at the very end of the film, when Jim leaves town, does she break down and cry in front of her board members, and then she literally chases him overnight in her car in order to declare her love. Now comes the "happy ending," with "first-half Alison" disappearing into "domestic Alison," whom Jim has hunted and tamed.

Allison shares characteristics with what Doherty describes as a pre-Code "bad girl," a "calculating agent of her moral decline and financial ascent who treats sex like any other business transaction," works her "wiles on dimwitted men as a way to wealth," and is "a determined female sexual predator" who "can break down the resistance of any male no matter how outwardly moral his exterior" (1999, 131, 132). While Allison certainly treats sex as a transaction, she gets pleasure, not money or goods, in exchange. When she moves from bad girl to good girl, she remains upper class (but loses her professional power). She has as much in common with the female protagonists of contemporary romantic comedy films, who choose marriage and the love of a man over autonomy and a satisfying career, as with her bad-girl counterparts.

There are at least two ways of interpreting *Female*. One is that the "happy ever after" conclusion offers a panacea for the empty experience of sex without romantic love. Another is that the pat romantic ending does little to diminish the glamour and appeal of Alison's free sexual expression and hedonistic lifestyle. Warner Bros. adopted a version of this latter perspective to sell *Female*. A theater manager named Stanley L. Citron is featured in the film's pressbook, claiming, "It will go big with women, as they watch Chatterton play the men by the same standards as the men play women. Besides the picture gives her an opportunity to wear lots of gorgeous gowns and new style creations." He urges owners to "get every woman's organization from the society club to the great number of shop and office girls to be among the first to see FEMALE" (*Female* Pressbook). The pressbook introduces ad copy for attracting female viewers: "Girls! See this story of a woman who made a business of bossing men! Maybe you think you know how to handle men—just because you've managed to handle one man! But could you do the same thing with any man—with scores of men as this girl does? Come and see how she does it—learn her system—and try it for yourself!" It also suggests that theaters do theme nights oriented around different "types" of females.

> 1st Day: A female who has what it takes to get her man.
> 2nd day: This female meets men on their own plane.
> 3rd day: This female has what it takes to lose her man.
> 4th day: This female has a way with men that gets 'em.
> 5th day: A female who makes love a career to get her man.
> 6th day: A clinging female who has love methods all her own.

Promotional poster for *Female* (First National Pictures, 1933). Digital frame enlargement.

Notably, the marketing largely avoids mention of the ending that sees Alison and Jim fall in love. The happy ending that shows her wild ways tamed isn't the implied point of this campaign, whose taglines emphasize action. Women "do," "have," "handle," and "get" rather than "fall," "meet," or "succumb." The campaign also plays on the idea—introduced by Jim—that Alison is many women at the same time, and that the female spectator can also "try on" multiple personae.

The casting of Ruth Chatterton as Alison aligned perfectly with this "multiple women" campaign. Chatterton was an Academy Award–nominated silent-film star, known as the "First Lady of the Screen" and highly regarded for her theater background and her nuanced performances in 1920s melodramas. In the early 1930s, her move from playing suffering, respectable characters to bad girls caused critics to wonder who the "true" Chatterton was. As a 1933 *Photoplay* story puts it, "Ruth has been a lady so long that she's kicked over the traces and decided to go 'baddie" for a while. . . . Nobody is sure that [she] is doing the correct thing in her 'right about face' from the roles of suffering ladyship to the ugly characters she has gone in for recently" (May Allison Quirk, "From Lady to Judy O'Grady," *Photoplay*, March 4, 1933, 57). The story continues, "The future of Chatterton's career is hanging in the balance. Is she to be a rowdy or a lady?" A *Picturegoer* piece, "A Chat to Chatterton," written in the form of a letter to the actress, laments the "studio policy of building up Chatterton into a queen of sex appeal. . . . If you keep this sort of thing up, you know, they will be calling Mae West the 'First Lady of the Screen' next" (Malcolm Phillips, *Picturegoer*, March 3, 1934, 8). These profiles of Chatterton reflect the same conflicting versions of Alison: there is the soft and feminine Chatterton versus the "baddie" Chatterton, the thespian genius versus the exhibitionist whose sexual audacity threatens to usurp Mae West's reign as 1930s cinema's bad girl. The film, its marketing, and its star all suggest that there are numerous ways to perform "femaleness."

Flamingo Road

Flamingo Road focuses on Lane Bellamy, a carnival girl tired of her peripatetic lifestyle who quits her job while stopped in Boldon City. When Fielding Carlisle (Zachary Scott), the deputy sheriff, comes to arrest the carnival's proprietor for unpaid bills, he meets Lane, is attracted to her, and offers to take her to dinner. His boss, Titus Semple (Sydney Greenstreet), sees them at the local diner and is immediately suspicious of Lane and how she might threaten his political plans for Field. Giving in to Titus's pressure, Fielding agrees to marry Annabelle (Virginia Huston), his more appropriate, wealthy girlfriend, and to drop his burgeoning relationship with Lane so that he can run for the state legislature. Meanwhile, Titus gets Lane jailed for prostitution. When she is released, she is hired at Lute Mae's (Gladys George) roadhouse, a spot frequented by political power-houses, including Titus and the businessman Dan Reynolds (David Brian). Although she still harbors feelings for the now-married Fielding, Lane becomes involved with Dan. They eventually marry, setting up a lavish home on the town's most prestigious street, Flamingo Road. A battle of wills over the gubernatorial election pits Titus against Dan, and leaves Fielding powerless, alcoholic, and depressed. After he commits suicide in Dan and Lane's home, the community tries to run Lane out of town. Fed up with the power that Titus wields, Lane goes to kill him, and when the two struggle with the gun, he ends up shooting and killing himself. The film ends with Lane in jail again but hopeful of exoneration after the evidence points to her innocence. Lane and Dan embrace in her jail cell, and she walks off to see the district attorney.

Understandably, this story was not greeted with open arms by the PCA. When Lou Edelman, an independent producer, and Paramount inquired about the story's suitability under the Production Code in the summer of 1946, Breen's assistant, Geoffrey Shurlock, responded that it was "extremely questionable" and a "sordid type of story" of the kind the industry had deemed "not suitable." He continued, "All of the characters are either crooked, engaged in adultery or illicit sex, as well as in crooked attempts to frame one another" (History of Cinema, *Flamingo Road*, 1949). Warner Bros. eventually acquired the rights in 1946, and Jerry Wald was attached to produce. Wald's biggest challenge in script development and revision was to establish a balance between the story's political and romantic aspects. In memoranda, Wald speaks about wanting to make sure that *Flamingo Road* would uphold Warner Bros.' commitment to substantive film-making. But with the House Un-American Activities Committee hearings in full swing and causing anxiety among industry players, he felt an apprehension about making the film too political (Robertson 1993, 99), which led to two years of rewrites. The studio sent several drafts of the treatment to the PCA in December 1946 and January 1947, finally receiving approval for the version dated February 10, 1947.

Predictably, Breen's notes focus on Lane's sexuality. He stresses the "need for the greatest possible care in the selection and photographing of the dresses and costumes for your women," and in page-by-page directions stipulates that "there must be no actual 'bumps' or 'grinds' or any other offensive movement" in Lane's carnival dance early in the film (History of Cinema, *Flamingo Road*, 1949). After the original director, Vincent Sherman, left the project, the script went through another year of revisions, which lasted through the film's production in November 1948. These phases addressed the PCA's renewed concerns, one of which was the film's depiction of political and moral corruption, and another was Lane being first a prostitute and then a kept woman. Eventually, the latter problem was resolved through script revision: Lane married Dan and was therefore no longer his mistress. Lute Mae's place becomes a roadhouse instead of a brothel.

Curtiz took on the film in 1948 under the Michael Curtiz Productions banner, acquiring rights to the property from the studio for $85,000. Wald still acted as producer. Once *Flamingo Road* was under the purview of Curtiz's unit, he oversaw every aspect of production: rewriting the script, selecting costumes and locations, and overseeing process shots. Wald responded positively to the dailies, stating in a memorandum to Curtiz: "No other director in the business has your ability to create mood and tension in the scenes as you do. It's really been a pleasure working with you" (Wald to Curtiz, October 6, 1948). Frank Mattison, the unit manager, wrote several memoranda to Warners' production manager, Tenny Wright, reporting on Curtiz's economical approach: "Mike shot 168 pages in 42 days, his shooting average 4 pages a day. I do not know how he did it, but he drove like a mad man. He was amenable and agreeable to any suggestions made which would cut the cost or save time in shooting" (Mattison to Wright, November 4, 1948). Curtiz's approach did not always sit well with Joan Crawford, however. Mattison writes, "For your information, yesterday, Monday, there was a blowup on the set between Curtiz and Crawford; they exchanged words rather sharp and pointedly, with the result Crawford went to her dressing room . . . We got her back on the set and continued with a little easier tempo for the balance of the day. My sympathy is with Crawford" (Mattison to Wright, November 2, 1948).

Curtiz had to go through significant negotiations with Warner Bros. to borrow the famously temperamental Crawford to play Lane. She was coming off her Oscar-winning success in *Mildred Pierce* (along with other popular post-*Pierce* films), and was in prime position to make demands with regard to billing and publicity. Once she signed on, they had in place the same group (Wald, Curtiz, and Crawford) that had made *Pierce* such a success for Warner Bros. a few years earlier. Because of the natural connections that the audience would make between *Pierce* and *Flamingo Road* (links that were formally forged through *Flamingo Road*'s marketing campaign), Curtiz's last round of script revisions focused on Lane's story. It had seemed logical to many whom Wald had consulted on the script that the film be geared toward a female audience. Collier Young, cofounder of the Filmmakers Company with the actor-director Ida Lupino, suggested that *Flamingo Road* was a "woman's picture" and that Wald should consider "tailoring it around a big woman star": Lane has the potential for "heroic proportions" (Young to Wald, December 12, 1946). Richard Brooks, brought in to do a major rewrite in early 1948, suggested changes that would maintain the characters and themes in the Robert Wilder and Sally Wilder source play but focus them around Lane. He imagined her:

> Independent, world-wise, completely adult (extremely more so than
> her male contemporaries), mature and striving for social, economic and
> political equality . . . She is a girl who can hold her own in almost any set
> of circumstances. Like most other American girls, she is a mass of contra-
> dictions. On the one hand, she is practical and realistic and, at the same
> time, she is romantic and sentimental. She is penny-wise and pound fool-
> ish. She believes in the Cinderella story. (Brooks to Wald, February 22,
> 1948)

Brooks's version of the script didn't make it to the screen. Curtiz, Crawford, and Wald instead chose to revise the early script by Robert Wilder, which had undergone an earlier rewrite by Edmund North (Wilder co-wrote the play on which the film was based). But the film maintains Brooks's highly contradictory representation of Lane. Indeed, to make such a sexually charged character suitable for PCA approval, she would need to possess multiple sets of opposing characteristics. Thus, she is world-weary and jaded but also optimistic and aspirational. That she wants to leave her "carnival girl" past behind and achieve upward mobility is introduced by her opening voiceover: "There is a Flamingo Road in every town. It is the street of social success. The avenue of achievement. The golden goal for all who struggle and aspire to reach the top, and sometimes find that from the top there is no other place to go." The film is calling attention to itself as a narrative of class mobility, which is intertwined with Lane's aspirations to become respectable.

In her first scene, Lane is seen dancing suggestively (though without bumps and grinds) as a part of the carnival's exotic burlesque show. Even when not dancing, she is perceived to be selling sex. When Fielding first appears in her tent, his body language and the scene's blocking indicate their mutual attraction. She initially assumes that she will have to exchange sex for the meal he offers, but then realizes she has mistaken him for the wrong kind of man. Her "experience," sexual and otherwise, is part of her display and speaks her lower-class status, which is made clear by a series of reverse shots of characters reacting to Lane when they first see her. She stands out as different—lower class and promiscuous—particularly in comparison with Field's longtime girlfriend Annabelle, whom he has stood up in order to spend the evening with Lane.

When Lane first hears about the affluence of Flamingo Road in the diegetic world of the film, she says, "Maybe one of these days, I'll get a place on Flamingo Road myself." The delivery of this line reveals the conflicting aspects of her character. When she says "myself," she seems to be suggesting that she will do it on her own. But will menial work (she is a waitress at this point) allow her to achieve that kind of mobility? Reading the film alongside *Mildred Pierce*, the audience might think otherwise, that Lane's only salable quality is her sexuality and that she can achieve class elevation only through romantic conquests. Unlike Alison in *Female*, Lane's efforts to move from sexual freedom to domestication are met with resistance, not acceptance. Even when she marries Dan and lives on Flamingo Road, her efforts at disguise by way of "enough clothes, furs and jewels to start a department store of her own" are met with disdain by those around her. Her performance as wife and homemaker seems convincing to everyone but Titus. She is free to live out her Cinderella story only after she facilitates his death. The film's final image is particularly telling. After Dan and Lane have embraced and Lane has admitted that she truly loves him now, she walks off to her trial. The final image of her is from behind as she is framed by the vertical bars of the jail cells that surround her. Her freedom is visually indicated by containment. She is free of Titus's constraints, but there is more than a hint that the new world she is entering might not be as idyllic as she imagines.

Flamingo Road's marketing focused on Lane as a "bad girl" rather than as the redeemed domesticated woman she becomes at the end. The ads also drew a direct link between the film and *Mildred Pierce*. Advertising spreads prominently featured a full-length picture of Crawford, a cigarette dangling from her mouth, with a variety of slogans, including: "When you see 'Flamingo Road' you'll be talking about the most exciting woman since 'Mildred Pierce,'" "A Wrong Girl for the Right Side of the Tracks," and "When you live on Flamingo Road you get talked about!" Indeed, the film was sold and received as a woman's film, and the political aspects of the plot were almost entirely ignored. In *BoxOffice* magazine, a

Promotional poster for *Flamingo Road* (Michael Curtiz Productions / Warner Bros., 1949). Digital frame enlargement.

theater owner in Quinlan, Texas, urged other theater owners to "aim for the female audience" and stated that the film was "too deep for most small town audiences," but that it was a "picture that is very well liked by the ladies so make sure your advertising reaches the women" ("Aim at Women Patrons, Advises L. E. Wolcott," *Boxoffice*, November 26, 1949). Reviews also discuss the film's appeal to women. The *Los Angeles Times'* critic writes: "Although its background is political, *Flamingo Road* is always the story of a woman, Lane Bellamy, and hence of Miss Crawford. Everything happens to her, to this paragon . . . whose lips may quiver and whose heart may break but who . . . turns her best profile to the wind, and . . . sees it through. That's our Joanie" (Philip K. Scheuer, "Joan Crawford Stars as Harassed Heroine," *Los Angeles Times*, April 29, 1949, A7). Lane in *Flamingo Road* is seen to be a logical extension of Crawford's public image as a complicated and powerful woman.

Stories written about Crawford around the time of the film's release found ways of equating Lane's transformative journey with Crawford's rags-to-riches, lower-class-to-upper-class real-life story. One profile claims that the film "is a turning point in the career of a grand actress." William Mooring adds that Crawford's career is a "story of shedding": "Shedding the kind of screen roles, which took their setting from the distant dancing days of smoky, half-lighted dives and dance halls to brighten it up into *Our Dancing Daughters* and other screen delights. This led gradually but inevitably towards more 'refined' roles as Joan herself shook off the limitations of her past to take on the enlarged but, in their own way, none the less imprisoning circumstances of screen success" ("*Flamingo Road*," *Picturegoer*, June 18, 1949, 8).

In keeping with Crawford's resilient image, a profile entitled "Joan Crawford's Other Life" supported this transformational class narrative. She started as a "very young and very shy" girl who was the only one at her "private co-ed school who had to work her way through its elegant halls" (Frances Clark, "Joan Crawford's Other Life," *Modern Screen*, June 1950, 60–61). At her first dance, "many an expensive gown on the sidelines was quivering with indignation as its wearer watched the girl in the gaudy bargain dress dominate the dance floor" (62). Once she got to Hollywood, she was "little more than a glorified extra-girl and a queen of the publicity department's cheesecake art" (63). After her debut film, *Dancing Girls*, in which she was still a "flapper so that she could put that on film well enough to make herself an overnight star," she "hit bottom career-wise . . . after leaving MGM" (63). But after *Mildred Pierce*, "everybody cheered and topped their cheers by giving her the Academy Award" (64).

As is commonplace in star profile pieces, Crawford's current success is described in relation to her home and the objects therein. Clark states, "As I looked about at the beauty with which Joan has surrounded herself, I was particularly impressed by the Gagni paintings. They are quite a far cry from the gaudy rhinestone dancing girl. . . . It seemed to me his technique keynoted Joan Crawford—standing out so vividly, so beautifully in her life today against the unhappy backdrop of her early years" (64).

Like Ruth Chatterton, Joan Crawford was profiled in relation to class, which, by extension, was wrapped up in her sexuality and domesticity. Her worthiness as an actress (and as a person) was connoted by her elevation to a world of display—her beautiful home, her paintings. Many Joan Crawford films of this era engage with romance and social mobility (*Mildred Pierce* is the most obvious example), but her rags-to-riches story has striking parallels with Lane's story in *Flamingo Road*. Curtiz saw to it that, as with Crawford's public image, Lane showed an acceptance of toughness, of "seeing it through" from bad girl to good.

This analysis of *Female* and *Flamingo Road* doesn't necessarily give us the answer to O'Neill's question: "What is the woman for Curtiz?" (2014, 103). For a director who made over 150 films, that would be a challenging assignment. What we do gain from examining these two overlooked films is a snapshot of Curtiz's career at two key moments, as well as insight into how his female characters at the time were often subject to contradictory expectations. During the height of the studio system, these expectations were particularly transparent because of PCA rules and regulations: in their essence, these characters are often in conflict with the choices they make in the films. In Alison and Lane (and Chatterton and Crawford), we have two women memorable beyond the narratives in which they are placed. *Female* and *Flamingo Road* may not be the best-known works in Curtiz's oeuvre, but they make transparent how class, sexuality, and display are central to how we define "feminine" and "female" in Hollywood cinema.

Archives

Margaret Herrick Library, Academy of Motion Picture Arts and Sciences, Beverly Hills. Files consulted include History of Cinema, Series 1, Hollywood and Production Code Administration.

Warner Bros. Archives, University of Southern California, Los Angeles. Files consulted include *Flamingo Road* Daily Production Reports (file 1490) and *Flamingo Road* Story Memos and Correspondence (file 1905).

Works Cited

Doane, Mary Ann. 1987. *The Desire to Desire: The Woman's Film of the 1940s*. Bloomington: Indiana University Press.

Doherty, Thomas. 1999. *Pre-Code Hollywood: Sex, Immorality, and Insurrection in American Cinema, 1930-1934*. New York: Columbia University Press.

Female pressbook. 1988. In *Cinema Pressbooks from the Original Studio Collections*, compiled by Warner Bros. Pictures and the Wisconsin Center for Film Theater Research. Reading, UK: Research Publications.

Four Daughters pressbook. 1988. In *Cinema Pressbooks from the Original Studio Collections*, compiled by Warner Bros. Pictures and the Wisconsin Center for Film Theater Research. Reading, UK: Research Publications.

Jacobs, Lea. 1995. *The Wages of Sin: Censorship and the Fallen Woman Film, 1928-1942*. Berkeley: University of California Press.

Kinnard, Roy, and R. J. Vitone. 1986. *The American Films of Michael Curtiz*. Metuchen, NJ: Scarecrow.

Landy, Marcia. 2006. "1949: Movies and the Fate of Genre." In *American Cinema of the 1940s: Themes and Variations*, edited by Wheeler Winston Dixon, 222-243. New Brunswick, NJ: Rutgers University Press.

O'Neill, Eithne. 2014. "Curtiz and Women." Translated by Lisa Joire. *Positif* 635 (January): 103-105.

Robertson, James C. 1993. *The Casablanca Man: The Cinema of Michael Curtiz*. London: Routledge.

CHAPTER 19

Devil-May-Care: Curtiz and Flynn in Hollywood

CONSTANTINE VEREVIS

In the 1930s, Warner Bros. initiated a cycle of costume-adventure pictures that combined the talents of the director Michael Curtiz and the upcoming stars Errol Flynn and Olivia de Havilland. The hitherto unknown Flynn had risen to stardom with *Captain Blood* (1935), a film that marked the studio's mid-decade shift toward more prestigious pictures, and between 1935 and 1941 Curtiz directed eleven of Flynn's seventeen films at Warner Bros.[1] Of these, five belong to a group of (just) six films—all of which star Flynn—that Nick Roddick dubs the "Merrie England" cycle (1983, 235–248). One of Warner Bros.' most recognizable products of the 1930s, the cycle begins with *Captain Blood*, includes *The Charge of the Light Brigade* (1936), *The Prince and the Pauper* (directed by William Keighley, 1937), *The Adventures of Robin Hood* (1938), and *The Private Lives of Elizabeth and Essex* (1939), and concludes with *The Sea Hawk* (1940). Although these pictures are devoted to different historical periods, Roddick argues that—following the example of *Captain Blood*—the films of the Merrie England cycle shared a common marketing strategy, and all six cohere around a central theme. Specifically, Flynn persistently plays "a man for whom moral and political decisions are unambiguous, and who is provided with the chance to put these decisions into practice through direct physical action" (235). Accordingly, Flynn becomes the "embodiment of Warners' philosophy of individual morality," whereby the "heroic acts of an individual" are at the "core of the narrative" and bear the "film's ideology" (236). This essay considers two of these pictures—*The Charge of the Light Brigade* and *The Adventures of Robin Hood*—as films that harnessed Flynn's flawless physiognomy and Curtiz's energetic visual style to (respectively) consolidate and mark out the pinnacle of the cycle.[2]

The Charge of the Light Brigade

Toward the end of 1935, Warner Bros. began to focus its attention on a recently secured contract player, twenty-six-year-old Errol Flynn, casting him in a new version of Rafael Sabatini's 1922 novel *Captain Blood* (previously filmed by Vitagraph in 1924) to be directed by Michael Curtiz. Ted Sennett writes that "the film was a popular success, making a major star of Errol Flynn and marking a turning point in Michael Curtiz' career at the studio" (1971, 150). Seeking to exploit the film's breakthrough, Warner Bros. immediately assigned Curtiz to *The Charge of the Light Brigade* (1936), a high-budget Flynn–de Havilland vehicle designed—in Jack Warner's description—as a "follow-up picture to *Captain Blood*" (quoted in Behlmer 1985, 31). Purchased by Warner Bros. following the major success of Paramount's *Lives of a Bengal Lancer* (1935), the original story, based on events of the Crimean War (1853–1856), was replaced by a totally fabricated narrative, one that reduced major historical figures such as Lord Raglan and Lord Cardigan to minor parts (Thomas, Behlmer, and McCarty 1975, 45–48; Behlmer 1985, 29). Specifically, the revised screenplay draws on Lord Alfred Tennyson's poem and memorialization of the suicidal charge by British light cavalry over open terrain in the Battle of Balaklava, but it stands more generally as a testimonial to the courage and tenacity of British soldiers stationed in remote outposts of the empire, namely, India and Crimea, during the mid-nineteenth century.

The Charge of the Light Brigade opens with a dedication:

> To the officers and men of the Light Brigade who died victorious in a gallant charge at Balaklava for Queen and Country
>   A.D. 1856

A second title card reads:

> The world is indebted to Alfred, Lord Tennyson, Poet Laureate to Her Majesty, Queen Victoria of Great Britain, for perpetuating in an epic poem one of the most distinguished events in history conspicuous for sheer valor . . .

The film's title and major credits come before a disclaimer stating that, while grounded in actual incidents, *The Charge of the Light Brigade* has little to do with the historical charge:

This production has its basis in history. The historical basis, however, has been fictionalized for the purposes of this picture and the names of many characters, many characters themselves, the story, incidents and institutions, are fictitious. With the exception of known historical characters, whose actual names are herein used, no identification with actual persons, living or dead, is intended or should be inferred.

In keeping with this renunciation, the final card—overlaid on a map of northern India—situates the action in the fictional province of Suristan, where—despite its title—the film spends the first three-quarters of its running time, moving to the Crimea only for the climactic charge.

As is evident from the film's 1936 theatrical trailer—one that announces a motion picture "Unmatched for spectacle and suspense" but also "A love story that sweeps from the palaces of India . . . To dangerous desert outposts"—the picture is first of all a romantic tragedy, one involving a love triangle between Captain (later Major) Geoffrey Vickers (Flynn), his fiancée, Elsa Campbell (de Havilland), and Vickers's younger brother and subordinate, Perry (Patric Knowles).[3] The romance is interwoven with the picture's political events, and the film is best remembered for action sequences that depict Geoffrey and his cohorts, the Lancers of the 27th Brigade, battling the forces of the duplicitous chieftain Surat Khan (C. Henry Gordon), a British ally who betrays Geoffrey's trust despite the fact that (early in the film) Vickers saved Surat Khan's life during a dangerous leopard hunt. Surat Khan begins his revolt by launching a surprise attack on the lancers' garrison at Chukoti, his massive army overwhelming the single company left defending the fort. Thinking to spare the lives of civilians, the British commanding officer—Elsa's father, Colonel Campbell (Donald Crisp)—reluctantly surrenders the fort, whereupon Surat Khan's forces open fire, massacring all but a few, including Geoffrey and Elsa, who manage to escape. The remnant of the brigade is subsequently transferred to the Crimea, whereupon Geoffrey suffers a further tragic blow when he comprehends that Perry's feelings for Elsa are reciprocated by his fiancée. Promoted to major, Geoffrey focuses on his military duties and, upon realizing that Surat Khan has moved to support the tsar against the British, proposes a daring frontal attack on the Russians. Accordingly, when the opportunity for the final charge arises, it is not (as historical fact would have it) a tactical blunder, but a move planned by Geoffrey, who—eager for revenge—deliberately falsifies instructions in order to lead survivors of the 27th Brigade in a charge on Surat Khan.

Vickers comes to his decision to disobey command and seize the opportunity to restore the honor of his regiment when he learns that British headquarters refuses to issue an order to fight Surat Khan. He makes an impassioned plea, saying not only that an attack is the lancers' best chance to avenge the Chukoti massacre but also that such a maneuver would occupy the Russians, allowing allied French, Ottoman, and British forces to attack nearby Sebastopol and likely "change the course of the war." Vickers's plan, described by his superior, Sir Charles Macefield (Henry Stephenson), as "admirably daring," is nonetheless dismissed as "too wild" in a dispatch that Vickers is ordered to personally deliver to the commander of the Light Brigade.

In the short, wordless sequence that immediately follows, Curtiz conveys Geoffrey's inner turmoil and imperative for moral and political action. Leaving Macefield's rooms, he enters the hall and then passes through a second door into his own office, turning left toward his desk, where he pauses to examine the dispatch. The camera moves in to frame his profile in close-up. Max Steiner's music rises, and—as the lancer turns his head—a prolonged chord underscores the expression of anguish on his face. The shot continues, following Geoffrey as he slowly moves back across the room to pause in front of a large lamp, its shade casting a dark (symptomatic) shadow over his brow. At this point, he turns decisively back toward his desk, where he sits to study a campaign map. A cut, to a close-up of the map in one hand and (in a slight reframe) to the dispatch in the other, tilts up to a medium close-up of Geoffrey, his stare fixed as he remembers the incident at Chukoti. The shot is held as scenes from the Chukoti massacre—five shots, each lasting two or three seconds, showing murdered women and children and the fallen officer, Colonel Campbell, an open Bible at his hand—are superimposed over his face. As he reaches down for his pen, the camera pulls back to a medium shot and then dissolves to show the order that he is forging for the Light Brigade to advance against the enemy position on Balaklava Heights.

Commenting upon these actions, Sidney Rosenzweig describes Vickers as a conflicted hero, one divided between military tradition, which demands that he follow orders, and human emotion, which insists that he defy this very authority so as to satisfy his desire for revenge (1982, 64–65). As Rosenzweig points out, even more than the external conflict between hero and villain, this internal tension determines both the political and the romance plots of the film. On one hand, Geoffrey falls on the side of tradition, initially refusing to recognize the relationship that has developed between Elsa and Perry. On the other, he is well aware of the blunders of British officials (he advised Campbell against the surrender of the fort at Chukoti) and ultimately takes matters into his own hands in the Crimea (64). The romantic (emotional) and military (historical) plots are intertwined throughout and come together in the short sequence, not quite one minute long, immediately before the charge, in which Geoffrey orders Perry to convey the forged dispatch to general headquarters (for a close analysis of this sequence, see Balio 1993, 109–116). The act of forcing Perry to deliver this order to a sympathetic adviser at once advances the military action and, by deliberately removing Perry from the suicidal charge, demonstrates Geoffrey's acceptance of Perry and Elsa's love for each other. Thinking that his older brother is trying to shame him by denying him a role in the action, Perry (under threat of court-martial) angrily accepts the order to deliver, not knowing that Geoffrey has already given Elsa permission to marry him. In the final shot of the sequence, an almost unnoticeable track forward—a stylistic display not uncommon in Curtiz's work—frames Geoffrey in medium close-up, emphasizing his (double) sacrifice: that of his reputation as a responsible officer, in order to avenge the fallen at Chukoti, and that of his brother's military honor, for the sake of Elsa's happiness. By intertwining the film's major plotlines, the episode resolves the romantic conflict and delivers the rebel-hero, Geoffrey-Flynn—"the embodiment of an action-based morality" typical of the Merrie England cycle (Roddick 1983, 236)—to the heroic charge.

Almost 100 minutes into the film's 115-minute running time, the flapping banner of the 27th Brigade marks the beginning of the charge sequence, the camera tilting down to show Geoffrey on horseback, instructing the bugler to sound the assembly. Addressing the troops, he announces: "Men of the 27th, Surat Khan is on the field with the opposing Russian forces. The same Surat Khan who massacred the women and children at Chukoti. Our chance has come. . . . Men of the 27th, our objective is Surat Khan. Forward!" A title card superimposed over wide panoramic shots of the advancing brigade gives the first stanza of Tennyson's poem:

Half a league, half a league,
Half a league onward,
All in the valley of Death
Rode the six hundred.
"Forward, the Light Brigade!
Charge for the guns," he said;
Into the valley of Death
Rode the six hundred.

Low tracking shots, intercut with medium shots and close-ups of Geoffrey
and other officers, show the advance of the cavalry, the horses gradually
increasing their tempo from a stately gait to a full gallop. As the brigade
mounts its charge, Surat Khan, observing from a vantage point high behind the Russian lines, scoffs at the "tactical blunder," declaring that the
"fools [are] riding to certain death." Bursts of deadly Russian cannon fire
are intercut with long shots and details of men and horses falling, while a
second card presents lines from Tennyson's third stanza:

> Cannon to the right of them,
> Cannon to the left of them,
> Cannon in front of them,
> Volley'd and thunder'd.

Flynn, waving his saber, urges them forward, shouting, "Onward, men,
onward!" Dynamic tracking shots from behind enemy flanks show Russian soldiers running to their positions and discharging rifles as the lancers
stream past. Despite suffering many casualties, the lancers break through
the first line of batteries, forcing the Russians to deploy a cavalry counterattack. Some eight minutes into the sequence, Geoffrey spills from his
horse, does a running mount of another, lifts a lance from a fallen trooper,
and vaults over the enemy barricades. Amid frenzied hand-to-hand combat, he finally finds himself face-to-face with his adversary, Surat Khan,
who discharges his pistol. Mortally wounded, Geoffrey still manages to
hurl his lance to kill Surat Khan, and lives just long enough to see others
in his company bury their lances in the villain's body. In repetition and
rhyme of the opening shot, the camera tilts up from the fallen Vickers to a
tattered but proudly flapping Union Jack, upon which are superimposed
the words of Tennyson's sixth and final stanza:

> When can their glory fade?
> O the wild charge they made!
> All the world wonder'd.
> Honor the charge they made!
> Honor the Light Brigade,
> Noble six hundred!

Unsurprisingly, *The Charge of the Light Brigade* is best known for its
final sequence, the charge often cited as one of the most spectacular action
sequences of the Hollywood studio period. James Robertson writes that

"Men of the 27th, our objective is Surat Khan." Major Geoffrey Vickers (Errol Flynn) in *The Charge of the Light Brigade* (Warner Bros., 1936). Digital frame enlargement.

Curtiz directed the sequence in collaboration with the second unit director and action specialist B. Reeves Eason, and delivered some 77,000 feet of footage to the editor, George Amy (1993, 38). Despite some controversy over its treatment of animals, *The Charge of the Light Brigade* became the studio's most successful film of 1936, earning in excess of $1.5 million, confirming Flynn and de Havilland as stars, and further consolidating Curtiz's position at Warner Bros.

The Adventures of Robin Hood

Initially considered for filming in 1935 with James Cagney in the lead role, *The Adventures of Robin Hood* was recast as a vehicle for Flynn and de Havilland as a follow-up to *Captain Blood* and *The Charge of the Light Brigade*. It was assigned an initial budget of $1.6 million, the largest sum for a Warner Bros. film to that time (Thomas, Behlmer, and McCarty 1975, 62). In January 1936, the producer Hal B. Wallis wrote to Jack Warner, saying he "had already spoken to the writers on 'Robin Hood' reference doing this [picture] for Flynn and feel sure we will have this to follow 'Light Brigade'" (quoted in Behlmer 1985, 44). Late in 1936, Rowland Leigh (co-writer, with Michael Jacoby, of the screenplay for *The Charge of the Light Brigade*) was appointed to prepare an initial screenplay, but Wallis expressed dissatisfaction with the script, providing detailed comments for improving the development of the relationship between Robin and Marian, as well as the script's stilted dialogue (45). Norman Reilly Raine, who wrote, or collaborated on, screenplays for a number of popular Warner Bros. films of the thirties and early forties, and, subsequently, Seton I. Miller, who later co-wrote *The Sea Hawk*, were assigned to revise the work. The final screenplay departed substantially (and necessarily, for reasons of copyright) from Douglas Fairbanks's United Artists version, *Robin Hood* (1922), drawing on traditional English lore and ballads to tell "the story of Robin Hood [as] the swashbuckling, reckless, rakehell type of character who, *by his personal adventures* has endeared himself to generations" (quoted on 47; emphasis in the original).

In September 1937, the cast and crew of *The Adventures of Robin Hood*, under the guidance of the director William Keighley, traveled to Bidwell Park in Chico, California, to shoot the picture's Sherwood Forest sequences. Eason was again assigned to film some of the second unit material, including a major jousting sequence (a legacy of the Fairbanks version) favored by Keighley to open the film, but dropped at the insistence of Raine and Wallis (Thomas, Behlmer, and McCarty 1975, 64; Behlmer 1985, 46–49; Behlmer 1965, 98). At the beginning of November 1937, the associate producer, Henry Blanke, wrote to Wallis that the production was already two weeks behind schedule, and by the end of that month (November 29), the unit production manager, Al Alleborn, had opened up a conversation with Curtiz regarding his taking over the picture, commencing with the shooting of the Nottingham Castle banquet sequence on the morning of December 1, 1937 (Behlmer 1985, 50). Within days, Alleborn wrote to the studio production manager, T. C. Wright: "I think this company with a new crew [Curtiz, and also the assistant director Jack Sullivan and the cameraman Sol Polito, who replaced Tony Gaudio] is moving along 100% better than the [former] crew," and noted Wallis and Blanke's approval of Curtiz's direction (52). Wallis still expressed mild concern that Curtiz's "enthusiasm to make great shots and composition" might further delay the production, but filming eventually closed on January 22, 1938, by which time the cost of the picture had risen to $2,033,000 (51–52).[4] Available accounts indicate that Curtiz—who shared final screen credit with Keighley—directed all the Nottingham Castle and town scenes, all other interiors, some of the archery tournament, and some additions to the Sherwood Forest action sequences begun by Keighley and Eason at Chico but later refilmed at Lake Sherwood, west of the San Fernando Valley (Behlmer 1965, 98; Robertson 1993, 43).

The enduring reputation of *The Adventures of Robin Hood*, sustained through its energy and vitality, is attributable to Curtiz's direction and Flynn's performance, and the film is a peak achievement in each man's career. Essential to this, as Rosenzweig (1982) notes, is the film's rhythmic organizing pattern, which consists, on one hand, of *action* in the court world of the self-appointed regent of England—the villainous Prince John (Claude Rains)—and his allies, the Norman lord Sir Guy of Gisbourne (Basil Rathbone) and the sheriff of Nottingham (Melville Cooper); and, on the other, of *counteraction* in the "green world" of those loyal to the absent King Richard (Ian Hunter): Sir Robin of Locksley (Flynn), Will Scarlett (Patric Knowles), Little John (Alan Hale), and Friar Tuck (Eugene Pallette). Moreover, as Ina Rae Hark points out, this contrasting pattern, never simply conveyed by plot or dialogue, is expressed through the film's mise-en-scène. Specifically, the court world is rigid and inflexible, whereas that of the forest is characterized by its spontaneity and motion: "The film . . . is structured around a series of episodes in which Robin and his band use their vitality to disrupt [the] static Norman geometry, until the final battle at Nottingham Castle destroys the deadening order once and for all" (1976, 9).

The two worlds find further contrast in and through the picture's three-strip Technicolor process, one that renders the closed interiors of Nottingham Castle in greys and dark crimsons and the open world of Sherwood Forest in sunlit greens. In these ways, Curtiz's visual style underlines an opposition between demonic and idyllic worlds that not only characterizes *The Adventures of Robin Hood* but figures to varying degrees in almost all the director's films: "court world and green world . . . stand [in the films of Curtiz] for a whole series of related oppositions . . . [namely, and as evidenced in *The Charge of the Light Brigade*] cynicism and idealism, imprisonment and freedom, war and love, public duty and private desire" (Rosenzweig 1982, 31).

The stature of the legendary stories of Robin Hood and his Merry Men, articulated in and through the film's contrasting castle and forest worlds, makes for spectacular—and sometimes, romantic—fairy-tale-like sequences. As Roddick notes, "If in *The Charge of the Light Brigade* the [final] action is the vehicle for morality [then] in *The Adventures of Robin Hood* the spectacle is the guarantee of the vaguely populist message" (1983, 242). The shift from action to spectacle is significant for the way that, in the latter instance, Robin-Flynn becomes the *embodiment* of moral justice.

This is plainly evident in the way that he commands the frame during two key sequences that establish and chart the progress of the conflict, namely, the opening feast at Nottingham Castle and Robin's ambush of Sir Guy in Sherwood Forest (Hark 1976, 9–16).

The first begins with two smooth craning shots that establish the interior of the great banquet hall, servants conveying platters of food and drink to the assembled party headed by Prince John, with Gisbourne and the sheriff seated to his right and Lady Marian (de Havilland) and the bishop of the Black Canons (Montagu Love) at his left. The order and formality of the court is interrupted by the sudden intrusion of Robin, who arrives brazenly carrying on his shoulders the carcass of a poached deer, which he unceremoniously dumps on Prince John's table. Invited to sit, Robin sets out to deliberately provoke, placing his feet on the table and rocking in his chair in blatant disregard of authority. The accompanying dialogue establishes both Robin's contempt for John (who announces, to the astonishment of all, that he has appointed himself regent of England) and Marian's disapproval of Robin and his outlaw methods. When Robin tells John that he will organize a people's revolt against his treachery, the prince calls for his guards to capture him. At this point, Robin springs into action, overturning tables and chairs, engaging the guards in swordplay, and eventually eluding the small army through his singular athleticism and unmatched proficiency with the bow and arrow.

The Nottingham sequence finds its counterpoint in the Sherwood Forest feast that follows Robin's recruitment of Little John and Friar Tuck, and the interception and capture of the sheriff, Gisbourne, Marian, and their guard as their royal caravan travels through the green wood to deliver a ransom, meant for saving King Richard, to John. In contrast to the banquet held in the rigid and artificially lit interiors of Nottingham Castle, the feast unfolds in a sunny clearing of Sherwood Forest, each shot a riot of movement and activity, with salient action often unfolding in midground while figures pass across the foreground of the frame. In the castle sequence, Robin ascended to high vantage points to thwart and elude his would-be captors. In the forest, he again assumes high positions, initially swinging from a vine to a high rock to cheerfully greet Guy and Marian ("Welcome to Sherwood, my lady") and, during the feast, by leaping upon a trestle to address his loyal band and mock Guy and the sheriff. The sequence is significant too for bringing the romance plot (and Marian's conflicted character) into line with the political action. Marian initially describes Robin as a "Saxon hedge robber" and the anarchic display of his assembled group as "revolting." But when Robin demonstrates that the captured money is not for his band but for Richard's ransom,

"I do begin to see, a little, now." Lady Marian (Olivia de Havilland) and Robin Hood (Errol Flynn) in *The Adventures of Robin Hood* (Warner Bros., 1938). Digital frame enlargement.

her admission that she "may have been hasty," accompanied by the first hint of Erich Wolfgang Korngold's evocative "Robin and Lady Marian" theme, marks her changing attitude. Still somewhat confused by Robin's methods, Marian is next escorted to a clearing in the forest where (in a trademark Warners scene, consistent with its "social problem" films) she meets peasants, Saxon and Norman alike, who have been persecuted by John's soldiers and tax gatherers and who have sought Robin's protection. As Robin and Marian make their way back to the main feast, her words—"I do begin to see, a little, now"—and a reprise of Korngold's love theme signal her shift in loyalty and newfound feelings for Robin.

The two feasts—action and counteraction—are followed by two spectacular set pieces. The first, in response to the audacious hijacking of the king's ransom, is the archery contest designed by the sheriff to lure Robin to the court. Unable to resist the temptation of securing Lady Marian's favor (she is to present a golden arrow to the winner), Robin wins the competition by impossibly splitting his opponent's arrow to score a double bull's-eye. The miraculous shot betrays Robin's identity, and he is captured and briefly held before making a daring escape (with Marian's assistance).

The second sequence, which follows upon the return of King Richard, is the disruption of John's coronation and the ensuing battle at Nottingham Castle, which culminates in a fencing duel between Robin and Sir Guy. Between the two is the castle chamber scene in which Robin climbs to Marian's room to thank her and declare his love. Underscored again by the warm orchestral textures of Korngold's "Robin and Lady Marian" theme, the passage is perhaps the most affecting of any in the Flynn-Curtiz catalogue, in part because, by declining Robin's offer to elope to Sherwood, Marian insists that they put public duty ahead of private desire until proper order has been restored to England (Rosenzweig 1982, 38). The dismantling of the false administration happens most decisively in the final duel—dramatic for Curtiz's use of expressionistic lighting that sees it partially played out as giant silhouettes upon a stone pillar—in which Sir Guy's defeat "resolves both the political conflict (Robin stands for Richard's policies as Guy stands for John's) and the personal (both combatants desire Marian's hand)" (Hark 1976, 16). A just government restored, King Richard declares a united Britain for Norman and Saxon alike, and the film concludes with Richard granting permission for the marriage of the Lady Marian and Sir Robin.

The Adventures of Robin Hood premiered on May 12, 1938, and despite its high negative cost, it was Warner Bros.' top-grossing film of the year (with profits of almost $2 million) and the winner of several major Academy Awards (Balio 1993, 405–410; Robertson 1993, 44). As Roddick points out, the completed film, deceptively effortless in appearance, provides an example of the Hollywood studio system "operating at maximum efficiency" (1983, 241), perfectly articulating the directorial skills of Curtiz and the roguish persona of Flynn, but also the talents of the producer (Wallis), writers (Raine and Miller), art director (Carl Jules Wehl), costume designer (Milo Anderson), editor (Ralph Dawson), and composer (Korngold). The story of Robin Hood has since been revisited many times—each telling a "quasi-independent adaptation" of the beloved myth, grounded in its own social-political context (Georgakas 1998, 70)[5]—but *The Adventures of Robin Hood* stands apart: not only a spectacular success and benchmark for subsequent versions, but a key achievement for Michael Curtiz.

Notes

1. The eleven Curtiz-Flynn films of the period are *Captain Blood*, *The Charge of the Light Brigade*, *The Perfect Specimen* (1937), *The Adventures of Robin Hood*,

Four's a Crowd (1938), *Dodge City* (1939), *The Private Lives of Elizabeth and Essex*, *Virginia City* (1940), *The Sea Hawk, Santa Fe Trail* (1940), and *Dive Bomber* (1941). The two men's reported mutual dislike intensified across this period until the direction of *They Died with Their Boots On* (1942) was reassigned to Raoul Walsh, who went on to direct Flynn in some of his best films of the 1940s. Curtiz also directed Flynn's first wife, Lili Damita, in several films in the 1920s.

2. For an indication of the reception and place of these two films, see Frank S. Nugent, "With a Bow to Tennyson, the Strand Offers 'Charge of The Light Brigade,'" *New York Times*, November 2, 1936, 24; and Nugent, "Errol Flynn Leads His Merry Men to the Music Hall in 'The Adventures of Robin Hood,'" *New York Times*, May 13, 1938, 17.

3. The extended trailer—which describes the climactic charge, filmed under the "skilled direction of Michael Curtiz," as "the most spectacular scene ever attempted in motion pictures," and includes behind-the-scenes footage—is available online at the Turner Classic Movies website.

4. For further production detail and background, see Behlmer (1979, 11–41).

5. As has been widely noted, the Curtiz-Flynn version is consistent with other Warner Bros. films of the thirties insofar as it espouses the New Deal politics of the Roosevelt administration, advancing a set of democratic values founded in the culture of the common people (see Georgakas 1998; Hark 1976; Roddick 1983).

Works Cited

Balio, Tino. 1993. *Grand Design: Hollywood as a Modern Business Enterprise, 1930–1939*. New York: Charles Scribner's Sons.

Behlmer, Rudy. 1965. "Robin Hood on the Screen." *Films in Review* 16 (February): 91–102.

———. 1979. *The Adventures of Robin Hood*. Madison: University of Wisconsin Press.

———, ed. 1985. *Inside Warner Bros., 1935-1951*. New York: Viking.

Georgakas, Dan. 1998. "Robin Hood: From Roosevelt to Reagan." In *Play It Again, Sam: Retakes on Remakes*, edited by Andrew Horton and Stuart Y. McDougal, 70-79. Berkeley: University of California Press.

Hark, Ina Rae. 1976. "The Visual Politics of *The Adventures of Robin Hood*." *Journal of Popular Film* 5, no. 1: 3-17.

Robertson, James C. 1993. *The Casablanca Man: The Cinema of Michael Curtiz*. London: Routledge.

Roddick, Nick. 1983. *A New Deal in Entertainment: Warner Brothers in the 1930s*. London: BFI.

Rosenzweig, Sidney. 1982. *"Casablanca" and Other Major Films of Michael Curtiz*. Ann Arbor: UMI Research Press.

Sennett, Ted. 1971. *Warner Brothers Presents: The Most Exciting Years—From "The Jazz Singer" to "White Heat."* New York: Castle.

Thomas, Tony, Rudy Behlmer, and Clifford McCarty. 1975. *The Films of Errol Flynn*. Secaucus, NJ: Citadel.

CHAPTER 20

Uncanny Effigies: Early Sound Cinema and *Mystery of the Wax Museum*

COLIN WILLIAMSON

A curious image from Michael Curtiz's *Mystery of the Wax Museum* (1933) shows a table lined with human heads, all inanimate and made of wax, except one. Between two of the wax figures is Hugo (Matthew Betz), an assistant in the wax museum where much of the film takes place. Hugo has crouched behind the table in such a way that, if viewers did not immediately recognize him from his earlier appearances in the film, they might take him for one of the artificial heads he is crafting in the museum workshop. Hugo eventually stands up, confirming that he is alive. His transformation from inanimate to animate increases the uncertainty of the image by suggesting that the artificial heads on the table might also come to life; or in a more horrifying vein, that they might not be wax at all, but rather the fleshy remains of once-living people.

Although it passes quickly, Hugo's appearance among the wax creations on the table invokes a long history of horror, spectacle, exhibition, and entertainment. The image resembles the playful displays of impossibly living heads on tables in Georges Méliès's *The Four Troublesome Heads* (1898) and *The Man with the Rubber Head* (1901), which are variations of earlier stage illusions that transformed horrifying spectacles of decapitation and dismemberment into entertaining optical effects. Curtiz's image also invokes the culture of death and violence that shaped the emergence of popular wax museums in the late eighteenth century. Building on the work of Philippe Curtius (1737–1794), Marie "Madame" Tussaud (1761–1850) famously populated her wax museums in Paris and London with figures molded through the use of death masks made from the severed heads of guillotine victims of the French Revolution, like Marie Antoinette. This formative intersection of waxworks and corpses continues to shape the image of the wax museum in the popular imagination. As Mark Sand-

Hugo working with wax heads, in *Mystery of the Wax Museum* (Warner Bros., 1933). Digital frame enlargement.

berg explains, "The dead body haunts the wax museum as an institution and has forever linked it, even if only subconsciously, to the macabre" (2003, 23).

Since the affinity between wax museums and death runs deep, it is not surprising that the waxwork figure is at the center of Curtiz's film. *Mystery of the Wax Museum* was the response by Warner Bros. to the success of the horror film genre in the early 1930s, a genre with strong roots in Gothic literature and, as James Fiumara (2012) has shown, in phantasmagoria shows, freak shows, world's fairs, natural history museums, and wax museums. The historical affinity between wax museums and horror accounts in part for the popularity of the wax figure in horror and mystery films such as Paul Leni and Leo Birinsky's *Waxworks* (1924), Karl Freund's *Mad Love* (1935), Harold Young's *The Frozen Ghost* (1945), and Hy Averback's Warner Bros. production *Chamber of Horrors* (1966), to name a few. As a space haunted by death and filled with human doubles that appear to be alive despite their lack of movement and speech, the wax museum offered Curtiz a rich setting to explore a genre that gravitated toward the macabre, the nightmarish, and the monstrous.

Set in the 1920s and 1930s, *Mystery* revolves around the investigation by a young newspaper reporter named Florence Dempsey (Glenda Farrell) into the disappearance of the body of Joan Gale (Monica Bannister) from a Manhattan morgue. (For a fascinating discussion of disappearing bodies in the context of seventeenth-century anatomy, see Guerrini 2015.) Florence's investigation leads her to discover that the missing body, along with several others, was encased in wax and put on display in a local wax museum run by an artist named Ivan Igor (Lionel Atwill). Igor's gruesome scheme of masquerading corpses as waxworks culminates and unravels when he attempts to murder Florence's roommate, Charlotte Duncan (Fay Wray), whose body he plans to turn into a sculpture of none other than Marie Antoinette (thus aping Marie Tussaud). Charlotte is spared at the last minute when the police shoot Igor in the basement of his museum and he falls, like the corpses he embalms, into a vat of boiling wax.

The film's macabre premise, that the waxworks are indeed corpses, its transgressive displays of the dead, and its inclusion of a "monstrous" though entirely human figure in the character of Igor have earned *Mystery* a prominent place in histories of the horror genre. Likewise, *Mystery* has been kept alive in popular culture by its horror remakes: André de Toth's *House of Wax* (1953) and Jaume Collet-Serra's 2005 loose version with the same title. It is important to keep in mind, however, that *Mystery* was released at a time when the horror genre was very much in transition. In the early 1930s, "classical" Hollywood horror films such as Tod Browning's *Dracula* and James Whale's *Frankenstein* (both 1931) were part of a broader filmmaking trend that embedded elements of horror in the well-established mystery and crime melodrama genres. Richard Koszarski has pointed out that whereas horror films before *Mystery*'s release were gaining momentum along these lines by weaving fantastic narratives together with displays of grotesque and otherworldly creatures, Warner Bros. maintained an investment in an aesthetic of "newspaper realism" and offered the wax museum as a site for investigating and demystifying uncanny events (1979, 10–11).

Warner Bros.' simultaneous appeals to horror and mystery recall, in a way, the history of wax museums. Although the reputation of modern wax museums was built on the bodies of the dead that haunt Tussaud's early waxworks, there is also a rich history of museum proprietors who attempted to distance their work from such a macabre association by appealing to middle-class sensibilities. Beginning in the mid-nineteenth century, many spectacles of death and violence were separated from primary waxwork display areas (and oftentimes relegated to museum basements) so that wax museums could be cultivated as respectable institutions of art and enlightenment. Rather than being simply "houses of horror," they were reimagined as spaces of wonder, investigation, and education, with strong ties to the uses of visual display in medical anatomy, the arts, and even newspapers.

This image of the wax museum as a source of both macabre spectacle and educational entertainment sheds new light on a film that has been studied almost exclusively for its place in the history of horror. *Mystery* undoubtedly provides valuable insight into how Warner Bros. negotiated the development of the genre in the 1930s, but there is much more to the film than its significance as an example of classical horror. What are we to make, for example, of the mystery premise of the film, and what might this tell us about *Mystery*'s relationship to the changing landscape of film in the early 1930s?

To answer these questions, I move away from the topic of genre and explore the broader cultural significance of Curtiz's choice to represent the wax museum in the early sound-film era. It is not coincidental that *Mystery* was released at the end of Hollywood's transition to synchronized sound (roughly 1927–1931), which renewed popular perceptions of the cinema as a mysterious medium. As I demonstrate, innovations in sound technologies fueled discourses about the uncanny properties of the moving image that resonated strongly with the waxwork's peculiar "illusion of life." This resonance between the cinema and waxworks suggests that for Curtiz, the wax museum in *Mystery* was not simply a suitable setting for a horror film; it provided a natural space for investigating, if you will, the mysteries of the cinema during a major transitional period in film history.

A Silent House of Wax: Life and Death in the Cinema

Although the film was successful, it would be easy to conclude from its reception that *Mystery* was rather unremarkable relative to the broader changes taking place in the landscape of the cinema. The film was heavily promoted for its use of two-strip Technicolor. But the novelty period for this early Technicolor process had ended by the late 1920s, and audiences were largely uninterested in the effects of color in Curtiz's film.[1] Coming on the heels of horror films like *Dracula* and *Frankenstein*, *Mystery* failed to stand out as a novel contribution to a genre with which audiences were already quite familiar. As a critic in *Variety* remarked, "'Wax Museum' would have been certain of better gate support a year ago. Recognizing this, the Technicolor and the hyper-weirdness apparently were manda-tory studio precautions to offset the element of a belated arrival" (Abel, "Wax Museum (In Technicolor)," *Variety*, February 21, 1933, 14). The per-ceived "untimeliness" of the film extended even to its relationship with the cinema's wondrous transition to sound. *Mystery* employed Warner Bros.' Vitaphone system, which the studio had showcased to great acclaim years earlier with *The Jazz Singer* (1927). Coincidentally, around the time of *Mystery*'s release, the film theorist Rudolf Arnheim cautioned against the implications of color and sound for the general development of film as the reproduction of reality, claiming that many people "do not see that film is on its way to the victory of wax museum ideals over creative art" (1957, 154).[2]

To say that from this perspective there was nothing new about Curtiz's film would be to overlook what does in fact make it such a timely and re-markable piece of early sound cinema. *Mystery* is not significantly *about* the novelty of color, horror, or sound in the way that many films during transitional periods in film history are about innovations that raise ques-tions concerning the nature of the medium. Rather, the film reflects some-thing older and arguably more essential than the changes in the cinema at the end of the silent era: the uncanniness of the moving image.

As with the emergence of the cinema in the 1890s, audiences responded to the transition to sound in the late 1920s with a mixture of wonder and unease. The unfamiliar experiences produced by innovations in sound filmmaking stemmed from a number of sources, including the novelty of synchronization and its attendant technical issues—for example, instances of actors' voices sounding unnatural, unreal, or phantomlike because of technological problems associated with recording and broadcasting them. In his book *Uncanny Bodies*, Robert Spadoni shows that adding sound to previously silent images promoted an acute awareness of the cinema as a strange and even monstrous machine whose images oscillated troublingly between reality and illusion. This awareness of the medium renewed early film audiences' deep fascination with the disturbing, ghostly, and appar-ently inexplicable qualities of silent moving images. Drawing on Tom Gunning's (1995) view of horror as a "ciné-genre"—a genre that explores the properties of the medium—Spadoni argues convincingly that horror films of the early 1930s were both products and reflections of audiences' renewed interest in the cinematic image (2007, 13–25).

Rather than treating *Mystery* as a reflection of the uncanny properties of sound—Igor's waxworks, after all, do not speak—we can approach it as a film that explores what Spadoni calls "the uncanniness of the recently extinguished silent cinema" (2007, 7). *Mystery* revolves around a blurring of the line between human and wax reproduction, which Curtiz promoted by periodically having live actors pose as waxworks in the film. The film gestures to this in its initial invocation of the waxwork as an exceptionally convincing reproduction of reality. Igor is introduced as an artist whose wax sculptures of historical figures such as Joan of Arc and Marie Antoinette are praised as perfect simulations. (At this point he is not yet encasing corpses in wax.) In the opening scene, Igor is shown walking a potential patron, Golatily, through his collection. When the men stop to behold a sculpture of the French Enlightenment thinker Voltaire, Golatily exclaims, "One might almost expect him to speak. I wonder what he'd say after all these years." Here, the waxwork's exceptionally convincing illusion of life is tempered by what it lacks—movement and speech—so that it appears to waver between the realms of the living and the dead, the animate and the inanimate, the real and the fake.

Golatily's experience closely resembles early responses to the cinema's reality effects. The cinematic image is deeply wedded to the living human body in motion, but it is also haunted by stillness and death (Mulvey 2006). It is now a commonplace in the study of early film history, for example, that the lack of sound and color in the novel spectacle of people moving on the screen inspired descriptions of the cinema as an uncanny medium, a silent domain of shadows and ghosts that appeared to be on the verge of coming to life. Golatily's playful remark that Igor has brought the real Voltaire back to life—"I wonder what he'd say after all these years"— calls to mind, too, discourses about the cinema's ability to preserve and reanimate the dead. As a photographic medium, the cinema inherited the idea that the still photograph, by virtue of being a literal trace or "index" of the person who appeared in front of the camera, "embalms" the subject—as André Bazin puts it—and preserves that person against the passage of time and the realities of death (Bazin 2005, 14–15). By introducing movement to still photography, the cinema garnered attention for its ability to figuratively breathe life into records of the past. Waxworks share this peculiar nature. As Marina Warner explains, "Wax cheats death; it simulates life; it proves true and false" (2006, 23). In *The Audible Past*, Jonathan Sterne makes a similar case for the "voices of the dead" reproduced by sound technologies (2003, 287–333).

The resonance of the waxwork with the cinema's uncanny illusion of life acquires another layer when Igor begins embalming dead bodies. Igor changes his method of creating waxworks after a fire destroys his original sculptures and cripples his hands, depriving him of the ability to manu ally craft the figures entirely from wax. To compensate, he uses a large machine in the basement of his museum to cover corpses in molten wax. He then offers them as sculptures to an unwitting public. The deception is interesting on several levels. The affinity between the wax corpse and the art of taxidermy points to the shared history of wax museums and displays of the dead. It is not insignificant, for example, that Igor procures Joan Gale's dead body from a morgue. Vanessa Schwartz has shown that in nineteenth-century Paris, the corpse was the common ground between wax museums and the public morgue, where the exhibition of unidentified bodies served as a form of entertaining spectacle (1998, 45–148). The cinema eventually became part of this culture of taxidermic visual display in the 1890s. (Igor's waxworks are affiliated also with a genealogy that extends from the famous nineteenth-century scientific curiosity known as the "Soap Lady," whose corpse was embalmed naturally in a waxy substance known as adipocere, to the recent and highly controversial anatomical displays of "plastinated" corpses—embalmed by using liquid plastic—in public museums as scientific specimens and works of art.)

More intriguing is the atmosphere of uncertainty that surrounds the wax corpse. An advertisement in the *Film Daily* on February 16, 1933, referred to waxworks like Igor's Joan of Arc and Marie Antoinette by posing the question: "Are They Women or Wax?" (For a good discussion of the representation of gender in Curtiz's film, see Bloom 2003, 113–139.) An advertisement in the *Motion Picture Herald* on January 7, 1933, promised that one could "See wax figures turn to human beings. . . . See human beings turn to wax!" This uncertainty about whether Igor's waxworks are real people or wax reproductions does more than simply drive the mystery narrative forward. One reviewer in the *New York Times* explained: "The human players in 'The Mystery of the Wax Museum' move among a variegated array of figures that to all appearance are human also, lacking only the breath of life. Some of these figures reproduce the physical appearance of living characters in the story" and effectively blur the line between live actors and their reproductions as waxworks ("In a Waxworks," February 12, 1933, 142).

For audiences, the question "Women or Wax?" is significantly complicated by the fact that, throughout the film, many of the "dead" waxworks are played by living actors. (A similar tradition in science fiction films involves actors performing as androids, a notable case being Ridley Scott's 1982 *Blade Runner*.) Fay Wray's first appearance in *Mystery*, for example, is not as her character, Charlotte Duncan, but as Igor's "true" waxwork reproduction of Marie Antoinette in the opening sequence of the film.

Wray's early appearance is justified by the fact that Igor is eventually inspired to murder and embalm Charlotte because of her uncanny resemblance to his original sculpture, which was destroyed in the fire. Wray's "regal" appearance as Marie Antoinette could also be seen as a playful gesture to her rising star status as the "scream queen" of the early sound era. Shortly after the release of *Mystery*, she appeared, famously, as Ann Darrow in *King Kong*. In any case, the strangeness of Wray posing as a waxwork stems from the fact that to the film's audience, she is obviously "alive"—a close-up shows her moving while trying to hold a pose—at the same time that within the story world, she is really "fake." Answering the question "Women or Wax?" is thus not as straightforward as the advertisement implies; Wray's Marie Antoinette appears to be both.

In the case of Igor's wax corpses, the lines between human and wax, living and dead, animate and inanimate become more complicated still. For example, when Florence begins to investigate Joan's disappearance, it becomes clear that the missing body was turned into a sculpture of Joan of Arc. Joan became "Joan." The wax corpse is displayed in several scenes throughout the film; close-ups that focus on Joan's face confirm that she is the woman whose photograph circulated in newspaper reports of her disappearance early on. Whenever the waxwork is shown, Curtiz alternates between shots of an actual wax figure and shots of Monica Bannister, the living actress playing the role of Joan, posing as the waxwork. With each of her appearances, it becomes increasingly (and surprisingly) difficult to distinguish between Bannister the human and Joan the waxwork as the two begin to double each other. Similarly, in a climactic struggle between Charlotte and Igor, it is revealed that Igor has all along been wearing a wax "face" (modeled on the face of the actor Lionel Atwill) to mask the fact that his real face was horribly disfigured in the fire that opened the film. In both cases—a live actress masquerading as a corpse masquerading as a waxwork, and a monster masquerading as a waxwork played by an actor—the real and the fake are woven together so tightly that the wax museum in the film becomes something like a hall of mirrors; the "real" is lost in a play of illusions.

Investigating the Secrets of the Wax Museum

Both Warner Bros. and audiences seemed to recognize that the ontological uncertainty of the wax corpse extended well beyond the story world of Curtiz's film. As part of a promotional campaign for the release of *Mystery*, the entrances and lobbies of the Warner Bros.' Hollywood Theatre in Los Angeles and Strand Theatre in New York were transformed into wax museums. Before moving into the main spaces of the theaters and taking their seats to grapple with the question "Women or Wax?" on the screen, audiences encountered three-dimensional reproductions of Fay Wray, Monica Bannister, and others from the film on display as waxworks. Among these wax figures audiences would also find the occasional "mechanical man" or "human automaton," a live actor posing as a waxwork or statue who would periodically move.[1] Other theaters offered similar exhibits. According to one report, the proprietors of a theater in New Haven, Connecticut, simply filled their lobby with a collection of sculptures borrowed from a wax museum at a local amusement park ("Real Museum," *Hollywood Reporter*, February 28, 1933, 3). Such exhibition practices, which were common to the horror genre, are noteworthy in the case of *Mystery* because they allowed and encouraged audiences to become part of the illusion that plays out in the film.

Using a movie theater as a space for reflecting on the waxwork's complex illusion of life resembles one of the earliest intersections of motion pictures and wax museums. In the 1890s, the famous Parisian wax museum known as the Musée Grévin exhibited cinematic images alongside its waxworks. Because of its striking reality effects, the cinema was seen as a natural extension of the museum's aesthetic, which was rooted as much in verisimilitude and authenticity as in the waxwork's status as a playful illusion. (René Clair points to this in a bizarre sequence at the end of his 1925 film *Le Voyage imaginaire*, wherein waxworks in the Grévin—including one of Charlie Chaplin—come mysteriously to life.) As Schwartz explains, "In film audiences would revel as they had in wax figures, in the lifelike and the real" (186). This revelry seems to have animated the exhibition practices surrounding the release of *Mystery*. More than a simple gimmick to draw crowds, the movement of the waxwork from the screen into the lobby of the movie theater blurred the line between the film and reality and invited audiences to see the cinema itself as a kind of wax museum, an uncanny space for reveling in spectacular illusions of life.

Extending the waxwork's complex game of perception in this way suggests that *Mystery* inspired the same highly participatory viewing practices that characterize the wax museum. Since at least the 1800s, wax museums have functioned according to the logic of what James Cook (2001) and Neil Harris (1975) call, respectively, "artful deception" and "operational aesthetics": a mode of visual display linked with P. T. Barnum's nineteenth-century hoaxes and cultivating a desire for information helpful in rationally explaining spectacles that appear to defy reason. As part of the nineteenth-century culture of popular entertainments that employed this mode—including magicians' tricks and automata—wax museums invited visitors to become detectives and investigate the waxwork's illusion of life. In *Mystery*, this viewing practice is taken up by Florence, whose inquiry into the mysterious disappearance of Joan's body from the morgue leads her to investigate the uncanny resemblance between Igor's Joan of Arc and the missing woman. The investigation is a macabre play on Sandberg's idea that "the corpse is the hidden secret of the wax museum" (2003, 22). Of course, Sandberg means that lurking behind the spectacles in wax museums are the dead bodies and death masks that artists like Tussaud used in creating exceptionally convincing wax likenesses. Igor's disturbing secret is that his sculptures appear so lifelike because they are in fact bodies. And the film's secret is that waxworks and actors oftentimes play uncanny doubles of each other on the screen.

Florence's investigation also speaks to the history of the wax museum as a form of popular visual education. As early as the seventeenth century, wax reproductions were used in teaching and studying human anatomy in Europe. Located somewhere between art and science, these waxworks were prominent fixtures of medical laboratories, where they were studied by students, and museums, where the public consumed the models as objects of wonder. Similarly, toward the end of the nineteenth century the Musée Grévin used the reality effects of waxworks to offer visitors sensational object lessons in historical and current events. The museum even modeled wax displays on headlines taken directly from Parisian newspapers, a practice that Warner Bros. employed as part of its commitment to the "newspaper realism" that influenced the mystery narrative of Curtiz's film. It is quite fitting from this perspective that Florence, a newspaper reporter, is the one who uses the waxwork to solve the mystery of life and death in the wax museum.

Waxworks play a minor but strikingly similar role in *Doctor X* (1932), a Warner Bros. film also directed by Michael Curtiz and starring Lionel Atwill and Fay Wray. Atwill plays Xavier, a doctor who becomes one of several suspects in an investigation by a newspaper reporter, Lee Taylor (Lee Tracy), into a series of murders involving cannibalism in New York City. To prove his innocence, Xavier invites all the suspects to be subjected to an electrical lie-detector machine as they are shown reenactments of the murders, some of which are staged with wax reproductions of the murder victims. The reenactments expose the real killer, Wells (Preston Foster), who attempts to make Xavier's daughter Joan (Fay Wray) his next victim until Taylor, posing as a waxwork, surprises Wells and pushes him out a window, causing him to fall to his death. As in *Mystery*, the interplay between human and wax is placed in the service of solving a mystery.

Mystery can be seen in this vein not only as a horror film set in a wax museum but also as part of the broader history of visual display that the wax museum represents. Consider, for example, that the nineteenth century was marked by a deep cultural fascination with the doubling of the human body in the form of what Sandberg calls uncanny effigies—for example, waxworks, automata, and photographs. The proliferation of these effigies created a world saturated with reproductions of reality that challenged peoples' experience of modern life. With the emergence of the cinema, this challenge became an enduring feature of modernity. Sandberg explains, "Our visual culture quite simply demands broad competency in effigies—not simply the mannequin [or waxwork] kind but an entire range of recorded and digital bodies" (2003, 3–4). Wax museums helped promote this competency by creating opportunities for people to play with and reaffirm the lines between categories that waxworks seem to blur. Curtiz shaped *Mystery* to reflect this playfulness in Florence's investigation, which allows her to navigate a world filled with artful deceptions, that is, to separate the real from the fake.

The museum's dual function as a house of horrors and a site of discovery is important for thinking about the cultural significance of Curtiz's evocation of the waxwork's illusion of life in the early sound era. In *Mystery*, the exploration of the waxwork as an uncanny spectacle located somewhere between life and death was no doubt influenced by the German expressionist and romantic traditions—including Robert Wiene's *The Cabinet of Dr. Caligari* (1920) and E. T. A. Hoffmann's *The Sandman* (1816)—that the Hungarian-born Curtiz brought with him to Hollywood in the 1920s (for more on this, see Koszarski 1979, 27–29). As I have argued elsewhere, such spectacular displays of illusion oftentimes teach audiences something about the cinema precisely because, as "mysteries," they invite audiences to learn more about the techniques and technologies used to produce them (Williamson 2015). In its narrative, exhibition practices, and the popular discourses it provoked, *Mystery* seems to have taken shape as an investigation of the properties that make the cinematic image uncanny. More specifically, the representation of the waxwork in the film functions as a kind of device for thinking about the cinema's ability to create "doubles" of reality, which the transition to sound brought firmly back to the center of film culture.

Approaching *Mystery of the Wax Museum* with this in mind sheds a revealing light on the film's grip on the popular imagination. When Warner

Bros. remade Curtiz's film as *House of Wax* under André de Toth's direction in 1953, the wax museum functioned as a setting for exploring the reality effects of novel 3-D technologies. Jaume Collet-Serra's 2005 version was released similarly in an atmosphere of intense interest in the effects that innovative digital technologies had on the line between reality and simulation. Although Collet-Serra's film was not a digital-effects vehicle, it is worth noting that at the time, motion capture and animation technologies were creating exceptionally convincing human simulacra—much like Igor's wax corpses—by digitizing the living bodies of real actors. (For more on these "virtual actors," see North 2008; Pomerance 2016.) Given the evoking of Curtiz's film during these recent periods of innovation, it is not difficult to imagine, as Michelle Bloom does (2003, 116), that *Mystery* will be conjured again when the cinema intersects with interactive virtual-reality technologies that promise to renew how we think about the nature of moving images. We might say that the waxwork haunts the cinema in the way that the corpse haunts the wax museum, that is, as a reminder of the cinema's endurance as an uncanny medium.

Notes

I am very grateful to the staff of the Warner Bros. Archives at the University of Southern California for helping with my research, and to James Fiumara, Adam Hart, and Murray Leeder for their helpful comments on early drafts of this chapter.
    1. Mordaunt Hall of the *New York Times* noted that the film's "ghastly details [were] accentuated by being filmed in Technicolor," but for the most part reviewers made little mention of the use of color other than to note that *Mystery* employed it ("Lionel Atwill and Fay Wray in a Gruesome Narrative about a Mad Modeler of Wax Figures," *New York Times*, February 18, 1933, 13).
    2. For Arnheim, the aesthetic potential of the cinema was to be found not in its capacity to imitate reality—a capacity exemplified by his idea of the "complete film"—but in the expressive qualities of the medium and the fundamental differences between film and reality.

Works Cited

Arnheim, Rudolph. 1957. *Film as Art* [1932]. Berkeley: University of California Press.
Bazin, André. 2005. "The Ontology of the Photographic Image." In *What Is Cinema?*, vol. 1, edited and translated by Hugh Gray, 9–16. Berkeley: University of California Press.
Bloom, Michelle. 2003. *Waxworks: A Cultural Obsession*. Minneapolis: University of Minnesota Press.

Cook, James. 2001. *The Arts of Deception: Playing with Fraud in the Age of Barnum*. Cambridge, MA: Harvard University Press.

Fiumara, James. 2012. "Grotesque Attractions: Genre History, Popular Entertainment, and the Origins of the Horror Film." PhD dissertation, University of Pennsylvania.

Guerrini, Anita. 2015. *The Courtiers' Anatomists: Animals and Humans in Louis XIV's Paris*. Chicago: University of Chicago Press.

Gunning, Tom. 1995. "'Those Drawn with a Very Fine Camel's Hair Brush': The Origins of Film Genres." *Iris* 19:49–61.

Harris, Neil. 1975. *Humbug: The Art of P. T. Barnum*. Chicago: University of Chicago Press, 1975.

Koszarski, Richard. 1979. Introduction to *Mystery of the Wax Museum*, 9–36. Madison: University of Wisconsin Press.

Mulvey, Laura. 2006. *Death 24x a Second: Stillness and the Moving Image*. Chicago: University of Chicago Press.

North, Dan. 2008. *Performing Illusions: Cinema, Special Effects, and the Virtual Actor*. London: Wallflower.

Pomerance, Murray. 2016. *Moment of Action: Riddles of Cinematic Performance*. New Brunswick, NJ: Rutgers University Press.

Sandberg, Mark. 2003. *Living Pictures, Missing Persons: Mannequins, Museums, and Modernity*. Princeton, NJ: Princeton University Press.

Schwartz, Vanessa. 1998. *Spectacular Realities: Early Mass Culture in Fin-de-Siècle Paris*. Berkeley: University of California Press.

Spadoni, Robert. 2007. *Uncanny Bodies: The Coming of Sound Film and the Origins of the Horror Genre*. Berkeley: University of California Press.

Sterne, Jonathan. 2003. *The Audible Past: Cultural Origins of Sound Reproduction*. Durham, NC: Duke University Press.

Warner, Marina. 2006. *Phantasmagoria: Spirit Visions, Metaphors, and Media into the Twenty-First Century*. New York: Oxford University Press.

Williamson, Colin. 2015. *Hidden in Plain Sight: An Archaeology of Magic and the Cinema*. New Brunswick, NJ: Rutgers University Press.

Michael Curtiz Filmography

European Productions

Unless otherwise noted, all of Curtiz's European productions are silent.

Az ezüst kecske
As Kertész Mihály
Kino-Riport (1912). Short.

Today and Tomorrow (Ma és holnap)
As Kertész Mihály
Projectograph (October 14, 1912).

My Husband's Getting Married (Házasodik az uram)
As Kertész Mihály
Projectograph (May 22, 1913).

The Last Bohemian (Az utolsó bohém)
As Kertész Mihály
Projectograph (November 6, 1913).

Captive Souls (Rablélek)
As Kertész Mihály
Uher Filmgyár (January 14, 1914).

Golddigger (Az aranyásó)
As Mihály Kertész
Projectograph (March 23, 1914).

The Princess in a Nightrobe (A hercegnö pongyolája)
As Kertész Mihály
Kino-Riport (May 6, 1914).

Prisoner of the Night (Az éjszaka rabja)
As Kertész Mihály
Projectograph (1914). Short.

The Undesirable (A tolonc)
As Kertész Mihály
ProJa Filmgyár (March 20, 1915).

The Borrowed Babies (A kölcsönkért)
As Kertész Mihály
ProJa Filmgyár (March 22, 1915).

Bánk bán
As Kertész Mihály
ProJa Fillmgyár (April 19, 1915).

One Who Is Loved by Two (Akit ketten szeretnek)
As Kertész Mihály
Terrus (December 6, 1915).

The Medic (Az ezüst kecske)
As Kertész Mihály
Kino-Riport (October 23, 1916).

The Strength of the Fatherland (A magyar föld ereje)
As Kertész Mihály
(Hungary, 1916).

The Karthauzer (A karthausi)
As Michael Curtiz
(Hungary, 1916). Silent.

Seven of Spades (Makkhetes)
As Mihály Kertész
(Hungary, 1916).

Mr. Doctor (Doktor úr)
As Kertész Mihály
(Hungary, 1916).

The Wolf (Farkas)
As Kertész Mihály
Kino-Riport (January 1, 1917).

The Black Rainbow (A fekete szivárvány)
As Kertész Mihály
Kino-Riport (January 8, 1917).

The Charlatan (A kuruzsló)
As Kertész Mihály
Phõnix Film (September 10, 1917).

Tatárjárás
As Kertész Mihály
Glória Filmvállalat (October 10, 1917). Short.

The Red Samson (*A vörös Sámson*)
As Kertész Mihály
Phōnix Film (November 21, 1917).

The Last Dawn (*Az utolsó hajnal*)
As Mihály Kertész
(Hungary, 1917).

The Fishing Bell (*Halálcsengö*)
As Mihály Kertész
Star Film (Hungary, 1917).

The Colonel (*Az ezredes*)
As Mihály Kertész
Starfilm (Hungary, 1917).

Tavasz a télben
As Mihály Kertész
(Hungary, 1917).

Secret of St. Job Forest (*A szentjóbi erdö titka*)
As Mihály Kertész
(Hungary, 1917).

Peace's Road (*A béke útja*)
As Mihály Kertész
(Hungary, 1917).

Nobody's Son (*A senki fia*)
As Kertész Mihály
(Hungary, 1917).

Master Zoard (Zoárd mester)
As Mihály Kertész
(Hungary, 1917).

Jean the Tenant (*Árendás zsidó*)
As Kertész Mihály
(Hungary, 1917).

Earth's Man (*A föld embere*)
As Kertész Mihály
(Hungary, 1917).

A Penny's History (*Egy krajcár története*)
As Kertész Mihály
(Hungary, 1917).

A víg özvegy
As Kertész Mihály
(Hungary, 1918). Musical.

99
As Mihály Kertész
(Hungary, September 2, 1918).

The Devil
As Kertész Mihály
(Hungary, October 4, 1918).

A skorpió I.
As Kertész Mihály
(Hungary, December 1918).

Magic Waltz (Varázskeringö)
As Kertész Mihály
(Hungary, December 4, 1918).

The Sunflower Woman (A napraforgós hölgy)
As Mihály Kertész
(Hungary, December 6, 1918).

The Ugly Boy
As Kertész Mihály
(Hungary, 1918).

Lulu
As Michael Curtiz
Phoenix Studios (1918).

Lu, the Coquette
As Mihály Kertész
(Hungary, 1918).

Júdás
As Mihály Kertész
(Hungary, 1918).

Alraune
As Mihály Kertész
Kertész Hunnia Filmvállalat/Phoenix (January 1919).

Jön az öcsém
As Kertész Mihály
(Hungary, April 3, 1919). Short.

Die Dame mit dem schwarzen Handschuh
As Michael Kertesz
Sascha-Film (November 21, 1919).

Liliom
As Kertész Mihály
Phoenix (1919).

Boccaccio
As Michael Kertesz
Sascha-Film (January 30, 1920).

Der Stern von Damaskus
As Michael Kertesz
Sascha-Film (September 3, 1920).

Die Gottesgeisel
As Michael Kertesz
Sascha-Verleih (September 10, 1920).

Mrs. Tutti Frutti
As Michael Kertész
Sascha-Film (January 14, 1921).

Good and Evil (Herzogin Satanella)
As Kertész Mihály
Sascha-Film (February 4, 1921).

Mrs. Dane's Confession (Frau Dorothys Bekenntnis)
As Michael Kertesz
Sascha-Film (October 7, 1921; United States, March 5, 1924).

Labyrinth of Horror (Wege des Schreckens)
As Mihaly Kertesz
Sascha-Film (November 11, 1921).

Sodom und Gomorrha
As Mihály Kertész
Sascha-Film (United States, March 26, 1923).

Der junge Medardus
As Michael Kertész
Sascha-Film (October 5, 1923).

Die Lawine
As Michael Kertesz
Sascha-Film (October 16, 1923).

Nameless
As Michael Kertész
Sascha-Film (December 28, 1923).

Harun al Raschid
As Michael Kertész
Sascha-Film (March 21, 1924).

The Moon of Israel
As Michael Courtice
Sascha-Film (October 24, 1924).

General Babka
As Michael Curtiz
(Austria, 1924).

Ein Spiel ums Leben
As Michael Curtiz
(Austria, 1924).

Red Heels
As Michael Kertesz
Sascha-Film (October 16, 1925).

Fiaker Nr. 13
As Michael Kertesz
Sascha-Film/Phoebus-Film AG (February 5, 1926).

The Golden Butterfly (*Der goldene Schmetterling*)
As Michael Kertesz
Sascha-Film/Phoebus-Film AG (July 31, 1926).

American Productions

Before 1940, the date given is for the first American screening, typically in New York. After 1940, dates are given for the American premiere screening, in any location.

The Third Degree
Warner Bros. (December 1, 1926). 80 m. Silent. Black and white.
1.33:1, photographed by Hal Mohr
Written by Graham Baker from a play by Charles Klein
With Dolores Costello, Louise Dresser, Rockliffe Fellowes, Jason Robards

A Million Bid
Warner Bros. (May 28, 1927). 70 m. Silent. Black and white.
1.33:1, photographed by Hal Mohr
Written by Robert Dillon from a play by Mrs. Sidney Drew [as George
    Cameron]
With Dolores Costello, Warner Oland, Betty Blythe, William Demarest

The Desired Woman
Warner Bros. (August 27, 1927). 70 m. Silent. Black and white.
1.33:1, photographed by Conrad Wells
Written by Anthony Coldeway from a story by Darryl F. Zanuck [as Mark
    Canfield]
With Irene Rich, William Russell, William Collier Jr., Douglas Gerrard

Good Time Charley
Warner Bros. (November 5, 1927). 70 m. Silent. Black and white.
1.33:1, photographed by Barney McGill.

Written by Anthony Coldeway, Owen Francis, and Ilona Fülöp from a story
  by Darryl F. Zanuck
With Warner Oland, Helene Costello, Clyde Cook, Montagu Love

Tenderloin
Warner Bros. (March 14, 1928). 85 m. Vitaphone (talking sequences). Black and
  white.
1.37:1, photographed by Hal Mohr
Written by Joseph Jackson and Edward T. Lowe Jr. from a story by Darryl F.
  Zanuck [as Melville Crossman]
With Dolores Costello, Conrad Nagel, Mitchell Lewis, Dan Wolheim

Noah's Ark
Warner Bros. (November 1, 1928). 135 m. Mono sound (talking sequences,
  musical score, and sound effects). Black and white.
1957 rerelease: 75 m.; 1990s restoration: 100 m.
1.33:1, photographed by Barney McGill and Hal Mohr
Music by Alois Reiser
Written by Anthony Coldeway from a story by Darryl F. Zanuck
With Dolores Costello, George O'Brien, Noah Beery, Louise Fazenda, Myrna Loy

Glad Rag Doll
First National Pictures (May 4, 1929). 70 m. Vitaphone sound. Black and white.
1.37:1, photographed by Byron Haskin
Written by Graham Baker from a story by Harvey Gates
With Dolores Costello, Ralph Graves, Audrey Ferris, Albert Gran

Madonna of Avenue A
Warner Bros. (June 22, 1929). 71 m. Vitaphone sound. Black and white.
1.37:1, photographed by Byron Haskin
Written by Ray Doyle and Francis Powers from a story by Darryl F. Zanuck [as
  Mark Canfield]
With Dolores Costello, Grant Withers, Douglas Gerrard, Louise Dresser

The Gamblers
Warner Bros. (June 29, 1929). 60 m. Mono sound and silent. Black and white.
1.37:1, photographed by William Rees
Music by Alois Reiser
Written by J. Grubb Alexander from a play by Charles Klein
With H. B. Warner, Lois Wilson, Jason Robards, George Fawcett

Hearts in Exile
Warner Bros. (September 14, 1929). 82 m. Mono sound. Black and white.
1.33:1, photographed by William Rees
Written by Harvey Gates from a play by John Oxenham
With Dolores Costello, Grant Withers, James Kirkwood, George Fawcett

Mammy
Warner Bros. (March 26, 1930). 84 m. Vitaphone sound. Black and white, with
  two sequences in two-strip Technicolor.

1.20:1, photographed by Barney McGill
Written by Joseph Jackson and Gordon Rigby from a play by Irving Berlin
With Al Jolson, Lois Moran, Lowell Sherman, Louise Dresser

Under a Texas Moon
Warner Bros. (April 1, 1930). 82 m. Vitaphone sound. Two-strip Technicolor.
1.37:1, photographed by William Rees
Written by Gordon Rigby from the novel by Stewart Edward White
With Frank Fay, Raquel Torres, Myrna Loy, Armida, Noah Beery

The Matrimonial Bed
Warner Bros. (August 2, 1930). 69 m. Vitaphone sound. Black and white.
1.37:1, photographed by Devereaux Jennings
Written by Harvey F. Thew and Seymour Hicks from the French original by
    Yves Mirande and André Mouézy-Éon
With Frank Fay, James Gleason, Lilyan Tashman, Beryl Mercer, Florence
    Eldridge

The Office Wife (uncredited directorial work with Lloyd Bacon)
Warner Bros. (August 23, 1930). 59 m. Vitaphone sound. Black and white.
Photographed by William Rees
Music by Alois Reiser
Written by Charles Kenyon from a magazine serial by Faith Baldwin
With Dorothy Mackaill, Lewis Stone, Natalie Moorhead, Joan Blondell

Bright Lights (a.k.a. *Adventures in Africa*)
First National Pictures (September 21 1930). 69 m. Vitaphone sound. Black
    and white.
1.20:1, photographed by Lee Garmes and Charles Schoenbaum
Written by Humphrey Pearson and Henry McCarty
With Dorothy Mackaill, Frank Fay, Noah Beery, Daphne Pollard

River's End
Warner Bros. (November 1, 1930). 75 m. Mono sound. Black and white.
1.37:1, photographed by Robert Kurrie
Written by Charles Kenyon from a story by James Oliver Curwood
With Charles Bickford, Evalyn Knapp, Zasu Pitts, J. Farrell MacDonald

A Soldier's Plaything (a.k.a. *Come Easy*)
Warner Bros. (November 1, 1930). 56 m. Mono sound. Black and white.
1.37:1, photographed by Barney McGill and J. O. Taylor (uncredited)
Written by Perry Vekroff and Arthur Caesar from a story by Viña Delmar
With Ben Lyon, Harry Langdon, Lotti Loder, Noah Beery, Jean Hersholt

Dämon des Meeres (a.k.a. *Demon of the Sea*; a.k.a. *The Sea Demon*)
Co-directed by William Dieterle (uncredited)
Warner Bros. (March 12, 1931, in Berlin). Mono sound. Black and white.
1.37:1, photographed by Sidney Hickox
Written by Ulrich Steindorff and J. Grubb Alexander from the novel *Moby-Dick*,
    by Herman Melville
With William Dieterle, Lissy Arna, Anton Pointner, Karl Etlinger

God's Gift to Women (a.k.a. *The Devil Was Sick*; a.k.a. *Too Many Women*)
Warner Bros. (April 13 1931). 72 m. Vitaphone sound. Black and white.
1.33:1, photographed by Robert Kurrie
Written by Joseph Jackson and Raymond Griffith from a play by Jane Hinton
With Frank Fay, Laura La Plante, Joan Blondell, Charles Winninger, Alan
    Mowbray, Louise Brooks

The Mad Genius
Warner Bros. (November 7, 1931). 81 m. Mono sound. Black and white.
1.37:1, photographed by Barney McGill
Written by Harvey Thew and J. Grubb Alexander from a play by Martin Brown
With John Barrymore, Marian Marsh, Charles Butterworth, Donald Cook

The Woman from Monte Carlo
First National Pictures (January 9, 1932). 65 m. Mono sound. Black and white.
1.37:1, photographed by Ernest Haller
Written by Harvey Thew from a play by Claude Farrère and Lucien Nepoty
With Lil Dagover, Walter Huston, Warren William, John Wray, Robert Warwick

Alias the Doctor
Co-directed by Lloyd Bacon (uncredited)
First National Pictures (March 26, 1932). 61 m. Mono sound. Black and White.
1.37:1, photographed by Barney McGill
Written by Houston Branch and Charles Kenyon from a play by Emric Foeldes
With Richard Barthelmess, Marian Marsh, Norman Foster, Adrienne Dore

The Strange Love of Molly Louvain (a.k.a. *The Tinsel Lady*)
First National Pictures (May 28, 1932). 73 m. Mono sound. Black and white.
1.37:1, photographed by Robert Kurrie
Written by Erwin S. Gelsey and Brown Holmes from a play by Maurine Dallas
    Watkins
With Ann Dvorak, Lee Tracy, Richard Cromwell, Guy Kibbee

Doctor X
First National Pictures (August 27, 1932). 76 m. Mono sound. Two-strip
    Technicolor.
1.37:1, photographed by Ray Rennahan
Written by Robert Tasker and Earl Baldwin from a play by Howard W.
    Comstock and Allen C. Miller
With Lionel Atwill, Fay Wray, Lee Tracy, Preston Foster

The Cabin in the Cotton
First National Pictures (October 15, 1932). 78 m. Mono sound. Black and white.
1.37:1, photographed by Barney McGill
Costumes by Orry-Kelly
Written by Paul Green from the novel by Harry Harrison Kroll
With Richard Barthelmess, Dorothy Jordan, Bette Davis, Hardie Albright

20,000 Years in Sing Sing
First National Pictures (December 24, 1932). 78 m. Mono sound. Black and
    white.

1.37:1, photographed by Barney McGill
Written by Wilson Mizner and Brown Holmes, adapted by Courtenay Terrett
and Robert Lord from the book by Lewis E. Lawes
With Spencer Tracy, Bette Davis, Arthur Byron, Lyle Talbot, Louis Calhern

Mystery of the Wax Museum
Warner Bros. (February 18, 1933). 77 m. Vitaphone sound. Two-strip Technicolor.
1.37:1, photographed by Ray Rennahan
Costumes by Orry-Kelly
Special effects by Rex Wimpy
Written by Don Mullaly and Carl Erickson from a story by Charles S. Belden
With Lionel Atwill, Fay Wray, Glenda Farrell, Frank McHugh

The Keyhole
Warner Bros. (March 25, 1933). 69 m. Mono sound. Black and white.
1.37:1, photographed by Barney McGill
Costumes by Orry-Kelly
Written by Robert Presnell from a story by Alice D. G. Miller
With Kay Francis, George Brent, Glenda Farrell, Monroe Owsley

Private Detective 62
Warner Bros. (June 10, 1933). 66 m. Mono sound. Black and white.
1.37:1, photographed by Tony Gaudio
Costumes by Orry-Kelly
Music by Richard Rodgers
Written by Rian James from a story by Raoul Whitfield
With William Powell, Margaret Lindsay, Ruth Donnelly, Gordon Westcott

The Mayor of Hell (a.k.a. *Reform School*)
Directed by Archie Mayo and Michael Curtiz (uncredited)
Warner Bros. (June 24, 1933). 90 m. Mono sound. Black and white.
1.37:1, photographed by Barney McGill and Merritt B. Gerstad (uncredited)
Written by Edward Chodorov from a story by Islin Auster
With James Cagney, Madge Evans, Arthur Byron, Allen Jenkins

Goodbye Again
First National Pictures (September 9, 1933). 66 m. Mono sound. Black and white.
1.37:1, photographed by George Barnes
Costumes by Orry-Kelly
Written by Ben Markson from a play by George Haight and Alan Scott
With Warren William, Joan Blondell, Genevieve Tobin, Hugh Herbert, Wallace Ford

The Kennel Murder Case
Warner Bros. (October 28, 1933). 73 m. Mono sound. Black and white.
1.37:1, photographed by William Rees
Written by S. S. Van Dine, Robert N. Lee, and Peter Milne; adapted by Robert Presnell
With William Powell, Mary Astor, Eugene Pallette, Ralph Morgan, and Asta

Female
First National Pictures (November 11, 1933). 60 m. Mono sound. Black and white.
1.37:1, photographed by Sidney Hickox
Costumes by Orry-Kelly
Music by Harry Warren
Written by Gene Markey and Kathryn Scola; suggested by a story by Donald Henderson Clarke
With Ruth Chatterton, George Brent, Lois Wilson, Johnny Mack Brown

Mandalay
Warner Bros. (February 10, 1934). 65 m. Mono sound. Black and white.
1.37:1, photographed by Tony Gaudio
Costumes by Orry-Kelly
Written by Austin Parker and Charles Kenyon from a story by Paul Hervey Fox
With Kay Francis, Ricardo Cortez, Warner Oland, Lyle Talbot

Jimmy the Gent (a.k.a. *Always a Gent*)
Warner Bros. (March 17, 1934). 67 m. Mono sound. Black and white.
1.37:1, photographed by Ira Morgan
Costumes by Orry-Kelly
Written by Bertram Milhauser from a story by Laird Doyle and Ray Nazarro
With James Cagney, Bette Davis, Allen Jenkins, Alan Dinehart

The Key (a.k.a. *High Peril*)
Warner Bros. (June 9, 1934). 71 m. Mono sound. Black and white.
1.37:1, photographed by Ernest Haller
Costumes by Orry-Kelly
Written by Laird Doyle from a play by R. Gore-Browne and J. L. Hardy
With William Powell, Edna Best, Colin Clive, Donald Crisp

British Agent (a.k.a. *Brutal Agent*)
First National Pictures (September 15, 1934). 80 m. Mono sound. Black and white.
1.37:1, photographed by Ernest Haller
Costumes by Orry-Kelly
Written by Laird Doyle from a book by R. H. Bruce Lockhart
With Leslie Howard, Kay Francis, William Gargan, Phillip Reed, Irving Pichel

Black Fury
First National Pictures (May 18, 1935). 94 m. Mono sound. Black and white.
1.37:1, photographed by Byron Haskin
Written by Abem Finkel and Carl Erickson from a play by Harry R. Irving
With Pau Muni, Karen Morley, William Gargan, Barton MacLane

The Case of the Curious Bride
Warner Bros. (April 13, 1935). 80 m. Mono sound. Black and white.
1.37:1, photographed by David Abel
Costumes by Orry-Kelly
Written by Tom Reed from a story by Erle Stanley Gardner
With Warren William, Margaret Lindsay, Donald Woods, Claire Dodd

Go into Your Dance (a.k.a. *Casino de Paree*)
Directed by Archie Mayo, Michael Curtiz (uncredited), and Robert Florey
    (uncredited)
Warner Bros. (April 20, 1935). 89 m. Mono sound. Black and white.
1.37:1, photographed by Tony Gaudio and Sol Polito (uncredited)
Costumes by Orry-Kelly
Written by Earl Baldwin from a story by Bradford Ropes
With Al Jolson, Ruby Keeler, Glenda Farrell, Barton MacLane, Akim Tamiroff

Front Page Woman
Warner Bros. (July 20, 1935). 82 m. Mono sound. Black and white.
1.37:1, photographed by Tony Gaudio
Costumes by Orry-Kelly
Written by Laird Doyle, Lillie Hayward, and Roy Chanslor from a story by
    Richard Macaulay
With Bette Davis, George Brent, Roscoe Karns, Wini Shaw

Little Big Shot
Warner Bros. (September 7, 1935). 78 m. Mono sound. Black and white.
1.37:1, photographed by Tony Gaudio and Byron Haskin (uncredited)
Costumes by Orry-Kelly
Written by Jerry Wald, Julius J. Epstein, and Robert Hardy Andrews from a
    story by Harrison Jacobs
With Sybil Jason, Glenda Farrell, Robert Armstrong, Edward Everett Horton

Captain Blood
Warner Bros./Cosmopolitan Productions (December 28, 1935). 119 m. Mono
    sound. Black and white.
Rerelease: 99 m.
1.37:1, photographed by Ernest Haller and Hal Mohr
Music by Erich Wolfgang Korngold
Written by Casey Robinson from the novel by Rafael Sabatini
With Errol Flynn, Olivia de Havilland, Lionel Atwill, Basil Rathbone

The Walking Dead
Warner Bros. (March 14, 1936). 66 m. Mono sound. Black and white.
1.37:1, photographed by Hal Mohr
Costumes by Orry-Kelly
Written by Ewart Adamson, Peter Milne, Robert Andrews, and Lillie Hayward
    from a story by Ewart Adamson and Joseph Fields
With Boris Karloff, Ricardo Cortez, Edmund Gwenn, Marguerite Churchill

Anthony Adverse
Directed by Mervyn LeRoy and Michael Curtiz (uncredited)
Warner Bros. (August 29, 1936). 141 m. Mono sound. Black and white.
1.37:1, photographed by Tony Gaudio
Music by Erich Wolfgang Korngold
Written by Sheridan Gibney and Milton Krims from the novel by Hervey Allen
With Fredric March, Olivia de Havilland, Donald Woods, Anita Louise,
    Edmund Gwenn, Claude Rains

The Charge of the Light Brigade
Warner Bros. (October 20, 1936). 115 m. Mono sound. Black and white.
Recut: 100 m.
1.37:1, photographed by Sol Polito
Music by Max Steiner
Written by Michael Jacoby and Rowland Leigh from a story by Jacoby and the
    poem by Alfred Lord Tennyson
With Errol Flynn, Olivia de Havilland, Patric Knowles, Henry Stephenson, Nigel
    Bruce, Donald Crisp, David Niven

Black Legion
Directed by Archie Mayo and Michael Curtiz (uncredited)
Warner Bros. (January 30, 1937). 83 m. Mono sound. Black and white.
1.37:1, photographed by George Barnes
Written by Abem Finkel and William Wister Haines from a story by Robert Lord
With Humphrey Bogart, Dick Foran, Erin O'Brien-Moore, Ann Sheridan

Stolen Holiday
Warner Bros. (February 6, 1937). 80 m. Mono sound. Black and white.
1.37:1, photographed by Sidney Hickox
Costumes by Orry-Kelly
Written by Casey Robinson from a story by Warren Duff and Virginia Kellogg
With Kay Francis, Claude Rains, Ian Hunter, Alison Skipworth

Marked Woman
Directed by Lloyd Bacon and Michael Curtiz (uncredited)
Warner Bros. (April 10, 1937). 96 m. Mono sound. Black and white.
1.37:1, photographed by George Barnes
Costumes by Orry-Kelly
Written by Robert Rossen and Abem Finkel
With Bette Davis, Humphrey Bogart, Lola Lane, Isabel Jewell, Mayo Methot

Mountain Justice
Warner Bros. (April 24, 1937). 83 m. Mono sound. Black and white.
1.37:1, photographed by Ernest Haller
Written by Norman Reilly Raine and Luci Ward
With George Brent, Josephine Hutchinson, Guy Kibbee, Mona Barrie

Kid Galahad (a.k.a. *The Battling Bellhop*)
Warner Bros. (May 29, 1937). 102 m. Mono. Black and white.
1.37:1, photographed by Tony Gaudio
Costumes by Orry-Kelly
Music by Heinz Roemheld (uncredited) and Max Steiner (uncredited)
Written by Seton I. Miller from a *Saturday Evening Post* story by Francis Wallace
With Edward G. Robinson, Bette Davis, Humphrey Bogart, Wayne Morris,
    Harry Carey

The Perfect Specimen
Warner Bros. (December 15, 1937). 97 m. Mono sound. Black and white.
1.37:1, photographed by Charles Rosher and Jack A. Marta (uncredited)

Written by Norman Reilly Raine, Lawrence Riley, Brewster Morse, and Fritz
Falkenstein from a magazine story by Samuel Hopkins Adams
With Errol Flynn, Joan Blondell, Hugh Herbert, Edward Everett Horton, May
Robson

Gold Is Where You Find It
Warner Bros. (February 12, 1938). 94 m. Mono sound. Technicolor.
1.37:1, photographed by Sol Polito
Music by Max Steiner
Written by Warren Duff and Robert Buckner from a *Cosmopolitan* serial story by
Clements Ripley
With George Brent, Olivia de Havilland, Claude Rains, Margaret Lindsay

The Adventures of Robin Hood
Warner Bros. (May 14, 1938). 102 m. Mono sound. Technicolor.
1.37:1, photographed by Tony Gaudio and Sol Polito
Music by Erich Wolfgang Korngold
Written by Norman Reilly Raine and Seton I. Miller
With Errol Flynn, Olivia de Havilland, Basil Rathbone, Claude Rains, Alan
Hale, Eugene Pallette, Patric Knowles

Four's a Crowd (a.k.a. *All Rights Reserved*)
Warner Bros. (September 3, 1938). 92 m. Mono sound. Black and white.
1.37:1, photographed by Ernest Haller
Costumes by Orry-Kelly
Written by Casey Robinson and Sig Herzig from a story by Wallace Sullivan
With Errol Flynn, Olivia de Havilland, Rosalind Russell, Patric Knowles, Walter
Connolly

Four Daughters
Warner Bros. (August 9, 1938). 90 m. Mono sound. Black and white.
1.37:1, photographed by Ernest Haller
Costumes by Orry-Kelly
Music by Max Steiner
Written by Julius J. Epstein and Lenore J. Coffee from a *Cosmopolitan* story by
Fannie Hurst
With Claude Rains, Jeffrey Lynn, John Garfield, Frank McHugh, May Robson

Angels with Dirty Faces (a.k.a. *Battle of City Hall*)
Warner Bros. (November 26, 1938). 97 m. Mono sound. Black and white.
1.37:1, photographed by Sol Polito
Costumes by Orry-Kelly
Music by Max Steiner
Written by John Wexley and Warren Duff from a story by Rowland Brown. Ben
Hecht and Charles MacArthur were uncredited writers.
With James Cagney, Pat O'Brien, Humphrey Bogart, Ann Sheridan, George
Bancroft, and the "Dead End" Kids

Blackwell's Island
Directed by William McGann and Michael Curtiz (uncredited)

Warner Bros. (March 25, 1939). 71 m. Mono sound. Black and white.
1.37:1, photographed by Sidney Hickox
Written by Crane Wilbur from a story by Wilbur and Lee Katz
With John Garfield, Rosemary Lane, Dick Purcell, Victor Jory

Dodge City
Warner Bros. (April 8, 1939). 104 m. Mono sound. Technicolor.
1.37:1, photographed by Sol Polito
Music by Max Steiner
Written by Robert Buckner
With Errol Flynn, Olivia de Havilland, Ann Sheridan, Bruce Cabot

Sons of Liberty (in Technicolor Specials 1938–1939 Season)
Warner Bros. (May 20, 1939). 20 m. Mono sound. Technicolor.
1.37:1, photographed by Sol Polito and Ray Rennahan
Written by Crane Wilbur
With Claude Rains, Gale Sondergaard, Donald Crisp, Montagu Love

Daughters Courageous (a.k.a. *A Family Affair*)
Warner Bros. (July 22, 1939). 107 m. Mono sound. Black and white.
1.37:1, photographed by James Wong Howe and Ernest Haller (uncredited)
Music by Max Steiner
Written by Julius J. Epstein and Philip G. Epstein from a play by Dorothy
    Bennett and Irving White
With John Garfield, Claude Rains, Jeffrey Lynn, Fay Bainter, May Robson,
    Donald Crisp

The Private Lives of Elizabeth and Essex
Warner Bros. (November 11, 1939). 106 m. Vitaphone sound. Technicolor.
1.37:1, photographed by Sol Polito
Costumes by Orry-Kelly
Music by Erich Wolfgang Korngold
Written by Norman Reilly Raine and Aeneas MacKenzie from the play by
    Maxwell Anderson
With Bette Davis, Errol Flynn, Olivia de Havilland, Donald Crisp, Alan Hale,
    Vincent Price

Four Wives
Warner Bros. (December 25, 1939). 110 m. Mono sound. Black and white.
1.37:1, photographed by Sol Polito and James Wong Howe (uncredited)
Music by Max Steiner
Written by Julius J. Epstein, Philip G. Epstein, and Maurice Hanline; suggested
    by a book by Fannie Hurst
With Priscilla Lane, Rosemary Lane, Lola Lane, Gale Page, Claude Rains

Virginia City
Warner Bros. (March 16, 1940). 121 m. Mono sound (RCA). Black and white
    sepia-toned.
1.37:1, photographed by Sol Polito
Costumes by Orry-Kelly

Music by Max Steiner
Written by Robert Buckner, Howard Koch (uncredited), and Norman Reilly
  Raine (uncredited)
With Errol Flynn, Miriam Hopkins, Randolph Scott, Humphrey Bogart

The Sea Hawk (a.k.a. *Beggars of the Sea*)
Warner Bros. (July 1, 1940). 127 m. Mono sound (RCA). Black and white, with
  sepia-toned Panama sequences.
Rerelease: 109 m.
1.37:1, photographed by Sol Polito
Costumes by Orry-Kelly
Music by Erich Wolfgang Korngold
Written by Howard Koch and Seton I. Miller
With Errol Flynn, Brenda Marshall, Claude Rains, Donald Crisp, Flora Robson

Santa Fe Trail (a.k.a. *Diary of the Santa Fe*)
Warner Bros. (December 13, 1940). 110 m. Mono sound (RCA). Black and white.
1.37:1, photographed by Sol Polito
Music by Max Steiner
Written by Robert Buckner
With Errol Flynn, Olivia de Havilland, Raymond Massey, Ronald Reagan

The Sea Wolf
Warner Bros. (March 21, 1941). 100 m. Mono sound (RCA). Black and white.
Rerelease: 87 m.
1.37:1, photographed by Sol Polito
Music by Erich Wolfgang Korngold
Written by Robert Rossen from the novel by Jack London
With Edward G. Robinson, Ida Lupino, John Garfield, Alexander Knox

Dive Bomber (a.k.a. *Beyond the Blue Sky*)
Warner Bros. (August 12, 1941). 132 m. Mono sound (RCA). Technicolor.
1.37:1, photographed by Bert Glennon and Winton C. Hoch
Music by Max Steiner
Written by Frank Wead and Robert Buckner from a story by Wead
With Errol Flynn, Fred MacMurray, Ralph Bellamy, Alexis Smith

Captains of the Clouds
Warner Bros. (February 12, 1942). 114 m. Mono sound (RCA). Technicolor.
1.37:1, photographed by Wilfred M. Cline and Sol Polito
Music by Max Steiner
Written by Arthur T. Horman, Richard Macaulay, and Norman Reilly Raine
  from a story by Horman and Roland Gillett
With James Cagney, Dennis Morgan, Brenda Marshall, Alan Hale

Yankee Doodle Dandy
Warner Bros. (May 29, 1942). 126 m. Mono sound (RCA). Black and white.
1.37:1, photographed by James Wong Howe
Music by George M. Cohan
Written by Robert Buckner and Edmund Joseph from a story by Buckner
With James Cagney, Joan Leslie, Walter Huston, Richard Whorf, Irene Manning

Casablanca
Warner Bros. (November 26, 1942). 102 m. Mono sound (RCA). Black and
   white.
Cut version: 82 m.
1.37:1, photographed by Arthur Edeson
Costumes by Orry-Kelly
Music by Max Steiner
Written by Julius J. Epstein, Philip G. Epstein, and Howard Koch from a play by
   Murray Burnett and Joan Alison
With Humphrey Bogart, Ingrid Bergman, Paul Henreid, Claude Rains, Conrad
   Veidt, Sydney Greenstreet, Peter Lorre

Mission to Moscow
Warner Bros. (April 28, 1943). 123 m. Mono sound (RCA). Black and white.
1.37:1, photographed by Bert Glennon
Costumes by Orry-Kelly
Music by Max Steiner
Written by Howard Koch from a book by Joseph E. Davies
With Walter Huston, Ann Harding, Oskar Homolka, George Tobias, Gene
   Lockhart, Eleanor Parker

This Is the Army
Warner Bros. (July 29, 1943). 121 m. Mono sound (RCA). Technicolor.
1.37:1, photographed by Bert Glennon and Sol Polito
Costumes by Orry-Kelly
With music by Irving Berlin and additional music by Max Steiner
Written by Casey Robinson and Claude Binyon from an Irving Berlin play
With George Murphy, Joan Leslie, George Tobias, Alan Hale, Charles
   Butterworth, Dolores Costello

Passage to Marseille
Warner Bros. (February 16, 1944). 109 m. Mono sound (RCA). Black and white.
1.37:1, photographed by James Wong Howe
Music by Max Steiner
Written by Casey Robinson and Jack Moffitt from the novel by Charles Nordhoff
   and James Norman Hall
With Humphrey Bogart, Claude Rains, Michèle Morgan, Philip Dorn, Sydney
   Greenstreet, Peter Lorre

Janie
Warner Bros. (July 25, 1944). 102 m. Mono sound (RCA). Black and white.
1.37:1, photographed by Carl E. Guthrie
Written by Agnes Christine Johnston and Charles Hoffman from a play by
   Josephine Bentham and Herschel V. Williams Jr.
With Joyce Reynolds, Robert Hutton, Edward Arnold, Ann Harding, Alan Hale,
   Robert Benchley

Roughly Speaking
Warner Bros. (January 31, 1945). 117 m. Mono sound (RCA). Black and white.
1.37:1, photographed by Joseph Walker

Music by Max Steiner
Written by Louise Randall Pierson from a book by her
With Rosalind Russell, Jack Carson, Robert Hutton, Jean Sullivan

Mildred Pierce
Warner Bros. (September 28, 1945). 111 m. Mono sound (RCA). Black and
     white.
1.37:1, photographed by Ernest Haller
Music by Max Steiner
Written by Ranald MacDougall from the novel by James M. Cain
With Joan Crawford, Jack Carson, Zachary Scott, Eve Arden, Ann Blyth, Bruce
     Bennett

Night and Day
Warner Bros. (July 2, 1946). 128 m. Mono sound (RCA). Technicolor.
1.37:1, photographed by Peverell Marley, William V. Skall, and Bert Glennon
     (uncredited)
With music by Cole Porter
Written by Charles Hoffman, Leo Townsend, and William Bowers from an
     adaptation by Jack Moffitt
With Cary Grant, Alexis Smith, Monty Woolley, Ginny Simms, Jane Wyman, Eve
     Arden

Life with Father
Warner Bros. (August 14, 1947). 118 m. Mono sound (RCA). Technicolor.
1.37:1, photographed by Peverell Marley and William V. Skall
Written by Donald Ogden Stewart from a memoir by Clarence Day and a play
     by Howard Lindsay and Russel Crouse
With William Powell, Irene Dunne, Elizabeth Taylor, Edmund Gwenn, Zasu Pitts

The Unsuspected
Michael Curtiz Productions/Warner Bros. (October 3, 1947). 103 m. Mono
     sound (RCA). Black and white.
1.37:1, photographed by Elwood (Woody) Bredell
Music by Franz Waxman
Written by Ranald MacDougall from an adaptation by Bess Meredyth of a novel
     by Charlotte Armstrong
With Joan Caulfield, Claude Rains, Audrey Totter, Constance Bennett, Hurd
     Hatfield

Romance on the High Seas
Directed by Curtiz with musical numbers staged by Busby Berkeley
Warner Bros./Michael Curtiz Productions (June 25, 1948). 99 m. Mono sound
     (RCA). Technicolor.
1.37:1, photographed by Elwood Bredell
Written by Julius J. Epstein and Philip G. Epstein, with additional dialogue by
     I. A. L. Diamond, from a story by Sixto Pondal Ríos and Carlos A. Olivari
With Jack Carson, Janis Paige, Don DeFore, Doris Day, Oscar Levant

My Dream Is Yours
Michael Curtiz Productions/Warner Bros. (April 15, 1949). 101 m. Mono sound (RCA). Technicolor.
1.37:1, photographed by Wilfred M. Cline and Ernest Haller
Written by Harry Kurnitz and Dane Lussier from Allen Rivkin and Laura Kerr's adaptation of a story by Paul Finder Moss and Jerry Wald
With Jack Carson, Doris Day, Lee Bowman, Adolphe Menjou, Eve Arden

Flamingo Road
Michael Curtiz Productions/Warner Bros. (April 28, 1949). 94 m. Mono sound (RCA). Black and white.
1.37:1, photographed by Ted McCord
Music by Max Steiner
Written by Robert Wilder from a play by Wilder and Sally Wilder
With Joan Crawford, Zachary Scott, Sydney Greenstreet, David Brian, Gladys George

The Lady Takes a Sailor
Warner Bros. (December 16, 1949). 99 m. Mono sound (RCA). Black and white.
1.37:1, photographed by Ted McCord
Music by Max Steiner
Written by Everett Freeman from a story by Jerry Gruskin
With Jane Wyman, Dennis Morgan, Eve Arden, Robert Douglas

Young Man with a Horn
Warner Bros. (February 9, 1950). 112 m. Mono sound (RCA). Black and white.
1.37:1, photographed by Ted McCord
Music adviser: Harry James
Written by Carl Foreman and Edmund H. North from the novel by Dorothy Baker
With Kirk Douglas, Lauren Bacall, Doris Day, Hoagy Carmichael, Juano Hernandez

Bright Leaf
Warner Bros. (June 16, 1950). 110 m. Mono sound (RCA). Black and white.
1.37:1, photographed by Karl Freund
Music by Victor Young
Written by Ranald MacDougall from a novel by Foster Fitz-Simons
With Gary Cooper, Lauren Bacall, Patricia Neal, Jack Carson, Donald Crisp

The Breaking Point
Warner Bros. (September 30, 1950). 97 m. Mono sound (RCA). Black and white.
1.37:1, photographed by Ted McCord
Music by Max Steiner
Written by Ranald MacDougall from the novel *To Have and Have Not,* by Ernest Hemingway
With John Garfield, Patricia Neal, Phyllis Thaxter, Juano Hernandez, Wallace Ford

Force of Arms (a.k.a. *A Girl for Joe*)
Warner Bros. (August 13, 1951). 99 m. Mono sound (RCA). Black and white.
1.37:1, photographed by Ted McCord
Music by Max Steiner
Written by Orin Jannings from a story by Richard Tregaskis
With William Holden, Nancy Olson, Frank Lovejoy, Gene Evans

Jim Thorpe—All-American
Warner Bros. (August 24, 1951). 107 m. Mono sound (RCA). Black and white.
1.37:1, photographed by Ernest Haller
Music by Max Steiner
Written by Douglas Morrow and Everett Freeman from a story by Morrow and
   Vincent X. Flaherty
With Burt Lancaster, Charles Bickford, Steve Cochran, Phyllis Thaxter

I'll See You in My Dreams
Warner Bros. (December 6, 1951). 110 m. Mono sound (RCA). Black and white.
1.37:1, photographed by Ted McCord
With songs by Walter Donaldson, Isham Jones, Vincent Youmans, and others
Written by Melville Shavelson and Jack Rose from a story by Louis F. Edelman
   and Grace Kahn
With Doris Day, Danny Thomas, Frank Lovejoy, Patrice Symore, James Gleason,
   Mary Wickes

The Story of Will Rogers
Warner Bros. (July 17, 1952). 109 m. Mono sound (RCA). Technicolor.
1.37:1, photographed by Wilfred M. Cline
Music by Victor Young
Written by Frank Davis and Stanley Roberts from Jack Moffitt's adaptation of a
   magazine story by Betty Blake Rogers
With Will Rogers Jr., Jane Wyman, Carl Benton Reid, Eve Miller, James Gleason

The Jazz Singer
Warner Bros. (December 30, 1952). 107 m. Mono sound (RCA). Technicolor.
1.37:1, photographed by Carl E. Guthrie
With music by Max Steiner (uncredited)
Written by Frank Davis, Leonard Stern, and Lewis Meltzer from a play by
   Samson Raphaelson
With Danny Thomas, Peggy Lee, Eduard Franz, Mildred Dunnock

Trouble Along the Way (a.k.a. *Alma Mater*)
Warner Bros. (April 4, 1953). 110 m. Mono sound (RCA). Black and white.
1.37:1, photographed by Archie Stout
Music by Max Steiner
Written by Melville Shavelson and Jack Rose from a story by Douglas Morrow
   and Robert Hardy Andrews
With John Wayne, Donna Reed, Charles Coburn, Tom Tully, Sherry Jackson

The Boy from Oklahoma
Warner Bros. (February 24, 1954). 87 m. Mono sound (RCA). WarnerColor.

1.37:1, photographed by Robert Burks
Music by Max Steiner, with music by Stephen Foster
Written by Frank Davis and Winston Miller from a story by Michael Fessier
With Will Rogers Jr., Nancy Olson, Lon Chaney Jr., Anthony Caruso, Wallace
    Ford

The Egyptian
Twentieth Century–Fox (August 24, 1954). 139 m. Four-track stereo (Western
    Electric). Eastmancolor. CinemaScope.
2.55:1, photographed by Leon Shamroy
Music by Bernard Herrmann and Alfred Newman
Written by Philip Dunne and Casey Robinson from the novel by Mika Waltari
With Jean Simmons, Victor Mature, Gene Tierney, Michael Wilding, Bella Darvi,
    Edmund Purdom

White Christmas
Paramount (October 14, 1954). 120 m. Mono sound (Western Electric) with
    Perspecta stereo sound in some prints. Technicolor. VistaVision.
1.85:1, photographed by Loyal Griggs
Music by Irving Berlin
Written by Norman Krasna, Norman Panama, and Melvin Frank
With Bing Crosby, Danny Kaye, Rosemary Clooney, Vera-Ellen, Dean Jagger,
    Mary Wickes

We're No Angels (a.k.a. *Angels' Cooking*)
Paramount (July 7, 1955). 106 m. Mono sound (Western Electric). Technicolor.
    VistaVision.
1.85:1, photography by Loyal Griggs
Written by Ranald MacDougall from a play by Albert Husson
With Humphrey Bogart, Aldo Ray, Peter Ustinov, Joan Bennett, Basil Rathbone,
    Leo G. Carroll

The Scarlet Hour
Paramount (April 1956). 95 m. Mono sound (Western Electric). Black and white.
    VistaVision.
1.85:1, photographed by Lionel Lindon
Music by Leith Stevens, with a song by Jay Livingston and Ray Evans
Costumes by Edith Head
Written by Alford Van Ronkel, Frank Tashlin, and John Meredyth Lucas from a
    story by Van Ronkel and Tashlin
With Carol Ohmart, Tom Tryon, Jody Lawrance, James Gregory, Elaine Stritch

The Vagabond King
Paramount (August 29, 1956). 86 m. Mono sound (Western Electric).
    Eastmancolor/Technicolor. VistaVision.
1.85:1, photographed by Robert Burks
Music by Victor Young
Written by Ken Englund and Noel Langley from a book by Brian Hooker and
    William H. Post and a play by Justin Huntly McCarthy
With Kathryn Grayson, Oreste Kirkop, Rita Moreno, Cedric Hardwicke

The Best Things in Life Are Free
Twentieth Century–Fox (September 28, 1956). 104 m. Four-track stereo sound
  (Westrex). Eastmancolor. CinemaScope.
2.35:1, photographed by Leon Shamroy
Music by Ray Henderson
Written by William Bowers and Phoebe Ephron from a story by John O'Hara
With Gordon MacRae, Dan Dailey, Ernest Borgnine, Sheree North

The Helen Morgan Story
Warner Bros. (October 2, 1957). 118 m. Mono sound (RCA). Black and white.
  CinemaScope.
2.35:1, photographed by Ted McCord
Written by Nelson Gidding, Stephen Longstreet, Dean Riesner, and Oscar Saul
With Ann Blyth, Paul Newman, Richard Carlson, Gene Evans

The Proud Rebel
Formosa Productions (May 28, 1958). 103 m. Mono sound (Westrex).
  Eastmancolor. Spherical.
1.85:1, photographed by Ted McCord
Written by Joseph Petracca and Lillie Hayward from a story by James Edward
  Grant
With Alan Ladd, Olivia de Havilland, Dean Jagger, David Ladd, Cecil Kellaway,
  Harry Dean Stanton

King Creole (a.k.a. *Danny*)
Wallis-Hazen/Paramount (July 2, 1958). 116 m. Mono sound (Westrex). Black
  and white. Spherical.
1.85:1, photographed by Russell Harlan
Written by Herbert Baker and Michael Vincente Gazzo from the novel *A Stone
  for Danny Fisher,* by Harold Robbins
With Elvis Presley, Carolyn Jones, Walter Matthau, Dolores Hart, Dean Jagger

The Hangman
Paramount (March 5, 1959). 87 m. Mono sound (Westrex). Black and white.
  Spherical.
1.85:1, photographed by Loyal Griggs
Written by W. R. Burnett and Dudley Nichols from a story by Luke Short
With Robert Taylor, Tina Louise, Fess Parker, Jack Lord

The Man in the Net
Jaguar Productions/Mirisch Corporation (June 10, 1959). 98 m. Mono sound
  (Westrex). Black and white.
1.66:1, photographed by John F. Seitz
Written by Reginald Rose from a story by Patrick Quentin
With Alan Ladd, Carolyn Jones, Diane Brewster, John Lupton

A Breath of Scandal
Titanus/Paramount (December 16, 1960). 97 m. Mono sound (Westrex).
  Eastmancolor/Technicolor. Spherical.
1.85:1, photographed by Mario Montuori

Costumes by Hoyningen Huene
Music by Alessandro Cicognini
Written by Ring Lardner Jr. (uncredited) from Walter Bernstein's adaptation of a
   play by Ferenc Molnár and Karl Schneider
With Sophia Loren, Maurice Chevalier, John Gavin, Angela Lansbury

The Adventures of Huckleberry Finn
Formosa/MGM (June 17, 1960). 107 m. Mono sound (Westrex). Metrocolor.
   CinemaScope.
2.35:1, photographed by Ted McCord
Written by James Lee from the novel by Mark Twain
With Tony Randall, Archie Moore, Eddie Hodges, Patty McCormack

Francis of Assisi
Perseus/Twentieth Century–Fox (July 12, 1961). 105 m. Mono sound (Westrex).
   Eastmancolor. CinemaScope.
2.35:1, photographed by Piero Portalupi
Music by Mario Nascimbene
Written by Eugene Vale, James Forsyth, and Jack Thomas from a novel by Louis
   De Wohl
With Bradford Dillman, Dolores Hart, Stuart Whitman, Cecil Kellaway

The Comancheros
Twentieth Century–Fox (November 1, 1961). 107 m. Four-track stereo
   sound in 35 mm mag-optical prints; mono sound in regular 35 mm prints.
   Eastmancolor. CinemaScope.
2.35:1, photographed by William H. Clothier
Music by Elmer Bernstein
Written by James Edward Grant and Clair Huffaker from a novel by Paul I.
   Wellman
With John Wayne, Stuart Whitman, Ina Balin, Nehemiah Persoff, Lee Marvin

Off to See the Wizard (1 episode)
Four Star/MGM Television (September 8, 1967). 60 m. Mono sound.
   Metrocolor.
1.33:1.
With Daws Butler, Mel Blanc, June Foray

Contributors

Rebecca Bell-Metereau is professor of English and director of the Media Studies Minor at Texas State University. She is co-editor of *Star Bodies and the Erotics of Suffering* and the author of *Hollywood Androgyny*, *Simone Weil on Politics, Religion and Society*, and chapters in *A Little Solitaire: John Frankenheimer and American Film*; *Stars of the 80s*; *Acting for America*; *Authorship in Film Adaptation*; *Cinema and Modernity*; *American Cinema of the 1950s*; *Film and Television after 9/11*; *Ladies and Gentlemen, Boys and Girls*; *Bad: Infamy, Darkness, Evil, and Slime on Screen*; and *Cultural Conflicts in Twentieth-Century Literature*. She has published articles in *Cinema Journal*, *College English*, the *Journal of Popular Film and Television*, and the *Quarterly Review of Film and Video*.

David Desser is emeritus professor of cinema studies at the University of Illinois. He has written and edited eleven books, most recently *Small Cinemas in Global Markets*. His best-known works include *The Samurai Films of Akira Kurosawa*; *Eros Plus Massacre: An Introduction to the Japanese New Wave Cinema*; *Reframing Japanese Cinema: Authorship, Genre, History*; *American Jewish Filmmakers*; *The Cinema of Hong Kong: History, Arts, Identity*; and *Ozu's Tokyo Story*. He is a former editor of *Cinema Journal* and a founding co-editor of the *Journal of Japanese and Korean Cinema*. He provided commentary on Criterion DVD editions of *Tokyo Story* and *Seven Samurai*. He also wrote the program notes, along with audio introductions and extensive commentary, on the films of Kiju Yoshida from Arrow Films in the UK.

Seth Friedman is associate professor in the Department of Communication and Theatre, and director of the Film Studies Program, at DePauw University. He is the author of *Are You Watching Closely? Cultural Paranoia, New Technologies, and the Contemporary Hollywood Misdirection Film*. His essays have been published in *Genders*, the *Journal of Film and Video*, the *Journal of Popular Culture*, and the *Quarterly Review of Film and Video*.

Mark Glancy is reader in film history at Queen Mary University of London. He is currently writing a biography of Cary Grant and contributing to the documentary *Becoming Cary Grant*. His previous publications include the books *Hollywood and the Americanization of Britain*; *"The 39 Steps": A British Film Guide*; and *When Hollywood Loved Britain: The Hollywood "British" Film, 1939–1945*, and, as co-editor, *The New Film History: Methods, Sources, Approaches*.

David Greven is professor of English at the University of South Carolina. His books include *Intimate Violence: Hitchcock, Sex, and Queer Theory*; *Queering "The Terminator": Sexuality and Cyborg Cinema*; *Ghost Faces: Hollywood and Post-Millennial Masculinity*; *Gender Protest and Same-Sex Desire in Antebellum American Literature*; *Psycho-Sexual: Male Desire in Hitchcock, De Palma, Scorsese, and Friedkin*; *The Fragility of Manhood: Hawthorne, Freud, and the Politics of Gender*; *Representations of Femininity in American Genre Cinema: The Woman's Film, Film Noir, and Modern Horror*; and *Manhood in Hollywood from Bush to Bush*.

Julie Grossman, professor of English and communication and film studies at Le Moyne College, has published numerous scholarly essays on literature, film, gender and culture, and adaptation. She is the author of *Rethinking the Femme Fatale in Film Noir: Ready for Her Close-Up* and *Literature, Film, and Their Hideous Progeny: Adaptation and ElasTEXTity*. She is the co-author (with Therese Grisham) of *Ida Lupino, Director: Her Art and Resilience in Times of Transition*. She is a founding coeditor (with R. Barton Palmer) of the Palgrave Macmillan book series Adaptation and Visual Culture, and, with R. Barton Palmer, co-editor of *Adaptation in Visual Culture: Images, Texts, and Their Multiple Worlds*. She is the co-author (with R. Barton Palmer) of *Major Performers in Hollywood Noir* (forthcoming).

Kristen Hatch is an associate professor of film and media studies at the University of California, Irvine. Her work focuses on gender, race, and sexuality in studio-era Hollywood and on the relationship between film and other popular arts. She is the author of *Shirley Temple and the Performance of Girlhood*.

Nathan Holmes is the author of *Welcome to Fear City: Crime Film, Crisis, and the Urban Imagination* (forthcoming), and has taught film and media studies classes at the University of Iowa, the University of Chicago, and Loyola University Chicago.

Bill Krohn is the author of *Hitchcock at Work* and monographs on Hitchcock, Stanley Kubrick, Luis Buñuel, and Joe Dante. He writes regularly for *Cahiers du cinéma* and the *Economist*.

Katharina Loew is an assistant professor of German and cinema studies at the University of Massachusetts Boston. Her research focuses on film technology and special effects. Recent publications include essays on early German film theory, 3-D cinema in the 1910s, and Fritz Lang's *Woman in the Moon*. She is currently completing a book manuscript that investigates the impact of special-effect technologies on German film during the silent era.

Robert Miklitsch is professor in the Department of English Language and Literature at Ohio University. His work on film and television has appeared in *Camera*

Obscura, *Film Quarterly*, the *Journal of Film and Video*, the *Journal of Popular Film and Television*, the *New Review of Film and Television Studies*, and *Screen*. He is the editor of *Psycho-Marxism* and the author of *From Hegel to Madonna; Roll over Adorno*; and *Siren City: Sound and Source Music in Classic American Noir*, which was named a Choice Outstanding Academic Title of 2011. His edited collection *Kiss the Blood Off My Hands: On Classic Noir* was nominated for an Edgar Allan Poe Award (Criticism) by the Mystery Writers of America and named a Choice Outstanding Academic Title of 2015. His most recent book is *The Red and the Black: American Film Noir in the 1950s*.

Deron Overpeck is an assistant professor in the School of Communication, Media and Theatre Arts at Eastern Michigan University. His research, which focuses on the American entertainment industry after 1950, has appeared in *Film History: An International Journal*, the *Quarterly Review of Film and Video*, the *Historical Journal of Film, Radio and Television*, and *Moving Image*, as well as in the edited volumes *New Explorations in Cinema History* and *American Cinema of the 1980s*.

Landon Palmer is a historian of film, media, and popular music who teaches in the Department of Communication at the University of Tampa. His research, which centers on the relationship between music performance and moving-image media industries, has been published in *Music, Sound and the Moving Image*, *Celebrity Studies*, and the *Journal of the International Association for the Study of Popular Music*.

R. Barton Palmer is the Calhoun Lemon Professor of Literature at Clemson University, where he directs the World Cinema program. He is the author or editor of numerous books on literary and cinematic topics, including, most recently, *Shot on Location: Postwar American Cinema and the Exploration of Real Place* and, with Amanda Ann Klein, the edited volume *Cycles, Sequels, Spin-Offs, Remakes, and Reboots: Multiplicities in Film and Television*.

Homer B. Pettey is professor of film and comparative literature at the University of Arizona. For Edinburgh University Press, he serves as the general and founding editor for two series: Global Film Studios and International Film Stars. He also serves as the general and founding editor of a series for Rutgers University Press, Global Film Directors. With R. Barton Palmer, he co-edited two volumes on film noir, *Film Noir* and *International Noir* (2014). He and Palmer co-edited the collection *Rule, Britannia! Biopics and British National Identity* (SUNY Press, 2017) and, with Steven M. Sanders, the collection *Hitchcock's Moral Gaze* (SUNY Press, 2017). Palmer and Pettey are assembling the collection *French Literature on Screen* for Manchester University Press (2018). Currently, Pettey is completing a book on Cold War film genres for Edinburgh University Press.

Murray Pomerance is professor in the Department of Sociology at Ryerson University and the author, most recently, of *A King of Infinite Space; The Man Who Knew Too Much; Moment of Action: Riddles of Cinematic Performance*; and *The Eyes Have It: Cinema and the Reality Effect*. He edits the Horizons of Cinema series for SUNY Press, and for Rutgers University Press, the Techniques of the Moving Image series, the Screen Decades series (with Lester D. Friedman), and the Star Decades series (with Adrienne L. McLean).

Steven Rybin is assistant professor of film studies in the Department of English at Minnesota State University, Mankato. He is the author of *Gestures of Love: Romancing Performance in Classical Hollywood Cinema*, and the co-editor, with Will Scheibel, of *Lonely Places, Dangerous Ground: Nicholas Ray in American Cinema*. His other books include *Michael Mann: Crime Auteur* and *Terrence Malick and the Thought of Film*.

Michele Schreiber is associate professor of film and media studies at Emory University. She is the author of *American Postfeminist Cinema: Women, Romance, and Contemporary Culture*, and the co-editor, with Linda Badley and Claire Perkins, of *Indie Reframed: Women's Filmmaking and Contemporary American Independent Cinema*. Her work on gender, genre, and authorship has appeared in the *Journal of Film and Video* and in several anthologies.

Constantine Verevis is associate professor in film and screen studies at Monash University, Melbourne. He is the author of *Film Remakes* and co-author of *Australian Film Theory and Criticism, Vol. I: Critical Positions*. His co-edited volumes include *Second Takes: Critical Approaches to the Film Sequel*; *After Taste: Cultural Value and the Moving Image*; *Film Trilogies: New Critical Approaches*; *Film Remakes, Adaptations, and Fan Productions: Remake/Remodel*; *B Is for Bad Cinema: Aesthetics, Politics, and Cultural Value*; *US Independent Film after 1989: Possible Films*, and *Transnational Television Remakes*.

Colin Williamson is assistant professor of film and screen studies at Pace University (New York City). He is the author of *Hidden in Plain Sight: An Archaeology of Magic and the Cinema* and has published articles and essays in *Animation: An Interdisciplinary Journal*, *Leonardo: Journal of Arts, Sciences, and Technology*, the *Moving Image*, and in the anthology *Thinking in the Dark: Cinema, Theory, Practice*. He is a reviews editor for *Animation: An Interdisciplinary Journal* and serves on the executive committee of Domitor, the International Society for the Study of Early Cinema.

Index

Of Human Bondage (1934, John Crom-
well), 69
O'Hara, Maureen, 85
Ohmart, Carol, 16, 19, 22
Oland, Warner, 240
"Old Fashioned Garden" (song), 63
Old Maid, The (1939, Edmund Gould-
ing), 76–77
Olivier, Laurence, 73, 81, 193
Olsen, Moroni, 216
O'Neill, Eithne, 249
O'Neill, Henry, 200
One Way Passage (1932, Tay Garnett),
240
On the Waterfront (1954, Elia Kazan),
160
Oscars, 26, 29, 33–34, 39n4, 43, 69,
78n1, 103, 105, 169n2, 258
Our Hearts Were Growing Up (1946,
William D. Russell), 37
Our Hearts Were Young and Gay
(1944, Lewis Allen), 36–37
Outlook (publication), 209
Overpeck, Deron, 12
"Over There" (song), 83–84
Owen, Dean, 209

Page, Gale, 251
Pallette, Eugene, 273
Palmer, Landon, 11
Palmer, R. Barton, 11
Palm Springs, California, 131, 208
Paramount Decree (1948), 42
Paramount Pictures, 6, 16, 36–37, 42,
107, 134, 159, 168, 174–175, 177–
178, 180–182, 225–227, 229–231,
223, 240, 250, 257, 266
Paramount v. the United States (1948),
159
Paris, 58, 85, 129, 134, 245, 278, 284,
286, 287
Paris (play), 57
Paris, Barry, 87
Parker, Colonel Tom, 173, 174,
180–181
"Passionate Shepherd to His Love,
The" (poem), 75–76

Passover, 49–51
Pastrone, Giovanni, 134
Peck, Gregory, 34
Peckinpah, Sam, 213
Peet, Creighton, 209
Pépé le Moko (1937, Julien Duvivier),
121
Perkins, Ray, 208
Pettey, Homer B., 10
Philo Vance (book series), 7–8
Photoplay (publication), 256
Pickford, Mary, 29, 39nn1–2
Picturegoer (publication), 102, 256,
262
Pierce, David, 208
Pietà (sculpture), 78
Pinkard, Maceo, 150
Pinkertons, 197, 200
Pitts, Zasu, 30, 33
Plank, Bob, 99–100
Playhouse 90 (TV series), 25
Play It Again, Sam (1972, Herbert
Ross), 131
Poe, Edgar Allan, 108
Poland, 204
Polito, Sal, 100, 210, 215, 272
Pomerance, Murray, 10, 73, 289
Porter, Cole, 12, 37, 56–66
Port Royal, Jamaica, 109
Positif (publication), 249
Possessed (1947, Curtis Bernhardt), 76
Postman Always Rings Twice, The
(1946, Tay Garnett), 104
Postman Always Rings Twice, The
(novel), 96
Powell, William, 7, 30–35, 130, 159,
187, 192, 194
Presley, Elvis, 11, 168, 171–183
Pride of the Marines (1945, Delmer
Daves), 96
Prince and the Pauper, The (1937,
William Keighley), 265
Prinz, LeRoy, 56, 62, 87
Private Lives of Elizabeth and Essex,
The (1939, Michael Curtiz), 5, 13,
68, 74, 107, 167, 250, 265
Production Code, 9, 20, 31–32, 56–57,